NO SILVER BULLET

BURSTING THE BUBBLE OF THE ORGANISATIONAL QUICK FIX

No Silver Bullet: Bursting the Bubble of the Organisational Quick Fix

© Steve Hearsum, 2024

Paperback ISBN: 978-1-7385538-0-8
ePub ISBN: 978-1-7385538-1-5

British Library Cataloguing-in-Publication data
A catalogue record for this book is available from the British Library.

Edited by Dr. Paula Hearsum, Mark Cole and Liz Bourne.

Management in Five Acts, on page 50 is taken from The Wiggly World of Organization by Chris Rodgers (Routledge, 2021). Reproduced by permission of Chris Rodgers Consulting Ltd. All rights reserved.

NO SILVER BULLET

BURSTING THE BUBBLE OF THE ORGANISATIONAL QUICK FIX

STEVE HEARSUM

Foreword by Dave Ulrich

Contents

Chapter 11:

To my daughter Maya, for being you.

Acknowledgements

After four odd years, it is unsurprising I have a few people to thank. First and foremost amongst these are Simon Cavicchia, who has been my thought partner and key contributor from the off; Paula Hearsum – not only for living through this with me but also editing the first complete draft; Mark Cole, who both edited it to make sure I was true to myself and consented to be interviewed; and Liz Bourne who completed the final edit from a publishing perspective. James Willis at Spiffing Covers, plus his lovely team, for making the thing publicly available; and Simon Bottrell, who did not just design the cover and accompanying marketing collateral, he climbed into my head to make sure it was true to who I am and what I wanted to say. Also thanks to Amy Purnell and Rhian Pearson at The Book Publicist for drumming up some interest in this tome.

Then there are the many people who I interviewed, those that I can name and many who must remain anonymous. The former, in no particular order, were Eva Appelbaum, Dr. Eliat Aram, Alex Boulting, Gervase Bushe, Stefan Cantore, Rachel Cashman, Dr Richard Claydon, Mark Cole, Dr Graham Curtis, Dr Glenda Eoyang, Dr Susanne Evans, Linda Holbeche, Lucian Hudson, Keith Jones, Joost Minnaar, Neil Morrison, Tom Nixon, Dr Wendy Shepherd, Geoff Marlow, Michael Jenkins, Martin Parker, Ollie Roberts, Mel Ross, Jesse Segers, Sue Sjuve, Naomi Stanford, Perry Timms, Matt Wells, David Wilkinson, Diana Wu David Matt Wyatt, and Bernd Zimmerman. Others who have contributed or helped along the way include: Chris Bolton, Alexa Fitzpatrick, Shelly Hossain, Sara Jones, David Lines and Matthew Moore.

Particular thanks must also go to Dave Ulrich, for being so generous with his time and support, and for writing the foreword; Toby Lindsay for being a relentlessly positive sounding board; and Simon Bottrell, for being a wonderful friend as well as being alongside me throughout to help translate my wibblings into something visually engaging.

I will no doubt have forgotten someone, and if I have let me know, because the wonders of print on demand publishing means I can add you with ease …

So, thank you all. It has been a ride.

THE ALMANAC OF THE HONOURABLE GUILD OF THE SILVER BULLET

PURVEYORS OF SILVER BULLETS

SINCE WAY BACK

A STUPENDOUS COMPENDIUM OF VELOCIOUS REMEDIES TO PERPLEXING CONUNDRUMS

Illusion & Collusion

Myth & Fantasy

Hope & Victory

SOLUTIONS FOR EVERY ORGANISATIONAL OCCASION!

AVOID FAILURE

DEFEAT SHAME

ENSURE SUCCESS

Enquire Within

In some ways, we're all unwitting members of the 'Honourable Guild of the Silver Bullet'.

21st century life is fast. It is swipes, clicks, instant gratification, fix-it-for-me-nowness, profile, and ego gratification. That all takes place in increasingly messy social, political, societal and environmental complexity. And we work in that.

Whilst this book is about organisations, organising, business, consulting, leadership and change, it would seem that how we make decisions, the choices we make and the action that results is as if the Honourable Guild, it's thinking and members were real.

To be seen to lead, perform, deliver, be efficient, sustainable, competitive etc., we try to take the fastest route we can. Because that is the right answer. Really?

The Guild is obviously a fictional creation, used here to bring a little bit of humour, and it's also a way of identifying some of the real Silver Bullets that organisations reach for regularly, and with predictable outcomes.

The membership of The Guild is open to both commissioners and practitioners of change, purveyors and consumers of Silver Bullets and consultants and experts of all flavours. We subscribe to its annual membership without a thought; we are members until we realise that Silver Bullets do not really exist. Until then, the collusion carries on, perpetuates, demand and supply. And round we go.

What does it take to find the courage to suggest taking the longer path and to hand back our membership cards? To be OK with not immediately knowing how to solve a complex problem and instead see complexity and the accompanying mess as, well, just complex?

This book emerged out of my experiences in organisations and with clients, and writing it has challenged me along the way, connecting me with some remarkable people, all of whom have their own take on this subject. The book's primary purpose is to get us all to think a little more deeply. And to inquire.

Want to inquire with me? Say hello@hearsum.com.

FOREWORD

by

DAVE ULRICH

Foreword

By Dave Ulrich

Rensis Likert Professor, Ross School of Business, University of Michigan

This book brings to mind a number of experiences.

In coaching an individual receiving some negative 360 feedback, she pleaded with me, "Just tell me what to do!" My response, "What do you think?", did not meet her needs for clarity.

When helping redirect their career, they played the 'if only …' game. If only I had taken that assignment, seen the political implications of my recommendation, not made that stupid comment, etc.

In a workshop where I was facilitating dialogue about building organisation capabilities, a participant pointedly asked me to just tell him what capability matters most so he could make it happen.

In redesigning an organisation, the leader met with the team and set the expectation of producing an organisation chart with roles and responsibilities.

In each of these (and many other) settings, people want easy, simple and memorable answers to the challenges they face. In this thoughtful and thorough book, Steve challenges this inevitable search for what he calls 'Silver Bullets' that derail personal, organisational and customer progress.

Over the years, the dysfunctions of Silver Bullets have been described in many ways:

- Shiny objects lose their lustre.
- Quick fixes create long-term cycles of cynicism.
- Fads fade.
- Simplistic solutions go unsolved.
- Pithy answers meant to reduce fear and anxiety often lead to more questions that increase angst.
- Clever slide decks have little sustaining power.
- Repackaging the past obfuscates the future.

Building on this logic, Steve reinforces that Silver Bullets often misfire or miss their target, causing more harm than good.

While dysfunctional, at one time or another, we have all wanted to discover the magic elixir or quick fix with the false hope that we could easily change ourselves, others, our organisation, or our work with customers. In reality, change requires enormous effort, persistence and dedication.

Steve's book does a marvellous job of laying out the false hopes of Silver Bullets, the reasons why they exist and persist (fear/anxiety), and their sources (poor business education, social media 'likes', and clever packaging of ideas to name a few). I could leave the book with a curmudgeon attitude that Silver Bullets will continue to exist causing more harm than good.

But Steve goes beyond the downsides of Silver Bullets to offer more realistic guidance about moving beyond them. His work reminds me that simplicity without complexity is simplistic; while simplicity on the other side of complexity enhances performance and enables change.

As we all know, the world is complex. There are 118 elements on the periodic table; over 10,000 diseases someone might catch; nearly 300 mental illnesses in the Diagnostic and Statistical Manual (DSM) of mental disorders; and numerable actions organisations can take to improve. To change there are so many places to source ideas: webinars, magazines, conferences, social media, books, articles, training programmes, coaches, peers, podcasts and beyond. It is easy to be so overwhelmed with the complexity that it paralyses action. Avoiding the trap of Silver Bullets requires sifting through this complexity to find tailored solutions that may be simple, but not simplistic.

Steve's work reminds us that the siren song of Silver Bullets with simplistic answers exists and will continue to do so, probably even more with AI which requires even less reflection and attention to process. Steve's book helps me realise that when simplicity on the other side or complexity (divergence and convergence) exists,

- fads can become personal journeys;
- shiny objects turn into grounded identities;
- quick fixes cumulate to sustained results;
- pithy answers lead to more challenging questions and a spiral of progress; and
- Silver Bullets can morph to discover ways to make change happen.

Steve's personal journey to move from Silver Bullets to peaceful change, from answers to questions, fads to identities, results to process, and answers to questions can be a blueprint for each of us who want to improve with confidence that we can change.

This book reminds us that the complex challenge of changing human systems can be navigated; polite compliance can be morphed into thoughtful creativity; undiscussable problems can be dialogues for moving forward; anxieties that lead to helplessness can turn into decision making that leads to hopefulness; uncertainty can be replaced with certainty; learning occurs where the past is prologue for a future; advisers help others discover their strengths.

The solution to overcoming Silver Bullets is not another quick fix, but a thoughtful commitment to the process of change which requires divergence and convergence, independence and collaboration; sharing and co creating; listening and acting; and savouring uncertainty to find certainty.

This messy process of discovering simplicity on the other side of complexity requires new ways to question, think, act, experiment, reflect and learn.

Steve, thanks for sharing your journey and turning your insights into our experiences.

Explanations exist; they have existed for all time; there is always a well-known solution to every human problem — neat, plausible, and wrong.

H. L. Mencken, 1920[1]

1. Prejudices: Second Series by H. L. Mencken, Chapter 4: The Divine Afflatus, Borzoi: Alfred A. Knopf, New York: 1920

A Wee Preamble to Set the Scene

Once upon a time, there was a CEO responsible for the European division of a large global managed services company. Let's call him Sergio. In post for a few years, Sergio was wrestling with a challenge: in an organisation of several thousand people spread across multiple countries, profitability was not as high as it should be. Various parts of the business were not as efficient as he thought they could be and key to that was how the different country operations were led and managed, reflecting their local culture, rather than 'one company culture'.

So, he had a plan. A cunning plan. A two-step Silver Bullet to bring his organisation together. What if he a) stripped out a load of people (saving money and setting the stage for culture change), and b) set expectations for 'one way of working' across Europe?

Luckily, Sergio latched on to an approach to working with culture that would lead to a set of 'simple rules' that could be rolled out across the business and be the basis for how everyone worked, regardless of intercultural differences. These rules would transcend *values* and be focused specifically on the *behaviours* that they wanted to see more of. He got his HR and Organisation Development people on board. An external consultant came in, worked with a large group of senior leaders across Europe and they co-designed new simple rules that were to apply to everyone. They made a lot of sense on paper:

1. *Be clear about what you can and can't do in time.*
2. *Suggest a solution with every problem.*
3. *Celebrate success and excellence.*
4. *Invite the opinions and ideas of others.*

These were to inform how people operated and acted from now on – at all levels of the organisation. The vision was clear and outlined in a company communication: "One goal. One team. One set of 'simple rules', designed to respond to a business environment [that] continues to change."

Sounds great, doesn't it? Four rules rolled up into one 'code', an intervention and solution to a complex challenge that was going to change organisational culture. It was uniform across countries and set out to achieve consistency regardless of differences. Yet as I reflect on this now, I notice my own cynicism and despair at the language and wonder how those on the end of this intervention must have felt. Actually, based on what transpired next, I think I know.

Reality bites back

Some months later, the redundancies and restructuring were done, and the pan-European leadership team assembled at a swanky airport hotel for a leadership retreat. The retreat's agenda included a session run by two external facilitators. Both were qualified in the methodology the client had used to arrive at the Simple Rules and were invited to run a two-and-a-half-hour session, to reinforce the messaging and extrapolate how things were going.

Enter reality stage left, wearing large hob-nailed boots. Reality can take many forms. Sometimes, it is external factors, e.g. the economy, regulation, COVID, etc. Even when it is, these then unfold at a human level, as those within organisations try and make sense of things and seek a suitable and meaningful response. That in turn unfolds at the level of people, culture and in groups, which is what happened here.

The facilitators quickly noticed something was amiss in the group. Participation was patchy and reeked of polite compliance. Part way through, the clients (the CEO and Heads of OD[2] (Organisation Development) and HR (Human Resources)) were smiling, nodding and indicating they thought it was going well. The facilitators were reassured but something niggled. As the session progressed, many of the sixty-odd people in the room seemed unwilling to be open, honest and truthful about what they were thinking and feeling.

At the end of the workshop, Sergio was pleased and appreciative, and the participants seemed mostly positive. The facilitators left, relatively satisfied if a little baffled by what they had experienced. Three weeks later, the evaluation data revealed that the session had left many people dissatisfied and, in no uncertain terms, they trashed the facilitators.

Which was rather disappointing, as I was one of them.

It is entirely possible we were awful and ran a poorly designed session, yet the client feedback in the room was positive to a design they approved. Feedback from the (previously happy) Head of Organisation Development was along the

_____

2. Whenever I say 'OD' I am referring to Organisation Development rather than Organisation Design. If I am referring to the latter I will do so explicitly

lines of 'nice people but we don't want to work with you again'. Three months after the workshop, Sergio suddenly left his role as CEO.

How can we explain it? Culturally we appear to have an unhealthy attachment, nay obsession, with quotes from old – and predominantly white – men, dead or alive. You probably know that Peter Drucker quote that has become a meme on LinkedIn and elsewhere, that 'Culture eats strategy for breakfast' – which he never actually said by the way,[3] but hey, never let that get in the way of oversimplification and making the complex a little less uncomfortable. Well, in this case Culture lurked in the shadows, licked its lips then lumbered out and tore Strategy into small and very bloody pieces. I think it took part of my left leg as well and evoked my own sense of shame and fragility as a consultant.

---

3. One of the things that fuels a sense of shame for leaders – which will be unpacked more in Chapter 2 – is the fear that you must know everything. You don't, and nonetheless I will fill in the gaps where I can. These nuggets are only here to help you make sense of the narrative in the book. So …

Peter Drucker was an Austrian-born American management consultant, educator and author, who is possibly best known for the eponymous Global Forum that takes place each year, the theory of 'management by objectives' and this one, short quote. Useful as it is, it has the effect of turning culture into a 'thing', rather than something that has to be worked with and in, that is co-created by all. Making culture a thing means it is easier for consultants and experts to sell solutions to clients to 'fix it', denying the less conscious dynamics around individual and group needs.

As for the 'culture eats strategy for breakfast thing', he never said it, as the Drucker Institute website state in their 'Did Peter Drucker Say That' section (https://drucker.institute/did-peter-drucker-say-that/). What he *actually* said is more nuanced: "Culture – no matter how defined – is singularly persistent."

Why did I Write this Book and Who's it for?

My overarching goal here is to encourage more critical thinking, to consider that, maybe, reaching for the obvious or accepting the smooth and convincing sales patter of a pedlar of Silver Bullets may not be the best option. I also hope that, by focusing on both sides of the buyer/seller relationship, the reader will develop more empathy and simultaneously flex their muscles for independent thinking and acting with integrity.

This is a book for clients and those that seek to help them by selling solutions or consultancy. It invites the different players to stand in each other's shoes and, crucially, understand why they are behaving the way they are. It is imperative that each engage in inquiry and dialogue around how all parties are complicit in this functional and defensive collusion. Such collusion works because services are bought and sold, revenue is generated (and wasted), and there is anxiety that business models and revenue streams may need to evolve. There is fear also of a loss of rich pickings within a capitalist model of market managerialism which seeks to defend itself, while lurking beneath is the ultimate existential anxiety of our mortality. To explore why we are smitten by Silver Bullets requires us to delve into our psyche and ways of relating.

If you are a client reading this: yes, it is important you read the chapter on consultant practice and ethics, because you need to get in their heads a bit.

Equally, consultants and practitioners of every sort, experts and gurus: it behoves you to go beyond a superficial understanding of 'client need' and get into the mush more, even when that means looking in the mirror and seeing you may not be as ethical or effective as you thought you were.

To that end, unless I say otherwise, the 'you' I address is anyone engaged in the buying and selling of Silver Bullets. If I am talking specifically to, say, the client, I will make that clear.

This book, ultimately, is an attempt to bridge the gap between logic and irrationality.

A brief word on stupidity

There is a risk in writing this book that you are left with the impression that I come from a place of pure judgement, that those of us who embark on quests for simple answers or quick fixes are there to be pitied or looked down on. Far from it. I recognise in myself the temptation – even desire – for someone or something to reduce the anxiety I sometimes feel when faced with things I cannot control.

Mats Alvesson and André Spicer, both academics specialising in organisational behaviour, and interested in "why smart people buy into stupid ideas" (2016: 8) coined the term 'functional stupidity' in their book *The Stupidity Paradox* (2016), which is "the inclination to reduce one's scope of thinking and focus on the narrow, technical aspects of the job" (ibid.: 9). The three tell-tale signs of this phenomenon are (ibid.: 78):

- Not thinking about your assumptions (reflexivity)
- Not asking why you are doing something (justification)
- Not considering the consequences or wider meaning of your actions (substantive reasoning)

What follows resonates with these ideas and seeks to go deeper in an attempt to understand how it is we seem particularly susceptible to Silver Bullets, and why we seem to find it hard to engage in thinking that is both the antithesis to functional stupidity and would go a long way to disrupting the market for fads, quick fixes and simplistic solutions.

What's on the menu

Introduction looks at the origins of the Silver Bullet alongside how and why the idea has infiltrated organisations and the work of consultants.

Chapter 1 explores in more detail what, exactly, a Silver Bullet is in the context of organisational change.

Chapter 2 explores the psychological roots of the anxiety that drives the need for certainty, and in turn for simple solutions and quick fixes to alleviate that discomfort.

Chapter 3 considers whether those of us that sell, design and deliver leadership development are really doing our jobs, given how prone our clients seem to be, still, to look for simple solutions to complex problems. Further, it questions whether 'leadership development' is actually part of the problem, both in terms of how it is understood and delivered.

Chapter 4 looks at the institutions that have been a fertile breeding ground for Silver Bullets over the past seventy odd years: business schools and institutes offering Executive Education. While acknowledging they have a useful role to play, it suggests that there is a co-dependent relationship that can often fuel anxiety.

Chapter 5 shifts the spotlight to gurus, thought leaders and experts who either explicitly cultivate a profile that leans into the idea they have Silver Bullets, or equally end up, through no fault of their own, having the mantle of saviour foisted upon them because their clients are so desperate for someone to have 'The Answer'.

Chapter 6 examines how theories and methodologies end up as Silver Bullets, and how the complex and contradictory data that might make them less attractive is edited out, ignored or quietly forgotten.

Chapter 7 swerves back towards institutions that are in many ways the most powerful and influential when it comes to Silver Bullet narratives: the big global consultancies and professional service firms. It considers both their utility and culpability.

Chapter 8 builds on this, exploring consulting practice in more detail, considering the ethics and competency of consultants themselves rather than the firms they work for. It suggests that they have a key role to play in either perpetuating the myth of the Silver Bullet or supporting their clients to make more informed choices.

Chapter 9 looks at another set of players in the landscape of Silver Bullets, namely the 'fields of practice': HR, Change, Organisation Development, Organisation Design and more. While they have a role to play in creating communities of practice, this chapter argues that they also are complicit in maintaining the idea that Silver Bullets exist, in no small part through the need to protect their own identities, income and existence.

Chapter 10 focuses on a series of case studies that draw the threads of the preceding chapters together, illustrating how the pattern of functional collusion is pervasive, and largely hidden.

Finally **Chapter 11** considers what one might do in the absence of Silver Bullets. No easy answers or quick fixes are offered; some useful starting points are.

Throughout, commentary from over thirty semi-structured interviews with clients, consultants, thinkers and academics is woven in to deepen the narrative.

INTRODUCTION

Introduction

The Mythology of Silver Bullets

Silver Bullets have their origins in fairy stories, passed down via oral tradition and captured by the Brothers Grimm (Grimm and Grimm, 2015) in the tale of 'Two Brothers'. Here a bullet-proof witch is finally killed by being shot with silver buttons. Watch any werewolf movie from the past fifty years and it is likely that the protagonist will scrabble for the single silver bullet they have just dropped, loading into the chamber of their gun in the nick of time, and dispatching said monster. Like the Lone Ranger, riding in on a white stallion with a belt full of silver bullets for every baddy, this is a well-used and recognisable narrative.

Like most mythology, the problem is that it breaks down as soon as you examine it with anything approaching logic or reason. Even if werewolves were real, manufacturing and firing silver bullets is expensive and problematic. You can certainly find people experimenting with the process, and videos of how to do it, but it is not a simple task: as silver is lighter than lead, you would have to mix it into an alloy, there might be gun barrel pressure issues, and so on. In short, the simplicity of the myth, much like the simplicity of the four Simple Rules earlier, is a myth in and of itself.

Even the mythical figure of the Lone Ranger begins to tarnish upon closer inspection. Notice how Tonto has been written out of the story, so it fits better with the notion of 'Leader as Hero'. Similarly, the narrative of the charismatic leader or consultant who will singlehandedly save an organisation's culture conveniently ignores the many helping hands required along the way.

The Silver Bullet became a metaphor for a guaranteed solution to an apparently intractable problem. A Google News search[4] for the phrase in October 2023 for 'there is no silver bullet', demonstrates how far it has penetrated modern discourse by returning nigh on 500,000 results, revealing for example that there is no Silver Bullet for:

- reputational risk: 'Why there is no silver bullet for Qantas' reputational crisis' – Smart Company, 27-09-2023;

---

4. A search of academic articles on one of the research portals reveals the same, with over 20,000 papers with the term 'Silver Bullet' in the title alone.

- hiring staff: 'There Is No Silver Bullet For Hiring, But These 5 Principles Can Help Improve Your Odds' – Forbes, 16-03-2023;
- carbon-free energy: 'There's no silver bullet to carbon-free energy but hydrogen could be part of the solution', The House 26-03-2023;
- war: 'There's no silver bullet for Ukraine against Russia' – Times of India, 22-03-2023;
- migration: 'Suella Braverman warns there is no 'silver bullet' to solve Channel migrant crisis' – The Daily Mail, 14-011-2022.

COVID, climate change, health, transport, alcohol consumption, football, Brexit, crime, shark attacks, flooding, farming, education, poverty, gambling, porn filters, gender pay gaps, government policy, racism … You can find a story for each about the absence of Silver Bullets, a recognition that easy answers are hard to find for complex problems. Either explicitly or implicitly, many are leadership challenges. The problem is, the myth that Silver Bullets are real seems to pervade organisations, and the people in the middle of that are leaders and by extension their employees.

Here we run the risk of stepping into the dichotomous leader vs manager quagmire, which I'll come back to in Chapter 3, and for now let's assume that *both* will have a challenge along the lines suggested above. For you will never find the perfect solution, only the one that is the best fit based on your understanding of the situation and the assumptions you are making. What happens next will be a function of your willingness to experiment and learn through doing, with no guarantees. Because what you face as leaders or managers may seem big, hairy, scary and coming at you with teeth bared, but unlike a lupine threat, your challenges will not be felled by a Silver Bullet.

But … but … the Lone Ranger!

> "There is no silver bullet, but sometimes there is a Lone Ranger." — G. Weinberg (1994: 1, in Highsmith, 2013: 179)

Even when we accept there may be no Silver Bullet, the temptation is still to hope that a handsome, Stetson-wearing hero may, Lone Ranger style, ride to our rescue. Weinberg acknowledges the lack of a Silver Bullet, but Highsmith reframes this by noting that these Lone Rangers may have "arsenals of bullets for different situations" (ibid.); and the hard part for most managers lies in "understanding the different types of bullets and the situations in which each is most likely to succeed" (ibid.).

We love a good story, not just writing them, but also telling and then re-writing and re-telling. In that process, what gets omitted or edited out? For example, a word of warning from a client of mine that sharpens this:

> "Organisations are people and people are complex things and there is never one thing that fixes everything. Even the term: the use of the word 'bullet' implies you are going to cause harm."[5]

At the outset, notice that the idea of a Silver Bullet in and of itself implies the death of someone or something, if it is to work. In my own career, both as an employee and then as a consultant, I have seen multiple examples of this, including the classic move of bringing in consultants to solve a problem because the belief is that the skills and knowledge did not exist in-house; inspirational speakers wheeled in to inspire and fill a void; the elevation of a model or methodology because *if you just follow it* then everything will be OK … and so on. In many instances, there has been an unnecessary human cost. That is worth holding in mind as you read on.

And yet the allure of Silver Bullets is strong …

> "Often people want a Silver Bullet – to be able to take a successful initiative from one place and replicate it in their own. In reality, this rarely works. It is like breaking off the tip of an iceberg and trying to get it to float somewhere else, without the structure below that underpins it. That is because the real change is not the new initiative per se, but the learning and consequent transformation of people, relationships and systems which gave rise to the particular initiative." Celia Carrington (in Kalman Mezey, 2023)

This book is an exploration of the phenomenon of seeking Silver Bullets for complex problems, an attempt to reveal our psychological desires for them, the damaging patterns that result and what we might do about them. For clarity, by 'complex' I am thinking of the kind of challenge Professor Emeritus at Warwick University, Keith Grint, uses to define his particular understanding of a Wicked Problem, i.e. "more complex, rather than just complicated – that is, it cannot be removed from its environment, solved, and returned without affecting the environment. Moreover, there is no clear relationship between cause and effect. Such problems are often intractable" (Grint, 2008: 12). It might also fall within

---

5. Interview 20th May 2020

the domains of what consultant and founder of the Cynefin Company, Dave Snowden terms either Complex or Chaotic challenges (Snowden & Boon: 2007) or Heifetz and Laurie's (1997) Adaptive Challenge. Regardless of your preferred definition, while many believe they have The Answer, this book argues these simple solutions and quick fixes do not exist.

Perhaps you are a manager or a leader, or maybe hope to be one someday. The challenges you will face are many and varied, all of them requiring a response of some sort from you. Much will be expected of and projected on to you, and if you search against the term 'look to leaders for' the results are revealing of just how much we expect, including but not limited to what behaviour, customs, attitudes and ways of communicating are acceptable; guidance, security, direction and stability; and the almost messianic notion that we look to them for notions of what is 'good'. The modern malaise of leadership and leading is that we are still addicted to the crack cocaine of heroic leadership, more of which in Chapter 3.

One key thing we need our leaders to do is make decisions, that is why they are paid so much, isn't it? You may be faced with the disruption wrought by COVID. Perhaps technological advancements mean that you need to rapidly move to becoming more digital, or to digitise or digitalise your business (and to know the difference). Maybe your competitors are innovating their socks off and you need to become more fleet of foot in response; customers are demanding more sophisticated products and services; your efficiency is plummeting and shareholders are twitchy; you are struggling to retain your young talent and are looking at the possibility of an ageing workforce without the ability to recruit for the long term; your workforce is increasingly monochrome in appearance and/or thinking, and on and on it goes …

Maybe you are even beginning to suffer from 'Silver Bullet Syndrome', which Techwalla describes as "the belief that the next big change in tools, resources or procedures will miraculously or magically solve all of an organisation's problems. This assumption is almost invariably erroneous."[6]

What … do … you … do? Well, that's easy, because there are plenty of people who say they have The Answer, The Fix, The Solution, The Cure. If you look long enough, you can find that magical Silver Bullet that will take the pain away and make addressing the challenge if not easy, then certainly less troublesome.

---

6. https://www.techwalla.com/articles/what-is-silver-bullet-syndrome

If someone told you it would do that, it must be true, and there are plenty of places offering Silver Bullets, in one form or another. Business schools, large consultancies, small consultancies, thought leaders, gurus and experts. If that is not enough, you can find purveyors and pedlars of methodologies and tools that promise, with varying degrees of certainty, to be The Answer. Failing that, go to one of the specialist practitioners of HR, Organisation Development, Change or Organisation Design who have their own communities of practice and bodies that represent them, offering a particular lens that tallies with their world view.

The expectation, maybe even incentive, is to offer as much certainty as possible, making whatever is proposed *seem* sensible, rational and, crucially, entirely realistic. You as the leader, after all, *want* to believe. So your pain points will have a light shone on them and the reasons for your anxieties will be mirrored back to you, with a few risks added in just to emphasise the acute need for the presenter's services. Finally, a recommended solution will be proffered up as the most logical and attractive available: the Silver Bullet to make it all go away. The right solution, though, is rarely obvious. Opinions may differ within the senior leadership team around what approach to take, complicating decision making further. Even if you can agree on the response and come up with a strategy, execution is a whole other ball game as the gap between theory and reality often results in a rude awakening. What looked so neat in a beautiful slide deck starts to unravel the further away it gets from the sanitised and hermetically sealed environment of the boardroom.

Confusion, anxiety, shame … let's dance!

Underneath all of this, one fundamental truth exists: Silver Bullets do not exist. There is no quick fix to complex challenges in human systems. The evidence for that statement is simple: if there were one answer, all leaders would be buying the same book or going to the same person or vying for the services of one consultancy. That is not happening, though, is it? Yes, you may have your go-to resources and people, and many are talented, helpful and knowledgeable. The problem is, they cannot *guarantee* success and what works in one context, at one moment in time, may not work in another.

What intrigues me is *why* we persist in believing there are simple solutions to complex problems. In recent years I have mulled ever more on this. I noticed how clients would look to me for certainty, and the resultant discomfort when I chose not to collude with that.

For example, I lost out on one piece of work with an internationally renowned cultural institute for a leadership development programme because I all too accurately reflected back the dysfunction in the system and suggested an approach to working with that. Here the tensions revolved around the behaviour of the CEO, and in turn the way in which the narrative surrounding middle managers was evolving. My assessment was bang on, I was told, but the client selected another provider because they were not ready to deal with the main issue and wanted to start with the managers. Remember: I had been told my diagnosis of the situation was accurate. What was too anxiety-inducing was any real attempt to engage with the primary issue.

I noticed among fellow consultants and practitioners, and myself, a propensity to look to our favourite 'tools' and models, the approaches we believed worked. Sometimes that might mean an instrument and intervention being proposed because it meant we felt more comfortable and at ease, rather than exploring more deeply what might be required. To be clear, I still have my favoured lenses and approaches, the question is can I recognise when I may need to step into my own discomfort with not knowing what the best approach might be.

Ten years or so ago I developed an interest in undiscussables – those things that are left unsaid in organisations and groups. I become fascinated by them, not so much *what* is undiscussable, but *why* we find it hard to talk about some things in certain contexts. I interviewed various people and started a blog on what I learned. My fascination with this remained long after I closed the website.

This fuelled my interest in the relationship between certainty and anxiety, starting with myself. I wrestled for years with my fear of conflict and how I struggle to make and maintain contact in relationships when under pressure (not ideal for a consultant). As the son of an alcoholic this is probably my life work, and I have learned a lot from it. In no small part, my ability to read what is going on in groups below the level of conversation comes from years of being trained to read non-verbal signals around the family dinner table.

Alongside this, I had started to reflect on shame. Initially my own, and increasingly, as I became more comfortable with the territory, wondering how it might relate to what I experienced in my client work. How is it people seem to be able to identify the problem they are facing and what it might consist of, yet struggle with the idea there may not be a guaranteed solution? Why is there such a strong narrative that we all, apparently, do not believe in mythical Silver Bullets yet simultaneously seek them out? And why are there an equal number of people colluding with that need, selling solutions, tools, methodologies and more that offer quick fixes and certain outcomes? It struck me that there was some kind of dance going on, one where buyers and sellers both know something does not exist yet collude *as if* it did. My confusion would sharpen when I moved from conversations that were grounded in acceptance that complex problems are inherently messy and there is no easy solution to them, to others where I was being asked to offer certainty; or others still when I was struck by the earnestness and absurdity as people discussed uncertainty with certainty that there was an answer. Like the emperor who was wearing no clothes in the Grimm fairy tale, to which I will return, I found myself the boy wondering why all the grown-ups were not willing to tell him.

As I began writing, therefore, I knew this was about Silver Bullets and certainty. What I had not done was make sense of the deeper psychological processes at play. The epiphany came via talking with Dr. Graham Curtis, Director of Operations at Roffey Park Institute Institute, and reading his PhD dissertation.

A lurking dynamic driving human behaviour

Curtis's work explores what he terms a 'functional collusion' that emerges in groups and communities, and by extension organisations. In essence he describes unconscious patterns of relating, and accompanying behaviour, that people engage in to avoid uncomfortable emotions. Prime among these is shame, as people collude in an attempt to be seen as competent. The functional element is that the collusion serves a purpose, namely to defend against anxiety. It is also functional in the sense that it happens through people acting in specific roles, in the context of this book these being the buyers and sellers of Silver Bullets, which often means senior leaders and the experts who cater to them.

While collusion has negative connotations, given it is seen as synonymous with conspiracy, Curtis is using it to specifically talk to how *a form* of collusion might have a function.

Here, collusion is integral to relating and relatedness, and is an ongoing and unfolding process that takes place over time and space. Functional collusion, Curtis suggests, might consist of two important factors.

1. Contextual history: this is key to understanding how collusion emerges and is maintained, and does so without any explicit planning or discussion between those involved.

2. Absence of discussion: the collusive patterns result in a disabling of conversations, further burying what is really going on.

Thus "functional collusion is a social phenomenon in which patterns of relating emerge over time as interdependent people interact with one another to maintain their ways of being together" (Curtis, 2018: 86). How these patterns arise connected deeply with what I had been observing and reflecting on in my own research. Curtis argues that it is as people seek to avoid the discomfort of emotions such as shame that the collusion arises, and in turn maintain existing power dynamics. He then links this directly to the notion of undiscussables, suggesting that patterns of collusion emerge *without discussion* and *between* people: this is a co-creation. That dance between buyers and sellers of Silver Bullets, where no one really admits they do not exist? This was it.

The question that then arises in Curtis's work is what it takes to discuss these, and that is a thread that runs through this book, culminating in Chapter 11. The decision as to whether to make the undiscussable discussable becomes one that is highly context dependent, relies on both the practical and relational skills of those involved, and the ethical judgements they choose to make – or not make.

Without using the words Silver Bullet, Curtis makes the link to my own work: these dilemmas born of functional collusion "cannot be solved simply through the application of universal rules" (Curtis, 2018: 2). He also makes the important point that nobody is at fault here, or as he terms it "there are no rogues deliberately setting out to fool everyone" (Curtis, 2018: 7). What drives these patterns is a need to be seen as competent, and people collude unconsciously to achieve that. This is key, because it talks to how both buyers and sellers of Silver Bullets – both client and helping sides – need to maintain their ego ideals, i.e. that of the leader who 'makes the right decisions', or the consultant who 'has the answers'. So "participants are required to collude with one another in what they hold to be true and what they assume to know for them to go on relating together", in no small part due to the "anticipation of shame" (Curtis, 2018: 6).

Curtis goes a long way to explaining the kind of mental gymnastics that go on in organisations and the minds of consultants/practitioners hired to help them, whereby we're able to pretend we're changing things while working hard to keep them the same. It also talks to our comfort with not knowing. Dr Eliat Aram, the CEO of the Tavistock Institute of Human Relations, points out that "shame is an affect of not knowing" and is "related to feelings of inferiority" (2001: 10). She goes on to highlight how it is an affect that is triggered when "panicking around not knowing because we have learned to link not knowing with a sense of inferiority" (ibid.). This is key to understanding how functional collusion happens, particularly when it comes to Silver Bullets. What arises in us if we do not know what to do, or do not know what the answer is to a client's problem?

With this in mind that I invite you to read on and consider where you and I might be engaging in functional collusion.

The challenges of being a 'modern' leader

"Good managers [and leaders I suggest] fail when they attempt to use silver-bullet solutions to complex problems" (Highsmith, 2013: 179). Given that a leader's main challenge is "creating an organisation that can thrive and change, or at least be comfortable in change", according to Diana Wu David,[7] that creates tension. Wu David is a former *Financial Times* Executive, was a management consultant and is currently a lecturer on Columbia Business School's EMBA Global Asia. Twenty years ago, through the advent of Lean, Six Sigma and Deming inspired approaches to efficiency,[8] leaders were encouraged to become experts at 'just in time'. Wu David says, that leaders "got good at 'just in time' and are having to get used to 'just in case'." Leaders have "got used to focusing on whatever crisis is at hand and extrapolating on that, rather than looking beyond that" and seeing the bigger picture and context, says Wu David. This is not helped, suggests Dr Richard Claydon (Chief Cognitive Officer of EQ Lab), by the "the degree to which many executives are wedded to the complicated strategies, expensive frameworks, and outdated developmental

---

7. Interview 21st April 2020

8. Lean is a production method that grew out of Toyota's 1930s operating model, *The Toyota Way*. The term 'lean' was coined by John Krafcik in 1988 before James Womack and Daniel Jones refined it into a set of five key principles in 1996. There is a cultural context to Lean that is worth mentioning, as it grew out of Kaizen, a Japanese approach to continuous improvement that covers all functions and employees, top to bottom.

Six Sigma is a set of techniques and tools for process improvement that was created by engineers at Motorola in the 1980s, and became more widely known as a result of its adoption by Jack Welch at GE In the 1990s. It had a foothold in manufacturing particularly.

Lean Six Sigma is the union of the two approaches, as they are complementary and ideas from both have been combined to create (another) methodology that is open to organisations who are looking to change.

W. Edwards Deming was an American engineer, statistician, professor, author, lecturer and management consultant whose thinking has been highly influential in the world of manufacturing and continuous improvement. His Plan-Do-Check-Act cycle is particularly well known.

methodologies, also favoured by business schools and big consultancies" (2023: 8). He goes on to point out the promises being made, and the inherent absurdity of that expectation, which reflects a central premise of my own arguments regarding the buying and selling of Silver Bullets.

My own experience, through observing myself and others in organisations, is that we reduce anxiety by 'doing', i.e. taking action. Silver Bullets meet that need, promising quick fixes while simultaneously leaders are under corporate, reputational and narcissistic/egoic pressures to be seen to be potent and capable. This often drives short termism and unintended consequences. These can never be fully prevented, but their negative impacts could be mitigated to some extent or adjusted to through reflection and ongoing monitoring.

This book seeks to explore these and other tensions, implicitly talking about different forms of knowing, being and doing that fundamentally challenge the dominance of the managerialist paradigm. In this book, I see learning as being about questioning the status quo, and I seek to offer an emancipatory ethic.

For many leaders, the reality is that you simply *do not* and *cannot know* what will work, yet the pressures and expectations, both those you place on yourself and what is projected onto you by others, have the potential to generate anxiety, fear, distress and other uncomfortable thoughts and feelings, as you wrestle with the reality of not knowing what, precisely, is the best course of action to pursue.

Functional collusion presents another challenge to exploring these tensions, in that it connects directly with shame. After all, those of us comfortable enough to talk about how our shame may be influencing our behaviour and decisions are few. There are inherent risks of being seen to make the 'wrong decision', of being exposed as a fraud or having your persona as an infallible leader challenged.

The ask, aside from addressing whatever you are facing organisationally, is to get more comfortable with not knowing the answer. One clue to how you act when faced with situations like this might be the COVID pandemic, which provided a global case study on how to respond to something that is a personal unknown and has no obvious answer. While the scale and magnitude of change and uncertainty may differ, the challenge is similar in terms of understanding how we as human beings respond to 'not knowing'. As we saw in the very public responses of politicians and leaders across the planet, those that were able to work *with* and *in* a state of not knowing ended up appearing far more in touch with reality. They did not make promises they could not keep, and they were better able to respond to what was emerging in a rapidly changing crisis. To offer just two examples, compare Jacinda Ardern and Donald Trump. It's hard to find a bigger contrast in modern leadership than those two in humility, humanity, collaborative practice and the ability to *respond* rather than *react*. You can decide which leader is which in this comparison.

I leave you to draw your own conclusions, but merely ask that you use these circumstances and examples to make that judgement, rather than leaping to conclusions, which is where the armoury of Silver Bullets is often to be found.

If there is no Silver Bullet, then what's the point of doing anything?

Having burst your balloon (sorry about that), now let me move to the upside. For starters, if you can move away from an anxiety-driven need for certainty, then you are on the way to recognising that the answer to successful change lies in a willingness to conduct experiments and to learn from them. You will begin to become less dependent on various 'experts,' and to see them as collaborative partners rather than saviours.

Doing so will reveal a range of possibilities opening beyond the ones habitually reached for. Some will be old ideas rehashed but still relevant and useful, others may be re-frames and spins on what came before. Occasionally, *very* occasionally, you may stumble upon that rare thing: a genuinely novel, new and different 'Answer'.

Like unicorns, these are rare animals, very hard to find. They often turn out to be a horse with a glittery plastic horn strapped on its head rather than anything more fantastic. If you are lucky, it's a horse, because a fair few will probably be well-disguised donkeys. To be clear, donkeys have utility, but not when you are paying over the odds and are expecting a unicorn farting rainbows.[9] Of course this metaphor brings us back to the central problem: that unicorns are fairy tales, and we need to get beyond these in leadership, consulting and organisational theory to something closer to reality.

This book *does not* give you easy answers or quick fixes. Nonetheless, it will suggest there are things you can do that might shift your experience so that you start to see different possibilities, begin to engage in more useful conversations

---

9. Hat tip to Olu Jenzen for this lovely turn of phrase.

and feel a lightening of the emotional load. Will all anxiety and stress evaporate through reading one book? Will you have got The Answer? Unlikely.

What I hope is that you will understand your own decision-making processes a bit better, get more comfortable with not knowing, and be ready to conduct an experiment or have a conversation that you would not have done before reading this book.

Postscript: that AI thing

You will notice AI barely gets mentioned. Hardly anyone raised it in my research, and it is interesting what happens when you do an internet search on 'is AI a Silver Bullet?'. It becomes just one more 'tool' or 'thing' being weighed as a panacea for both organisational and wider societal problems, and found to be falling short. Rightly so, because on its own AI cannot 'fix' things like climate breakdown, culture, conflict, behaviour, organisational transformation and the panoply of complex challenges we face.

My own take on this is based on two observations. Firstly, my experience of trying to set up Lasting Power of Attorney for my mother with a UK bank that has removed *all* routes to talking to them other than a declining number of branches and one telephone line for complaints (if you search long and hard for it) suggests that the problem remains the people. The automated sections of the process worked reasonably well; it was the utter inability of the humans that remained to take responsibility and help join the dots that was the problem.

Which takes me to the second point. The logical solution may be to remove the remaining people and create a joined-up process run by AI. This is the scary scenario: one route to solving many complex challenges in organisations is simply to remove the people, because if your challenge is in part or whole cultural, behavioural, to do with decision making or other areas where we sometimes display our collective capacity for dysfunction, swap out the nodes that are prone to that.

I am already hearing clients, colleagues and friends, from the Civil Service through to law, executive coaching and those in middle management roles in differing sectors, wondering if their days are numbered. Based on current predictions by, amongst others, the International Monetary Fund, they are right to be worried: 60% of jobs in advanced economies are exposed to AI and half of these may be "negatively affected" – a euphemism if I ever heard one ('AI Will

Transform the Global Economy. Let's Make Sure It Benefits Humanity', IMF. org 14-01-2024). Others are thinking and writing about the social, political and ethical issues around AI. As far as this book is concerned, add AI to the list of things that are no Silver Bullet, and read on.

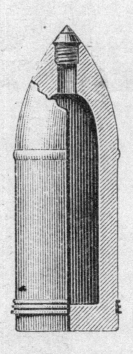

SILVER BULLET NO. 9

REGURGITATED OLD IDEAS

Our approach is a three-step change model that looks nothing like all the other ones
but in reality it still has three steps. They work because lots of people have them,
but ours really is different. Honest.

THE LIFE CYCLE OF A SILVER BULLET

OR: TRYING TO PIN THIS THING DOWN

Chapter 1:
The Life Cycle of a Silver Bullet

"Models, methodologies, processes, or even consultants serve as psychological support for the denizens of corporate-land, much in the same way as teddy bears or security blankets provide three-year-olds with a sense of security that serves to facilitate emotional development." David Wastell (1996: 'The Fetish of Technique: Methodology as a Social Defence')

"The Silver Bullet is based fundamentally on assumptions of command and control, of prediction, and response." Glenda Eoyang[10]

When I started research for this book, I was sure others would have already come to similar conclusions or made the same argument. In patches that was true and an early example was when several people who knew of my work sent me the link to a post by Chris Bolton, entitled 'The Lifecycle of a Silver Bullet'. His thinking, and that of fellow Welshman Matt Wyatt,[11] inform this chapter on the nature of Silver Bullets in organisational contexts.

I touched on the mythology of the Silver Bullet in the Introduction, and now we come to what that mythology looks like when transmogrified into solutions that offer guaranteed outcomes for organisations. 'Transmogrified' seems the right word here, because it means 'to transform in a surprising or magical manner', and Silver Bullets are nothing if not magical.

'The Life Cycle of a Silver Bullet' was the subject of a 2003 paper in *The Journal of Defense Software Engineering* written by Sarah A. Sheard, a researcher and consultant in software engineering. It neatly describes the trajectory that many Silver Bullets take, from inception to eventual decline and either death or ignominious neglect. Chris Bolton, a Welsh consultant and blogger, helpfully translated Sheard's paper into a graphic and accompanying explanation.[12]

---

10. Interview 5th May 2020

11. There is a coven of complexity thinkers in Wales who do interesting and useful work e.g. www.complexwales.com

12. https://whatsthepont.blog/2017/05/29/the-life-cycle-of-a-silver-bullet/

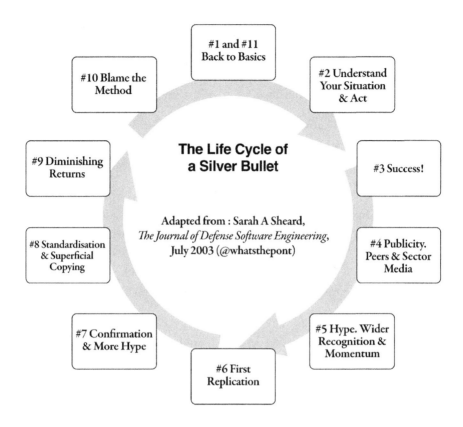

Stage #1 Back to Basics. This involves throwing out all of the existing Silver Bullets and having a good look at your organisation, because you really should know it better than people from outside.

Stage #2 Understand Your Situation & Act. The most important part. This involves a proper examination of what does and doesn't work for the organisation. Done by the people who are involved in the actual work, not external consultants. Managers listen (properly) and help to make good things happen.

Stage #3 Success. The organisation reaps the rewards of having people working at the jobs they understand and are good at.

Stage #4 Publicity. Peers and Sector Media. People start to notice good things happening and case studies and other reports start to emerge. I'm not against case studies, but beware. There is always a tendency to 're-imagine' what happened in getting from A to B, so that it all neatly fits together and looks like there was a glorious plan (Hindsight Bias).

Stage #5 Hype. Wider Recognition and Momentum. People start to pay attention now and look at how they might copy the recipe for success. This really helps if the original approach is given a name (say the Balle-Argentee Method, to add some Francophile elegance to the term 'Silver Bullet') and a 'model' created that you can easily draw on office flipcharts.

Stage #6 First Replication. Things haven't gone horribly wrong YET. The first people to replicate do a lot of work to understand why the Balle-Argentee Method works. They probably talk closely with the people who originally used it, and modify the process to suit their own circumstances.

Stage #7 Confirmation and More Hype. The First Replicators have success in using the method. This confirmation is all that is needed for the sector media and other commentators to 'cash in' and produce literature promoting the method. This is where the management consultant and others get involved offering to help organisations implement the Balle-Argentee Method. (Does any of this sound familiar yet?)

Stage #8 Standardisation and Superficial Copying. This is where things really start to go wrong. In a world of tight budgets, conflicting demands, initiative overload and dubious leadership, the people within organisations are forced to implement the Balle-Argentee Method. This will be fresh on the heels of the last improvement methodology that head office has sent down the line. Just to make things worse, it has been standardised and simplified by the Central Team so that anyone can understand it (this might get called 'designing out the idiot' in some organisations …).

Stage #9 Diminishing Returns. No surprise here. Staff resist having something else forced upon them and the Balle-Argentee Method fails to solve the problems of the organisation.

Stage #10 Blame the Method. The Balle-Argentee method is discredited. This is backed up by evidence from front-line delivery where staff complain that the method makes them do stupid things (this always helps in getting shot of something).

Stage #11 Start Afresh & Back to Basics. Someone sensible throws out the Balle-Argentee Method. They have a good look at their organisation, because they really should know it better than people from outside. And the whole cycle starts again, just like a Silver Boomerang.

This life cycle contains an erroneous assumption: that the unique is also universal. It shows up in the love that clients have for case studies, plus the willingness of purveyors of Silver Bullets to offer them. The gritty reality is we may not get the same nourishment from following the same recipe: therein lies the off-the-shelf smoke and mirrors of doctor-patient consultancy, rather than the self-awareness and self-efficacy of collaborative and process consulting to create bespoke, context-specific solutions. What other people did 'there and then' is of interest, but only insofar as it inspires or provokes us to notice what we might choose to do 'here and now'. The challenge this presents is that it requires you to resist the temptation to use – or provide – a case study, except by way of reflective practice for introspection and further self-awareness.

Management fads

> "In the face of sagging fortunes, companies become noticeably more willing to experiment with new ideas." Richard Pascale (1990: 18)

Management fads – those business ideas that periodically emerge, become popular and then lose credence over time – share key characteristics of Silver Bullets. Management theorist Richard Pascale documents fads from 1950 to 2000 in *Managing On The Edge* (1990). He covers everything from theory X/ theory and management by objectives, through to value chains, quality circles, 'wellness', 'excellence', Kanban, one-minute managing and more. A fad for every day of the month, and all to varying degrees pedalled with certainty that, this time, we had 'the answer' to something challenging. As Pascale notes, with a sigh you can almost hear, "not surprisingly, ideas acquired with ease are discarded with ease" (ibid.: 20).

Some 'fads' are useful and offer value, even if they are not Silver Bullets e.g. if you explore the history of Total Quality Management (TQM) it morphs into Business Process Re-engineering (BPR), before Lean becomes all the rage, and then Six Sigma appears and Lean Six Sigma is the go-to approach. More of methodologies as Silver Bullets later in Chapter 6.

In a certain irony, given its propensity for being a channel through which many new ideas and fads are disseminated, the *Harvard Business Review* (HBR) in 2002 neatly offered a simple guide to spotting management fads, for they tend to be:

- simple
- prescriptive
- falsely encouraging
- one-size-fits-all
- easy to cut-and-paste
- in tune with the zeitgeist
- novel not radical
- legitimised by gurus and disciples

Silver Bullets, in other words. The question is what distinguishes these from thoughtful experimentation? I like Pascale's framing, when he suggests the difference is one of "commitment and follow through, *whether or not* the initial attempt is a success *or* a failure. When a new idea fails, we give up instead of investigating the causes of failure and addressing them systematically" (ibid.: 21). As we will see in Chapter 10, this 'giving up' can cost hundreds of millions of $, all because it is easier to write that off than investigate.

The Wizard of Oz Factor

OZ'S VOICE: Do not arouse the wrath of the great and powerful Oz! I said come back tomorrow!

DOROTHY: If you were really great and powerful you would keep your promises!

OZ'S VOICE: Do you presume to criticise the Great Oz! You ungrateful creature! Think yourself lucky that I am giving you audience tomorrow instead of twenty years from now ... The Great Oz has spoken. Oh ... pay no attention to that man behind the curtain. The Great Oz has spoken.
DOROTHY: Who are you?

OZ'S VOICE: Well, I – I – I am the Great and Powerful – Wizard of Oz.

DOROTHY: You are?

WIZARD: Uhhhh ...

DOROTHY: I don't believe you!

WIZARD: No, I'm afraid it's true. There's no other Wizard except me.

SCARECROW: You humbug!

LION: Yeah!

WIZARD: Yes-s-s – that … that's exactly so. I'm a humbug!

The Wizard of OZ (1939)

The truth is often far less impressive or neat when we finally see how things really are. Like Dorothy in *The Wizard of Oz*, the short man frantically pulling levers behind a curtain is an approximation of what really happens when Silver Bullets are devised.

Matt Wells, another of the community of complexity and change practitioners I found in Wales, commented on a blog that most Silver Bullets are the product of muddling through. This muddling through is then opportunistically monetised:

> "… they look back over what they did (which is never documented very well) and make up a perfectly plausible and rational explanation of the steps they took to succeed, as if they were there all along and followed from the beginning. They were not … they just don't really understand how they actually did the stuff themselves and kid themselves into believing their own hype." (Matt Wells, 22-05-2027 at 6:43 pm, comment on Chris Bolton, *Silver Bullet Syndrome and Richard Pascale's Management Fads,* on What's The Pont blog 14-05-2017)[13]

Believing in one's own hype, when you are in the business of selling Silver Bullets, is a good example of the logical fallacy of assuming that one thing caused another merely because the first thing preceded the other.[14]

I love this idea of muddling through because it is far closer to what really happens. To muddle through we need reflection and connection, and we cannot do it alone. This means paying attention to relationship and relating and working together. Silver Bullets offer an illusory way of bypassing and avoiding that work.

---

13. https://whatsthepont.blog/2017/05/14/silver-bullet-syndrome-and-richard-pascales-management-fads/

14. "Post hoc, ergo propter hoc" – "after this, therefore because of this" https://rationalwiki.org/wiki/Post_hoc,_ergo_propter_hoc

Just like the Wizard of Oz, behind the smooth consultancy offering snazzy slide decks stuffed with impressive models and graphs, things are messier and less functional than they'd have you believe. The Life Cycle of a Silver Bullet is in part sustained because we choose not to look behind the curtain and acknowledge the muddling. The 'expert' who is prepared to own their fallibility and imperfection is not as common as it could be, which is to our collective detriment.

How to dodge a Silver Bullet

In her paper, Sheard suggests that the morals of her story are as follows:

1. A sequence of steps, each consisting of decisions made for good reasons, does not necessarily lead to a good result.
2. For best results, start at Phase 1 and stop at Phase 3.
3. Only by really looking at your company's problems can you solve them. Other people's strategies worked for them because the strategies were made for them. If you want to make real improvements, you have to do the work of determining your business problems and applying methods that make sense to fix them.
4. Do not assume that people who claim to be using a method really are using it.
5. There is nothing like the original. Do not read everyone else's interpretation of a method, read the original. If possible, talk to the creator. Find out the principles behind the steps, so you can ensure your adaptation is consistent with the principles.
6. The ROIs of multiple improvement initiatives do not add; they interfere. Focus on what problems you want to solve, and work out as executives how the initiatives contribute to solutions. Determine where the initiatives will appear as conflicting to the workers and reconcile them. Display a unified front to the workers.
7. Do not assume other companies' ROI numbers will apply to you. They started from a different place and made different investments.

These morals, I suggest, serve as a backdrop to what you will read in subsequent chapters, and reinforce Sheard's argument.

She goes on to offer guidance on how to avoid Silver Bullets, which Bolton (*The Life Cycle of a Silver Bullet*, on What's The Pont blog 29-05-2017) helpfully summarises as:

EVERYONE – Remember that methods are just a means to an end.

EXECUTIVES – Understand your organisation, and also understand the methods you are promoting and listen to messages from below.

MANAGERS – Really need to understand the methods they are pushing.

PROCESS/POLICY STAFF – Push back if things don't look sensible, especially any targets imposed.

Finally, Sheard's 'big message' is that it is crucial to understand your own context and situation, and not rely on someone else's, which are a form of 'second generation Silver Bullet'. This is a leitmotif in this book.

Let's just pretend the world is a lot neater than it really is

Chris Rodgers, in *The Wiggly World of Organisation* (2021), simplified the Lifecycle of the Silver Bullet. Here we see how the messiness of organisational activity (Phase 1) is post-rationalised into a story that makes sense of our experience and edits out the uncomfortable elements (e.g. mistakes, pain, loss, failure, shame, etc.) into a more comfortable narrative for future storytelling (Phase 2). These neatened stories are further word smithed and polished by academics and practitioners into generalisable theories that, crucially, "reinforce the myths of rationality, predictability and control" (Phase 3 below). Lastly (Phase 4), we get the full transformation of the generalisable into idealised prescriptions and solutions that can be sold with certainty to clients who are looking for, well, certainty.

Management in five acts…

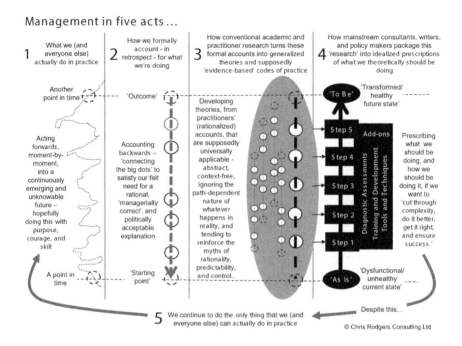

© Chris Rodgers Consulting Ltd

This is reminiscent of Wile E. Coyote from the Warner Brothers cartoons. Wile is a lovely example of leadership addicted to Silver Bullets. The coyote seemingly faces the same core problem again and again, namely, how to catch the roadrunner. However, he fails to acknowledge how circumstances are subtly changing over time. He endlessly goes back to Acme to buy different supposed solutions to his problem … and fails on each occasion, not because the instrument is faulty, but because he fails to attend to what is happening around him and prefers action to thought, as everything he does has to be done at speed.

In Rodgers' model we see more clearly the collusion that exists between all the parties involved, and how clients, in many ways, sow the seeds for them to be sold solutions that emanated from their own contexts and learning. There is a certain irony in clients being sold things they have, in essence, come up with themselves.

It also highlights how collusion has a function as a defence against anxiety (something we will explore more in Chapter 2) and is functional in the sense of being a workable and useful strategy/orientation, even if it cannot offer a guaranteed solution. Thus collusion can be simultaneously defensively functional and pragmatically dysfunctional.

Understanding the Lifecycle of a Silver Bullet is not enough

Firstly, if understanding the Lifecycle of a Silver Bullet was sufficient, then these ideas would have travelled far and wide and we would all be a lot less susceptible. Given the sheer number of people with a vested interest in maintaining the fiction, it should not be a surprise that a few lone voices are struggling to be heard.

Secondly, I am not convinced that there is a sufficiently deep understanding of either the psychology of Silver Bullets, or just how pervasive the functional collusion that sustains them is.

The rest of this book, therefore, is an attempt to peel the curtain away more fully, a little like the small dog in *The Wizard of Oz,* so that the fiction of Silver Bullets for complex organisational challenges can be seen more clearly. Maybe, at that point, there might be a little less easy acceptance of the bellowing macho voices, glamour, smoke and lights emanating from behind the curtain.

Reflective Questions

- What Silver Bullets have you picked up and sought to use – and how did that work out for you?
- Have you ever been bedazzled by the smoke and lightshow of a wizard? What will stop that happening again?
- Have you ever hired a Lone Ranger, or played that role with a client?
- What myths do you still believe in, even though part of you know they are not really true?
- What management fads are you susceptible to?

SILVER BULLET NO. 12

TOP 3/5/10 WAYS TO...

We have put together a list of the top things
you need to do to address your problem.
This is it. There are no others.
I mean, when things are in a Top 3/5/10,
that means it's all ok, doesn't it?..

PREPARING THE GROUND — WHAT PSYCHOLOGICALLY DRIVES THE NEED FOR SILVER BULLETS?

OR: FURTLING AROUND IN OUR MESSY UNCONSCIOUS

Chapter 2:
Preparing the Ground – What Psychologically Drives the Need for Silver Bullets?

Before getting into the meat of the book, I want to linger for a moment on why it is human beings find Silver Bullets so attractive. At face value it is obvious: kill the monster, get rid of the threat, lessen the chances of injury or death. How does that translate into an organisational context, and what is going on psychologically? Silver Bullets appeal to lonely heroes, disconnected from their vulnerability and supportive connections with others, perhaps in the grip of and needing to maintain narcissistic fantasies of greatness. Looking for the next thing that will give them a competitive edge over others.

This book and chapter in particular are heavily influenced by Simon Cavicchia, a consultant, coach and supervisor. His thinking underpins much of it, through conversations, email exchanges, sharing of ideas and his published works.

Starting with an exploration of some of the factors that drive the need for certainty, I move on to explore the idea of psychological defences, till the soil on shame, as it applies to organisations and leadership specifically, and pull on several threads which may help us understand the unconscious and collusive behaviours that lead to Silver Bullet questing.

The Expert Tension

Experts and expertise play a key role, as they are who we normally go to for Silver Bullets (after all, would you buy a Silver Bullet or stake from an amateur monster hunter?). This relationship with experts and expertise is … complicated. On the one hand, we love them when it comes to many of the things we depend on, e.g. medical procedures, the design of aeroplanes, our personal finances, etc. At other moments, the relationship is more fraught, if we do not like what they are saying – politically or morally – or are terrified, e.g. think about the mixed responses to COVID experts on everything from vaccines to lockdown. In a 'post truth age', the expert is whoever you agree with.

In organisations, complex challenges often involve many people needing to work together, ideally towards a common objective, but equally they may not even be able to agree on that. In that situation, someone who offers certainty to cut through the noise, well, they are welcomed with open arms. The person or thing that promises to fix things will likely find an audience, even if in a different context we might well treat their confidence with slightly more scepticism.

I'll come back to experts later in the book, but for now let's explore certainty.

What drives the need for certainty?

We need to start here, and unpick what might underpin certainty, because it is what creates receptivity for the market in Silver Bullets. From the research interviews, several themes emerged, many recurring:

- Expectations – of leaders, followers, stakeholders, shareholders, etc. which necessitates that a lot of weight is put on clarity, certainty and coherence.
- Pace – the need to be seen to be doing something right now and the need for speed. Rachel Cashman, who works with executive teams on psychological safety, suggests this creates a psychologically unsafe platform for boards to operate in, increasing the tendency to grasp for anything.[15]
- Archetypes of 'great leaders' – e.g. fast, decisive, confident, heroic, charismatic, etc.
- Laziness – because, bluntly, it is too much like hard work (or too uncomfortable) to stop and think.
- Myth of fixability (Cole & Higgins, 2022) – laziness in part underpinned by assumptions about the nature of change.
- Fear and anxiety – of failure; of what might be discovered or revealed, about either the situation or oneself; existential anxiety; discomfort with ambiguity; of being exposed somehow as 'not knowing' or being seen as incompetent; of being held accountable; of simply being and bringing oneself to work, e.g. in the C-Suite and executive level more widely, how OK is it to 'be you', really? And underpinning all of that – shame.
- Inability to cope with not knowing – not knowing what to do, why something is happening, what will happen if I do/do not act, etc.

---

15. Interview 12th May 2020

- Anxiety born of privilege that is found to be built on sand – when you realise all the things you had as Silver Bullets do not in fact work, and all our models and tools and thought leaders do NOT have the answer.
- The need to please – parent/child behaviour is rife in many organisations for the simple reason they reflect the humanity of those that work there. Part of this dynamic is the need for some leaders to be liked, to please employees and peers by being seen, for example, to have found the solution to a problem.
- Regression – Jesse Segers suggests that thinking in terms of Silver Bullets is 'childlike' in the oversimplification, and potentially indicates a lack of emotional maturity. "If it's too big, cognitively, [simplifying] gives you the illusion of certainty."[16]
- Displacement – the need to make someone – or something – else responsible. Joost Minnaar from Corporate Rebels suggested "many leaders want this recipe or Silver Bullet, because then the responsibility is on the bullet or the recipe and not on them, creating one".[17]
- Mindset – if your background is one that tends to a view that the world is inherently plannable or you have a high need for precision, that will increase the need.
- Cognitive overload – all this 'stuff' is just too much to bear.
- Risk reduction – in commercial environments less a need for certainty, rather to quantify, manage and/or externalise risks as best as possible. However, 'risk' can be deeply personal and subjective, even if coached in business-speak.

And to wrap things up, a nice list from Rob Briner, Professor of Organisational Psychology at Queen Mary University London:

Magical thinking, incentives and rewards for leaders, cognitive biases, lack of training in decision-making, limited accountability, few evaluations and "management 'theatre' where being seen to be doing something is more important than what you actually do".[18]

Given all of that, it is hardly surprising that leaders are receptive to offers of certainty in the form of Silver Bullet solutions. I feel the pull myself, particularly when I think about the more existential challenges we face societally and globally. Who wouldn't? Wishing something were true is not the same thing as

---

16. Interview 20th April 2023
17. Interview 18th May 2020
18. Email 17th February 2024

it being so, and the way we construe the world, and interact with it as it really is, is key.

The maps we use influence our destination

Maps have their uses. They help us from A to B, to the hotels when we go on holiday, rendezvous with loved ones, both familiar and illicit (oo-err). They enable us to contain anxiety in the face of what we experience as novel, unknown and overwhelming. Once we contain anxiety, like soldiers in a battle trying to make sense of their position relative to the enemy, we gain perspective and begin to collaborate and strategise for plotting our way through uncharted territory, one step at a time. Maps can support us to make sense of what is complex, multi-layered, nuanced and defies a total, complete 'once and for all' understanding. What they cannot do, even if they are closer to the territory they purport to orient us towards, is reflect all the contours and unique features. That is why people get lost, even with satnav, or run the risk of walking off cliffs because Google maps told them to.[19] Maps have a function, therefore, but they may not be accurate.

All maps for understanding human systems, including the many created for corporate clients, consultants and experts, embrace implicit and inherent biases, assumptions and theoretical underpinnings. They also illuminate aspects of the complex fields we and our clients operate in and miss other dimensions. This means we need to be aware of the maps we use and bring a degree of critical reflexivity to them so that we can be simultaneously aware of their uses and limitations.

One of the hypotheses of this book is that the maps we use to come up with solutions to complex problems are not always fit for purpose, and in some cases are downright dangerous. They may not lead to people falling off cliffs, but they do lead to job losses, lost livelihoods and a significant impact on the emotional and psychological well-being of many of those involved. The problem is, until we acknowledge what might be going on underneath the surface – that which is hidden by functional collusion – we cannot begin to accurately describe what is really going on nor how best to address that. If we believe COVID is just a common cold, for example, and ignore data that says otherwise, then we might end up seriously ill.

---

19. https://futurism.com/the-byte/google-maps-walking-directions-off-cliff

What follows is an overview of the psychological topography of some of the features of the terrain we are exploring that might be worth thinking about, if we want to better understand what drives the need for certainty.

Anxiety and rabbit holes

There is a risk here of going down a Freudian rabbit hole (no pun intended), as Freud is often referenced when it comes to anxiety. For clarity, he considered there were three types:

- *Objective anxiety* – results from a real threat in the physical world to one's well-being, as when a ferocious-looking dog appears from around the corner.
- *Neurotic anxiety* – results from the ego feeling overwhelmed by the id, which threatens to express its irrationality in thoughts and behaviour. There is a fear of external punishment for such expression.
- *Moral anxiety* – based on a feeling that one's internalised values are about to be compromised. There is a fear of self-punishment (e.g. guilt) for acting contrary to one's values … Whatever the anxiety, the ego seeks to reduce it. Operating at the unconscious level, it employs defence mechanisms to distort or deny reality.[20]

At points, all three will be alluded to, but my primary focus here is organisations, because they are just as prone as individuals to suffering from the symptoms of anxiety, the impact of which will be a potential reduction in strategic adaptability and effectiveness (Stein, 2021: 226).

To understand the role of anxiety in organisations it is helpful to consider how social systems work and the defences that arise when things become too uncomfortable. Anxiety increases in times of uncertainty, when being aware and increasingly conscious of how we make meaning about our experience is vital. The alternative is to assume meaning is pre-determined and fixed based on past experience, i.e. we act based on past events, regardless of whether that is an appropriate response. Silver Bullets are the ultimate defence against a threat which defies reason and all known or traditional remedies. Silver Bullets as metaphors offer a promise of salvation from that which represents our worst fears and a universal treatment for all that ails us.

---

20. From a neat online summary of Freudian anxiety: https://bit.ly/3PC3kRI

Psychoanalysis has long described the fear human beings have of the irrational, the instinctual and the unconscious, whether that be the blood-sucking lust of vampires or toothy hairiness of the werewolf. In the context of contemporary life, the bogeyman who haunts apparently rational and reasonable human behaviour is anything that is experienced as new, potentially overwhelming, unknown and which threatens to destabilise our constructions of a social, ordered and controllable reality. The anxiety gets even worse when our resulting identities based on images of mastery and domination are challenged. Examples of when reality might erode our sense of identity include:

- The complex change programme that defies all attempts at 'management', with complex human system dynamics (i.e. those pesky people) just not following the plan;
- A rapidly changing competitor landscape threatening the viability of an organisation, evoking anxiety and calling for responsive innovation in order for the organisation to survive; and
- Human emotions, needs and vulnerabilities, which are often hidden or denied, bubble up and exert powerful influences on how people think, relate and effectively coordinate (or not!) as they attempt to change ways of working.

From a psychoanalytic perspective, total mastery and control are an illusion. Not only do people behave as if they have control when they do not, or overestimate the control they have in the face of complexity, they are as likely to under-estimate how much they actually have – in short "people make imperfect estimates of their level of control" (Gino, Sharek & Moore, 2011: 104).

What is real, and no better demonstrated than in the COVID pandemic, is that we live in a precarious, contextual and interdependent world of far greater unpredictability and potent natural forces than we are able to tolerate psychologically. Pause for a moment to consider not just the predictions of climate scientists, rather look at the insane temperatures in 2023 across the globe (and those you may have experienced personally) and check how easy you find that to dwell on.[21] So, we construct all manner of elaborate defences, which are necessary to cope with anxiety as it arises. The problem comes when defences are unacknowledged, because then they can become established patterns of behaviour and impede or block learning and change.

---

21. They terrify me.

Basic defences include repression, denial and displacement, i.e. the ability to push away and out of conscious awareness anything we perceived as threatening to the narratives we have constructed to soothe ourselves. Elliott Jaques, a Canadian psychoanalyst, social scientist and management consultant often regarded as the originator of concepts such as 'corporate culture', 'mid-life crisis', and 'requisite organisation' (among others), was the first to put forward a theory of social defence in organisational life (Stein, 2021: 227).

Jaques' ponderings on organisational change and the dynamics that hold many an organisation in stasis are worth considering, as he proposed:

> "(i) the central hypothesis of social defence systems …; which includes (ii) the idea that social defences provide a kind of institutional glue or binding function; (iii) the interrelatedness of task and dynamics; (iv) the fact that changes bring about a disruption to the defences established over time and hence change will be resisted for unconscious as well as conscious and more obvious reasons." (Stein 2021: 229)

To translate: if we have an organisation struggling with how to (re-)organise, then one way to defend against the anxiety that it may all be about to go to hell in a handcart is to latch onto the offer (aka glue) of a methodology that promises to make it happen with minimum fuss, even if that means trampling over the psychological and emotional dynamics. Any disruption that occurs that is not 'in the plan' may be resisted, including the views of people pointing out why the plan is not working. One of the most obvious examples of these social defences against anxiety are the pronouncements of companies announcing job losses. Two examples, from LinkedIn and Rolls Royce, released within days of each other:

- "While we are adapting our organisational structures and streamlining our decision making, we are continuing to invest in strategic priorities for our future and to ensure we continue to deliver value for our members and customers. We are committed to providing our full support to all impacted employees during this transition and ensuring that they are treated with care and respect." (*LinkedIn to lay off hundreds of people amid broader restructuring*, Axios, 16-10-2023)
- "… a simpler, more streamlined, organisation in the next phase of its multi-year transformation. The new structure will create a more agile business that is better able to serve customers and continue to create and maintain world-class products … The changes being proposed will also

remove duplication and deliver cost efficiencies." (*Rolls-Royce to create simpler, more efficient and effective organisation to continue to deliver world class products,* RR press release, 17-10-2023)

The Rolls Royce release is a perfect example of how compassion expressed towards the people affected by change is typically in inverse proportion to the number of buzzwords used. The less language about people and how they might be feeling, the easier it is to deny one's own emotions or the consequences of one's actions.

Organisation as a container of anxiety

Isabel Menzies Lyth (1960), who along with Jaques (1951) was part of the Tavistock Institute of Human Relations' rise as a centre of Organisation Development grounded in system psychodynamics, is another key figure. Specifically, her work drew attention to the way in which organisations act as containers of anxiety for everybody in them, to which the success of any social institution would be intrinsically linked. So any action which weakens that sense of safety releases anxiety across the system. This means that every glittery change exercise driven from behind the curtain by the wizards in the boardroom will inevitably generate discomfort for those impacted.

The kicker in all this, organisational consultant James Krantz noted, is that "what makes social defences so effective is that they either eliminate situations that expose people to anxiety-provoking activity altogether or they insulate people from the consequences of their actions" (Krantz, 2010: 192). That is the Silver Bullet solution in a nutshell: it embodies a social defence against anxiety, in that, if we really believe they exist, we both minimise anxiety – 'phew there IS something that will fix this intractable problem and take the pain away' – or we have the ultimate excuse – 'it's not my fault, the damn bullet didn't work as it was supposed to'.

It's worth acknowledging a subtle distinction between Menzies Lyth and Jaques. The former's seminal 1961 paper developed Elliott Jaques' (1955) work on social defence against anxiety (Krantz, 2010: 193). Where she differs is in suggesting that an organisational system reflects more than just its unconscious dynamics.

"[The] elements of organisational life – structures, practices, policies, technologies, methods of working, patterns of decision making, the distribution of authority, and so on – are the 'stuff' of social defences. While these aspects of organisational life exist to facilitate work, they come to be utilised for the additional purpose of helping people manage anxiety." (Ibid.)

To put it another way: every project plan, strategy, Target Operating Model (TOM), process map, job description, positioning statement, values model, competency framework and memo, one way or another, they all serve as containers for anxiety. You know that organisation that you worked in that frustrated the hell out of you because of all the bureaucracy? That is because the anxiety was likely so high, systemically, that people were trying to manage it with evermore process and procedure. Similarly, the workplace that feels unsafe and chaotic, where you have no sense of where the edges and limits of work and permissible behaviour are? Not enough containment. For all the bling and shininess of organisational models and theories, of change gurus and experts, underneath it all remains the fun and games of human beings trying to make sense of the world and their relationships with each other.

The more rigid the attachment and narrow the defence of often reductive ideas the greater the echo of the underlying terror human beings face when they begin to experience a reality that is far more complex and unpredictable than they imagined possible. It therefore cannot be controlled, only related and responded to. Taking and defending fixed positions operate as a defence and is at the heart of any form of fundamentalism, whether that be religious, political or organisational. It gives the illusion of mastery over the un-masterable and offers inclusion and community within factions of shared belief. They are thought collectives, which we will explore more in Chapter 9.

The price we pay for this is a reduction in the capacity to face complexity collectively and work together to optimise responses. This is why the importance of Menzies Lyth's work here cannot be overestimated, for "underlying the entire body of work was an affirmation of the developmental and reparative potential of work and the belief that one of the most important gratifications of adult life is the ability to work well" (Krantz, 2010: 194). Her emphasis on "practicality – developing theory that is judged by its usefulness – which was formalised as 'Action Research methodology'" and "the interdisciplinary integration of different perspectives" (ibid.) is something we would do well to remember and continue to learn from, especially when considering Silver Bullets. These are, after all, a mental and social construct, an idea, a belief in something that will be a magical and complete answer. As such, the pursuit of them points simultaneously to what we fear and how we attempt to manage those fears through magical thinking and a desire for any suffering to be spirited away. This sits in sharp contrast to the existential philosophical view that a certain amount of uncertainty and suffering are an inevitable part of the human condition which we need to and can tolerate. Which is precisely why they are so seductive.

Context and assumptions matter. Seriously, they really do.

In the organisational sphere with which this book is concerned, the context in which the buying and selling of Silver Bullets persists is characterised by several assumptions and orientations.

Despite developments in organisational and leadership theory and practice over the last thirty years, the world of organisations is still steeped in often unconscious, and therefore untested, assumptions about what an organisation is. The fact we assume it is a 'thing' may be the first problem: it is not, it is an abstraction, and only exists because the people in it decide it is one. I will come back to this tendency to 'thingify' complexity into oversimplified abstractions as part of the defence against anxiety.

For now, I want to turn to the question of where does human aversion to anxiety and threat of the unknown, along with the deep desire for suffering to be spirited away, come from? What makes us tick at a deeper level? This will necessarily be a light touch signposting, as there is a lot here, and it is important to acknowledge some of what lies beneath the apparent rationality in the world of work.

It's in the genes

Brace yourself reader, because we are going into some concepts that at first may feel a bit remote from the workplace, but on closer examination are not. I want to touch on the evolutionary perspective of the development of an autonomic nervous system. This plays an important role in keeping us safe, in that it causes us to respond to physical danger and pain, which is necessary for our survival. Many living organisms have this capacity, unsurprisingly, because we need to work out whether what is rustling in the bushes is a fluffy bunny or a sabre-toothed tiger, or worse, a sabre-toothed bunny. As a species, our brains have been evolving for millennia and neuroscience continues to reveal how our brains form part of a complex nervous system, which includes and processes stimuli from other areas of the human body including the human gut. Among many autonomic functions (automatic functions which happen without us needing to think or act) such as controlling respiration, temperature and heart rate, our nervous systems have evolved to keep us safe. Safe however is not the same thing as logical, rational or able to make good decisions, which is what makes it relevant here.

The autonomic nervous system acts as an early warning system alerting us to the possibility of threat and enables us to take effective protective action in the form of sympathetic responses such as fight, flight or parasympathetic responses, e.g. freeze or submit. Should we accidentally pass our hand over the spout of a kettle which has just boiled, we will have recoiled, or at least started to recoil, from the burning steam ahead of consciously registering what has happened and remembering that steam is hot and best avoided. In organisations, walking into a meeting to discover a well-known volcano prone to erupting is sitting around the table may elicit a similar response. The speed with which these reflexes happen demonstrates the degree to which we are neurobiologically wired to withdraw from threat or pain.

One way to withdraw from pain in the workplace therefore is to ensure that we minimise the risk of attack from those in power – whether above us or peers – who through their anxiety might go on the attack if their needs are not met. A good way of doing this is to move as quickly as possible to that which resolves or minimises the sense of a loss of control, i.e. the Silver Bullet solution.

Nurture – yes: mum, dad and that childhood stuff has an impact

We start off small in relation to a world of adults who are, from an infant's perspective, experienced giants upon whom our survival depends. Psychoanalytic writers (Winnicott, 1958) have described the need of children to believe adults know what they are doing and can be relied upon. This sets up fantasies of omniscient others who can relieve us not only of physical suffering but emotional and psychological distress, for example loneliness, isolation and fear of abandonment to which as a species we are particularly sensitive.

As far as we can tell from what we currently presume to know (given that we cannot know what we do not know!), the human species has developed neurologically beyond the functioning of the autonomic nervous system of the reptilian brain (MacLean, 1990) to include the limbic system (social brain) and neocortex, or newest part of the brain which supports awareness and consciousness of our experience of existing. So, in addition to driving the recoil from physical threat and pain, as human beings we also experience movement towards social and psychological pleasure and away from psychological pain.

The neocortex is also the part of the brain in which we construct and hold meanings about ourselves and the world and the relationships we form with others and the systems in which we are situated.

Early childhood experiences have been shown to have a significant role in shaping how an individual makes meaning from experiences throughout infancy and adult life, known as mentalisation (Fonagy *et al.*, 2002). The more unreliable and inconsistent the responses of adult caregivers, the more likely an individual is to be ambivalent and anxious about the world and his relationships. This foundation of insecurity will find its way into making meaning informed by this undercurrent of anxiety and low trust, leading to rigidity of thinking and position taking, even fundamentalism, as a form of defence. These processes underpin developmental capacity for thinking and reflecting on experience, which means that how we think and reflect in organisations is directly related to early life.

Importantly, the quality of the early neurobiological dance between infants and their caregivers is also vital to the development of a capacity for empathy and understanding of others. If we cannot understand or acknowledge another's subjective experience, and feel secure in the face of that, then we are in the realm of 'what I believe to be true'. Where empathy and the capacity to appreciate and be interested in the different perspectives of others without feeling threatened is undeveloped, the scene is set for the pursuit of, and dependency on, certain versions of reality which can only ever be partial and limited. They will need to be defended at all costs in the face of any data or wider perspectives that might call the sanctity a particular version of reality into question.

These perspectives and versions of reality can persist into adult life. So it is no surprise then that when anxious, we seek an external source to heal us – a Silver Bullet – in the form of experts and theories. Of course, some suffering requires an appropriate professional, but when the nature of a problem – such as organisational change – is complex and nuanced, there may be an over-reliance on external expertise. Yet outsourcing the solution to this anxiety has considerable limitations.

Uncertainty and the fight/flight/freeze thing

Neuroscience research has shown that when experiencing anxiety and stress, because of the amygdala activating the flight/fight or freeze responses to threat, human beings suffer a reduction in their ability to reflect, analyse data, consider different perspectives on a problem, evaluate options and consciously choose their responses (Siegel,1999). Research into trauma has shown that individuals can learn to regulate their nervous system activation and this is finding its way into organisational life in the form of mindfulness and resilience programmes.

Yet there is a long way to go. When faced with the unknown or the overwhelm of multiple complex challenges along with anxieties about performance, reputation and career progression, leaders and followers tip into automatic, non-reflective reactivity becoming headless chickens. When in this state, the promise of an all-knowing consultant with a Silver Bullet can be particularly seductive.

De Berker *et al.* (2016) demonstrated the relationship between actual or perceived uncertainty and nervous system activation and stress responses. A central idea in the neuroscience and psychology of stress is that this is reduced when there is balance between the stimuli experienced and the ability to respond effectively. When an individual is faced with experiences that are familiar and where they have an existing capacity to understand these experiences based on past events, and an existing repertoire of strategies and ways for effectively responding, stress and anxiety are reduced, and reflection and perspective-taking protected. Conversely, in the face of something unknown or new, balance is disrupted with an increase in stress or anxiety.

> "The paradox here is that if we remain within the comfort zone of our familiar experiences and responses we may experience reduced stress, but we will also not have the opportunity to develop new perspectives and strategies necessary for responding to the novel situation we find ourselves in." (Simon Cavicchia)[22]

In some ways, this is the nub of this whole book. By outsourcing the containment of anxiety to consultants, clients experience temporary relief, but never develop the resources to contain anxiety in themselves, thus creating and maintaining dependency on the individuals and organisations who serve them, and the Silver Bullets they sell.

------

22. Conversation 20th July 2023

Enabling and supporting individuals to tolerate and bear the inevitable disorientation that new learning and development brings, so that they can discover and develop their own internal resources for navigating complexity, seems to me an essential and necessary requirement. Contrast this with approaches to consulting that exploit clients' anxiety and the outward search for the parent/saviour by actively amplifying the nature of the problem and promising unrealistic and once-and-for-all solutions requiring vast investment in utilising specific resources … which just happen to be held exclusively by the consulting firm (more on this in Chapter 7).

From this brief foray into the neurobiological and developmental foundations of human experience, we can see that we are fundamentally wired to react to that which is experienced – or perceived – as painful or threatening.

The age of disconnection and the fuelling of narcissism, among other things

> "Given how the human personality develops through the influence of others and the environment, it is also inevitable that many of us … can get caught in identifying more rigidly with certain self-images and striving to live up to those images which are also sanctioned by the society and organisations that we live and work in." (Cavicchia & Gilbert, 2018: 145)

Simon Cavicchia's thinking underpins much of this section, in particular *The Theory and Practice of Relational Coaching: Complexity, Paradox and Integration* (2018), as does my experience of working alongside him with clients. Different individuals identify with their beliefs and contents of their minds with varying degrees of attachment and rigidity. Someone who is very identified with the belief 'I don't like foreign food', based on past negative experiences, may not be inclined to try *any* unfamiliar flavours, thereby denying themselves the possibilities of new and potentially pleasurable experiences among the vast array of new taste opportunities. This is akin to the Einstellung effect, which is when approaches to problem solving are negatively affected by previous experience. It stems from the work of American psychologist Abraham Luchins in the 1940s, and "the effect occurs when a repeated solution to old problems is applied to a new problem even though a more appropriate response is available" (Binz & Schultz, 2023: 526). The effect is particularly relevant to experts as well, which this book is also concerned with in several chapters. Sternberg (1996: 347) noted: "… there are costs as well as benefits to expertise. One such cost is increased rigidity: The expert can become so entrenched in a point of view or a way of doing things that it becomes hard to see things differently." Which is maybe why some experts cling onto their models and theories for so long when their efficacy is increasingly in doubt.

Similarly, a leader may be strongly wedded to beliefs about the importance of hierarchy and command and control as being the only legitimate and appropriate way to achieve organisational effectiveness and personal success. Their identity might be fused with images of being authoritative, potent and controlling of the environment. As such, they may struggle to adjust and develop the skills and behaviours necessary to negotiate and co-construct meaning and strategy where multiple stakeholders with different subjectivities and perspectives may need to participate in this process. This adherence to a particular world view that then shapes presence and practice is a reminder that the idea of 'leadership development' is illusory in so many instances.

Leaders, like the rest of us, have an inner world of self-images and ideals that have been shaped through life experiences and the influence of cultural discourses. These are then further shaped by the dominant assumptions about what is required to be successful and happy. The end result is that personality and ego come to dominate: they are privileged and characterised by narratives of what we associate with success and aspiration. That is how organisations end up favouring particular styles, and why leaders bend themselves out of shape to ensure they progress. As Cavicchia and Gilbert suggest, "we risk becoming in thrall to a virtual reality based on images" rather than connection to what it means to be really human (2018: 145).

A further consequence of this need to identify with particular images is *egoic striving*, suggest Cavicchia and Gilbert. This is an often unconscious process of maintaining the intactness of the ego, images and ideas with which an individual is identified e.g. strength, knowledge, power, status, capability, competence, success, etc. The problem is that this image is a narrow and inaccurate representation, disconnected from reality and our lived experience (Cavicchia & Gilbert, 2018: 145). So long as we believe that this image is reality, and are attached to that, we have an unconscious need to maintain it. If we do not have this image, and are threatened, that can feel existential, and we will defend ourselves based on the image we hold in mind, e.g. through trying to "control others and our environment, the accumulation of wealth, happiness, knowledge, status, and the acquisition of all that is associated with it" (ibid.). Defences in place, reality has little chance of really breaking through.

Over time, self-esteem and identity become overly fused with achievement and accumulation, "a permanent striving for the next bigger and better acquisition, promotion or experience" (ibid.). The result is a "failure to live up to these ideals [and] also causes shame as a feeling of being unworthy" (ibid.). This in turn fuels patterns of functional collusion.

Defining narcissism is a bit like Whack-A-Mole

"If there is one personality constellation to which leaders tend to gravitate it is the narcissistic one." Kets De Vries & Miller (1985: 583)

"Part of the confusion in research and practice on narcissism stems from the existence of multiple 'flavours' or forms of narcissism", observed Campbell *et al.* (2011: 270). They suggest that while there is broad agreement that there are two primary forms of narcissism – grandiose and vulnerable – "despite voluminous literature investigating narcissism, coverage of this construct is somewhat spotty in the organisational sciences" (ibid.: 272). So we need to tread lightly here, as the fixation on image and the discounting of deeper, painful experiences of emptiness and vulnerability are at the heart of narcissism. I am not interested in pathological narcissism, more in the idea that it is an inevitable part of the human condition. We need a little bit of healthy narcissism, as it is linked to personality development. Without it, there is no development of self-esteem or a sense of self-worth. This reflects a schism among researchers on what might be construed as 'bright side' and 'dark side' narcissism (ibid.: 272), but that is a spat we will leave here. For our purposes, I offer a definition from Simon Cavicchia:

> "Individual narcissism [in an organisational context] is the process whereby human beings defend against feelings of emptiness and deficiency by constructing grandiose self-images or 'ego ideals' with which they identify. They need to maintain these by behaving in ways associated with the ideals or demanding that others see them the way they wish to be seen, e.g. clever, knowing, powerful, competent, certain, assertive, etc."[23]

That can be compounded by the notion of the organisation ideal, which stems from Howard Schwartz's seminal book *Narcissistic Process and Corporate Decay* (Schwartz, 1990). This is when individuals, often out of conscious awareness, become preoccupied with living up to the expectations the organisation and its cultural norms place on them.

---

23. Email 4th November 2023

The risk is that excessive narcissism in an organisational context ultimately leads to performative leadership. The relationship between action (performance) and complex reality is severed in favour of maintaining images of greatness in the face of often devastating consequences and realities. 'Get Brexit Done!' in the UK is a recent example of leadership reduced to performative slogans disconnected for any real appreciation of the complexities. Trade deals which empirically have been proven to be tiny in comparison to what was earned by the UK when a member of the EU are described, along with any other activity, as 'world beating'. This performative aspect is subtle though:

> "... although CEO narcissism was unrelated to mean firm performance, narcissistic CEO's lead firms characterised by financial volatility and extreme levels of performance in both directions. In other words, narcissistic leaders are a force for change in organisations; however, this change can either lead organisations to unprecedented success or abject failure." (Campbell *et al.*, 2011: 283)

Lurking in here is how narcissism influences decision making, particularly when it leads to an inflated confidence in oneself and one's abilities, which ultimately leads to unpredictably risky decision making and impulsivity across a range of behaviours (ibid.: 277). Which is not the ideal state of mind to be in when considering how best to address a complex challenge.

Ultimately, there is an important distinction to be made here between what may be *actual* qualities of capability and competence, which an individual has and can draw upon, and the *image* of being competent and capable with which an individual is identified, and which is threatened every time life challenges it, temporarily, into question. Again, this is where shame potentially lurks and as Aram notes, some in the psychoanalytic field have "connected the process of shame with narcissistic processes to do with feelings of inadequacy, low or no sense of self-worth, immaturity, aggression and regression" (2001: 2).

Identification means that we experientially take ourselves, often unconsciously, to *be* the images and beliefs that we hold about ourselves. Given that "narcissism is often the driving force behind the desire to obtain a leadership position" (Kets De Vries & Miller, 1985: 587), that can explain why sometimes there is such a strong need to either ensure that there is a solution, or to deny that something has gone wrong when things do not work out as planned. It also talks to why change and transformational learning can be difficult. In truly changing a core belief, relaxing identification with a particular self-image and opening up to the implications of a different world view to one we have held for a long time, we change our identity. A leader, finding their familiar way of seeing themselves and operating in the world challenged by the context they find themself in, may experience confusion and disorientation as their familiar strategies, attachments and resulting identity fail to have the impact they desire. At that moment, unless they can work with their anxiety, this can feel, from the perspective of the ego, like a psychological death, which in turn can generate anxiety and resistance, and lead to reaching for solutions that promise to reduce that.

Leaders as gods

In organisational life, the ego ideals of omniscience and omnipotence are particularly relevant. These often contribute to the lonely hero archetype that still holds many leaders in its grip and can disconnect them from reality. Founding Executive Director of Human Systems Dynamics Institute, Glenda Eoyang, observed that leaders often:

> "… pretend that there's certainty when there's not. And that comes up in several ways. One is they blame others when they're not able to control events so they assume certainty and someone else is just making errors. The second is that they simply get into a delusional state and think the world is doing what they tell it to do. The third is they frame their world so small that they can predict and control it."[24]

In other words, they seek to become omnipotent. Omnipotence refers to a set of beliefs, assumptions, images and feeling states associated with the ideal of being able to achieve anything one puts one's mind to and directs activities towards. This understanding of the notion stems from Freud's idea of "omnipotence of thought" (1912: 13a).

"Omniscience is a state of mind where we imagine and feel as if we know all we need to know in order to function successfully in a particular context", suggest Cavicchia and Gilbert (2018: 149). For clients and consultants, particularly the latter who prize their identities as 'experts' and need to be right and all knowing, this is familiar. Both omnipotence and omniscience have their roots in individualism and positivism, which values only what can be logically or scientifically verified. Managerialism is a neat fit with this given its emphasis on mastery and individual success (Cavicchia & Vogel, 2020). It is a short

---

24. Interview 5th May 2020

hop, skip and jump to states of mind that orientate to being "grandiose and disconnected from the complexities of a social reality where knowledge and meanings are subjective, emergent, partial and provisional, and where certainty and predictability prove to be unreliable" given the reality of the contexts they find themselves in (Cavicchia & Ready, 2018: 149).

These ideals are no small things; they have influence over people, such that the pressure to know what to do, have the answer, make the right decision, etc. is considerable. "Failure to live up to these ideals results in feelings of shame and an anxious preoccupation with whether we are acceptable in the eyes of others" (ibid.).

As Cavicchia and Gilbert emphasise, having expertise or knowledge is not a bad thing per se, it can be incredibly useful, obviously. The problem lies when the need to be seen as all-knowing and all powerful is so strong that it overrides their capacity to consider anything other than the map of the world they hold that is underpinned by assumptions born of shame and anxiety. The pursuit of an illusion of certainty, omnipotent control (including Silver Bullets) and the protection of ego ideals and reputations dominate with room for little else.

Ego and the allure of things that puff that up

Another part of the jigsaw is how our individual ego ideals become fused with the ideals of the organisation. In our need to please, we "become preoccupied with living up to the expectations the organisation places" on us and "with maintaining the particular image the organisation wishes to promote to the world – the 'organisation ideal'" (Cavicchia & Ready, 2018: 149).

This is in part why whistle-blowing is so difficult, even in the face of overwhelming evidence that an organisation is involved in dangerous, unethical or illegal behaviour. We edit out or deny the evidence of our own ideas, and can even turn this into a form of wilful blindness, which Margaret Heffernan (2011) described in great detail in the book of the same name. This is where we choose not to act even when we see or hear something we know to be wrong or requiring intervention. It is the difference between observing abuse in a care home and walking by, and reporting it. The term itself came from the instructions of the presiding judge to jurors in the 2006 Enron accounting fraud trial. He said it was not enough for defendants to say they did not know what was going on if it was in effect in front of their eyes, causing a fair few twitches in the corporate world. In the face of anxiety that an ideal of competency and/ or effective leadership may not be all that it seems, it is hardly surprising that egoic defences kick in and there are so many stories of whistle-blowers being ignored or even punished (Steve Hearsum, 'Whistleblowing: removing the wilful blindfold', *HR Magazine*, 05-02-2015).

All of this makes individuals extremely vulnerable to being seduced by the promise implicit in any Silver Bullet (which could take the form of a model, slide deck, flavour of the month idea, strategy, theory or fad) – 'if you use me you will be relieved of your feelings of doubt and be supported to shore up your images of competence and control.' In a sense they become transitional objects, like cuddly toys, soothers or blankets in childhood.

An additional layer of security is offered whereby, should a consultant hold up a mirror to practices and behaviours that in some way burst the illusion of the organisation ideal, they can be quickly scapegoated in an organisation unwilling to look at its shadows and the effect of these on culture and performance.

Consultants, practitioners and their clients risk unconsciously entering into (and frequently do) unholy alliances and mutual protection rackets along the lines of 'I the practitioner will help you to achieve what you need to achieve to look good and my success in achieving that will in turn make me look good'. Just think about this set-up for a moment. Where there is an unconscious alliance around preserving mutual reputations predicated on achieving predetermined outcomes, all are likely to experience anxiety at the prospect of failure or deviation from intentions – an increasingly familiar probability given the seismic shifts occurring at social, political, market and planetary levels.

This in turn can lead to coercion, gaslighting and game playing (the hallmarks of narcissistic processes) when the complexity of a particular consulting engagement begins to reveal itself. It also explains why Silver Bullets in the form of a particular methodology or approach need to be promoted, defended and protected even in the face of data that suggests they might be limited or unfit for purpose in a particular context or application. There is that pattern of collusion again: we all need to agree this works even if it does not. To admit it has not may be perceived as reputational risk and would raise anxiety because of the experience of imperfection and temporary powerlessness in the face of a more complex reality. Some of the cases in Chapter 10 are stark examples of this.

This explains why slick presenters and purveyors of pseudo-certainties can often be more successful in pitches than those consultants who from the get-go embrace complexity and seek to engage potential clients in a collaborative inquiry into the complex realities of their situation. Simon Cavicchia suggests:

> "Purchasers, seeking to alleviate themselves of anxiety in the face of complexity, often want to buy (an illusion of) quick fixes, solutions and answers, not what might actually be required in the form of access to skilled inquiry, dialogue and reflection to enable new learning, improved relating and organising and novel resolutions to complex problems to emerge and be discovered together."[25]

The purveyors of Silver Bullets, in addition to the commercial need to promote and convince others of the infallibility of their particular Silver Bullet, need to protect their own identification with the sanctity of their model in order to defend their own sense of self. If they can't, shame lurks.

Shame, the ultimate organisational undiscussable

Let's end with shame, which lurks when our needs are not met at a psychological and often unconscious level. It's important to make the distinction between vulnerability (I feel at risk), guilt (I made a mistake) and shame (I am a bad person) (Bazalgette & Harrison, 2020: 11). When the latter kicks in, it is likely panic will too, which is hardly conducive to critical reflection or thinking. What makes it so difficult to surface, let alone talk about, is that it is largely non-verbal in nature and out of awareness, mainly because it originates in infancy (Aram, 2001: 5). It starts, Aram suggests, when "infants are unable to make sense of why parents react the way they do" (ibid.), and so conclude, but never articulate, that they are 'not enough', that they are somehow defective. It is also non-verbal, and self-related, is deeply felt and connects to something elemental about who we are and where we come from. Hardly any wonder that it is not talked about, particularly in the context of organisations and the competition and comparing that characterise them. Aram's research (2006) suggests that shame is an integral part of any learning process, especially any potentially transformative one that may challenge our identity. An uncomfortable truth lurks here, in that shame here has a paradoxical affect: it is both deeply challenging *and* key to transformative learning, and therefore does not fit the linearity of traditional thinking about development.

---

25. Conversation 26th October 2023

Just because it is non-verbal and out of sight doesn't mean its power and intensity is to be underestimated, for the direct experience of shame "is characterised by feelings of exposure, self-consciousness, inner torment, judgement, comparison with others and often vicious self-criticism" (Cavicchia & Ready, 2018: 148).

Couple that with the fact that shame is inherently relational, i.e. we experience it in the context of our relationships with others, it is no surprise it is both present and denied. If that context is a high-stakes organisational one, where either the outcomes of a decision may result in one being seen to have failed to make the right call, or you have been asked to deliver/bring a solution and there is anxiety you may not deliver, it is hardly surprising that the parties involved will:

a) not want to admit to themselves let alone anyone else that they may feel shame or panic; and

b) when things go wrong, seek to avoid further pain by doing whatever they can to avoid a conversation about that failure, *even if there might be huge learning on offer.*

In Chapter 10, we see this dynamic play out in full, and it will also bring to life how even when "experienced in solitude, it is experienced relationally with reference to the feelings, desires, standards, rules, principles, limitations, and so on of a larger relational context" (Lee, 1996, in Aram 2001: 4). Aram emphasises that shame fundamentally "arises in relationships, in the process of interacting, and is individually felt *at the same time* as it is a social phenomenon" (ibid.: 6). Think about the relationship between the buyer and seller of a Silver Bullet for a moment: this is a relationship that exists at a moment of high organisational need, likely with strong emotions lurking, where failure and the fear of being fired might exist for both parties if things do not go to plan, and there is a lot of money possibly at stake. In that context, is it any wonder that a calming slide deck and the safety of a meeting room away from the actual challenge is so seductive? This talks to Cavicchia and Gilbert's belief that "one of the useful functions of shame is to maintain norms and social cohesion" (2018: 148).

The irony in the sophisticated and yet largely unconscious colluding that goes on to avoid discussing, if not the shame itself then what has triggered it, is that this process is an essential part of what it means to be human, and of our developmental journey. As noted earlier, our childhood experiences set the conditions for us as adults, and our self-narrative that unfolds from that is key. If I speak from my own experience, I can taste the shame of early childhood, whether that be from being teased as an overweight kid, to being ostracised as a teenager, through to how I responded to the moments of inevitable rejection in my courting days. That is before I get to any of the deeper-seated facets of shame to do with my immediate family system. I notice when I run sessions on undiscussables with groups, that the most powerful way to get participants to understand and access how what is hidden might impact them and therefore how this might relate to how they show up in their work, is to ask them simply what is undiscussable in their families or personal relationships. I do not ask them to share, although occasionally people do, and shame is often not far away.

Implications of all of this

Consultant and organisational psychologist Keith Jones summarised how much of the above drives the need for certainty, in that it is:

> "… the spiking of unmet needs that exist outside of consciousness … whether it be the need for certainty, connection, variety, recognition, etc. whatever those needs are, which for the most part would be managed in the constellation of someone's day-to-day work. But when it spikes, I need to have a solution to this problem, whatever that is. If that doesn't get fulfilled, then in some cases, anxiety drives consequential behaviour."[26]

In the face of complex realities, calling for moment-by-moment relating, experimenting and meaning making, Silver Bullets can be no more than a sticking plaster, a reduction of symptoms which doesn't address the underlying causes of dis-ease. The blind pursuit of Silver Bullets can be seen as an expression of neurotic anxiety where we attempt to contain and avoid existential anxiety through control predicated on magical thinking.

Woven into the mix is shame, which is a paradoxical process (Aram, 2001: 12) "where its social aspect of exclusion and inclusion happens in the private conversation of mind and gives rise to the emotion we call shame". In response, we adopt the defensive function of seeing strategies as Silver Bullets (which can only ever disappoint given any approach's limitations), outsourcing anxiety management to the purveyors of quick fixes, and use the intelligence and illumination of different maps and approaches contained in them to support

---

26. Interview 28th October 2021

our own sense making, creativity and lifelong learning in relation to working, engaging with and navigating the previously unknown, the complex and uncertain. If we *don't* do this, then there is the risk of exposure, and that is what functional collusion ultimately defends against.

If this is what is going on inside us, driving patterns of behaviour that enable us to deny or hide the anxiety and shame we feel, how does that manifest in reality? Who are the players who benefit (or suffer) from our collective inability to work through discomfort to respond to what might be really happening rather than what we wish were? This brings us to what currently dominates organisational thinking, and the following chapters explore how Silver Bullet thinking has become highly profitable and entrenched, starting with the field of leadership development.

Reflective Questions

- How aware are you of what drives your own need for certainty – and what thoughts do you initially have as to how you might manage that?
- What is your self-image based on? What stories do you tell yourself about how you 'need to show up'?
- How do you, in fact, show up?
- How do you know, and what impact do you actually have?
- What are you most worried others might learn about you?

SILVER BULLET NO. 1

LEADERSHIP RETREAT

Turbocharge your leadership and maximize your potential for impact
in a new era. Learn in lush surroundings, and escape from the drudgery
of your organisation to learn how to become a great leader.
The food is pretty fancy too.

LEADERSHIP DEVELOPMENT

OR: HOW SO MUCH EFFORT GOES INTO SOMETHING THAT HAS QUESTIONABLE IMPACT

Chapter 3:
Leadership Development

"It shouldn't be surprising that leaders are often deluded. Much of the talk about leadership propagates misleading ideas, and these have built a huge leadership industry…that specializes in selling seductive images to managers and other leader-wannabees." Alvesson & Spicer (2016: 103)

The last chapter laid out all-too-human reasons for why decision making is not as rational or clear-sighted when it comes to addressing organisational and leadership challenges. I want to build on that by addressing a conundrum: why is so much money spent on leadership development and training when the evidence for it working is patchy at best? Furthermore, how is it that Leadership Development (the field) has become a space where those that sell leadership development (the activity) are complicit in the Silver Bullet problem? And to what extent might we see 'leadership development' as a Silver Bullet itself?

I begin by framing the nature and size of the sector, then lay out the case for why leadership development rarely has the intended impact, before moving on to consider how we ended up in this place, e.g. by discussing the various 'Schools of Leadership' as a fractal of the Silver Bullet problem, the significance of how we construe the nature of learning, and what the implications are for those that buy and sell leadership development.

In doing so, I will weave in primary data from interviews I conducted as part of my research, as well as examples from my own practice. The aim is to challenge some of the certainty and rhetoric that exists around how leadership development is presented as a Silver Bullet, either overtly or covertly.

The question here is simple: how is the current provision of leadership development made to appear (and get sold as) a simple solution, and what might the implications of that be? Given how much we are told that development affects engagement ("Great leaders attract, hire, and inspire great people", according to the Centre for Creative Leadership in *4 Reasons to Invest in Leadership Development*, 20-11-2021), satisfaction (which a 2015 meta-analysis of 318 studies found had medium-level positive effect, Cakmak *et al.*, 2015) and retention (Eruca Keswin, *3 Ways to Boost Retention Through Professional Development, HBR 2022*), how is it that year after year there is little to indicate improvement (Pfeffer, 2015: 14)?

To sharpen that, if more investment in leadership development was the answer to, say, the many issues that the NHS faces in the UK, then all would be rosy by now. Regular reports by, among others, The Kings Fund (2011) and Nuffield Trust (2023) over the years would indicate we are a long way from demonstrating that 'leadership development' is the answer, and certainly does not represent a Silver Bullet.

Why is that?

The Leadership Development Industrial Complex

According to TrainingIndustry.com, in 2018 organisations around the world spent about $3.4 billion with leadership development solutions and programme vendors, which is just a sliver of the far larger $366 billion that was spent on training more widely.[27] A lot of time and money is being spent on developing leaders – and by extension managers, who often make up the numbers on programmes as they are groomed to step up.[28] The players in this market fall into a number of categories:

- Business Schools and universities, often in the form of their Executive Education or Management Education arms (more on this in Chapter 4).
- Institutes and colleges operating in an adjacent space to the above that either offer programmes and/or signpost to providers, e.g. the Institute for Leadership and Management in the UK,[29] Roffey Park Institute Institute (where I worked),[30] etc.
- Professional bodies, e.g. the Chartered Institute for Professional Development,[31] the Chartered Management Institute,[32] etc.
- Professional Services firms and big consultancies, e.g. KPMG, Deloitte, etc. (more on Big Four firms in Chapter 7).
- Leadership development and training companies of various sizes.
- Independent/sole traders.

---

27. https://trainingindustry.com/wiki/leadership/the-leadership-training-market/
28. Mark Cole, who has decades of experience in the NHS, suggested to me an unwelcome side effect here: "The focus on leadership has arguably erased management at every level, meaning development tends to be around ethereal notions of leadership rather than the hard practicalities of managing people, process and resources to deliver a good or service." (Email exchange with author, 02-10-2022)
29. https://www.i-l-m.com/
30. https://www.roffeypark.ac.uk/
31. https://www.cipd.co.uk/
32. https://www.managers.org.uk/

To varying degrees, these all operate interdependently. People move between them, and sometimes facilitators and consultants are associates of multiple entities. I, for example, have my own direct clients and work as an associate with several other providers. So, we all form part of a wider 'thought collective', a concept I will discuss later in Chapter 9, as these collectives play an important role in the Silver Bullet story.

In the list above, there are many talented and experienced people who are excellent at what they do, and have positive intent to be of service to their clients. They are also commercial entities, and it is in their interest to market what they do in such a way as to suggest that leadership development works. Simply search for leadership development online and notice the language used to describe the offers – they are 'expert led', 'you'll walk away with …', frameworks are 'proven', 'mastery' will be developed – the list is endless.

Compare this to how other products and services are sold. Avis, famously, marketed themselves as being 'only' Number 2 in the market in the early 1960s. It was a campaign that took them from 18% market share to 34%. Their promotional material cleverly included a list of ways that, as the number two company, they had to go to extra lengths to impress and deliver since they did not enjoy the complacent position of the number one firm.

Volkswagen launched the Beetle and did not deny but embraced the reality of its appearance, stating 'Ugly is only skin-deep' and thus proudly and confidently owning the arguably eccentric design of the Beetle car's body, and there are other examples. [33]

The certainty in how leadership development is sold, however, seems at odds with the messy reality of organisations which people come onto programmes to grapple with. There is also often a lack of precision in terms of a shared understanding of what 'leadership' might be, in contrast to the tasks and activities that go to make up management. With leadership, we tend more towards idealistic notions of 'great' or 'good' leadership, which is highly subjective. After all, to one audience Nelson Mandela is the epitome of 'great leadership', to another Adolf Hitler, to another Queen Elizabeth and so on.

To sell a product with such confidence requires evidence of impact. The problem is that in many if not most cases, the impact is not felt beyond an individual or team level, and at best only for a short period. Leadership

---

33. https://velocitypartners.com/blog/6-examples-of-insane-honesty-in-content-marketing/

development and training often fails to have the desired impact on the organisations that leaders and managers work in, as this data from the DDI Global Leadership Forecast 2021[34] illustrates:

- 58% of managers say they did not receive any management training.
- 63% of millennials say their leadership skills were not being fully developed.
- Only 10% of CEOs believe their leadership development initiatives have a clear business impact.
- Only 11% of organisations report they have a "strong" or "very strong" leadership pipeline.

When rhetoric meets reality

My own experience of selling, designing and delivering leadership development in no small part was a catalyst for the thinking that has informed this book. I spent four and a half years at Roffey Park Institute Institute. When I joined in 2013, it was regarded as one of the leading centres of Organisation Development and Leadership Development in the UK. More importantly for many, it had a restaurant renowned for its endless supply of food with a dessert trolley to die for.[35] So we had menus in both settings: one offering a smorgasbord of leadership models and approaches to self-development, the other sugary puddings.

We prided ourselves on offering 'deep personal development for leaders and managers', rather than training; clients were 'participants' not 'students', and we orientated to a view of organisations as complex human systems, where navigating social processes was key. 'Chalk and talk' – the idea that learning was best achieved by having an expert or someone with a PhD stand at the front of the room and decant their knowledge into your brain – was anathema, and I began to learn about leadership development as a practitioner rather than participant.

---

34. https://www.ddiworld.com/global-leadership-forecast-2021

35. I once counted eleven different desserts in one day. Given that no one would stop you going back for more, the weight gain that some new staff experienced was hardly a surprise. I can't help thinking that this is a metaphor pointing to human desire for aesthetic pleasures that is completely disavowed in the hyper rationalism of managerial discourse. That and the need for soothing (via pudding) in the face of anxiety.

Whether it be through your own anecdotal experience or reading and watching the news, you probably have a view on whether investment in leadership development is worthwhile. The evidence, however, is damning. In a 2016 Harvard Business Review article entitled 'Why Leadership Training Fails – And What To Do About It', Beer *et al.* break down and evidence how the Return On Investment (ROI) for all those billions is actually poor because, "for the most part, the learning doesn't lead to better organisational performance, because people soon revert to their old way of doing things". If the primary reason, Beer *et al.* suggest, that senior executives and HR invest in development is to make their leaders and organisations more effective, "the results on that front have been disappointing". Citing research as far back as the 1950s, the authors illustrate the flawed assumption that interventions aimed at individual and team development are in and of themselves enough – they are not.

> "The problem was that even well-trained and motivated employees could not apply their new knowledge and skills when they returned to their units, which were entrenched in established ways of doing things. In short, the individuals had less power to change the system surrounding them than that system had to shape them." (Beer *et al.*, 2016)

Opening their eyes to this fact through leadership development is more destructive than constructive, as it highlights the employee's lack of self-determination on the most efficient ways to achieve their work goals. They now 'know better' but are forced to do it the old way to succeed within a construct of an organisation and ways of organising that are not evolving to support the (apparently) desired change.

Nested in that is the issue that HR functions too often view changing organisations as a function of *developing individuals*, and organisations as an "aggregation of individuals" (Beer *et al.*, 2016). This assumes that if you develop individual competencies then systemic change will follow. Ummm … No. I suspect part of this is down to the individualism of the Global North, and partly down to the fact it is a lot easier to construe individual development as the route to successful organisational change. The alternative, that it may be a little more complicated than that, means wrestling with mess and interventions that are not as easy to purchase as a place on a programme.

As Beer *et al.* go on to point out, organisations are "systems of interacting elements". Mark Cole, author of *Radical OD*, commented to me on "the endless corporate fascination with the 'team' as a key facet in successful delivery", and the tension that creates. If HR and Learning and Development, through their focus on finding and developing 'talent', make the individual leader their central focus, that is ideologically interesting if teams and their working are truly what makes things work well. If the 'Leader' is the defining factor in team effectiveness, why might that be, and is there evidence to support that?[36] That level of critical thinking seems to be missing in much of the conversation between clients and providers and segues into the next point.

Things are further compounded by the inability of many in organisations to speak truth to power, plus the unconscious assumptions about hierarchy, belonging and safety in homogeneity. This is not just about HR as these patterns are often, in my experience, merely a reflection of wider organisational culture, particularly at a leadership level whereby:

"… companies are often reluctant to change their board practices due to fear of change and the unknown. [There is] strong and consistent data showing that most new board members are recruited from the small, pre-existing networks of current board members." (S. Johnson 14-05-2018, *What Amazon's Board Was Getting Wrong About Diversity and Hiring* in HBR)

When I worked at *The Guardian* in the late 1990s on a large organisational change programme which I will touch on again later, the main body of work was accompanied by a review of broad process, which was buried and not acted upon. I never got to the bottom of why, but it talks to this reluctance to change.

Unsurprisingly, the homogeneity is not good business practice, and damages profits. For example, when CEOs increase the demographic diversity of their boards, profits go up, although at the expense of their own pay (ibid.). Johnson also goes on to point out that twelve years of Fortune 500 data allowed researchers to demonstrate that "demographically diverse boards are more likely to challenge the authority of the CEO and curtail CEO pay". Which might be a clue as to why some (white and male) CEOs are not so keen on the idea. Black civil rights activist Assata Shakur puts it well: "No one is going to give you the education you need to overthrow them".

---

36. There is also some useful research that challenges the individualistic paradigm of leader-led team effectiveness. Alex Pentland's work at MIT showed that "individual reasoning and talent contribute far less to team success than one might expect. The best way to build a great team is not to select individuals for their smarts or accomplishments but to learn how they communicate and to shape and guide the team so that it follows successful communication patterns." Pentland, A. 2012 *The New Science of Building Great Teams* HBR Available at: https://bit.ly/2ZpF5fe

An upshot of this is a resulting "failure to execute on strategy and change organisational behaviour [which] is rooted not in individuals' deficiencies but, rather, in the policies and practices created by top management. Those are the things to fix before training can succeed longer-term" (Beer et al., 2016). That makes it all the easier for HR to make employees' competencies the problem and training the clear solution, a far more palatable outcome for many senior leaders.

CEOs will only hear it if someone speaks up, and even then there is a question of how meaningful a reflection of reality that will be, given the propensity of the need to please senior leaders. The pattern of avoiding uncomfortable conversations is common in virtually every organisation I work in, to some degree. In my own practice, I have become increasingly direct in challenging clients to think about the wider context, and not seeing leadership development as in and of itself a solution. For example, working with leaders in a global manufacturing business, it was necessary to link the notion of 'going to the balcony' – the idea that one needs to step back and above the fray to see the patterns in what is happening in order to decide on the next action – to self-care and challenging cultural norms. It was a business where long hours and crisis management were the norm, something they were actually very good at. The flipside is they were poor at innovation and had high instances of workplace stress. Here going up on the balcony translated into some individuals experimenting with – Shock! Horror! – going home at 5:30 pm. This meant there were some crunchy conversations as the rhetoric of culture change – 'we need to work differently!' – encountered people doing just that …

Part of the problem is that the question that the development is designed to answer is unclear at best, and on a surprisingly regular basis has not been properly thought through or articulated. Leadership development is commissioned on an aspirational basis with a pick and mix of terms that fit a well-worn template of what everyone thinks leaders need, which is not necessarily the same as what would serve the organisation.

The inability to speak truth talks to some of the anxieties I spoke about in Chapter 2 and will crop up again as a thread in subsequent chapters. The inability of human beings to engage in constructive conflict and dialogue is, in my view, at the root of many of the issues that Silver Bullets are designed to address. An example of this is the rhetoric around collaboration. Most clients will answer in the affirmative to the question: do you collaborate? When I follow up by asking whether, when push comes to shove, they favour the preservation of harmony over working through differences, which may require what is sometimes termed constructive conflict, then the number who say they collaborate falls dramatically. Collaboration, which to me is about an outcome where all parties achieve a result they can live with, often requires some heat. Think of successful resolutions to industrial disputes or marriage break-ups. Both parties need to leave feeling and experiencing that they are no worse off and as well off as the other.

If there is not a willingness to engage in constructive conflict, and sometimes that may be for understandable reasons (e.g. power imbalances or poor behaviour makes it unsafe to do so), then the next best thing may well be something that has the appearance of resolving tensions, of dampening the anxiety in effect. If the problem is that people in the organisation are not collaborating or being straight with each other around, say, performance or accountability, it is a lot easier to send people off to learn to be better leaders than scaffold the conversation that needs to take place.

Leadership? Management? Same or different?

Briefly I want to attend to the difference – or not – between these. Definitions of both abound, and how they differ from 'manager' and 'management'. On many leadership and management development programmes, the question of how they differ is a staple. I have facilitated that conversation many times.

For example, one view, from Mark Cole, author of *Radical OD* (2020), is that "the leader is invariably distanced from the work of the organisation – and unlike the manager they are not defined by their proximity and engagement with the work. Hence, you can perhaps only be thought to be a leader if one has been immersed in leadership development, as opposed to developing skills in relation to live tasks, such as a manager might need to undertake. Leadership development is more akin to baptism into a sacred caste rather than upskilling around practical activity."[37]

Whether you agree or not with that statement is less important than what you think about the implications. Getting learners to *think critically* and *ask better questions* has to be a key outcome of any development, because otherwise all you get is more of the same, or a 'better sameness'.

---

37. Conversation 10th September 2020

I am not going deeper on this point, as the onus is on you to think about how *you* and the *organisation you work in/for/serve* define these terms, and their relationship to/with each other and the wider organisation. My own view is that the differences are too often overemphasised, and I align with Mintzberg (2004: 6) who argues that the fashion for distinguishing between the two is flawed, primarily because "managers have to lead, and leaders have to manage". In a sense, they are interchangeable, and context determines which label may be (marginally) more appropriate.

Leadership – or management for that matter – is a socially constructed concept that many people have a view on. As you will see by the end of this chapter, there is not one way of 'doing it', although everyone has a view on where they get it wrong. "Being a successful leader involves working with particular situations with your unique personality, where a degree of judgement is required," suggests Richard Hale,[38] who specialises in action research and practice-based leadership development. "The results of doing leadership are not always predictable. All of the above points may sit uncomfortably if you are looking for a formula for becoming a better leader."

Leadership development is the answer to what question, exactly?

This is an important question, and, if you cannot answer it, why would you even consider spending money on developing yourself or your people? That may sound obvious, but the number of times I have asked that of clients – in relation to any challenge they are facing and not just leadership – and been met with a stumped look, is telling. If I follow that up with 'what do you want to be able to see/hear/feel a year after we have finished working together that will tell you it has made a difference?', the bemusement can increase before the simplicity of the question brings anything from relief through to a recognition some more thinking and inquiry needs to happen.

Leadership development, similarly, will be the answer to a question and often it will be framed around a specific challenge. I believe that leadership development exists to help leaders, and by extension their organisations, to better meet the challenges they are facing *in a specific* context, which is key but sadly often skipped over. In interviews for this book, I asked people what they saw as the biggest challenges leaders face today.

---

38. Email 8th March 2024

I break this down into perspectives that were offered from the different positions the interviewees hold relative to organisations and leadership. Let's start with some of the voices from within organisations.

Leadership Voices (Internals)

A Human Resources Director (HRD) of a major UK insurance business said the challenge was "the confidence to make choices more than ever and leave some options behind".[39] She saw leaders increasingly struggling both with the range of options open to them, the anxiety of picking the 'right one' – or being blamed by others for *not* picking the right one – and an inability to simply let go of those they have not opted for. This suggests that what might be needed is the capacity to live with uncertainty, resist the tyranny of perfection, be more experimental and deconstruct the idea of the perfect solution, along with a commitment to ego relaxation.

A Chief Human Resources Officer at an international building material group, said, "The biggest challenge leaders probably have now is how do you get out of the operational back-to-back meetings and actually create the space … to really think strategically about where the business is and where it's going?"[40] That raises a number of questions about the cultures that leaders co-create (including ones where operational execution is the be all and end all), the behaviours they model, their ability to say no and to focus on what is important. Another benefit of back-to-back meetings is that they serve as an illusion of work, a ritual that fills time, avoids important, meaningful and more difficult conversations, and ultimately achieving little.

A different perspective was offered by Neil Morrison, Group HRD at Severn Trent plc. "Social purpose is probably one of the biggest things we wrestle with … what's our relevance?"[41] This wider perspective, that leaders can no longer think solely in terms of their own organisations and immediate stakeholders, was sharpened given all the interviews that took place during the first few months of the Coronavirus pandemic.

---

39. Interview 7th July 2020
40. Interview 26th June 2020
41. Interview 26th May 2020

"I think the biggest challenges is to … break the corporate games[42] … we are trying to bring culture together with strategy so that they can 'have breakfast together' and not against each other, so to speak," said Bernd Zimmermann, formally Global Head of Organisational Development and Innovation at Siemens Healthcare GmbH and now an independent consultant.[43] Long term this also required they become 'ambidextrous'. 'Organisational ambidexterity' is a term popularised by James G. March over thirty years ago. He said, "The basic problem confronting an organisation is to engage in sufficient exploitation to ensure its current viability and, at the same time, devote enough energy to exploration to ensure its future viability" (March: 1991). In a nutshell, exploiting what you have already got while not losing sight of the need to innovate for the future, a tension many organisations struggle with, requires post-conventional thinking.

Organisation Development and Change Perspectives (Internals)

The perspective of three interviewees were striking, in terms of the observations they made of their leaders. The first, a senior change manager in a major UK retail business, said, "The biggest challenge is how to keep the organisation surviving financially in a world that is getting harder and harder to predict what the most appropriate choices are."[44]

The other two, as well as now having a client-side perspective in major global corporate brands, also came with substantial experience working as consultants in big consultancies. The first of these, now a Head of Organisational Development, said: "I think some of the biggest challenges they face is how to quickly respond to things … I see a lot of leadership where there's still this felt need and sense, that they should be on top of things … providing a level of

---

42. The irony of course is that to get to the top, leaders often have to be masters of playing corporate games, and by then it may be a bit late to think about breaking them. Many initiatives look for ways to accelerate people of colour and others into the upper ranks of the organisation but do not allow for the fact that this progression should also bring with it the licence to look around at where they have landed and redesign it to better reflect the diversity of thought and ideas that they bring to this setting. Graduating to the upper echelons is all consuming – and silences people who will have powerful observations and suggestions to offer as to how senior leadership might sensibly and effectively be reconsidered. It also raises questions, again, as to whether leadership development, as it is generally conducted, is fit for purpose when it comes to preparing people for that.
43. Interview 5th May 2020
44. Interview 1st May 2020

clarity and certainty 'at the top', and then realising that [reality] is messier and more complicated than that."[45]

The third client, a VP of Change, said it was about "the speed of change. And the complexity."[46] They also suggested that leaders in her organisation did not help themselves because there was a "cadre who believe they have all the answers and, they don't". The fear they observe in their leadership colleagues is in no small part due to the fact "that some of the stuff that they're dealing with has no playbook … there is no management text that's going to help them through".

The view from outside (External)

I had the privilege of speaking to some well-known names in the fields of change, organisation development and design. One of these was Naomi Stanford. She commented: "I think the biggest challenge is that leaders don't think about challenges", in this case complex and intractable ones. "They think about how much they are going to make in the next quarter or, instead of being outward looking. I think the biggest challenge for a lot of leaders I come across is (they are) inward looking."[47]

This is not a new idea, but it is telling that this pattern is still prevalent. In vertical development terms, time trajectories extend with the development of broader perspectives. There is a need to develop longer term orientations beyond quarters, half- and full-year-on-year cycles, 'managing' the present while also behaving in a way that is evolving an organisation for the future.

It also underscores the fact that a distinction between management and leadership does not meaningfully exist, in definitional terms. If the 'leader' is just focused on the bottom line of quarter-by-quarter results, then they are assuming a mantle that simply overlays the day-to-day work of a manager, seeking merely to meet shareholder expectations. The Gestalt concept of Field Theory, based on the work or Kurt Lewin, states the behaviour is a function of a person's environment, where past-present-future all overlap (Lewin, 1939). If we overlay that thought on organisations, the distinction between 'leadership' and 'management' is simply part of the field people operate in; it is socially constructed rather than what they do. That overlapping in part explains why organisations are often experienced as chaotic and unpredictable, and the

---

45. Interview 18th May 2020
46. Interview 18th June 2020
47. Interview 24th July 2020

anxiety that in turn drives increases the need for certainty, for something to help make sense of things or resolve them such that they are bearable, as per Chapter 2.

There is also something of a fascination with titles in organisations. People allow these labels to be put on them (and sometimes disappear into them, denying themselves the capacity to act across a wider domain than the one attached to the title), but in reality people are just getting on with stuff, regardless of the label they are given. Leadership development serves to emphasise the fascination with titles, as opposed to a focus on what needs doing and how should it be done.

A sense of leaders not being able to or not wanting to grapple with the messiness of organisational and business realities was a thread throughout the interviews. Not in an unkind or judgemental way; the tone was more often one of compassion for the struggles that people observed leaders going through, mostly at an all too human level, e.g. the impact on mental and physical well-being, personal/family lives being compromised, etc. Graham Curtis suggested this challenge was amplified by "the expectation of you to be certain. And how to respond to that need for certainty, in a way that is authentic and ethical, but doesn't cause the level of existential anxiety that will be caused, if we had to see it" (the uncertainty).[48]

This tension around our relationship with certainty and uncertainty, and the psychological impact, kept coming up. Gervase Bushe, a well-known Organisation Development scholar and consultant, said, "The biggest challenge is how to keep the organisation surviving financially in a world that is getting harder and harder to predict what the most appropriate choices are."[49] He also made the connection to anxiety: "I think they're scared. They're scared of the decisions they've got to make. And for some that makes them slower to make decisions, or they even freeze and don't make deci-sions; they just talk a lot about what their choices are without actually making any [decisions]."

Linking to this, consultant and business psychologist Keith Jones, suggested to me that the key challenges for leaders today are the need for "adaptability and the recognition of fragility".[50] That duality is a challenge, because if adaptability *is* linked to our capacity to inquire into our fragility, that connects once more to our experience of shame.

48. Interview 3rd July 2020
49. Interview 6th May 2020
50. Interview 28th November 2021

Technology, interestingly, came up very little. That may in part be because of the people I spoke with, and I suspect that had these conversations been happening pre-Coronavirus, technology and the questions raised by 'digital' would have been more prevalent. As it is, Eva Appelbaum, who has a long history of working with senior leaders and organisations wrestling with what it means to 'digitally transform', offered this perspective: "It's not just the fundamental disruption of technology, it's that the technology has opened up completely new models and frameworks and designs, not just for organisations but for society; and it puts us in a completely different space."[51] Therefore leaders can really struggle, because while on many levels they do understand how to deal with change and uncertainty or a new strategy, because they've been doing it for their whole careers, they're now doing it in a context where the rules are very different.[52]

This sense of time and history emerged as a strong theme in several interviews. Here the idea that the rules of the game are changing is counterbalanced by the view that there remain fundamental challenges of leadership that we have grappled with for decades, if not centuries. "The challenge that's always been there for leaders is the extent to which they can engage critically and meaningfully with their circumstances instead of just reacting to them. So, we're faced with an absence of thoughtfulness in leadership, the absence of a critical take on what's happening, the reliance on formulaic responses," said Mark Cole.[53] Given the fact that organisations tend to reward compliance and loyalty, maybe it is no surprise that people err on the side of caution and choose not to reveal their critical thinking or indicate they have done any.

An alternative yet complementary view was offered by Dr Richard Claydon, who is, among other things, an Organisational Misbehaviourist, Ironist and Antifragilist. He posited that we are "going through a transformational shift in organisational development/organisational design … the original model was 'what's the entity?' … the idea [was the] organisation was an entity, and it had a certain structure. And at the top of the structure was a leader and an organisational chart, and it was just this 'thing' that could be managed in a

---

51. Interview 8th June 2020
52. An embryonic line of inquiry that connects to this is how the personalities and perspectives of those developing technology shape the ways the technology then shapes us. With a high prevalence of autism and neurodiversity in technology companies, what are the long-term impacts on relating, leadership, culture, etc.?
53. Interview 3rd July 2020

certain way. So, the great leadership challenge is to work out how to lead in a contested version of reality."[54]

This last point, regarding contested realities, again connects to the idea that all organisational experiences are ultimately socially constructed, and are a function of individual and collective meaning making. This happens organisation-wide in the form of disputes between employers and employees – the NHS or rail strikes in the UK in recent years see expressions of radically different realities. It can also happen in one-to-one or group settings. I have helped clients work through conflicts that revolved around the difference between what one person said and the other heard, in effect a contested reality based on two sentences that catalysed months of conflict.

A further issue Claydon highlights is the preoccupation with the idea of a three- or five-year vision. "The idea that you can create a stable vision where you're leading the organisation over a five-year period to this future horizon, which you've imagined perfectly now … that's a real challenge. I don't think it's particularly realistic." Yet the importance of having a 'leadership vision' is a staple.

Michael Jenkins, a former CEO of Roffey Park Institute, with decades of experience in the field of leadership development, was the only person to mention a "trust deficit", which he viewed as the most foundational thing because "if a leader doesn't have trust, I'm not sure that they can achieve anything sustainable over time".[55]

Mel Ross, founder of Adapt2Digital and someone steeped in change wrought by digital technology, suggests the biggest challenge is recognising Silver Bullets are not the solution.[56] She also suggested that whereas previously we could rely on centres of excellence and specialised teams, e.g. for technology, marketing, sales, etc, the expectation now was that leaders have to understand and do these things themselves, in the context of ever faster unpredictable change.

The last perspective I offer is that of Glenda Eoyang, founder of the Human Systems Dynamics Institute. She, again, makes the case for uncertainty as "the biggest issue … full stop". So far so similar to others. However, her follow-up comment is particularly important:

---

54. Interview 4th May 2020
55. Interview 29th January 2024
56. Interview 14th February 2024

"All of our leadership principles and practices and methods and models have been based on the ability to predict and control the future. And even the ones that say they're about uncertainty are about getting things under control so you can predict."[57]

The implications of Eoyang's statement are profound, in the sense that the more you say you are getting uncertainty 'under control', the closer we are to an inherent absurdity: it's a contradiction in terms. Why do we, those who seek to help clients and the clients themselves, collude with this? I'll explore this in later chapters. For now …

Some implications

"Of all the hazy and confounding areas in social psychology, leadership theory undoubtedly contends for the top nomination. And, ironically, probably more has been written and less known about leadership than about any other topic in the behavioural science." Bennis (1959: 259)

Leadership development plays at least two roles in managing the anxiety that was discussed in Chapter 1. It offers a way for organisations to manage anxiety around developing talent – 'If we send our people on this programme with people who know what they are doing, they will come back better leaders' – and when presented neatly packaged with the trappings of expertise, it is not surprising that there is a reassurance. Simultaneously, it assuages the anxiety of consultants and facilitators offering development that they both know what they are doing and can make a difference. I took it at face value, as I started delivering more leadership programmes myself, that they would make a difference. The reality, according to Jeffrey Pfeffer ('Why We Don't Get the Leaders We Say We Want', 16-09-2015), is a little less neat:

"Literally scores of empirical studies show the relationship between instructor ratings and objective measures of what students learn is essentially zero, and the better, more accurate the measure of objective learning, the lower the already-tiny correlation between student ratings of their instructors and how much they learned is."

Reflecting on my own experience of working on leadership development programmes, the above criticisms ring all too true. Most of the programmes I

---

57. Interview 5th May 2020

bid for or worked on were beset by the problems outlined. I cannot think of one client who took up my invitation to evaluate an intervention over time. 'Happy sheets' or some ad hoc conversations with participants a little while after we finished were as good as it got, and even when the oft-quoted Kirkpatrick's 4 Levels[58] were mentioned, it never seemed to lead to anything rigorous. At the time of writing this, I was shocked to receive a Request for Proposal (RFP) from a client that explicitly asked for details on how I would evaluate the intervention. Evaluation is probably top of the list of things typically descoped due to budgetary constraints, and is rarely requested upfront by clients.

We have this peculiar situation where something – leadership development – is sold with certainty as offering the solution (e.g. a programme) to a problem (e.g. 'poor leadership'). Therein lies one of the core facets of the functional collusion that exists between providers and clients: it is in both parties' interests to agree that what is being bought and sold will make a difference, and there is a lot at money at stake if it turns out that this is not the sure-fire thing we'd all like to believe.

I'm going to spell out a few of the issues that fall out of all of this, starting with a superficially simple question of definition.

Issue #1: what is 'leadership development', exactly?

Let's assume that you know the question you need help answering. Great! Have you defined what you mean by 'leadership development', and what assumptions underpin that? If not, how can you assess what you are buying? Part of the challenge is that the precise definition of leadership is often hotly debated and contested,[59] as is its nature and style, and, more broadly, impact. There is also a debate around the difference between *leadership* development (programmes) and *leader* development (individuals).

A 2017 report by the University of Cambridge Institute for Sustainable Development[60] offers a few examples of the ideas that circulate around leadership:

---

58. https://www.kirkpatrickpartners.com/the-kirkpatrick-model/
59. Keith Grint's books on leadership are a good place to look if you want more on this.
60. See https://www.cisl.cam.ac.uk/resources/publication-pdfs/Global-Definitions-Leadership-Theories-Leadership-Development.pdf

"Rost (1991) describes leadership as 'an influence relationship among leaders and collaborators who intend significant changes that reflect their mutual purposes', while Kouzes and Posner (1991) believe it is 'the art of mobilising others to want to struggle for shared aspirations'. Common themes of influence, change and leader-follower collaboration emerge from these and other definitions. Senge *et al.* (1999), for example, describes leadership as 'the capacity of a human community to share its future, and specifically to sustain the significant processes of change required to do so'."

Most of these (and other) definitions explicitly or implicitly reflect the ideas of an underlying theory or school of leadership, and in the next section I look at these to begin to reveal how little has changed or is new, and how particular ideas still hold sway.

Issue #2: finding the 'right' flavour of leadership

"A wide range of stakeholders have vested interests in finding ways to develop leadership capability; these range from government to professional agencies, from in-house learning units to corporate universities, and from consultancy firms to business schools." Mabey (2013: 359)

The irony of having so many vested interests arguing for a particular philosophy or approach to leadership development is that the certainty with which many of those narratives are articulated is at odds with the uncertainty of knowing which one is 'right' in each context. As Mabey (ibid.) goes on to argue, "authors tend to remain committed to their favoured ontological approaches, with little constructive dialogue between them [which] has the effect of stunting debate and progress." The irony is that there is little evidence, if any, that there are inherently right or wrong answers when it comes to leadership development, rather just an endless process of abstraction.

Which is interesting, as leadership development programmes will be underpinned by a set of assumptions, typically associated with a particular 'school of thought', or 'leadership era' of thought (King, 1990: 44) which in turn will map to an accompanying set of assumptions about the learning experience. These may be explicit or not, and possibly out of conscious awareness of those designing it. Why? Because it takes effort to think about why you think about leadership the way you do, and where your assumptions come from. Transactional Analysis, one of the most well-known theories of personality, has the concept of a "life-script [which] explains how our present life patterns originated in childhood" (Stewart & Joines, 1987: 3). Bluntly, it takes effort to consider how interacting with, say, senior leaders today may be related to our relationship with authority figures from when we were young. That in turn will underpin some of how we think about leadership, in all likelihood, given leaders in organisations are authority figures also. Exploring assumptions can be cultivated as a skill, and might be a pillar of post-conventional leadership development going forward.

Thinking back to my time at Roffey Park Institute, our approach was heavily influenced by complexity-based theories of leadership and change, and relational approaches to organisations, particularly those associated with group dynamics, e.g. Gestalt. This was coupled with a philosophy of Self-Managed Learning, which signalled to clients something of our values, assumptions and what they could expect as a learning experience.

From the client perspective, the underlying assumptions about the nature of leadership can be more complex. There may be a real tension, for example, between the 'as is' style of leadership and that which the organisation may be seeking to move more towards. There may also be a further tension, which is not always as easy to spot and may in and of itself be undiscussable: what an organisation says it wants may be very different to how its leaders continue to behave. There may also be different views between, say, the leadership of an organisation and its view of 'effective leadership' and the people responsible for commissioning programmes, i.e. Learning and Development and HR functions typically.

In psychological terms, we might ask whether 'leadership' comes to act as a container for projections, because in some ways it is impossible to live up to the expectation of leaders as they are individually held. So those commissioning development, delivering and receiving it are unlikely to have the same idea of what is needed.

Dig beneath the surface of any initiative to change an organisation's culture, these and other tensions are often there.

So, buckle in as I take you on a whistle-stop tour of the history of Leadership Development, the full details of which are in the appendixes. Rummage around on Google and you will probably end up with a chronology that looks something like this:[61]

- *Great Man Theory (1840 onwards)*
- *Behavioural Theory (1950–1970)*
- *Contingency Theory (1967–1990)*
- *Leader-Follower Theory (1970 onwards)*
- *Transformational Leadership Theory (1985–2010)*
- *System Leadership Theory (2005 onwards)*

The rest

The above is by no means exhaustive. In researching for this chapter, I asked several former colleagues what they made of my putative list and whether I had missed anything. Suggestions came flying in. What about the more recent growth of Self-Management and the leadership that goes with that, as popularised by Frederic Laloux (2014)? Neuro leadership, as per the Neuro Leadership Institute? Meg Wheatley's work on New Science (2006)? Moral leadership (*What it means to be a moral leader*, HBR 22-09-2023)? Inclusive Leadership (Korkmaz *et al.,* 2022)? Joseph Raelin's leadership-as-practice (2016)? The work of Ralph Stacey (2012) and Patricia Shaw (2003) on leadership from a complexity standpoint? Dialogic approaches to leadership, based on the work of Gervase Bushe (2010; 2019)? Simon Western's approach to networked and eco leadership (2019)?

Is your head hurting yet? I found myself straining to come up with the 'right list', to make sure I framed all of this 'stuff' in such a way as to prepare the ground for making my argument. Then I realised that the point is that this straining for the full list is in and of itself an absurdity, a reaching for the Silver Bullet of leadership theories when no such thing exists. All of the above have relevance and utility. The challenge is not which one is 'right', rather which will be useful in your context. Which one matches your intentions and beliefs. Approaches to leadership evolve in relation to situational challenges and shifting knowledge/discourses.

Overarching all this theoretical development is a simple observation: that they are heroic and/or charismatic. So, we didn't see much public discourse about Boris Johnson's skill set in respect to managing a country; instead, it was dominated by abstract notions of whether he is a 'good leader' or not

---

61. This list is based on one of the search results, a useful summary that can be found here https://docplayer.net/56772249-A-short-history-of-leadership-theories.html

– with constant reference to the fact that he is an admirer (and biographer) of Churchill, who remains the leadership lodestone for much of the UK. As a fractal of wider conversations about leadership, it is interesting that discourse around Johnson was polarised into a camp identified with the 'heroic' myth that completely disregards any questions of values, morality and personhood – the cult of personality is what matters – and another that sees morality, values, principles and personhood as central questions in defining what constitutes (good) leadership.

Lastly, all the above is in addition to the fundamental issues with applying leadership theories and models beyond narrow cultural contexts. As *The Oxford Review* noted, "the majority of currently available leadership theories and models are western-centric, which makes them irrelevant in many contexts", many are US-centric representing "a form of cultural imperialism", and "are too idealistic and based on the mythical hero's journey that ends in a triumphant win … [thus] both unrealistic and impractical, especially in other cultural settings".[62] I recognise in myself a need to decolonise my own thinking and frames of reference around leadership.

Issue #3: the fallacy of the new and novel

> "There is no such thing as a new idea. It is impossible. We simply take a lot of old ideas and put them into a sort of mental kaleidoscope. We give them a turn and they make new and curious combinations. We keep on turning and making new combinations indefinitely; but they are the same old pieces of coloured glass that have been in use through all the ages." Mark Twain, in Paine (1912:208)

The notion that little truly new or novel exists in human thought, that rather we are engaged in a perpetual regurgitation and/or recombining of ideas that have come before, is in and of itself not new. If the schools of thought set an overarching context for Leadership Development, it is worth looking at a few specific examples of individual models, tools and theories that show up as part of many programmes.

---

62. https://oxford-review.com/how-to-make-leadership-training-more-cross-culturally-relevant/

Strengths-based approaches

In recent years, 'strengths-based approaches' have become increasingly popular, e.g. Gallup's StrengthsFinder, which profiles the intensity of your talents. All arguably owe a debt to the work of David L. Cooperider (1985, 1990) and the body of work that falls under the heading of Appreciative Inquiry. They are useful, and in some contexts can be experienced as radical, particularly in organisations led by people who take a problem-focused approach to change and/or behaviour change requires coercion or manipulation.

Motivational approaches

The many offerings framed as 'Leading with Purpose', 'Finding Your Why' or similar have utility, and ask important questions, but also offer nothing earth-shatteringly new regarding human motivation, which is well-trodden ground (e.g. Abraham Maslow (1943) and Frederick Herzberg (1959)). In a business/organisational context the names of Douglas McGregor (Theory X and Y) and Elton Mayo (1933)[63] among others, have trodden this path before. Daniel Pink, with his work on motivation (2011) and Simon Sinek (2011) are just two of the more high-profile recent examples.

Culture

Edgar Schein's 1980 model for understanding organisational culture – Artefacts, Values and Assumptions – spawned various derivatives. Roffey Park Institute had their own version when I worked there, but strip away the veneer and language, and you have Schein's model.

Group dynamics

Kurt Lewin was also one of the first to write about group dynamics and how the group itself influences behaviour of those within it. His definition still resonates today: "the essence of a group is not the similarity or dissimilarity of its members, but their interdependence" (1939: 84). Many of the modern approaches to group work, whether they be Gestalt or psychodynamic influenced, can trace their origins back to the work of Lewin and others in the Human Relations movement post WW2, and the urgency which many felt to better understand human relations to help avoid mass conflict of the kind many had just experienced.

---

63. Of the problematic Hawthorne Experiments fame, something I touch on in Chapter 6.

Change

"Scratch any account of creating and managing change and the idea that change is a three-stage process which necessarily begins with a process of unfreezing will not be far below the surface"[64] commented Hendy (1996) on how Kurt Lewin's Unfreeze/Move/Refreeze model[65] of the human responses to change lurks beneath many change models as an underlying set of assumptions or partial ones. It is probably the fascination with Silver Bullets that have led people to seize upon one passing remark by Lewin in an extensive and wide-ranging article and promote it thereafter as 'Lewin's model'. A simple three-stage imagining of change has been lifted from a bigger piece and turned into something it is not. Lewin didn't intend it to be a Silver Bullet, but people persist in declaring it is one. More on that in Chapter 6 where we explore how theories and theorists more widely are part of the problem in how they are construed and used.

What?/So What?/Now What?

This is a model I was introduced to by Glenda Eoyang of the Human Systems Dynamics Institute when I did my certification. In HSD, this is framed as the Adaptive Action Cycle, and is linked to Eoyang's innovative thinking around containers, differences and exchanges that appear in patterns of human interaction. Rolfe *et al.*'s 2001 model for critical reflection in the nursing profession offers the same three stages, and is often cited as a source, yet it appears first in a difficult to access book by Terry Borton published in 1970 entitled, *Reach, Teach and Touch*. Either that or search and see it show up in multiple contexts credited to someone else entirely or not at all.

NLP

A personal favourite is Neuro-linguistic Programming (NLP). For example, a number of the core approaches within it essentially lift, or are variants of, Gestalt (and other psychotherapeutic) approaches. Jay Hedley[66] sums this up by saying: "the originators [of NLP] *appropriated* it from Gestalt, and then failed to give full credit to its source. They stood on the shoulder of these giants and saw further, but did not fully acknowledge those shoulders." Examples of this

---

64. Hendry, C. (1996).'Understanding and creating whole organisational change through learning theory'. *Human Relations*, **48**, 5, 621–41.
65. In (over)simplified terms, this is the equivalent of melting ice to make it amenable to change (unfreezing). Then moulding iced water into the shape you want (Oh goody! Change!). Then solidifying the new shape (refreezing). Funnily enough, human beings have been found to be less predictable than ice …
66. Jay Hedley, 2016 (https://bit.ly/32m8aZC)

include the focus on awareness, patterns, the emphasis on authenticity and the focus on *how* rather than *why*. Steve Salerno (2005: 81) noted that "NLP has acquired particular cachet in business circles for its usefulness in business negotiations and conflict resolution – which is interesting because Grindler and Bandler [its founders] ultimately ended up in court unable to resolve their own conflict over who owned the licencing rights to NLP". That has not stopped many others offering derivative programmes or methodologies, possibly the most high-profile example of this is Tony Robbins, who is simultaneously a poster boy for Great Man theories of leadership.

The above critique, or my own irritation with, say, NLP, does not take away from the fact that they can and do have huge utility and relevance *in the right contexts*. Few are new nor can offer a guaranteed answer, which in part may explain the constant regurgitation and re-combining. The market in Silver Bullets is rife with buyers, sellers and thieves it seems. What interests me is how some of the most lauded ideas of recent years that set out what leaders and organisations need to be or do more of to be 'fit for the future', 'fit for purpose', 'fit for function', 'fit for digital', etc., are all reframes of previous ideas. While Leadership Development is built on a bedrock of useful ideas, they are not magical answers and rarely unique. Self-proclaiming 'once and for all solutions' (an artefact of the lonely hero, managerialist paradigm), they are more accurately maps for navigating the mystery of an ongoing, unfolding, lifelong process of learning and responding.

An example of questing for the Leadership Development Silver Bullet

The National Health Service is the UK's largest employer and at one time the largest single organisation in Europe, if you band together the hundreds of organisations that operate under it. In March 2019, it had over 1.2 million employees[67] [68] (notwithstanding the vast numbers of current vacancies in 2023) and a National Leadership Academy orchestrating development across the wider health system in conjunction with regional academies.

---

67. https://www.ethnicity-facts-figures.service.gov.uk/workforce-and-business/workforce-diversity/nhs-workforce/latest
68. Notwithstanding the vast numbers of vacancies in more recent years: https://www.theguardian.com/society/2022/sep/01/nhs-vacancies-in-england-at-staggering-new-high-as-almost-10-of-posts-empty

Since the inception of the NHS, it has been on its own perpetual quest to find the 'right' approach to leadership development. At the start, doctors who were in the main male, were the natural leaders therefore there was no need for leadership development because they were in charge and therefore de facto leaders. While discussions around how the health service should be managed started in the 1950s, it was not until the 1970s changes began to be made, and the concept of managers was visible. The Griffiths Report in the 1980s closed off hospital administration and welcomed in a private sector version of managerialism. This was followed by the introduction of 'New Public Management' by the Thatcher administration, and consolidated by Tony Blair's New Labour governments from 1997 onwards. The tensions between clinical, nursing and management tribes thus emerged in the 1970s and became further embedded by successive governments' own assumptions about leadership.

In 2011, The Kings Fund, an independent charity that works to improve health and care in England, produced a report on the future of leadership and management in the NHS that noted, "the health service has a long history of attempting to improve both management and leadership. Many reports have either touched on management and leadership or been specifically focused on it" (p.9). The report lists sixteen different reviews, all concerned with what kind of leaders the health service needs and how best to develop them, and supported by what theories.

Interestingly, in 2023 at a conference at The Kings Fund, once again it was agreed that they begin an inquiry into what 'good leadership' in the NHS looks like. I can't help but wonder what is being avoided by repeated attempts to reframe and redefine what leadership is and is not. Pondering is useful, if it is not simply covering the same ground to come up with remarkably similar answers. The essential challenges in what it means 'to lead' remain remarkably similar today as they did in the 1950s or 1960s; what changes is context, but the human aspects, the need to navigate social processes, the capacity to lead self and others 'through and in' change, these remain constant.

Talk to people in the NHS, and they will tell you how in the last twenty odd years the antidote to command-and-control/heroic leadership became Transformational Leadership, before Servant Leadership was latched onto. In the past fifteen years, which spans my own time working with NHS organisations, I have seen them move on to embrace Adaptive Leadership, then Systems Leadership, and in 2013 the NHS Leadership Academy published the new 'Healthcare Leadership Model – The Nine Dimensions of Leadership Behaviour'.

Scratch beneath the surface of all these, and the underlying challenges remain remarkably similar and the perpetual questing and shifting to find (yet another) model or framework for leadership development ceaselessly fails to provide an answer. In my work with clinicians, doctors, nurses and managers, the challenges remain largely unchanged:

- Collaboration is more vital than ever, but requires the ability to do conflict well, in a system that remains heavily beholden to the command-and-control leadership culture of central government.
- Many cultures within the NHS are far from open and transparent, which makes speaking truth to power both vital and challenging.
- Tribes and thought collectives jockey for position and defend territory.

Which begs the question, if leadership development is the answer, how come many within the NHS are still struggling with how to deliver effective care, collaboration and developing healthy work cultures? That is in addition to the challenges of workload, staff shortages, pay and funding constraints. What if struggling and navigating struggle was the work? Is the struggle made worse by assuming there shouldn't be one and that there should be a once and for all prescription for cure? The recent Messenger Review (2022), led by a former general is arguably (yet another) example of the quest for a Silver Bullet. It regurgitates many of the approaches that have been tried before, through a military lens. It is transfixed with leadership as the answer to all the ills of the NHS, forgetting that while the battlefield and A&E are superficially similar, the latter is but one small part of the whole. Then again, it is the most politically visible …

Here is where we start to get to the nub of the issue with Leadership Development, how it is part of the Silver Bullet problem, and the co-dependency it represents. Before that, however, I want to touch on one more tension, namely the challenge of articulating what is meant by 'learning' in this context.

Issue #4: are you clear what you mean by 'learning'?

Is leadership development really about learning? I believe that leadership development *should* be primarily a process of developing the capacity for critical reflection, crafting an understanding of the world and context you are operating in and honing the *practice of leadership*.

That, however, is not the prevalent view. What we have is something akin to the business of learning, where knowledge acquisition, self-development and getting better at 'doing' is the name of the game. If we go with the idea that leadership development is concerned with learning of that kind, there are still major issues because many organisations think about learning in a narrow way. It gets mangled in the language of HR and Learning and Development, of 'learning objectives', 'learning outcomes', 'programme outlines', 'learner experience', etc., without asking a simple question: what do you mean by 'learning', exactly?

> "When it comes to competence, especially to 'leadership', we are still largely in thrall to the individual … Leadership and personal development training tends to be focused on taking the individual out of their organisational setting – on 'retreat' – then return them to impose the new attitudes and behaviours on the workplace." (O'Hara, 2012: 66)

Maureen O'Hara and Graham Leicester (2012: 59) describe learning in 21st-century organisations and leadership as being a function of four modes, offering a simple framework for learning:

- Learning to *know*
- Learning to *be*
- Learning to *be together*
- Learning to *do*

Learning to know

"The real difficulty as a leader is the expectation of self and others that you will *know* what to do, and will be any good at doing it, when, in reality, you're pragmatically doing what makes most sense and seems most effective in the best way you can. The killer is the corporate and hyper-individualistic accountability for operational achievement over which you have no control and no ability to make any difference. Then you look for the magical thinking of the Silver Bullet." Alastair Wylie[69]

There is a distinction here between *knowledge* and *knowing*. The former can be defined as:

---

69. Conversation 5th September 2020

1. acquaintance with facts, truths or principles, as from study or investigation; general erudition
2. familiarity or conversance, as with a particular subject or branch of learning
3. acquaintance or familiarity gained by sight, experience, or report
4. the fact or state of knowing; the perception of fact or truth; clear and certain mental apprehension
5. awareness, as of a fact or circumstance. (Dictionary.com)

Typically, knowledge is learned at school, then by extension at university and on through further adult learning. So, is learning (a sufficient amount) about leadership as a concept and how it might differ, say, from management, enough?

The short answer is unequivocally no. Is it useful to learn about approaches, theories and models? Yes, but it is not sufficient without learning discernment. If it were, then you would go to university, study for a master's or PhD, or get your MBA from a business school, or attend a programme at an Executive Education centre or elsewhere, or simply read lots of books and watch TED videos and be sorted. Wielding, say, your understanding of the theory of Systems Leadership with only a conceptual and cognitive understanding is like asking a trainee brain surgeon to operate on you having qualified purely in an academic setting. Without other forms of learning that move beyond knowledge acquisition, you run the risk of letting people practise before they are qualified to do so in real-world settings.

'Knowing'

This is where we get to 'knowing'. *Experience* is the most primary form of knowing, which gets translated through meaning making, and ultimately, we get to a form of "*knowledge in action*" (Tosey & Gregory, 2002: 93). Experience does not lead automatically to knowing, it has to be processed mentally, so may be tentative knowledge. Crucially, knowing is *participative*, as the surgeon is not operating in a vacuum: there is a patient, plus a team who help them. To offer one example from my own practice, I have *known* for many years that one of the learning edges in my practice has been how I make and maintain contact with others, in Gestalt terms, a legacy of my own family context. While in the last fifteen years I have known – i.e. cognitively and intellectually understood something of what occurs within me – I did not really *know how* that process worked or was able to connect it to how I could work with it in the moment. It was a perfect example of why knowledge is not the same as knowing.

In organisations, what we are ultimately talking about is a form of situated learning, as described by the social anthropologists Jean Lave and Etienne Wenger (1991). By definition, it happens in a particular place and context, it is participative and involves people who may both come and go. That might mean becoming part of a community, and on occasions finding yourself expelled (see Chapter 9 for more on how particular groups protect themselves by expelling heretics, and how that relates to Silver Bullets).

There is a connection here to the language of 'tools'. When you wield that lovely new instrument or tool, as leader or practitioner you are *by definition* engaging in a participative activity and are in dialogue with others. That is true even if your approach is to impose change on others, for the simple reason that participation is still required even if it is only in the form of resentful compliance where you become the 'ever so helpful sadist' unwilling to consider the unique subjectivity of the other/s.

The implications of this are that when you consider what you might need to learn in order to develop yourself as a leader, you start with an assumption that it is all about models and theories. They have a currency for practitioners and consultants as well as leaders. I used to horde models, techniques and instruments, saving them up in digital and paper folders so that I could impress people with my breadth of 'stuff'. I would covet those held by others, imagining they had greater value because I did not possess them or, in some cases, understand them (there lies part of the shame of the consultant). And we then use this currency to bribe the commissioner of our services, laying out our resources and allowing them to pick up the shiny things that they like.

The trap you fall into is one akin to cramming for an exam – '*I need to understand all this stuff and acquire all this knowledge before I can lead differently*'. It assumes the learner is an empty vessel, which negates every aspect of their experience to date. In my work with leaders and managers who are leading themselves and others through change, I have noticed that the models I use to support inquiry are less important than how successful I am at creating a space for people to connect to their lived experience of change. Talking through how the Change Curve, a ubiquitous and popular model of which there are many variations, loosely based on Elizabeth Kubler-Ross's 1969 book on how humans experience death and grieving, is a banal and hollow exercise until you connect it to the visceral experience of what someone *knows* having lived through an experience that connects to the theory. Hearing a participant talk personally about their anger, frustration, fear and sadness and using that form of knowing to illuminate the usefulness of a change curve as a vehicle for shared understanding is to reveal how a model is a mere artefact in a museum cabinet, devoid of context and meaning, until it meets experience. It also shows why models *in and of themselves* are not Silver Bullets. The moment I saw a manager stand among her peers as we mapped their shared experience on the floor, and recognise how her own experience was utterly unlike that of her colleagues is not something you can teach. It arises in the moment, among a group of people, at a particular moment in time.

This is why limiting 'learning to know' to a form of data upload is to miss a fundamental point, that organisations are relational human systems. To learn to lead the people within them, or indeed the whole organisation, more effectively will not happen solely through learning about them in a training room, book or slide deck or without context.

The irony here is that Kubler-Ross's model is a prime example of a method of sense-making being adapted into a Silver Bullet for organisational settings. It speaks about grief and how we see that humans might process that, and then it's melted down, poured into a cast, and appears as something that can be deployed into the heart of how organisations might wish to approach 'transformation'. It is also another example of how we latch onto ideas with little empirical evidence to support them, for as Kastenbaum noted: "there is no clear evidence for the establishment of stage in general, for the stages being five in number, to be those specified, or aligned in the sequence specified …The few studies that have examined facets of stage theory have not supported this model" (2015: 131).

One way of managing the anxiety that was discussed in the previous chapter is to contain and constrain it with models and theories, which explain away complexity and propound a degree of certainty. The ultimate example here is possibly the organisation chart, and it's no surprise that some senior leaders seek solace in them as they are intoxicating in their apparent offering of a clear answer to often complex challenges. The reality is rather different. Anyone who has held down a job in an organisation of more than five or six people rapidly learns that the organisation chart does not reflect the reality of what you need to do to get things done at work. As Aaron Dignan has pointed out (2019: 8), the organisation chart as a mechanism for mapping organisations remains remarkably unchanged since its inception by the Scottish-American engineer Daniel McCallum, who is widely credited with being the first to create an organisation chart in 1854. This is in spite of the fact that how we work together has evolved in intervening years and is no longer predicated solely on notions of power exercised through hierarchies. The organisation chart is just a blueprint, yet it is often assumed to be the solution. In the same way that you wouldn't pack your bags, sit on a big printout of the blueprint of Boeing 747 and expect it to take you to Torremolinos, an organisation chart on its own will not suffice.

Knowledge acquisition is important, it is useful to learn about models and theories. It is crucial however to be aware that our responses are also predicated by our knowledge base and therefore the assumptions we carry. That in turn drives whether or not we actually know what we are doing, and do what we know.

The ideal, therefore, is to acquire knowledge while engaging your critical faculties and understanding that applying this in reality will be a relational and participative endeavour. This requires additional modes of learning and differentiating between knowledge and knowing. I may have read a book on brain surgery and understood it conceptually, it does not mean I know how to perform an operation. The same is true of leadership, management, change and other theories more generally. Doing a Prosci change management course, one of the most well-known and successful change methodologies which I will return to in Chapter 6, teaches you about all the parts, but does not equip you with the relational intelligence it requires to be successful. In *Hare Brain, Tortoise Mind (1998)*, cognitive scientist Professor Guy Claxton uses the example of clinicians who are highly knowledgeable and skilled in a particular discipline flailing to know what to do when a patient crashes, whereas an experienced nurse with many years of acquiring tacit knowledge *just knows* what to do even if they have not been able to make a diagnosis, which in emergency situations comes after arresting a rapid decline.

In leadership terms, then, Learning to Know has to be a function of knowledge acquisition on the assumption it is in service of increased embodied and whole person knowing.

Learning to Be

Learning to Be talks to the idea of self-awareness and other-awareness, the capacity to remain present and responsive rather than reactive to surrounding events. As I found my way into Leadership Development and designing programmes for clients when I was a Senior Consultant at Roffey Park Institute, it became apparent that, typically, we framed development around 'Leading Self', 'Leading Others' and 'Leading an Organisation'. Our Organisation Development Practitioner Programmes all followed a similar pattern of self/ group/system, and if you look at many leadership programmes, this approach is common.

The arrangement is like a Russian doll: the individuals pack into a team, the team into an organisation, the organisation into a wider system. But the very notion of organisation presupposes human agents choosing to connect collectively to combine to get something done. The model creates artificial breaks between a rich picture of interconnectedness – which could be an overarching critique of all leadership practice and the models (tools) in use, as an artificial and misleading way of imposing sense on reality (as opposed to reflexively and collectively working together to sense-make).

The 'self' part will invariably include things like emotional intelligence, influencing skills, listening, presence and impact, and maybe exercises that reveal your personal narrative/story. Do a search for 'Leadership Journey', and the individualistic nature of how we see leadership learning, particularly in the West, is clear. Even the language echoes the Great Man Theory, the idea that our hero must, Odysseus-like, go on a personal quest involving much hardship to emerge once more as a leader worthy of followership. The irony is Odysseus did not achieve all he did on his own: he had many followers to start with, lost them, made alliances, benefitted from the support of gods and ultimately prevailed with the help of his family.

Learning to Be Together

> "In the operating conditions of the 21st century it is impossible to be competent alone. Competence is a function of culture, which is a function of relationship ... we create our own lives in a pattern of relationship with other lives, and we always have done." O'Hara & Leicester (2012: 4)

The complex organisational change challenge that does not entail behaviour or culture change, either as an outcome or a by-product, is a rare beast. The project that does not depend on the behaviours of those involved **does not exist**. The behaviours/competencies that are particularly important in this context are all those to do with collaboration and include but are not limited to:

- sense-making skills (getting under the skin of your own and others' assumptions/stories)
- constructive conflict
- experimentation
- risk taking
- working in and with difference
- capacity to respect other views even when disagreeing
- genuinely willing and able to work towards win-win

Notice just how much of what you need to achieve in your day-to-day work is dependent on human interaction, therefore on *being together*.

The kicker here is this. I have spent many years developing my own 'self and other awareness' (and am still a work in progress); I work with many people who wrestle with this; there are whole industries – e.g. pop psychology, self-help, Executive Education etc. – that talk to the need for people/leaders to 'be', to 'know themselves' and/or to 'raise their awareness of self and others'. The latter fits beautifully with a dominant Western paradigm of individualism, which dominates how we see organisations and change, something that was hammered home to me when I became certified in Prosci.

The atomic unit of an organisation is often deemed to be the individual. I contend that is not the case, rather everything of substance and significance that happens in human systems does so in the context of groups – it is rare I meet someone who says their organisation has an effective 'meeting culture'. Without the capacity to 'be together', is it any wonder that our experience of organisational life is often underwhelming, disappointing, frustrating, depressing, etc.?

When change is in the air – which is when the clamour for Silver Bullets is most acute – the need for those involved to 'come together' and 'be together' in useful and functional dialogue is sharpened. In that context, Learning to Be is useful but insufficient.

Learning to Do

Finally, we come to the 'do' bit, arguably the most important, and often given the most value. Certainly, everything that comes before is moot if there is no change, no action or difference, and this risks de-valorising the vital relating and meaning making that needs to underpin action if it is to be effective.

However, if doing something was always a) the *most appropriate* response at a given moment in time; and b) when done, the correct *kind* of 'do', then organisations and society generally would be more efficient, profitable, healthier and happier. A glance at any news feed tells us that the quality of what is being 'done' often falls short of expectations, both of the 'doers' and those dependent or on the end of that activity.

If you have experienced change in organisations as something that is 'done to' rather than 'done with', it can be disempowering. While it is possible to construct an argument that some change initiatives require significant elements of the former, e.g. significant downsizing or restructuring, it is on the assumption that those involved *by definition* cannot be trusted to engage and work with what is being planned.

Too often leadership development – or learning more generally – goes straight from Learning to Know to Learning to Do, bypassing Learning to Be and hardly ever attending fully to Being Together. This is the space of 'done to' change, of 'just give me a tool or technique' development. As Steve Tarpey, a fellow consultant, put it during an online exchange:

> "The acquisition of wisdom takes time – lots of time – and practice – lots of practice – and reflection – lots and lots of reflection. We understand that mastery in music, art, carpentry, medical practice, etc. is the product of a long process. However, commodification of leadership development into schools of thought and particular theories means that we ignore this understanding and collude in the fantasy that there are quick wins."[70]

This is why it is important to understand that Leadership Development, as it is currently often construed and offered, is no Silver Bullet but can be sold as one. The implications for leaders and organisations are that you need to think more critically about what exactly you are buying, and why, because "learning in the world of leadership is about the application of judgement, knowledge and skills

---

70. A comment on a LinkedIn discussion thread I started around the question 'Is there a problem with Leadership Development? https://bit.ly/49SeoBF

in real situations," maintains Richard Hale.[71] This cannot be learned sat in front of a professor in a business school lecture theatre or a comfy room at a rural retreat. Rather deeper and genuinely impactful learning comes from those 'aha moments' as we gain insight self, others, the team or the organisation, not from "motivational talks have a limited shelf-life, measured in hours or days, and they do not necessarily lead to action on the part of leaders" (ibid.).

Issue #5: Leadership Development or Dependency

The risk ultimately is one of dependency, or rather a co-dependency, in no small part because there is a "lack of an adult development dimension in organisational learning theory", as Kegan and Lahey (2009: 5) say. This is not an academic argument, "as leaders increasingly ask people to do things, they are not now able to do, were never prepared to do, and are not yet developmentally well matched to do" (ibid.). Then we get to the crunch of their argument:

> "The field of 'leadership development' has over-attended to leadership and under-attended to development. An endless stream of books tries to identify the most important elements of leadership and help leaders to acquire these abilities. Meanwhile, we ignore the most powerful source of ability: our capacity (and the capacity of the people who work for us) to overcome, at any age, the limitations and blind spots of current ways of making meaning." (Ibid.)

The Silver Bullet problem exists in part because there are good sales people out there selling them, and more fundamentally because of blind spots, whether that be one of seeing the world in binary, either/or, black/white terms, an inability to think critically about the nature of learning required or an anxiety-driven desperation to block out everything other than what will make all the pain go away. The ask of you, then, is to understand better what is meant by 'human development', "what it is, how it is enabled, how it is constrained – what passes for 'leadership development' will more likely amount to 'leadership learning' or 'leadership training'" (Kegan & Lahey, 2009: 6).

---

71. Email 8th March 2024

Issue #6: the thinking at play

The Chief Human Resources Officer I quoted earlier made a powerful point that illustrates a fundamental problem with the thinking that goes on around the (re)sourcing of leadership development:

> "Too often we're driven by financial narrative that's quite narrow, and not spending time and interrogating, what's the problem behind the problem. And therefore, often the solutions that come out are actually just focusing on short-term fixes, or they're quite superficial by nature."[72]

Crucially, what is often overlooked is *context*, for the idea that what works in one situation will work in another is fundamentally flawed. This makes it even more absurd how often we collude with the client asking for 'case studies' that show how things have worked elsewhere. That is a problem for two reasons:

1. What worked 'there' is unlikely to work 'here'. Corporate Rebels spent two years travelling and learned about many different interventions and experiments. As Joost Minnaar said to me, not once did they find the same thing in two places.[73] Similar? Yes. The same, no. I was once asked to design and deliver an Action Learning-based intervention in one of the UK's largest consulting, transformation and digital services corporations. This was at the behest of a divisional CEO who had seen it work in their previous organisation. Here, there was a lack of willingness to engage in rigorous contracting and to explore exactly why they thought what worked in one context would work in another. In spite of repeated requests to meet with them to inquire into this, it never happened, and funnily enough, after a couple of pilots, the project was cancelled. Action Learning was no Silver Bullet.

2. The tendency to treat innovators, radicals, progressives, experimenters, revolutionaries and their ideas as case-study porn, a kind of 'conceptual tourism', visiting the exotic and being entertained by it. They are titillating to read and hear about, but at the end of the day, as Niels Pflaeging put it (2015 blog post), "we remind ourselves that they are somehow not from this world. They stake out land that appears unknown and foreign to us. *'That would never work for us here'* we say. *'We're just not ready for that.'* Or, *'I could never swing that with my team.'*

---

72. Interview 26th June 2020
73. Interview 18th May 2020

And *'We went to visit them and had a look; it sure was fascinating, but their approach is just not right for us.'*[74] We want to visit the zoo, but we sure as hell don't want to let the tigers roam in our own house.

As Naomi Stanford said to me, the development activities in programmes are too often "generic, not situation specific, [so leaders are] not necessarily able to solve problems or see opportunities or spot connections. To try and wrap up everything you need in a concept of leadership is not the best way or even a good way. A way we could start to think about leadership is: what are the qualities we need or capabilities we need to meet specific contexts?"[75] This requires the cultivation of reflective practices, and it may result in a recognition that taking gangs of leaders to sit in a hotel room for the purposes of leadership development creates too much of a gap between reality and the learning space.

One final point to make concerns power, because how that is exercised in your organisation, as you make buying decisions, is key. One of the most obvious manifestations of this is the organisation (which means almost all those I have worked with) that believes the higher up you go the more tailored an experience you need. This is another defence against anxiety and a narcissistic shoring up of an ego ideal of knowledge superiority rather than levelling and embracing the notion that learning is lifelong, nor are we ever the finished article as often implied in linear models of adult learning and maturation. There is also the shame that means this can rarely be acknowledged openly.

So why do senior leaders get this special treatment? Based on what assumptions? Have they reached a rarefied level where their development needs to be hidden or that they are already at the pinnacle? Are senior leaders more intelligent? More skilled? More complex? In need of more support and challenge? Are leadership development programmes just another form of luxury consumption? In my experience, the special treatment is down to several factors. Sometimes it is a form of reward (you have reached this level, have a few days working on yourself at a nice hotel); it can be a rite of passage (you hit this level, everyone does this programme); there may be a narrative that senior leaders' needs are different (they work on things and in contexts that are more challenging so they need more development).

---

74. https://www.linkedin.com/pulse/why-we-cannot-learn-damn-thing-from-semco-toyota-niels-pflaeging/
75. Interview 24th July 2020

While there may be some differences, e.g. the jeopardy they can face, the defended-ness, the scale of the projections, etc., they are not as significant as to justify the degree of streaming that goes on. One of my interviewees, a senior people leader in a UK insurance business, observed of the senior leaders they worked with:

> "I don't see often vastly more superior intellect. I don't see vastly more data analytical skills. I don't see vastly better influencing skills actually. And that has been a total shock to me."[76]

The moment you send your senior people on a programme designed just for them, several things can happen. Patterns of 'Them and Us-ness' kick in or grow. While there may be envy at seeing your boss swan off to a lovely Exec Education centre, what also grows is the sense of there being one set of rules/values for leaders and another for the rest. That can morph into resentment, or ridicule if what people experience is no change at best or at worst leaders who come back spouting new ideas while still failing to change. One organisation I worked with sent several hundred of its most senior leaders on a 'Voyager Programme'. The aspirations of the programme were laudable, but in a system that has a fundamental problem due to a parent/child leadership style and an obsession around levels/seniority, all that succeeded in doing was amplifying an existing dysfunction. This contrasts with another client, who designed and delivered a leadership programme aimed at *all* leaders and managers, regardless of level, delivered unaltered for all, that sought to build a common language and set of mental models, so that people would be able to better understand each other and work more vertically and horizontally.

The same senior people leader mentioned above told me that:

> "… a talent development programme in a business of 25,000 people in the UK is where we put our money. I struggle to believe that that pipeline of five potential General Managers will move the dial substantially on organisational performance in the competitive landscape. But the decision makers saw the business case and signed it off, they are the ones who are therefore going to outsource their own direct reports' leadership development."

For her, this raised a question about how senior leaders can end up becoming a self-reinforcing elite that regards itself – if not in thought then in act – as better

---

76. Interview 7th July 2020

No Silver Bullet

than those around them. This links to narcissism and maintaining self-images, and the negative impact of this on maintaining critical reflexivity and openness to evolving knowledge and innovation.

Now what?

The late Ralph Stogdill, who was one of the first to point out that trait-based leadership on its own was flawed unless it considered the social context leaders operated in, once commented that "there are as many definitions of leadership as there are persons who have attempted to define it" (1974: 7). Fast forward to July 2023, and David Wilkinson, an organisational psychologist and founder of *The Oxford Review*, sat opposite me on Zoom and did a quick search. At that moment in time, in 2023 there had been 10,900 research papers published on leadership development thus far, out of a total of over half a million over time. As Wilkinson said to me, "The question is: why? We haven't got the answer. Because if we had the answer all that wouldn't be needed." Some progress.

Leadership development is as much about marketing and sales as it is about learning. Much of what is packaged and sold by providers is essentially drawn from the same broad body of knowledge, slanted and flavoured by the world view of the people designing the interventions. As one consultant familiar with the material used by an organisation that is the largest global provider of leadership development outside of business schools, said, "they have a phenomenal marketing and business machine that delivers large scale solutions. You strip it all the way down, and what you end up with is a series of discrete models that you would find [easily elsewhere]. It's a series of models that are put together in a particular sequence, and then rolled out and dressed up and then dressed up even further."

Much leadership development, therefore, argues Pfeffer (2015: 6), "has become too much a form of lay preaching, telling people inspiring stories about heroic leaders and exceptional organisations, and, in the process, making those who hear the stories feel good and temporarily uplifted while not changing much of what happens at many workplaces".

Pfeffer has the good grace to make some recommendations in terms of what leaders and organisations might more usefully pay attention to, although tellingly comments, "if these recommendations were comfortable and easily implemented, they already would have been" (2015: 8). No Silver bullets here either, then.

122

Leadership development – or development period – may be useful, and it might make a difference to organisations, although even that is debatable, as Pfeffer and others have argued. What we need to do is learn not to see it as like how we buy other products and services where its features and benefits are uniform and clear. We are not talking about hairdressers, car mechanics or construction engineers, where it can be assumed that what is being bought can be known in advance. Neither is development like buying dairy herds, which is ironic as I once had to negotiate the final rates on a major talent programme with someone in a purchasing department whose last job was buying and selling beef. That made for an interesting and frustrating negotiation, although to be fair some organisations see their people as meat to be farmed and culled at points so maybe that was appropriately ironic.

The need in organisations is arguably for 'vertical' transformational learning/ development and to learn about how to 'relate' and organise as sentient beings; to being more open to messiness and developing the knowledge, confidence and skill to sit with the unknown. Knowledge here becomes part of learning about orienting frameworks not 'answers'.

Develop your people then, and please do as otherwise I will be out of work, but do it in a way that genuinely supports people to work with and in the messiness of organisations, to influence rather than control, and to have the humility and capacity to both not know and be better able at working with that.

All of which brings us to …

The MIT Sloan Review noted, following a review of leadership development programmes at several dozen business schools globally in 2023, that "few programme directors we surveyed could identify how the design and evaluation of their leadership development offerings consistently meet scientific standards of desired impact" (*Leadership Development Is Failing Us. Here's How to Fix It*, 06-12-223).[77] Instead of documenting improvement in participants' capabilities, for example, the majority (70%) said they settled for "positive reactions to

---

77. The article is worth reading in full. It includes some useful questions that people might ask when it comes to procuring leadership development. I particularly liked these two. The 'comfort' of participants in learning tends to get weighted more heavily than the useful discomfort they may need to experience.
Instead of asking 'Is it easy enough?' *ask* 'Is it appropriately complex?'
Instead of asking 'Will participants be comfortable?' *ask* 'Will participants learn, even if they're uncomfortable?'

the programme or evidence of knowledge gained, at least in the short term (63%)" (ibid.). Echoing some of the earlier criticisms in this chapter, none of the MIT researchers "linked their programming to changes in participants' career trajectories, followers' attitudes or performance, or team- or organisation-level outcomes". Ouch. They go on to note that interviews with forty-six HR executives revealed that leadership development programmes are selected less on evidence, and more on somewhat superficial criteria, namely the 'looks' of a programme, such as the accompanying attractiveness of the website or charisma of the faculty as if it were a dating app (ibid.). Maybe my background in having launched a dating service for a UK national newspaper earlier in my career is being underutilised in the field I now work in ...

More importantly, this latter research leads us neatly to our next port of call: business schools.

Reflective Questions

- What assumptions do you hold about 'leadership'? And 'development'?
- What is your model for an effective or 'great' leader?
- How do you manage the tension between knowledge acquisition and developing leadership practice? Do you see a difference at all? If not, why not?
- How do you measure the impact of leadership development in your context?
- Do you believe that we should continue to entertain the notion that those who get christened as leaders should persist in trying to lead? If so, what are the implications for them and for you?

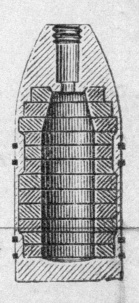

SILVER BULLET NO. 2

MBA

Exceed your expectations. Grow your network. Up your salary.
Increase your impact. Push the limits of modern management and leadership.
Go on, you know you want to.

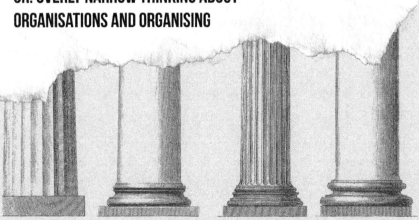

THE BUSINESS SCHOOL PROBLEM

OR: OVERLY NARROW THINKING ABOUT ORGANISATIONS AND ORGANISING

Chapter 4:
The Business School Problem

"The time has come to recognise that higher education management rests on a fatal fallacy: the idea behind the contemporary Business School is that preparing future business managers means training them in a discipline called business management. After 100 years of fruitless attempts to produce such a discipline, it should be clear that it does not exist … business schools as they are presently constituted are at best superfluous." M. Stewart (2010: 291)

"Business School 'thinking' has become piffle, hiding its cliches and self-interest in plain sight." John Higgins[78]

University departments that teach leadership and management, and inform wider thinking about the nature of organisations and organising, are important players in the functional collusion described. They are influential in propagating new ideas, as well as sometimes offering the illusion of novelty, with which corporate life is so obsessed. They also play a key role in reinforcing and amplifying thinking that feeds the market for simple solutions to complex problems. Often that is inadvertent, or a by-product, even when they are ostensibly attempting to help clients become less rigid in their thinking.

This chapter will illustrate the role business schools and Executive Education play in reinforcing governing assumptions which merely amplify the propensity to look for simplified solutions, rather than challenge that.

The development hierarchy

I joined *The Guardian* and *Observer* in 1995. This was my first experience of working in a large organisation that had a Learning and Development department, with an accompanying strategy for developing leaders and managers.

There is an unspoken hierarchy at play when it comes to leadership and management development which speaks volumes about not only the size of the

---

78. https://www.gameshift.co.uk/business-school-thinking-has-become-piffle-hiding-its-cliches-and-self-interest-in-plain-sight-says-john-higgins/

budgets available, but it also talks to 'in' and 'out' groups, and who, ultimately, will be anointed for promotion.

The Institute of Leadership and Management (ILM) helpfully suggest six levels,[79] so let's begin there:

- Level 2: Team leader/Supervisors
- Level 3: Junior managers (First-line manager or Supervisor)
- Level 4: Middle managers – new
- Level 5: Middle managers – more experienced, with bigger teams/ responsibilities
- Level 6: Senior managers (Director of smaller organisations)
- Level 7: Senior leaders (CEO, Director of large divisions)[80]

When I started at *The Guardian* and *Observe*r, I was probably a Level 4. My role was unusual, as I was brought in to help set up an innovative commercial division, so I didn't 'fit' neatly. Nonetheless, I was soon earmarked for development. Maybe someone deemed I was 'talent' – how exciting!

I did various in-house training programmes, I was MBTI ®'d,[81] and, having been stamped as an ENTP,[82] I was selected to go on that Developmental Rite of Passage (DVP), the Off-site Development Programme.

This is a stage in the development cycle that suggests you are moving up the learning pecking order:

79. https://www.i-l-m.com/learning-and-development/leadership-and-management-qualifications
80. This kind of thinking can be seen in the NHS in the UK post the Messenger Review, mentioned in Chapter 2. Approaches grounded in systems leadership and supporting people to make sense of their work challenges seems to be being superseded by a reversion to oversimplified levels of management and leadership dependent on the completion of some form of certificated course.
81. Myers Briggs Type Indicator. It is one of the most well-known and popular psychometric instruments, with a somewhat problematic history. I touch on this in Chapter 6, as it is another subset of Silver Bullets sold by an industry that pedals personality and type tools as offering a certainty around defining who we are and what that means for our personal relationships. They run the risk of merely serving to segment the workforce into the deserving and undeserving. I have worked with clients who have been bent out of shape and damaged by the way in which instruments like MBTI, Disc and Insights are used.
82. Extraverted, Intuitive, Thinking and Perceiving profile, which apparently means I am "bold and creative, deconstructing and rebuilding ideas with great mental agility. They pursue their goals vigorously despite any resistance they might encounter." So says the official MBTI website https://bit.ly/3uu5lI5

1. The language shifts from 'training' to that of 'development'.
2. You get to stay over in a hotel or conference centre for a night or two.
3. The format of the programme is less classroom and more conversation and inquiry based: you start to talk about yourself as a leader/human.
4. You are less a *student*, more a *participant*.

My first foray into this learning nirvana was in Bournemouth for a negotiation skills course. Later, I knew I had moved up another level when a smaller, more select group were sent to a country house venue for a presentation skills course. The clue that this was a step-up was the presence over dinner of one of the organisation's directors. That is another DVP: the presence of a senior leader, where someone from 'up there' comes 'down here' and, for one night only, breaks bread with their minions. There is a semblance of equality, yet it still smells of a beauty parade, as people jockey subtly and socially for favour, or at least to become more visible.

It was around this time that I began to ask questions about what other opportunities there were for development, and that is when I first heard of places like Ashridge and the London Business School.

The Frat Houses of Executive Education

> "To develop better managers is one thing; to develop better organisations in the process of developing better managers, rather than as a consequence of developing them, is quite another." Henry Mintzberg (2004: 336)

Large organisations often send people to a business school, which alongside its purely academic programmes offering things like MBAs, may also have an Executive Education arm, to engage in knowledge transfer between academia and business. Their stated aim is to improve leadership and ultimately organisational outcomes. Often their actual aim, as a business in a crowded space of sellers, is to create a market through their research and 'thought leadership' for the products they create in response to this.

There are a couple of issues that are worth noting at the outset when discussing Executive Education. Firstly, there is a long-standing debate within universities around the tension in business education between academic rigour and real-world relevance. This doesn't just show up in business schools, as it also plays out in other disciplines, as career academics work alongside those who come from a practice ('real-world') background – I have seen it in law, journalism and medicine, to name but three. Wherever it shows up, the accusation from one side is that practitioners may have the experience, but where is the evidence to support what they do? In turn, practitioners accuse academics of being stuck in ivory towers pontificating, too far removed from the pain of their clients and students. At its heart is the belief that research, and publishing research in recognised academic journals, trumps practice, however impactful and deep.

What gets missed is that both have merit. It behoves those who work on real-world issues to do sufficient research and inquiry to understand *why* what they do and *how* they do it works, or does not, so that learning can be better understood and amplified. Equally, academics who have become so far removed from the issues that they write and research about, and the real-word implications of what it takes to actually *change* things, need to understand that no amount of journal articles or PhDs will help a leader wrestling with an intractable problem if you cannot translate that knowledge into practice. In my own work, I eschew conventional leadership development and favour a practice-based approach to learning.[83] Here, theory is subservient to practice and is introduced wherever possible in response to the emerging needs of the client. It is 'inside out' rather 'outside in' development, and assumes that starting with the assumption that I might know what my client needs and can 'prescribe' an appropriate theory is to infantilise them from the off. Clearly there is a tension, and sometimes I may need to suggest a model or theory, but it is done with co-design in mind, not prescription.

Stefan Cantore, who teaches Organisation Development and Change Management at Sheffield University Management School, put it rather nicely in a webinar I ran as part of my research:

> "Executive Education sits very uncomfortably within many business schools because there are many tensions around even the notion of practice and supporting practice development. Many business schools are not particularly geared up for thinking that way.

> They're thinking about a particular frame of reference and a world view around what knowledge is and how knowledge is generated, how knowledge is managed and who owns knowledge … Is that knowledge about practice or knowledge about theory? It creates huge tensions."[84]

---

83. This has been influenced by working alongside colleagues at Mayvin, a specialist people and change consulting practice.
84. Comment during a webinar entitled *Business Schools & Exec Education: purveyors of Silver Bullets?* 24th September 2021

Which is why, in the context of modern organisational life and what it takes to change how we organise and create value, the nature of practice and how that relates to research is so important. Higher education is preoccupied with research and evidence-based practice. The risk is this diminishes the importance of practice-based evidence. If it cannot find a way to allow these perspectives to interlock, then where is the place a learner whose curiosity about the world might best be addressed by both research and an active interrogation of its impact on said world? It's also noteworthy that so much business research is conducted through the lens of scientism, when the complex interconnectivity of humans in this realm cannot be fully reflected through this kind of methodology. More on practice later anyway.

The second tension related to Executive Education is the relationship between the business school – or School of Management as some are labelled – and the wider institution. Increasingly, and particularly in the UK, universities have become disproportionately reliant on the income generated by business-related education. It is not unheard of for a business school to generate as much as 25% of all income for an entire university.

That creates an imbalance and distorts the conversation about the nature of learning both in terms of which courses are judged as being worth running (increasingly anything that attracts international students in large numbers) and those that are not (e.g. arts and humanities).

An additional friction can exist where research and theorising is undertaken by people who can be conveniently labelled as engaging in Critical Management (or Leadership) Studies (CMS), but whose work in this context isn't seen to be marketable in a corporate context. A recent example of this is the cull at the University of Leicester in 2021 of its entire CMS faculty.[85] If CMS research cannot be monetised, there is a deep ethical issue at play here, for if all research activity *by definition* has to generate an income, then universities are no longer centres of learning, first and foremost they are businesses.

Nonetheless, to go on an Executive Education programme is a status symbol. It signals that you are being invited to mingle not just with other managers and leaders, rather the tantalising prospect of joining the ranks of executives is being dangled before you. The more famous and expensive the business school, the greater cachet and kudos that rubs off, as the gap between where you aspire to

---

85. Well-documented here: https://ulsb16.com/

be and where you have come from widens. You might *just* be about to join one of the more powerful alumni networks in society. Lucky you.

That may sound flippant, yet a glance at the MBA and business school league tables, where two of the key metrics are the earning potential of graduates and the alumni network which you will ultimately become part of, rams home the message that, just like when deciding where to do an undergraduate degree, there are economic, social and class considerations.

With a business qualification, these are sharpened and the commercial implications of deciding where to study come to the fore. If you are spending tens of thousands of £ or $ on a course, then understandably the marketing for these programmes needs to offer a degree of certainty as to the value exchange. Not all, but many, institutions sell courses with language which amplifies a sense that if you do this programme, then you will achieve greater success. A few examples from institutions across the world (correct at time of writing and these do change regularly):

> "Helping you develop your leadership strengths to drive positive change for yourself and your organisation."[86]

> "We help leaders and their organizations to change. From supporting strategic transformation to mastering personal visions of leadership, we enable you to inspire, guide and galvanize, releasing the full and diverse capacity of all your people to be change-makers."[87]

> "Empower your future"[88]

> "Join a global community of learners. Build the skills to shape the world."[89]

> "We empower future leaders to reshape global business and society.[90]

Notice the certainty and aspirational quality of the language: 'deliver', 'drive', 'empower', 'doors' will be opened, etc. 'Change makers' is particularly problematic, as it continues the fetishization of change, notwithstanding how this might be experienced by people on all that change that the makers are

---

86. https://www.sbs.ox.ac.uk/programmes/executive-education/online-programmes
87. https://bit.ly/49lGkhs
88. https://www.insead.edu/master-programmes/master-business-administration
89. https://bit.ly/49lGAwW
90. https://www.jbs.cam.ac.uk/masters-degrees/mba/

initiating. Other phrases that appear regularly are 'world-leading', 'cutting edge' and 'internationally', all emphasising the elite company you will be in.

Hold in mind that these are programmes that are designed to 'equip' leaders to lead, change, manage, transform, grow, develop and otherwise improve organisations. As we have seen already, when it comes to complex challenges, the more intractable they are and less willing to be moved by force of will, the surety that comes with having a qualification from a big institution becomes most enticing.

The Silver Bullet that spawned the modern business school

Business education is often traced back to the bachelor's programme in business at the University of Pennsylvania (1881), thanks to Joseph Wharton, who ultimately founded a school in his own name (Mintzberg, 2004: 21).[91] Mintzberg points out that others trace the roots of business education back to the "Prussian school of bureaucratic statecraft" (2004: 21), and ultimately this is moot.

Matthew Stewart, a former management consultant, is the author of *The Management Myth* (2009), an excellent book that sets out to debunk modern business philosophy. He unpicks the history and influence of two of the big gurus and influencers, Frederick Taylor and Elton Mayo.

For our purposes, the modern business school as an institution can, in some ways, be traced back to the advent of Frederick Taylor and the birth of Scientific Management, in particular the notion of the 'one best way'. This set out to determine the most efficient way to organise work and people on the shop floor (1911: 36–37). Taylor concluded that prosperity and harmony for both workers and managers could be achieved by following four principles:

1. Develop a science for each element of an individual's work, which will replace the old rule of thumb method.
2. Scientifically select and then train, teach and develop the worker.
3. Heartily cooperate with the workers to ensure that all work is done in accordance with the principles of the science that has been developed.
4. Divide work and responsibility almost equally between management and workers.

---

91. https://www.wharton.upenn.edu/history/

What became popularised as the fifth principle stemmed from this:

> "… to work according to scientific laws, the management must take over and perform much of the work which is now left to the men; almost every act of the workman should be preceded by one or more preparatory acts of the management which enable him to do his work better and quicker than he otherwise could." (Taylor, 1911: 26)

Taylor was instrumental in shaping how Harvard Business School evolved in the early part of the 20th century. Edwin Gay, the man who essentially opened Harvard, was greatly influenced by Taylor's work, and the latter was a regular visitor, lecturing to students from 1909 to 1914 (Stewart, 2009: 40). The influence of Scientific Management can still be felt today, as can the positioning of Taylor as a credible researcher. Britannica.com,[92] which as a source is an important educational influence, goes as far as saying:

> "Though the Taylor system provoked resentment and opposition from labour when carried to extremes, its value in rationalising production was indisputable and its impact on the development of mass production techniques immense."

In a 1992 National Academy of Engineering report on *Manufacturing Systems: Foundations of World-Class Practice,* Heim & Compton critique Taylor's work and concede that the dehumanising aspects of the 'one best way' might be a bit much. They also say:

> "We know that Taylorism worked and worked well in the early part of this century."

Really? That depends on your assumptions about the nature of work, organising, power and distribution of wealth. Seen through the lens of a factory worker in the early part of the 20th century, Taylorism is an invitation to give up any idea of agency and autonomy, or that you might have some good ideas worth implementing. Just doff your cap and be grateful for however your manager feels inclined to reward you, assuming they think you are efficient enough to retain. Through the lens of a factory owner or manager, at least on paper, it is a Silver Bullet: do all this and you will produce more and make more money, remember you always know best, and replace people who are not up to scratch.

---

92. https://www.britannica.com/biography/Frederick-W-Taylor

Enter Silver Bullets, stage left

Hold in mind that Taylor's work was universally applauded as being a solution to the challenges of how to improve efficiency in business. It was sold as a scientifically researched and grounded approach that could be replicated in different contexts if you followed the 'one best way'.

It is arguably the very first Silver Bullet of modern management, with implications for how leaders are developed and how we organise. It was a 'thing' that could be bought from consultants – Taylor labelled himself as a 'consulting engineer for management', so maybe was the world's first management consultant (Stewart, 2009: 29) – *and* taught at business schools on the embryonic MBA programmes of the time, the first of which Harvard offered in 1908.

Indeed, as Wikipedia points out on the page for MBAs, they "originated in the United States in the early 20th century when the country industrialised and companies sought scientific management".[93]

In a nutshell, Scientific Management was key to the growth of the modern business school, and heavily influenced the thinking within them.

This focus on a 'one best way' and scientific management introduced the notion that if you do *this*, then *that* will follow: the promise of a scientifically proven best way to achieve success in business. It is the embodiment of certainty, and the genesis of the notion of 'best practice', a phrase much loved in business and by many consultancies because it exudes certainty through its pores, and something that will crop up throughout this book.

It is another convenient myth, one that sets an expectation that if you only follow this series of steps, then things will just … work. This linearity – if I introduce action A then outcome B will surely follow – seeks to completely deny the essential reality of the social domain, namely that it is uncertain and unknowable. Leadership, as it is often taught, represents an imposition of certainty and the capacity to direct the world – and the educational superstructure that has grown up around reinforces this.

Miriam Webster[94] suggests 'best practice' was first used in 1927, and it seems not unreasonable to suggest that 'one best way' is a short hop, skip and jump

---

93. https://en.wikipedia.org/wiki/Master_of_Business_Administration
94. https://www.merriam-webster.com/dictionary/best%20practice#h1

to the idea of 'best practice'. That what works in one context will work in another, an inherently absurd notion and is easily disproven by simply starting with Taylor:

> "In a 1914 study of 35 plants said to have adopted the Taylor system, Robert Hoxie concluded that 'no single shop was found which could be said to represent fully and faithfully the Taylor system… and no two shops were found in which identically or even approximately the same policies and methods were established and adhered to throughout'. Just as the science wasn't a science so, it seems, the system wasn't really a system." (Stewart, 2009: 51)

'Best practice' does have its place, but only in contexts with low complexity, e.g. fixing cars, installing equipment, etc. The more moving parts there are, the greater number of wonderfully unpredictable, irritating, emotional, intuitive, diverse and unique human beings are involved. 'Best practice' unravels as it comes face to face with humanity.

The kudos of the business school

> "For the most part, business schools all assume a similar form. The architecture is generic modern – glass, panel, brick. Outside, there's some expensive signage offering an inoffensive logo … The door opens automatically. Inside, there's a … receptionist dressed office-smart. Some abstract art hangs on the walls, and perhaps a banner or two with some hopeful assertions: 'We mean business.' 'Teaching and Research for Impact.'
>
> A big screen will hang somewhere over the lobby, running a Bloomberg news ticker and advertising visiting speakers and talks about preparing your CV. Shiny marketing leaflets sit in dispensing racks, with images of a diverse tableau of open-faced students on the cover." Martin Parker ('Why we should bulldoze the business school', *The Guardian*, 27-04-2018)

I worked for four and a half years at Roffey Park Institute Institute. While not a business school *per se*, for most of its seventy-plus years' existence, it was a leading centre in the UK for a relational and human-centred approach to leadership and organisation development. As a Senior Consultant, I regularly competed for work with business schools, and we too had sliding doors, female receptionists, a screen (not a big one) and leaflets and glossy brochures featuring participants and clients.

My job was to sell leadership development, and over time my curiosity grew as to why clients would sometimes choose business schools over other providers. Was it simply because they had better offers? If so, why?

One proposal I was involved in was for a large UK-based NGO. They wanted a leadership programme for their top twenty-five "aspiring leaders", who were "already demonstrating the three meta-competencies of 'ability to learn', 'agility in the world' and 'flexibility and adaptability'". Notice here that these are competencies that are demonstrable solely through changes in behaviour. Knowledge transfer, theories, models and great ideas alone do not catalyse behaviour change – it requires experiential learning, reflective practice and experimentation.

One of the reasons we were not awarded the contract and a larger, 'more prestigious' business school was, came down to the client's belief that having academics and professors would be more impactful.

Now, there are many brilliant academics and great practitioner researchers in business schools, but the *de facto* assumption here was that the kudos of business-school-based Executive Education was the difference that made a difference. There was no discussion as to which programme would have the greater impact on the organisation, or those they were there to serve.

It is difficult not to look at business schools through the lens of status, class and privilege, as they reflect a hierarchy that exists in the corporate world. The way money flows, how programmes are priced depending on the location and league table position of an institute reflect wider patterns in society. Jesse Segers, now Dean at SIOO,[95] an Organisation Development institute and an alternative business school in Holland, recalls being charged out at between €8,000 and €12,000 a day when working for a more mainstream institution. Faculty in business schools, in particular professors, have projected onto them (and are marketed as having) an aura of expertise, knowledge and certainty that helps smooth the wrinkled brows of clients who want to be reassured, stroked and, sometimes, learn. This is also evidence of the outsourcing of leadership thinking. Instead of taking the time to consider matters themselves, some senior leaders – under the pretence of being too busy with extremely important matters –

95. https://sioo.nl/

assume that 'knowing' is not something that human beings come to do through engagement with the world and other people's understanding of it, but instead is merely a commodity that can be bought and brought in. Learning then remains knowledge rather than practice-based.

Dr Richard Claydon works for one of the top business schools in Australia, ranked at time of writing top ten in the world for the global MBA programme. He told me that "the essay quality for the top-level students is just the same [as those from students on a less prestigious programme in Nepal] but they didn't have any money. They got an MBA from an institution that no one rates so they don't get the jobs."[96]

Ultimately, the perceived cachet and status of the institution, while important, is less significant to many that the mere fact it is a business school. The same may also be said of 'institutes', of which there are a number as well offering leadership and organisation development.

A nice and cosy relationship

The relationship between the buyers of learning within organisations and purveyors of Executive Education is important.

One of the HR leaders I interviewed saw Executive Education as "a racket", based on a collusion between business schools and L&D functions in organisations:

> "The problem I still see with L&D or leadership development functions is that the budget owners and the decision makers overwhelmingly are the ones that put the spotlight on themselves.

> So, they spend a hundred grand on one person doing an MBA or a couple doing a master's degree, when that money could have been used to transform the entire middle management permafrost layer that most businesses experience – the glut in the middle." [97]

Here power is exercised in service of amplifying the potential of an elite cadre of leaders, and by extension the assumptions that underpin that as being a good return on investment. What this story also raises is a question of how business schools are perceived more generally.

96. Interview 4th May 2020
97. Interview 7th July 2020

Among the webinars I ran as part of my research were two with Dr Wendy Shepherd from Cranfield University (Webinars, 05-05-2021 & 12-05-2021). At the beginning of each session, I asked participants a simple question: what is the primary function of a business school? The responses were as follows:

- "Help to develop better business professionals with ethical values."
- "To make money to pay for other non-money-making stuff (I don't agree)."
- "To prepare individuals to be purposeful in business life."
- "To provide high-level Executive Education for organisations."
- "To make money for the business school."
- "To equip learners to be better able to solve the problems they encounter in their businesses, to grow better businesses."
- "Develop relevant skills and knowledge for business success."
- "To return a healthy surplus to a university parent."
- "Larger scale delivery of learning. Standardisation of curriculum. Give an elitist edge to those who attend."
- "To create wealth, to provide learning space and career developments for people in 'business' including creating networks."
- "To sell MBA courses."
- "To equip people to lead and follow."
- "To educate businesspeople in good practice across the spectrum of business and challenge and improve notions of good practice."
- "Equip learners with an understanding of business."
- "If only we knew!!"

The audience consisted of a mix of people with experience as independent consultants, leaders, managers, plus current and former teaching staff in business schools. Who were less well represented were commercial clients of business schools, although there were several people with MBAs and other master's-level qualifications.

Nonetheless, this was a group interested in the role of business schools and arguably knowledgeable of the sector, hence their attendance. What strikes me is the extent to which business schools were seen here as more commercial than other learning organisations, and the extent to which they exist to teach people how to thrive in commercial entities rather than any other kind.

Is that all business schools cater for? No, even if some people hold that view. It does invite a different question though: what exactly are the kinds of problems that business schools can help with, and how do we measure the impact of that?

'The problem' problem

> "The profession of management has been created on the back of the belief of problems and the existence of problems. If you didn't have problems, why would you need managers or leaders?" Stefan Cantore[98]

Notwithstanding this, there is a more fundamental question. The way in which we construe problems, how we frame them, the assumptions that underpin this and our beliefs about how best to deal with them, is critical.

Organisations, and arguably society more widely, are obsessed with problems and the notion of problems. We do not tend to see challenges in organisations as things we address by building on strengths and what is in place, despite the increasing popularity of appreciative approaches to change sparked by David Cooperrider's PhD research in 1985 that in turn spawned a whole field, i.e. Appreciative Inquiry.

A good example of this is how organisations typically address the 'we need to save £x' or 'make savings of y%' or 'lose z headcount'. These are perfect examples of what Stefan Cantore described to me as "the essence of a problem", i.e. a set of boundaries and is "really an exercise in power".[99] Who has that power, of what type and over whom is it being wielded are key questions.

I have been involved in many conversations with clients over the years about the 'we need to ...' type of problem outlined above. What is rare is the client – or consultant given the tendency of consultancies to sell their services based on their ability to cut costs and hence people – who understand that the 'we need to save £x' problem can also be addressed by proposals that may involve investing money to generate revenue instead.

It is, however, "mutually advantageous to maintain the illusion of the world as a place of a lot of problems", commented Cantore, because it "maintains a stuckness" (ibid.). That in turn means there is always a new problem, and a pattern of problematising. The issue with problematising the world is that it leads to the need for the business school, and professional services firms more generally. It legitimises the narrative that not only are problems always intractable and often requiring specialist knowledge, we need experts who can tell us how to address them. It is an ethical challenge, because unless we agree with the idea that

---

98. Email 7th April 2020
99. Email 7th April 2020

'there is a problem', there is no need for business schools, Executive Education, consultancies or consultants – including me.

The irony, and a gnarly truth that lies underneath this, is that many challenges in organisations are not inchoate 'problems', on the contrary they are about sharing, relating, working with difference and similarity. It is rarely neat, as Naomi Stanford, a well-known organisation design practitioner, teacher and author observed:

> "One of the most common mistakes in finding a solution is that [clients] try and find a solution. They don't accept that there *isn't* a solution. There are only ways of acting and operating that may be better or worse, but you don't know until you start acting on them … I am absolutely fed up with the phrase 'what is the problem we're trying to solve?' [It] tries to simplify something into such a solvable problem, if you start to look at whatever is going on, there may be multiple problems but there also may be multiple opportunities, but the phrasing is around 'problems to solve'."[100]

The language that irritates Stanford adds a quantitative measure to the work, which allows those selling solutions to creep in and charge for fixing a problem that they themselves defined. Instead of reflecting the soup of complexity, ambiguity, emotion, assumption, story, ritual, shame, ego, narcissism, rivalry, power, politics and more that 'problems' are made up of, much writing about leadership and organisations has a utopian seasoning. It represents a yearning for a world of quick fixes and certain solutions that does not exist. Academic writing, and hence Executive Education that is offered off the back of that, often seeks to make sense of the mess, to reduce the anxiety and offer answers, even if they are oversimplifications, or marketed as packaging learning interventions.

The narrative around 'problems' presupposes that the main response must be that of an individual leader, doing something active and heroic, potentially marshalling their 'followers' to carry out their orders. But the stress of that individualised focus sends these all too human individuals into the arms of those who are peddling Silver Bullets, whether that be an MBA, leadership programme or change methodology.

The role of the leader, though, should not solely be about defining a problem and giving a contract to someone to fix it. They should instead create a space for the workforce to pool their collective intelligence to have a conversation about

---

100. Interview 24th July 2020

their experiences and how they might be improved. The job is too big for an individual – but the collective exists around them. What gets in the way of genuinely empowering employees, maybe, is that it shatters the illusion of the power of the great leader. As we will see in Chapter 11, when considering what to do in the absence of Silver Bullets, creating the conditions for inquiry is vital.

The underlying world view

The roots of management education and much of the thinking that stems from that "is based on a set of world views and assumptions, including the veneration of capitalism, and organising that supports that", suggests Cantore.[101] Mark Cole provocatively suggests:

> "… what you're up against is machine ideological reproductive apparatuses that keep that [world view] going, viz business schools and the professional services companies. So, while they're sitting there, churning out their drivel, people like us will struggle to engage with leaders in their field of practice, because they're listening to that, because that's what carries … prestige."[102]

The challenge for leaders therefore is to have time, space and permission for *their own* sense making and meaning making, to get clear on how they are constructing a 'problem'. Which brings us back to business schools, as centres of thinking and learning, and places that ostensibly can help with that. The problem with that is how business schools tend to mirror business, and, suggests Naomi Stanford, "that's why they're called business schools … they're not called 'critically reflective schools' because that's the philosophy department … they're set up as mirrors, to kind of 'production line' people into business in a way that business wants. That's a collusion."[103]

A CEO of an investment bank I worked with in early 2024, at the end of three days with myself and a colleague, said he had just come back from ten days at an international business school with lots of other CEOs. He said it was great, and that he had learned more in two and a half days with us than he did in ten days there. This talks to the idea of Zombie Leadership, which I will touch on shortly, and how this kind of executive leadership development can often be more an exercise in ego stroking than actually developmental.

---

101. Email 7th April 2020
102. Interview 30th July 2020
103. Interview 24th July 2020

Even when business schools succeed in creating genuinely reflective and impactful learning interventions, they risk doing so within a paradigm that ultimately is self-reinforcing, perpetuating existing ways of being, doing and organising rather than offering radical alternatives. MBAs epitomise this and are complicit in feeding certainty.

MBAs: the superficial passport to exec-level learning and success

Why do people choose to do an MBA, arguably the most well-known offering from business schools?

Dr Wendy Shepherd is Director of Individual and Organisational Impact at Cranfield University. She said: "You've got to ask the question 'why do people invest in MBAs?' In many cases, people use it as a badge. It's a way of proving that they have established a certain attainment in terms of their knowledge and understanding, which can help them to get promoted and when they apply for jobs, they can use it as a way of demonstrating what they know … some people do it to become better leaders. Some people do it because of the badge. Some people because of status."[104] The other reason is financial, as epitomised by the salary calculator and MBA.com.[105]

Mintzberg's *Managers Not MBAs* (2004) is arguably the go-to text for a detailed critique of MBAs and by implication business education more widely, arguing that "MBAs train the wrong people in the wrong ways with the wrong consequences" (2004: 6). He goes into detail how MBAs result in the wrong consequences, corrupting managerial practices as well as established organisations and social institutions, and breaks down how this translates into education for managers and leaders that is far removed from what it means to practice effectively.

Development programmes should help people become better at leading and managing, and at solving problems. The MBA is a perfect example of this but does not always have the impact the brochures promise. Look at the outline for any MBA and it is essentially a list of things aimed at helping you with problems that may arise.

---

104. Interview 29th September 2020

105. https://www.mba.com/business-school-and-careers/salary-and-roi/estimate-your-post-mba-salary – apparently my salary would go up by 35%. Woo hoo!

Mark Cole believes "an MBA should start with a week's residential that says: what do we know about organising? And that will be your inquiry, that will be your starting point. Whereas I expect if you went to Imperial or LBS you'd be starting with 'let's do finance. We'll start with the spreadsheets, crack on and then the world will make sense to you'."[106]

This echoes one of Martin Parker's central ideas in his book advocating the closure of all business schools: "The Business School only teaches one form of organising – market managerialism" (Parker, 2018: 9) and "teaches capitalism and the inevitability of the corporate form". He goes on:

> "These quite specific organisational models and their paper cut-out rational egoists are then assumed to provide general lessons for all sorts of other organisations, which is a bit like assuming … that the documented behaviour of elephants must be the same as that of fleas because they're both animals.

> If management is to become a subject worthy of the name, then it must study and teach more than just management." (ibid.: 98)

Parker points out "that fascism, feudalism, slavery and the mafia are ways of organising" (ibid.: 132), among many others that can be found in human societies, and one of the omissions in Executive Education is a thread that runs through the learning that genuinely supports inquiry into the political and ethical implications of *different* ways of organising.

In essence, Parker's is a critique of business schools and Executive Education that suggests they have a world view that is peculiarly narrow and, by extension, what leadership is required. In a sense, we are talking about a 'taken for granted' kind of thinking, which, by definition, limits what is taught, and therefore we would be better bulldozing business schools and replacing them with Schools for Organising. While we might be waiting a long time for the bulldozers, as a thought experiment it is worth engaging with: what if the real need is not to learn about 'business' rather it is about learning how to 'organise'?

John Higgins, an academic and researcher with a particular interest in power in organisations, has deep experience of the sector including at Hult Ashridge. He commented in 2021 that "it has become obvious to me that business school theory and management practice is built on sand. It denies and

---

106. Interview 20th July 2020

hides the self-serving nature of its perspective and its lack of any meaningful intellectual rigour."[107]

This narrowness Higgins, Parker and Cole refer to I encountered when considering doing an MBA or similar programme in 2004. I wanted one that took a relational and systemic approach to change in organisations and couldn't find one. I ended up doing an MSc in Change Agent Skills and Strategies, which was steeped in relational and systemic approaches to change.[108]

Anecdotally, my own conversations with MBA graduates have revealed that often the most useful modules they have taken are those few that talk to the psychological and behavioural aspects of organising. One MBA student talked to a former colleague of mine about the choices available to them in terms of further development, and their experience after the first year of an MBA. They came to the UK because, as they put it, "that's what you do if you want to get on but I'm so bored. It's crap what we're learning. I'm not learning anything that I can actually use."[109]

Disconnected from reality

The issue is that the world that the MBA is designed for is arguably no longer there, if indeed it ever was. Neil Morrison, with his background as a senior leader, suggests MBAs "teach a methodology for a world that, to a certain extent, is no longer playing by the rules of the methodology. I would argue that MBAs probably teach groupthink in quite a dangerous way. They don't generally lead to the diversity of thought and opinion that some of these problems need."[110]

Morrison then makes a case for a more fundamental problem with the MBA: "They breed that sense of: if you just apply these models, you'll come up with the right answer."

Martin Parker, who I quoted earlier, echoes Morrison, arguing that:

> "… institutions play a role in solidifying a chaotic world. So, the buzzing confusion of the world is reduced to a particular set of certainties and positions and certain sort of transactions."[111]

107. https://bit.ly/4am0VCk
108. The programme no longer exists as it ultimately, I gather, became to uncomfortable and radical for the School of Management at the University of Surrey to house it.
109. From a now no longer available blog post by Tom Kenward that appeared on the Roffey Park Institute website.
110. Interview 26th May 2020
111. Interview 24th May 2021

That certainty encourages people to see the world in certain kinds of ways. Universities – and by extension business schools – are incredibly effective at boxing particular pieces of knowledge. They say there are boxes for 'leadership', 'management', 'change', as if these were territories in the world. As Parker went on to say, "all the interesting action takes place on the boundaries between these territories" (ibid.).

More than anything, maybe, these are institutions that play a role in managing collective anxiety, in part evidenced by the mimetic nature of their strategies, because "they're all doing the same stuff, and none of them really have the courage to go and try something new" (ibid.). Universities' increasing reliance on international students amplifies that pattern, as it is easier to sell certainty than messy reality.

All of which makes Silver Bullet solutions a perfect fit. An alternative and more positive view is offered by Dr Wendy Shepherd, who argues:

> "Executive Development creates a pause for reflection in the busy flow of activities. Tutors and other participants provide new lenses to view old challenges. These lenses are often communicated through the use of models and frameworks.
>
> The lenses help broaden perspectives, promoting new insights and variety into the participants' repertoire of responses for handling complex challenges. Often leading to a change in priorities or the initiation of new actions."[112]

Both things can be true. There *are* business schools and people within them offering wonderful learning of the kind described by Shepherd. What is required is an awareness of the tensions inherent within this: the need to recognise what is working, and a wider need to support learning that goes beyond conventional frames of reference.

Teaching certainty is disconnected from reality

> "Deconstructing real-world problems to puzzles that can supposedly be solved with the 'secret' generalisable formulae is illusory and delusive."
> Richard Hale, OD & Leadership Consultant[113]

---

112. Interview 29th September 2020
113. https://bit.ly/3T9UIm7

If learning takes place in a wonderful building, with possibly some of the most advanced and well-resourced learning facilities on the planet, then the learning on offer is coloured by the certainty of the world views offered by the teaching faculty. Even if you are lucky enough to do an MBA that has practical application, success in part depends on the reputation of the place of study.

So what *exactly* is the benefit, from a student and learner's perspective, of going to a business school? Is it mere anointment? Whether the employer pays and allows for study release or the student pays for themselves and does the work in their spare time, the graduate comes out bearing the sheen of the MBA. Beneath that sheen, what is it that one can learn there that has utility and relevance, and how new is that? In a sense I am talking about impact, which I will turn to in a moment, and novelty. If there is one thing that is as alluring as a Silver Bullet, it is the New and Sexy Silver Bullet.

The past hundred years should therefore have seen lots of new and sexy Silver Bullets, as management thinking and education has evolved, but I doubt it. I tend to agree with Matthew Stewart, who argues that management is a neglected branch of the humanities. He goes on to suggest that, if anywhere, it would sit better within the history of philosophy. "Management theorists lacked depth … because they have been doing for only a century what philosophers and creative thinkers have been doing for millennia. This explains why future business leaders are better off reading histories, philosophical essays, or just a good novel than pursuing degrees in business" (2009: 11).

Reflecting on the gloss of Executive Education evokes again the lights and smoke from the Wizard of Oz. For all the glamour, behind the curtain there is a bespectacled white, middle-aged man pulling some levers and making a lot of noise. What is behind the curtain here?

The elephant (not) in the room

My own quest for an MBA that majored in the psychological aspects of leadership and organisations had in part been sparked by a conversation several years earlier with a graduate of the London Business School MBA programme, who commented that the one module that they found they continually drew on, in comparison to all others, was that of human behaviour. I have long wondered why this was the case, and Mintzberg offers a partial explanation.

"… soft skills simply do not fit in. Most professors do not care about them or cannot teach them. While most of the younger students are not ready to learn most of them. And few of these skills are compatible with the rest of the programme – they get lost among all the hard analysis and technique. So rather than *teaching* the soft skills, the business schools have tended to 'cover' them, in the two meanings of the word: review them and obscure them." (Mintzberg, 2004: 41)

Given the penetration of MBA graduates in the higher echelons of organisations, with some data suggesting as many as a third of CEOs have one,[114] maybe it is little surprise that there are low levels of understanding when it comes to human behaviour – of self and others – and social processes in organisations. They are inherently messy (not good or bad necessarily) and do not lend themselves well to bar charts, graphs and simplistic reductions of messy humanity into palatably digestible gobbets of business school-speak.

There is also another grey and trunky thing that lurks in the corner, namely whether it is even possible to 'teach' leadership. Mintzberg's work is key in raising this challenge, and Richard Hale argues that "trainers and consultants in this field are often performative, perfecting the art of being liked, entertaining and tricking their audiences into believing they have the Silver Bullet in the form of a new taxonomy or a colourful psychometric. Liking or even loving an entertainer should not be confused with learning from them."[115] I recognise that performative element, and have felt in myself the invitation to perform, the desire on the part of participants to ensure that they 'like' me, and my own counter transference as I admit to being partial to the odd stroke. That a recipe for creating the conditions for useful discomfort in service of learning does not make.

The impact of Executive Education

Maybe the above in part explains why Mintzberg is so scathing about business schools, arguing they have lost their way.

"They claim to develop managers yet turn out staff specialists who promote dysfunctional styles of managing. They are meant to be institutions of thoughtful scholarship, yet are increasingly drawn to

114. https://careerattraction.com/what-c-level-executives-think-about-mba-degrees/
115. Email 8th March 2024

promotional hype … Many cannot make up their collective minds whether to tone down their material for 'relevance' or ratchet it up for 'rigor', when they should be repudiating both." (Mintzberg, 2004: 377)

Ouch. Are business schools a 'bad thing'? In terms of how they operate, there are questions to be asked in terms of intent and outcomes, the learning on offer and the way in which that is sold to collude with the idea that there are guaranteed outcomes and certainty to be had in tackling complex problems. As Sumantra Ghosal commented in the wake of the Enron scandal, "Business schools do not need to do a great deal more to help prevent future Enrons; they need only to stop doing a lot they currently do. They do not need to create new courses; they need to simply stop teaching some old ones" (2005: 75).

There are great people working, thinking, writing and agitating within their walls, and challenging the neatness of the narrative. Yet there is also an inbuilt inertia. Parker spoke to me straight after a meeting with his institution's VC of Research, looking at their research strategy. These were people who had "already made it", and therefore had "a lot already invested" in the idea of certain sorts of disciplines, departments, students, funding streams, etc.

"So as soon as he [the VC] starts to pitch to them the idea that we need to reinvent the university, there's a kind of 'Wah! It's been working all right for the last 150 years, hasn't it?'"

Is there a case for shutting business schools down, therefore, as Martin Parker suggests? If that is the only way to change the conversation about how we organise and teach people to lead and change the places they work in, unlikely as it may be, it's appealing to me.

More realistic is that learning to organise – whether that be in Parker's School of Organising or in some other form – becomes both acknowledged as a need and is done in a way that reflects the many other ways one might do that rather than offer a narrow version of reality. The challenge is that, while managers and leaders concern themselves with the *organisation* – fixating on structure and org charts and Target Operating Models – others are busy with the business of *organising*. This is a praxis-oriented[116] activity that arises from people coming together with a common ambition to get things done. Here the leader needs

---

116. Praxis/Practice – sometimes used interchangeably, praxis is often associated with Karl Marx. Here I am thinking of praxis as Kemmis (2010: 11) defines it: "action aimed at self-conscious change of people's circumstances and of themselves (self-change)."

to challenge their reassuring fiction that they are the sole agent that ensures shit gets done. This requires letting go of the traditional image of a leader in favour of finding a way of being part of the collective, which may mean letting go of the desire to climb ever higher.

Ultimately, however, this all boils down to impact. Dr Wendy Shepherd's work is important in this context, because she is unusual: a professor and insider at a leading business school, who has done research into the real-world impact of Executive Education. Shepherd herself observed how vague the value proposition was for MBAs when she completed her own at Cranfield and then became faculty herself, so she is open about the tensions.

> "When it comes to the impact of Leadership Development, what leaders *actually do* as a consequence of their development is of higher importance than what they *know*. This is because knowledge that cannot be applied will soon be forgotten."[117]

Her research reveals the link between critical reflection, learning, behaviour change and impact. What she does not do is collude with the idea that leadership development at Cranfield or anywhere else guarantees success.

In conversation with me, her own frustration with clients who ask to be told what impact a programme would have is palpable. "I found that overly simplistic that people were asking … 'can you tell us what outcomes we'll have? Can you tell us how this has worked in another organisation, so we can know what to expect?' And of course, life's not like that."[118]

What is interesting is how she and Martin Parker agree, as he notes that "the messy reality of actual organising is rarely as simple as neat theoretical distinctions would suggest" (2018: 140).

Both advocate learning that supports inquiry, critical reflection and offers as wide a range of perspectives as possible (although Parker is advocating for a far wider range than I suspect would be found in any business school currently, given that the moment you expand your frame of reference to consider ways of organising that are *not* underpinned by market managerialism, there is greater permission to look beyond what is currently construed as 'relevant').

---

117. https://www.linkedin.com/pulse/results-dr-wendy-shepherd/
118. Interview with the author

I do wonder why universities persist on calling these places of learning 'business schools'. It seems to me far more relevant, appropriate and important to frame them as 'Schools of Organising, Work and Business' – in that order. Business as a container is not only limiting, but ethically problematic at this time. As Singhal *et al.* note, "a long-stated objective of management education is to transform graduates' value systems and lift them to their better selves" (2023: 2). Singhal *et al.* question whether business schools are either set up practically or philosophically to do this, and whether they are capable of looking "beyond their own self-interest and confined world views to fully appreciate the urgency of the challenges we collectively need to address" given their fixation on teaching about profit maximisation (ibid.). They go on to call for the following, although I would argue it applies to many of the other organisations and entities that 'help' leaders and organisations: "We argue that business schools should purposefully design in opportunities for reflexivity to stimulate epistemic humility and create leaders fit to tackle the [UN's] Sustainable Development Goals" (ibid.).

Lastly, it is worth mentioning that the problems raised in the last chapter regarding leadership development apply here, because business schools are the source of much that is ultimately published by way of thinking on leadership and organisations. It is self-reinforcing, because those theories are part of the portfolio of things that business schools sell. It is in their interest to construct a narrative that emphasises how learning about them in these institutes *will* have a positive impact.

John Quiggin's 2012 book *Zombie Economics,* which posited that there are dead ideas that still walk among us, has recently been applied to leadership, and is worth reflecting on having just spent two chapters on leadership theory and some of the places it is taught. Haslam, Alvesson and Reicher (2024: 1) suggest that "ideas about leadership that prove particularly hard to kill are those that simplify a knotty social process while at the same time legitimising the privileges of social elites and the leadership industrial complex that supports them", namely the mix of coaching that fuels egos, expensive development programmes, and literature that reinforces that. They suggest that this legitimisation takes at least three forms:

1. We, the masses, are incapable of looking after ourselves and need "a hierarchical society with strong leaders at the top in order for social order to emerge and endure" (ibid.).

152

2. Leaders deserve to be at the top due to their specialness that sets them apart from mere mortals, where men are generally implicitly the prototype.

3. Any success is ultimately down to the wondrousness of the leader, thus attributes any success that a group might have to the actions of its leader, thus marginalising others in terms of having had any part in that, with "the flow of attention, esteem and resources towards that leader and away from (others)" (ibid.).

This is another way in which market managerialism retains its grip on thinking about leadership and organisations. Zombie Leadership acts as a mechanism that excludes many from power, reinforces the existing social hierarchy and provides a justification of the superiority those in power feel "that is at the same time both comfortable and comforting" (ibid.). It is a form of functional collusion, and works remarkably well at preserving the status quo. In light of this, suggesting that the most useful thing we might start to do is simply encourage leaders to think that they may not, in fact, know best or have all the answers feels, literally, transgressive and revolutionary.

Reflective Questions

- What is the attraction of business school or executive education to you, precisely?
- To what extent do you feel that the curricula at business schools reflect the knowledge and skills needed to participate effectively in corporate life?
- What is the anxiety that going to a business school to learn might quell in you?
- If we bulldozed business schools, what would you replace them with? Schools for organising? Something else?
- Which voices are not being represented in executive education? Who is being silenced?

SILVER BULLET NO. 5

THOUGHT LEADER

As the global head of thought leadership for a major consultancy,
I focus on how technology is changing the future of interactions,
human behaviour, and business. I have big thoughts.

OF GURUS, WIZARDS AND THOUGHT LEADERS AKA 'EXPERTS'

OR: WHY WE ARE IN THRALL TO THOSE WHO ARE GOOD AT MARKETING THEIR IDEAS

Chapter 5:
Of Gurus, Wizards and
Thought Leaders aka 'Experts'

"A veritable army of people have a vested interest in hyping the gurus, and almost nobody gains by criticising them." Mickelthwaite & Wooldridge (1997: 57)

I met Pim De Morree and Joost Minnaar at a Holacracy[119] workshop in Brighton in 2016. At that time, they were two escapees from corporate life who were looking for alternatives to organisations they experienced as "characterised by inertia, bureaucracy and a lack of motivation. We simply couldn't accept that the world of work – for far too many – is a place full of misery and despair."[120] They set off on a trek around the globe to meet people who they hoped would inspire them to "make work more fun".

At the time I worked at Roffey Park Institute, and we invited them to come and share their experiences. A couple of years later, we repeated the exercise, and that session was the genesis of this book.

During the session, Pim made the observation that when they had started their journey two years previously, they thought that by the end of it they would find 'the magic bullet'. Tellingly, they rapidly concluded that there is no magic bullet – gold, silver or otherwise – but here is what caught my attention, and in turn how the energy for this book arose.

Having shared his observation, namely that there is no Silver Bullet, several times during that session members of the audience asked questions that came from a place of 'but there is one really, isn't there? Go on, what is it?' After all, if you abandon serfdom and go on a quest in search of the Holy Grail, and make a noise about it, you are expected to come back with something.

---

119. Holacracy was one of the first great hopes of approaches to organising that expanded on the idea of self-management. It was the brainchild of Brian Robertson, who distilled the working practices of his technology company into the methodology in 2007, before it was latched onto by some as a Silver Bullet for how to decentralise management and organisational governance. Funnily enough, it wasn't.
120. https://corporate-rebels.com/about/

I discussed this with Pim and his colleagues in the break, and they'd noticed that pattern as well. So here we had a group of Organisation Development, Change and HR practitioners – consultants, coaches and facilitators all – and even here defaulting to a hope that somewhere, out there, there is a guaranteed answer or a quick fix.

In the years that followed, they have founded Corporate Rebels, published a book on how to change modern workplaces (2019), been nominated for awards and listed among the Top 30 Emergent Management Thinkers by the Thinkers50 Institute. In a way they have set themselves up to be another party to whom the difficult thinking can be outsourced, and that will always be a challenge for anyone who, intentionally or unintentionally, gets set up as having answers. While they may be perceived as gurus, gurus typically do not challenge their own thinking as much is Joost Minnaar did in his interview with me, tellingly observing:

"Management thinking and management, or at least in the popular management literature, all those books have 'the magic formula', or they claim to have it. I think the stuff that gets really popular, that many people read or share, always has some kind of universal answer. Just look at Simon Sinek, *The Golden Circle*.[121] It's widely popular … is it really true? I don't think so. It's a good story and it fits our mind. I think we'd like to believe that. So, when we started our journey, we also were looking for that Silver Bullet … I think we got more radical and [know] that there is no Silver Bullet …

I would say there's not a model or solution you can copy from another organisation and [put] it into your organisation and think that will be successful … We have never seen one organisation doing exactly the same as the other."[122]

You don't sell many guru t-shirts with that lack of certainty, but Corporate Rebels have done a good job of marketing what they are certain about in the context of uncertainty. That you need to appear like you know what you are talking about, that you have ideas worth listening to, is key to the market in Silver Bullets, and again explains why business schools and consultancies are so successful, as they have the resources to combine these two elements into saleable packages.

---

121. This is a reference to what made Sinek famous, namely a TED talk and the book based on that, *Start With Why* (2011). More on him later.
122. Interview 18th May 2020

The veneration of personality over substance

There are tens of thousands of people on LinkedIn who describe themselves as a 'thought leader', and several dozen companies even have the term as part of their name. Many of them are 'dynamic', offer a 'shift in perspective', are 'ground breakers' or offer 'the very best thinking from the world's brightest thought leaders'. Some can help YOU, dear reader, become one yourself. I have, occasionally, been described as a thought leader, and when that happens, I refute that, and try not to look too much like a cat that is hacking up a furball.

So, what is a 'thought leader'? Denise Brosseau, author of *Ready To Be A Thought Leader?* (2013) says on her website:[123]

> "Thought leaders are the informed opinion leaders and the go-to people in their field of expertise. They become the trusted sources who move and inspire people with innovative ideas; turn ideas into reality, and know and show how to replicate their success. Over time, they create a dedicated group of friends, fans and followers to help them replicate and scale their ideas into sustainable change not just in one company but in an industry, niche or across an entire ecosystem."

Brosseau is part of an industry that helps others to become thought leaders in their own right – hers is one of many books that will help you become one. Why wouldn't you want to be when "as a recognised thought leader, you will have the *power to persuade*, the *status* and *authority* to move things in a new direction, and the *clout* to implement real progress and widespread innovation"? [my emphasis] It almost sounds like you will qualify for your own throne.

A more measured definition of thought leadership is that it is "the expression of ideas that demonstrate you have expertise in a particular field, area, or topic,"[124] which arguably accurately describes everything written about leadership development referenced in Chapter 3, and the output of business schools.

In an interview with *Business Daily News*, Jake Dunlap, founder CEO of a sales consultancy called Skaled, said that "thought leaders draw on the past, analyse the present and illuminate the future to create a comprehensive, unique, and impactful view of their area of expertise".[125] Another definition is that "a thought

---

123. https://thoughtleadershiplab.com/what-is-a-thought-leader/
124. https://www.wgu.edu/blog/what-thought-leadership2012.html#close
125. https://www.businessnewsdaily.com/9253-thought-leadership.html

leader is someone who is seen as an expert in a specific field; they're capable of introducing new ideas and influencing other people in the industry to make certain decisions or take certain actions. Thought leadership, or thought leadership marketing, is the process of developing your expertise and leveraging that into leadership over others."[126] A more cynical view is that "thought leaders tell very particular stories that in another guise would be described as simple and deceptive. They choose topics which enough people have heard of but too few understand."[127]

A more recent study by Harvey *et al.* (2021: 1) points out that thought leadership is both well-known and simultaneously, a poorly understood concept. They go on to say: "It has attracted growing attention from certain knowledge-intensive firms, namely, professional service firms (PSFs) who are creating large volumes of practitioner material distributed through magazines, white papers, blogs, podcasts and videos. As demand grows, 69% of these organisations have a specific head of thought leadership" (ibid.). Now I know why I feel swamped by bright ideas and brain farts coming at me from all directions, as indeed are many clients, for whom "far too much of it fails to connect" (ibid.).

Harvey *et al.* go on to identify a fundamental problem that Brosseau and others fall foul of:

> "… the diffuse nature of thought leadership is complicated by the interplay between the individual, the organisation and the industry context in which it occurs. Problems such as producing thought leadership that is supposedly rare and unique, yet the sheer demand for thought leadership puts pressure on people and organisations to find ways of delivering quantity at the expense of quality … Hence, it is not surprising that some scholars and practitioners consider it as yet another management fad." (2021: 2)

The key question is what is thought leadership *for*? Primarily, say Harvey *et al.*, it is about developing and disseminating knowledge, and one view is that it is about helping managers and leaders become more effective. However:

> "… not everyone can be a thought leader because if everyone is challenging the status quo, there is no status quo to challenge. Yet, a survey of CMOs [Chief Marketing Officers] found that 82% of clients

---

126. https://www.entrepreneur.com/article/359058
127. https://medium.com/swlh/why-you-shouldnt-be-a-thought-leader-4c87907e1bf

expected that firms will be thought leaders and produce insightful content." (2021: 13)

In short, there is a functional collusion at play here: clients want PSFs – and others – to be thought leaders and to be insightful, i.e. to come with case studies, suggestions and answers. At best it is a tacit cry of 'we need help', and at worst another example of case study addiction. What we have ended up with is the commoditisation of thought leadership, it has become something to be created, marketed and sold as a product, or as marketing collateral as part of a sales process.

Harvey *et al.* (ibid.) go on to suggest there are nine tensions, three at an individual level, which serve as a useful backdrop to what follows:

How can individuals balance the risk of thought leadership with the safety of thought followership, so they do not damage their reputation among salient stakeholders?

How do individuals balance using the thought leadership derived from client engagement, with the restrictions of client confidentiality and intellectual property?

If thought leadership is supposed to be rare, how can it become common for individuals to consistently produce?

If you have to say you are a thought leader, you probably aren't

The pattern that emerges is that thought leaders are viewed primarily as *experts* in a particular domain. In some instances, these experts become so 'thought leader-y' that they take on the lustre of gurus and are imbued with God-like qualities.

The reality is that there is a long history in human civilisation of endowing certain people with attributes that elevate them above others. Wisemen/ women, witch doctors, shaman, sages, philosophers, wizards and witches, among others, have been elevated into positions where they are seen as having special knowledge or skills, or both, that set them apart. They are special, 'other', somehow of this world and yet not, which is what in turn leads to them occasionally being cast out – we want to benefit from their power and wisdom, until the awe shifts from reverence to fear, or in the case of some, ridicule.

John Micklethwait and Adrian Wooldridge's critique of this area, *The Witch Doctors: Making Sense of the Management Gurus* (1997), has aged well. It was written at a time when business guru behemoths such as Tom Peters, Peter Drucker and their ilk were at the peak of their fame. Gurus were an accepted part of the management and self-help landscape, from Princess Diana calling on Anthony Robbins to Newt Gingrich "preparing for his job" by reading Drucker (Micklethwait & Wooldridge, 1997: 3), and in 2023 we may have reached Peak Guru, for it is possible to buy a website with a '.guru' domain. And yes, I have checked: Hearsum.guru is available for £3.99. Watch this space, for when my ego gets big enough …

What all gurus have in common is the projection onto them of expertise and the label that goes with that – 'expert' – and how they seek to capitalise on that by exuding and marketing themselves back out as voices to pay attention to. These are the ultimate purveyors of Silver Bullets, and organisational entities such as business schools and consultancies are on the end of similar projections.

Nonetheless, let's start with what happens when it is the individual 'expert' who sets themselves up as having the answer, or conversely finds themselves having to disabuse their clients of that notion, often repeatedly. To do that, we need to unpack the history of 'expertise'.

What is an 'expert'?

"The word itself originally comes from the Latin *experiri*, which is a derivative of the word for 'experience' and translates literally as 'experienced in', or 'having experience of'" (Skovholt *et al.*, 2016: 2). In its original sense, it refers to "someone whose fluency of skill in a given domain is grounded in an accumulated set of experiences in that domain" (ibid.). Chaucer, who offers one of the first instances of the word in written form, "described experts as those who acquired mastery through an accumulation of relevant experiences" (ibid.), which could also be in several domains, not just one.

We must wait until the 20th century for a systematic definition of the term 'expert', and research into what distinguishes the latter from a 'novice'. For example, brothers Stuart and Hubert Dreyfus (1980) researched how air force pilots acquired their skills. This has become known as the Dreyfus Model of Skill Acquisition (Benner, 1982: 402), and posits that skills acquisition goes through five stages:

- Novice
- Advanced beginner
- Competent
- Proficient
- Expert

That fifth stage is the guru and thought leader's nirvana. Experts "see the words, pieces, or notes within a context of accumulated experience, knowledge, and wisdom. This allows the expert to see deeper, faster, further, and better than the novice" (ibid.). What is interesting here is that we can already see that 'knowing stuff', having knowledge of schools of thought, approaches, methodologies, tools, etc., is useful but not sufficient. That applies however knowledge is acquired, whether through a master's, PhD, MBA or other qualification.

What is 'expertise'?

The main problem here is that there does not seem to be a commonly accepted definition of 'expertise' in the literature (Frensch & Sternberg, 1996 in Skovholt *et al.*, 2016: 6). There is a general assumption that experts have a unique combination of talents and motivation needed to undertake the necessary training and practice to reach a point where they have achieved the requisite level of expertise (Ericsson & Lehman, 1996 in ibid.: 6), which is confirmed by Frensch & Sternberg's definition (1989 in ibid.: 6): "The ability, acquired by practice and experience, to perform qualitatively well in a particular task domain."

It is at this point we get to the crux of the matter, in a sense how our understanding of 'expertise' and 'experts' has become subtly but significantly detached from actual meaning. The definition above brings clarity to our understanding, it "simultaneously reduces a complex phenomenon to a few highlights" (Skovholt *et al.*, 2016: 6). In a nutshell, that is also what a Silver Bullet is: the reduction of the complex into easily digestible and bearable components.

So 'expertise' and the 'experts' that proffer it have become increasingly untethered from their original purpose. In organisations that manifest in the propensity to look for quick answers and easy solutions, and more widely in society it reflects an increasing disdain. A graphic example of this is Dr Anthony Fauci in the US, who became the bête noire of those who did not like what most medical experts were saying about COVID. There we see how the term has become almost an insult and expertise is to be derided unless it supports a particular ideological or political position. In the UK, while arguably a more nuanced relationship with expertise arose around COVID, Brexit showed we can be equally dismissive, e.g. Michael Gove's attacks on experts during Brexit, on the assumption that the British population had had enough of them. This set the London Business School off in defence of their expertise (and arsenal of Silver Bullets).[128]

In short, we pick our experts based primarily on whether they agree with us, and less so when they challenge our thinking. We choose views of the world that affirm our own, so never step out of a place where we are insulated from any to our own perspective. Maybe this is why contract after contract is handed out to people who say things that feel just edgy enough but without ever any real risk of tearing down the shibboleths of conventional thinking in corporate life.

The pedestal problem

A lot of relations in corporate life are defined and mediated by the relationships not between people but between the labels that they assume or are ascribed to them. If someone declares that they are a leader, we will typically fall into either a follower or a rebel role, wilfully disrupting the balance of life in the organisation. Similarly, the expert will guide and steer the leader, as they are immersed in their role of arranging people around them to develop and deliver their vision (however illusory their ability to do that may be). We seem endlessly – and sometimes exclusively – fascinated by those we elevate in terms of their status, whether as leader or expert.

Underpinning the particular focus on the 'expert' lies the obsession with novelty. We all – clients and consultants – seem to endlessly chase the latest thinking, idea, technique and model; we become fixated on fads and fashions. This suggests that we are holding an extremely traditional view of innovation, where we pursue new ideas that emerge from some heroic individual. In so doing, we neglect the way in which an 'innovator' can be someone who keeps previous ideas firmly to the foreground – and works to adapt and/or adopt them to suit contemporary challenges. Innovation can be cyclical, bringing old ideas back into vogue, something the fashion industry is particularly good at, and even in organisations, we see recycling (or more accurately regurgitating in some cases) of old ideas, e.g. change curves, four box models, pyramids, etc.

---

128. https://www.london.edu/think/who-needs-experts.

In finding experts we agree with, we then place them on pedestals, such that what they say is taken maybe far more seriously than they merit, or is relied on in a way that the speaker never intended or expected. It gets more complicated with experts who know what their expertise might lead to and are aware of the risks, e.g. J. Robert Oppenheimer, the 'father of the atom bomb', as he is sometimes referred to.

Let's consider how we view experts, 'names', leading figures in the fields we work in ... I first met Simon Cavicchia, who has contributed much to this book, in 2005 when I did my master's. My initial experience of him was an exercise in phenomenological inquiry[129] that had a profound effect on me. It brought into my awareness aspects of my behaviour and how I showed up that, in the months and years that followed, were life changing. From that moment on, I relished the opportunities I had to work with Simon, and slowly but surely and unbeknownst to him, constructed a lovely pedestal that elevated him 'above' me.

Fast forward a few years post master's, and Simon and I get to know each other better and start to collaborate. At the start of this, we sat in a coffee shop and had a conversation about our fears and anxieties we might have about working together. Mine was simple: I still had him on his pedestal and held him in such high esteem that my own practice as a facilitator paled. Simon, on the other hand, feared me discovering how he really was and that he could not match up to my and his own expectations – an imposter syndrome of sorts. Having had this conversation, our work has evolved and remains a joyous experience. I learned loads, and the pedestal was slowly but surely dismantled.

Clearly what I was doing was comparing myself to Simon, and this goes on all the time for humans. From a young age, we learn to compare ourselves to others. First family members, and then peers in school. Marks and grades actively reinforce this comparison across all aspects of school life. We compare ourselves to fictional and non-fictional characters we are exposed to, and that carries on through education and into work, where we are constantly comparing and being compared, and more broadly in life. So much so obvious, and comparing is one way we learn about ourselves and what it means to fit in.

When we compare ourselves to experts, that process is at work as well, and for me it has always been a good test of how my own internal imposter syndrome is

---

129. Phenomenology is the study of phenomena as they manifest in our experience, or in other words how we know the world, our subjective experience. In this exercise, Simon and I sat opposite each other and reported moment by moment what we were experiencing in the here and now.

doing. I have had the pleasure of meeting various people who, from afar and by virtue of the stories that surround them, are regarded as experts, even regarded as 'thought leaders' or 'gurus', in their field. One such is Naomi Stanford.

The reluctant gurus

I heard about Naomi Stanford when I joined Roffey Park Institute. She was regarded as 'the' person to talk to regarding Organisation Design and was a regular guest. From afar, I was intimidated by her reputation, the many books she has written, which amplified my own insecurities (do I know enough? Am I a good enough consultant/facilitator? Etc.). In recent years, I have got to know her, starting when I shared a coffee with her as we discussed her speaking at a conference I was involved in designing, and more recently as we have discussed all things Silver Bullet related. What I know now is that Naomi is humble, witty, generous and a rare thing: an expert who is always learning, evolving, challenging her own thinking and sharing as she goes. Her own view on the label of 'guru' is revealing:

> "I reject that concept, but in the Middle East that's what the colleague I work with there sells me as. But I think my personality quickly dispels the myth that I have all the answers because I keep on saying I haven't a clue. No one has any answers."[130]

I was struck by Joost Minnaar's stance. Corporate Rebels do a good job of marketing and positioning themselves as an alternative to mainstream thinking, albeit they now have to manage the tension of no longer being newcomers, rather they are established. What gets missed is the stance that lurks beneath. Minnaar asked:

> "What actually is 'organising'? How do we organise truly differently? What are the dimensions of organising? This is more of the work I'm in now and our book is more an entry level 'adventure book'. And if you got interested in this work, you cannot do too much with it, to be honest. You can create some nice experiments; you can open your mind a bit about different ways of doing things. But it doesn't go deep into the things you mentioned. I think you have to read that between the lines … our book was a conversation starter."[131]

---

130. Interview 24th July 2020
131. Interview 18th May 2020

Glenda Eoyang, founder of the Human Systems Dynamics Institute, notices that when she begins to work with clients:

> "… they begin to think of adaptive action, pattern logic and inquiry as Silver Bullets. Now they're 'go to' processes, but the answer belongs to you. So the agency for coming to the solution is that…Some people come in expecting me to have the Silver Bullet [but] that doesn't last very long."[132]

Similarly, Gervase Bushe is keen to disabuse others of the notion that he is a guru. While recognising that people in the OD community will "make up stuff" based on what they have read about him, he has come to terms with that: it goes with the territory. It happens for him with clients as well: "I'll get clients coming at me where there's that initial [hope I have a Silver Bullet], which I try really hard to disabuse as quickly as possible."[133]

Dave Ulrich is another worth mentioning. Well-known in the field of Human Resources (HR), he is a prolific writer and speaker, best known for what has become known as the 'Ulrich Model', one of the major innovations in HR thinking in the past thirty years that advocated reconfiguring key HR roles to better create value and serve an organisation. Dave and I connected during my research for this book, and he is another who struggles with the projection onto him of a status and story he is not comfortable with. Remember the description of an expert from earlier: experts "see the words, pieces, or notes within a context of accumulated experience, knowledge, and wisdom." Compare this to how Dave sees his work:

> "I hope I create ideas that will have impact, that build on the past, that rely on relevant theory, that are research based, and that are useful.

> If someone labels them a 'Silver Bullet' that is more their agenda to likely discount my ideas and promote theirs. I get frustrated by misrepresentation of my ideas, but it is what it is."[134]

Ulrich now has the benefit or the curse of forever being associated with his 'Ulrich Model', even though his thinking has and is continually evolving, in particular deepening and extending what it really means to build capability within not just HR but an organisation more widely. We, the audience, find it

---

132. Interview 5th May 2020
133. Interview 6th May 2020
134. Email 24th February 2021

easier to frame him in a convenient way and edit out anything that does not fit, not least that he genuinely doesn't believe he has The Answer.

It was clear from my interviews that many of those regarded by their peers and clients as experts in their given field clearly know the risks of colluding with the fantasies and projections of others. Yet there are those that indulge their clients and audiences, using that adulation to elevate their status and reputation. This is part of the shadow of expertise, and where it meets thought leadership and guru-dom.

"So true!"

"Simon [Sinek]'s major breakthrough happens when a local TEDx event decides to invite him to share his theory. There are only fifty people in the room to witness an almost historical moment. The video of how Simon passionately unfolds his Golden Circle theory goes viral on YouTube and TED and turns Simon Sinek instantly into a management guru."[135]

If you spend much time on LinkedIn, it probably won't be long before someone in your network likes a post by Simon Sinek, whose popularity is founded on books about finding your 'why'. More recently, he has started talking a great deal about 'the infinite game', and he does a brilliant job of framing and selling ideas, whether that be his own or the repackaging of other peoples. What interests me is *how* Sinek shows up and markets himself, and how people *respond* to him. Many of his posts are short, pithy sayings that border on 'The Word of Sinek' delivered from Mount Why.

When Sinek speaks it is with a serious intensity, a masculine certainty that seems to signal 'Disagree with me at your peril, for I am right', and it smacks of either a conscious or unconscious intent to hold a heroic position, with all the shadow that comes with. This is increasingly how our polarised political discourse feels. Truths are held to be self-evident, those who disagree are unspeakable in their absurdity or evil or both, and simple assertions are made notionally from 'the right side of history', all of which denies dialogue. The latter is what Sinek's axioms do, whether that is the intent or not.

---

135. https://corporate-rebels.com/meeting-simon-sinek/

Simon Sinek
Optimist and Author at Simon Sinek Inc. - Taken from LinkedIn

The value of our learnings multiplies when we share what we learn with others

---

Simon Sinek
Optimist and Author at Simon Sinek Inc. - Taken from LinkedIn

Great leaders don't blame the tools they are given.

Great leaders work to sharpen them.

Simon Sinek
Optimist and Author at Simon Sinek Inc. - Taken from LinkedIn

Any worthwhile conversation starts with listening

Simon Sinek
Optimist and Author at Simon Sinek Inc. - Taken from LinkedIn

The selfish fear change.

The selfless lead it.

Simon Sinek
Optimist and Author at Simon Sinek Inc. - Taken from LinkedIn

Bad leaders may edit the truth for fear of causing discomfort. Good leaders accept that the truth is often uncomfortable.

Simon Sinek
Optimist and Author at Simon Sinek Inc. - Taken from LinkedIn

A bad leader cares more about others hearing their ideas.

A good leader cares more about hearing ideas from others.

These are a case study of thought leadership guru-ness, and follow a set of easily identifiable rules:

1. Speak in simple language.
2. Use juxtapositions wherever possible, and always frame things as binary, either/or statements.
3. Assume universal notions of 'goodness', 'badness' and 'greatness'.

And above all else:

4. Say something inspiring, however meaningless, established truism or a rehash of well-established ideas it is.

And yet …

His posts inspire by turns fawning admiration – 'So true!', often a tell for uncritical thinking – and ridicule by a small minority who suspect the emperor may indeed be wearing no clothes. The numbers of people liking and commenting positively are in the tens of thousands, critics not so much. His popularity personifies a diminished public discourse and wider practice. It begs the question of what social need is being met. His pronouncements have a quality of religiosity about them, and maybe in uncertain times, that is what sells more.

Gary Vaynerchuk, an American businessman, speaker and author, is another example of using strength of personality to create an aura of guru-ness, in particular through savvy use of the internet. He has millions of followers across LinkedIn, X, Facebook, YouTube and Instagram, where he is known as Gary Vee, and evokes stronger positive and negative reactions even than Sinek. His books shout with a shouty, grim and muscular machismo, with titles like *Jab, Jab, Jab, Right Hook: How to Tell Your Story in a Noisy Social World* (2013), *Crushing It!: How Great Entrepreneurs Build Their Business and Influence – and How You Can, Too* (2018) and *Crush It!: Why NOW Is the Time to Cash In on Your Passion* (2009).

What strikes me about both is that they express little doubt; every message, whether in written form or speech, is delivered with an unwavering certainty. Watch videos of either and what is offered are ideas presented as a truth that you can rely on, which come from a place of expertise and knowing. There is oodles of charisma on display, amplifying the sense that these men are experts and have the answers, thus colluding further with the tacit belief that this is how those offering expertise should be.

It's a reassuring and intoxicating invitation: follow me because I have the answer. Clearly, there are plenty of other examples of business gurus, e.g. Brené Brown, Elon Musk, Gary Hamel, Richard Branson, Peter Drucker, etc. Expand your frame of reference a little to include popular psychology and self-help, and we can add the likes of Tony Robbins to that list, another figure of towering self-confidence, inspiring an almost religious fervour. So too TED Talks, which, for every insightful session may also have a quasi-TV evangelist quality, making liberal use of pathos to evoke a response from watchers (Ludewig, 2017 & Di Carlo, 2015).

When people become so deified that they cannot be questioned – and TED Talks interestingly do not have Q&As, reinforcing the sense of them being sermons – or they are held in such high esteem that they are believed to offer The Answer, that is the point we enter Silver Bullet territory.

Dominance dynamics, or why we *really* like to be told what to think

One of the questions that has been bugging me is how and why we seem so in thrall to thought leaders. As well as meeting our need for certainty and the allure of the expert, another possible reason presents itself in the form of what anthropologists call dominance dynamics. This is illustrated by when discussion is dominated by one or two people, leading to the suppression of insights from other group members, particularly introverts. Leigh Thomson, who specialises in research into dominance dynamics, suggests that in a typical four-person group, "two people do 62 per cent of the talking, and in a six-person group, three people do 70 per cent of the talking" (Syed, 2020: 109).

What is possibly more telling is that she notes that "the people doing all the talking don't realise they are doing it … They are adamant that everyone is speaking equally, and that the meetings are egalitarian. The reason is that they often lack self-awareness. So, if you point it out to them, they bristle, and you often get into an escalating conflict" (ibid.). The result is that the dominant players end up having their ideas parroted back at them, creating a feedback loop that reinforces the esteem in which they are held.

On a platform like LinkedIn, we see how technology and language can reinforce these patterns. In the past year, LinkedIn has invited members to contribute to posts that are AI generated. This is coupled with an initiative that entices you to invest time contributing with the promise that if a) you write frequently enough and b) you get sufficient likes, you can earn a 'LinkedIn Top Voice' badge.

Now, being the minx that I am, I decided to play and see how long it would take to become a Top Voice. A couple of weeks and some pontificating (and to be fair some quite good pontificating) is all it took before I earned my 'Top Voice in Facilitation' badge. Another couple of weeks saw me earn my 'Top Voice in Change Management' badge. What interests me is the language: why the need to ascribe to contributors the label of 'Top Voice'? Why not useful, provocative, interesting, stimulating or critical voice? Why the need to invoke hierarchy? It implies some voices are better and cleverer than others, feeding an ecosystem that strokes the loudest and most strident players. Do a search for 'LinkedIn Top Voice' on the platform and what you see is evidence of how the label is actively adopted by those who wish to promote their 'thought leadership' and thus profile. Visibility and followers are the key metrics in this hierarchy rather than the quality of thinking or learning on offer. Are there good ideas in this stew of ego and attention seeking? Absolutely, and I believe that is secondary to the creation of more thought leaders and gurus who can be elevated in the LinkedIn hierarchy. The clue that something is off remains for me what happens when dissonant and dissenting voices appear, as with my experimentation on Simon Sinek's feed. It reminds us that thought collectives will only take so much heresy, and I wonder whether LinkedIn's 'Top Voices' are merely another fractal of a collective defence against anxiety, creating the conditions for the birth of more experts to whom we can look for reassurance.

Why are we so receptive to bullshit? ...[136]

One other factor is worth mentioning here that contributes to the ease with which thought leaders, gurus and experts are so successful in influencing others. A 2015 study by Pennycook *et al.* looked at how people process information, and the degree to which this impacts bullshit receptivity, in particular the perception that meaningless information/data is somehow profound. The results suggest that people who are more likely to rely on a faster, more intuitive (i.e. less analytic and reflective) thinking style are more susceptible to falling for bullshit. They are more reflexively open-minded (i.e. they are more accepting of all kinds of information because they are less likely to put much effort into

---

136. This section was heavily influenced by an exchange with Shane Littrell, a researcher with a particular interest in bullshit. I recommend his work if you wish to learn more.

processing and reflecting on it). Modern organisations, with their emphasis on speed and narratives around, say, how technology requires us to do things with ever greater pace increase the pressure on us to process information more quickly.

This fuels the market for neat, pithy and easy-to-consume stuff (hello social media and populist news channels) that we do not have to put much thought into. We are also sometimes dazzled and impressed by fancy buzzwords and jargon that we don't understand but are too cognitively lazy to ask a thought leader to define (Littrell *et al.*, 2021). The danger in these types of situations is clear: when we fail to engage our critical thinking skills at the appropriate times, we are more likely to just accept whatever a thought leader or guru is saying and respond by exclaiming 'So true!' (Spicer, 2020).

This is, in part, why thought leadership fuels the market for Magic Bean management tricks and Silver Bullet solutions: they wrap lame slogans and empty promises in impressive-sounding jargon and serve them directly to the intuitive parts of our brains in bite-size, easy-to-digest morsels of anxiety-relieving sweet treats. As the old saying goes, "if you can't dazzle them with brilliance, baffle them with bullshit!" (Pennycook *et al.*, 2015; Spicer, 2020).

An important thing to keep in mind is that thought leaders and gurus often use language that is full of confusing buzzwords and jargon (this is especially true in the corporate world). People don't often understand what the words mean (the thought leader likely doesn't either) but they are often perceived as superficially impressive because they sound fancy, innovative and high-concept. In these situations, some people will fall for bullshit (especially 'business bullshit') because, when they encounter this inscrutable, confusing jargon, they fall back on a cognitive heuristic that tells them 'if it sounds smart/impressive, it is smart/impressive!'. Or at the other extreme, the potential for shame evoked by the possibility we do not understand the cleverness leads us to pretend we do.

The moral of the story? Question stuff. Yes, even if what you think I am saying is clever. Really. Go on. Question it.

When gurus wander into organisations

A senior HR leader in a major insurance company in the early 2000s went through several gurus. In my interview with them, they first recalled Dr Paul Stolz, who "is considered [by his website at least] the world's leading authority on the integration and application of grit and resilience. He is author of five international bestselling books on the subject — printed in seventeen languages — including the top-selling business book in China, and was voted by *HR Magazine* as 'One of the Top 10 most influential global thinkers,' and by *Executive Excellence* as 'One of the 100 Most Influential Thinkers of Our Time'."[137]

The Top 10s and Top 100s, and the Thinkers 50 that is, apparently, "the world's most reliable resource for identifying, ranking, and sharing the leading management ideas of our age"[138] fuel the guru industry. They apply a veneer of celebrity, another social construct originally arising out of entertainment that is now leaching into other domains, onto those that it elevates. I know lovely folk who have appeared on such lists, and undoubtedly it can be a validating experience and good for business. It is also true that they represent a fractal within the guru-sphere that fuels the market for Silver Bullets.

The glitter does not mean that Stolz does not know his stuff or do good work, however in this organisation the impact was different:

> Interviewee: "He was all about campers and climbers and peak performance, like literally climbing a mountain. And the summer before I joined, they'd all literally been in massive conference centres with carabiners and rope … [the leaders] had these guru books on their shelves … So, he was the first guru and that lasted about eighteen months. His whole selling point was I buy shares in your firm because I know I'll make a difference to your share price – and everyone bought it."
> Me: "What was the outcome and what difference did he make?"
> Interviewee: "People just took the piss. I mean these books on the shelves [took up] five to eight inches (of space) … Each leader got this stuff – it was something to be derided. I didn't see or hear or feel it get under the skin of team or leader performance at all."
> Me: "So they liked the rhetoric and the buzz?"
> Interviewee: "Well, the HR team who bought it liked the buzz and the old CEO, but it bore no resemblance to what the organisation was about."[139]

---

137. https://www.peaklearning.com/dr-paul-g-stoltz/
138. https://thinkers50.com/
139. Interview 7th July 2020

To be clear, in a different context, Stolz may well have been the difference that made a difference. Here that was not the case. Interestingly, the same organisation did have a better experience with another guru figure, Eric Boles, who "helps organisations collapse time, achieve goals quickly and function within their purpose and values. The results organisations experience are real and powerful."[140] Notice again the reassuring certainty in the marketing. My interviewee described Eric as being like:

> "... Tony Robbins, but athletic. And he was all about the affirmations, and the mindset shift for success. Now that did better, and ... some people became total sycophants to the method. And for some people, it really changed their personal and professional lives. But again, it was a very British sort of scepticism about this very charismatic American ... you could almost see the eyes rolling in those first months."

Even where the expert has a positive effect, it is not universal, so it cannot be a Silver Bullet, largely because we are all too different as people to accept one guru, plus often invested, for good or ill, in the past. In the same way it is not possible to get everyone to agree on one god, why on earth do we accept people in organisations to swallow whole the ideas of one expert?

When I worked at *The Guardian*, my sole guru experience was at an annual sales conference, where the guest 'inspirational speaker' was Frank Dick, a former Olympic coach. He said some good stuff, was entertaining and had great stories. Some of it I found vaguely inspiring, much of it not, in large part because his wonderful tales of what it takes to be a successful coach or Olympian did not relate to my own life experience, personal challenges and aspirations, or context.

There is also an ethical challenge here and the psychological processes at play are worthy of a book in themselves, for in all this ego and adulation so reminiscent of fans of popular music icons we need to ask:

- Do experts and gurus ever disabuse clients of the fact they do not have a Silver Bullet? (The same question can be asked of many consultants incidentally.)
- To what extent do they need to collude with the fantasy they have The Answer to build credibility and thus their own business, and/or cope with their own inadequacies?

---

140. https://thegamechangersinc.com/about-eric/

- Does the way in which these experts 'show up' at an embodied level play a disproportionate role in amplifying dependency, and what happens when they do not play the game? Are they no longer 'gurus' if we become aware of our projections?

To expect experts or gurus to have the answer or Silver Bullet is both unrealistic and unfair even if they in part collude with the idea they do. Yet we do, and this shows up in spaces where you might not expect it to.

When consultants, coaches and others lose perspective

Most fields of practice have their experts and gurus. HR has Gary Hamel and Dave Ulrich; Organisation Design has Naomi Stanford and Andrew Campbell; change has people like Kurt Lewin (a serious thinker upon whom people posthumously bestowed guru status) and John Kotter (who was highly skilled at (re)packaging and marketing on his eight-step change model in *Leading Change* (1996)); Digital Transformation has Didier Bonnet and the brains at MIT Sloan; Organisation Development has Gervase Bushe, the late Mee-Yan Cheung-Judge and more, and leadership development has too many to count.

Of these, I am probably most familiar with the patterns of interaction in the Organisation Development (OD) community, having attended many OD conferences, been involved in running them, and been the co-chair of the OD Network Europe. Roffey Park Institute was also a community of OD practice. The conferences are interesting places, because you get to see us OD folk as we gather and interact with those we hold up as our models and idols. It is also where you get to observe, to varying degrees, the deference we show our idols, elders and what are sometimes referred to as 'the greats in our field'.

There is a difference between respect and deference when coupled with uncritical thinking, where a thought collective becomes so rigid in its thinking or subtly intolerant of difference that anyone who challenges the orthodoxy is a heretic. Cohesion and community are important and useful; groupthink is not, even if it is an understandable response to managing individual and collective anxiety.

For "when 'teacher' becomes 'cannot be questioned or challenged', then how is growth, idea development and the rest possible? Followers/disciples hanging on to every word believe that by doing so they become imbued with the divine without realising that in doing so they diminish themselves and the one they follow."[141] This was something Toby Lindsay, a fellow consultant and former colleague, told me as he relayed his own experience of an OD conference that we both attended in Amsterdam in 2019.

One of the sessions offered a critique of OD as being too values-driven rather than pragmatic and offered Mee-Yan Cheung-Judge as an example. Whether or not the critique was valid is less important than the reaction this argument elicited from some, which Toby described as "fierce". There was a sense that Cheung-Judge's work was uncriticisable. This defensiveness is a fractal of the admiration and adulation she receives, not least because she was one of ODs most important, influential and impressive scholars and practitioners of the past thirty years. That, however, does not mean that her ideas, or how they are interpreted by others, are off limits. If we cannot discuss and critique the ideas of those we look up to, then we are indeed in the realm of a religion or cult and not a field of practice. The wonderful irony here is that Cheung-Judge was profoundly human in her owning of her own blind spots and failings, and never shied away from robust debate.

Big brains are useful but not sufficient

We are talking about people here with undoubted intelligence and sizeable intellects (which are not the same thing) as we were when discussing those who work in business schools. There seems to often be a default assumption, when someone is elevated to guru and expert status, that they 'know stuff'. The problem is that may not be true. Friedrich A. Hayek, the economist and political philosopher, may have been thinking more about intellectuals in a political context, but his ideas resonate here. In an introduction by John Blundell to Hayek's *The Intellectuals and Socialism* published by the London-based Institute for Economic Affairs in 1998, he comments:

> "According to Hayek, the intellectual is neither an original thinker nor an expert. Indeed, he need not even be intelligent. What he does possess is:
>
> a) the ability to speak/write on a wide range of subjects; and
> b) a way of becoming familiar with new ideas earlier than his audience."[142]

---

141. Conversation 23rd February 2023
142. https://bit.ly/49ctj9f

Sound familiar at all?

Someone mentioned to me the air of 'Queen Bee'-ness to some of the best-known thinkers and gurus in OD. The Urban Dictionary's definition of 'Queen Bee'[143] resonates here, as does its sexism:

> "A girl who, usually in a high school setting, is the 'leader of the pack'. She doesn't always have to be the prettiest, but she is extremely confident, and because she thinks she's hot, others do too. She knows all of the 'important' gossip, and people emulate her style. If the queen bee wears something new and different, others will wear it the next day. She always has the hottest boyfriend, and is at all the parties. Everyone always talks behind her back about how much they hate her, even though everyone secretly wishes they were her friend."

For 'pack', read thought collective, e.g. HR community. 'Important gossip' is a bit like new ideas and trends. The emulation comes as we seek to integrate the expert's ideas into our own map of the world, whether with or without attribution. As they come up with sparkly new ideas and thinking, we rush to adopt those too. The parties they attend – for that read conferences – attract more visitors to hear their ideas, and yes, there may occasionally be envy and jealousy that leads to resentment.

Sometimes, we adults behave in remarkably teenage ways.

We need thought partners, not thought leaders

What strikes me about the language of 'thought leader' and 'thought leadership' is the peculiar straining for attention that accompanies it. I often wonder if those who are most attached to the description are the least secure in themselves.

One strand of leadership theory talks to the importance of followership. Derek Sivers' 2010 TED Talk became a popular example of this and was based on footage of a lone dancer at a music festival slowly gathering followers. The video became a 21st-century folk tale and exemplar for what leadership followership looks like. I am still waiting for the parallel growth in 'thought followership'. I wonder why?

---

143. https://www.urbandictionary.com/define.php?term=queen%20bee

What clients need are fewer thought *leaders* and more thought *partners*. Real ones, not merely the lip service of someone agreeing with them, which talks to what that requires of practitioners and consultants, which is explored in Chapter 10.

The fundamental problem …

In a 1999 paper, Karl Weick wrote about the trade-offs inherent in writing good theory, and this is crucial because so many Silver Bullets are, essentially, positing that a particular theory or ideas or opinion offers The Answer. Weick argues there is a trade-off in theory development regarding three attributes: generalisability, accuracy and simplicity, and he suggests you can only ever have two out of three. Dr Richard Claydon offered some good examples to bring this to life in the context of the ideas being discussed in this chapter and more widely the book.

- A theory that is simple and accurate cannot be generalisable to a whole population, e.g. "case studies and autobiographies … are really interesting. And you can read them and they're quite powerful, but you can't generalise them because that leader's life and how they act is not necessarily going to be relevant for your organisation, which has a different geography, different clientele, different products, different strategy, etc." I'd add that as this work concerns human agents, that is what makes it impossible to generalise at all.

- A theory that is simple and general will never be accurate, e.g. many leadership models: "*Start With Why* – generalisable and simple, gets a big audience but it's not actually very accurate. Just Starting with Why doesn't make you a good leader."

- A theory that is accurate and general will never be simple, e.g. "[these are] your Heifetz and your Torbets and it takes a long time to get people up to the complexity of understanding [and] reading those to say 'Yes, I get that. So it's not a Silver Bullet because it takes effort to get there. And you're possibly never going to get 'there', you're just going to get closer to understanding."[144]

---

144. Interview 4th May 2020

Here is the essential problem again: our need for certainty, to minimise and dampen the anxiety of 'not knowing' leads us to oversimplify and ignore or filter out anything that will challenge the idea that there is a solution. As Claydon went on to say:

> "We tend to (choose) the wrong ones, rather than the ones that might be a bit more helpful because the ones that are helpful take away all the certainty."

Given that the most useful books that a leader could read are likely to be a little denser, as they cover complex ideas and attempt to help the reader think for themselves, is it any wonder Claydon went on to observe, that "airport novels or an airport leadership book is much more likely to catch their attention than anything that's really going to be helpful?" This echoes Harvey *et al.*'s comment regarding thought leadership, namely that it:

> "... should intrigue, challenge and even inspire people already familiar with an organisation by generating new ideas and pushing boundaries, what Timo Elliott calls 'Return on Interesting' or 'Return on Ideas'. This generates new and unsettled knowledge with potentially high but uncertain returns that can be potentially relevant to several parts of an organisation, though which parts and in what ways is initially unknown." (2021: 12)

This leads us to the uncomfortable truth that much of what leaders in organisations rely on is explicitly and/or implicitly built on sand. We seek experts, thinkers, theorists, consultants, indeed anyone who is selling something that will take away that uncertainty and anxiety. The quest for a generalisable theory or tool or model that is guaranteed to work is probably futile given that much of the work in organisations concerns human beings. That is what makes it impossible to generalise at all. The observation by Heraclitus that no one ever steps in the same river twice because it's not the same river and they're not the same person, may apply equally well here. Human interconnection is like the flow of a river and arises in the here and now, which makes generalising it impossible.

So, before we get to the pinnacle of the Silver Bullet Sales Pyramid underpinned by consultants and consultancies, let's consider how theories have come to hold such a grip on us.

Reflective Questions

- What thinkers or gurus do you revere? Why?
- Whose thinking are you taking at face value that you might usefully critique more deeply?
- Are you a guru or thought leader, or like the idea of being seen as one? How does that serve clients, exactly?
- What are you expert in? How do you know? Do you ever disabuse others of that notion?
- How do you respond when others see you as a thought leader? Lap it up or challenge?

SILVER BULLET NO. 3

NEAT METHODOLOGY

Master the art and science of change management.
Our proven framework for individual and organisational change
will help you successfully manage your change initiatives.

THE MYTHOLOGISING OF THEORIES AND THEORISTS

OR: GETTING HOT AND BOTHERED OVER CLEVERNESS

Chapter 6:
The Mythologising of Theories and Theorists

"A dilemma is throwing out all insight and advice when removing the quick fix ideas. There is a market for thoughtful insights that deliver sustainable value. Discerning them is never easy, but important to do."
Dave Ulrich[145]

Theories are useful. They help us make sense of things and offer a way to scaffold thoughts and feelings in such a way as to explain the world around us. That world however is always shifting and evolving, so they need to be constantly checked against experience. A theory cannot be a fixed thing, it needs to be regularly critiqued if it is not to ossify into a dogma or simply be out of date.

They often get codified into methodologies and a variety of 'tools' and methods, and a by-product of that process is we risk creating legends out of theory makers, rather than critiquing their ideas. We create 'greats' in given fields, yet often do so without asking whether myth reflects reality, either of their own time or our own.

The uncomfortable truth is that time doesn't just heal, as the saying goes, it helps smooth out the wrinkles by omitting inconvenient truths, even if unconsciously or with the best of intentions. The books and thinkers who are the most popular are invariably the ones that offer 'an answer', and almost always with unwavering positivity.

In an age of information overload, we have information anxiety and dampening the clutter/noise is always welcome. Maybe that is why we end up doom scrolling: because we think we've had things algorithmically tailored to us as we are so time poor – the irony of course is that it's a timewaster. Into this mix come those we imbue with the authority of the 'trusted adviser' or 'expert', who if they say some impressive things and talk confidently about a theory that addresses how we might alleviate the problem we are facing, then, dear client, you can relax.

---

145. Email 3rd December 2023

That runs the risk of fantasy and pandering to the lazy consultancy – and in turn client – who swallows whole the stories, regardless of whether they are true or not. Add to that a tendency towards the fetishization of science and the scientific method, which Mark Cole argues is the "assumption that if you apply some reasoned process to an issue that you face, if you *really* push that reason into the mess of the problem, by doing that you generate an answer. And it is an answer with a capital A".[146]

(Another way to) alleviate the pain

This is key to understanding the functional collusion described here, for our relationship with theories and theorists isn't particularly rational. We seek theories that explain the unexplainable to alleviate anxiety, whether that be why the big shiny thing in the sky vanishes each day and mysteriously comes back, or irritating behaviours in our organisation.

The more existential the threat, the greater the likelihood we will filter out inconvenient truths. Dan Ariely (2009 & 2011) and others in the field of behavioural economics, such as Daniel Kahneman (2012), have done much to disabuse us of the notion we are entirely rational in our decision making. Another Dan – Dan Gardner, who writes about decision making and psychology – describes in detail how "so much of what we think and do about risk does not make sense" (2008: 11).

Gardner explains how our relationship with risk is largely configured by existential anxiety and fear more than anything else, particularly when it comes to social, political and ecological issues. Nested in his argument is another question: if we are that poor at assessing and working with risk in those domains, are we any better at it in organisations? Short answer: no. In this context, risk is merely bureaucratised. The Risk Register reassures everyone that issues of concern are openly acknowledged and 'mitigation' is taking place. As with many administrative functions, completing this form becomes a superficial game, a self-referencing practice that quickly floats free of the realities of organisational life, and genuinely wrestling with what we construe as risk, how we feel about that and what we will (or will not) do in response.

More recently, Ariely (2023) explored risk in more detail, connecting it to the psychological processes that result in people believing in conspiracy theories

---

146. Interview 3rd July 2020

and misinformation. Given all of this happens in societies more widely, it is unsurprising similar patterns exist in business and organisations more widely.

Taking one high profile and global example, namely the assessments made by many countries in relation to pandemics, and the ways in which those risks were mitigated, is a case study in the relationship we have with existential – or merely serious – threats. While *on paper* many risks were identified, the *actual* plans put in place sometimes bore little relationship to them. The UK's Joint Committee on the National Security Strategy, for example, bluntly reported that the "Government failed to act on its security plans for a pandemic"[147]

At a more prosaic and local level in organisations, there is a big difference between a risk register with a traffic light system and engaging in both the reality of perceived risks and what might constitute an appropriate and thoroughly costed response. An example of this is how local authorities plan for climate change. I spoke to the coastal engineer for my local authority in Brighton a few years ago about their planning for climate change, in particular coastal erosion. He said they had three scenarios: worst case, median and best case. Which did they cost for? The median one, as it was politically and financially the most palatable.

Experts: to revere or ridicule

A key thread in Gardner's argument is how we treat experts, in that we tend to pay more attention to polished and loud media-friendly types than we do duller and more detail-orientated thinkers. That sounds uncannily like how we view leadership, management and organisational theories. It is far easier to consume a gobbet of Sinek than a course of, say, Kurt Lewin because a rhyming couplet and easily swallowed Sinek-ism requires less thinking than being open to the possibility that there are no easy answers. Sinek offers us answers – if a leader does X, Y will surely follow. Lewin requires more self-reflection and brain sweat.

I will now consider three key patterns in relation to how we use theories and treat the thinkers behind them, starting with what happens when theories and methodologies that derived from them become disconnected over time from reality, squeezing uncomfortable truths out of our collective narrative. Secondly, I will examine how particular methodologies, which are often grounded in theory, amplify that pattern. Lastly, I will look at what this might mean for a

---

147. https://bit.ly/3TyHmA2

particular body of knowledge that all Silver Bullet offerings are essentially built on – what might loosely be termed change theories.

Standing on the shoulders of giants (or not)

When I joined Roffey Park Institute in 2013, I became part of an organisation that embodies Organisation Development theory and practice. On our OD Practitioner Programme, we covered many theories and methodologies, and a key artefact we used was a 'Map of the Field', graphically displaying a range of models, theories, methodologies and accompanying theorists/practitioners, to help participants understand how much is out there, some of the connections, how things evolved and how impossible it is to ever know everything.

Nestled in it was a graphic of a light bulb, representing the Hawthorne Experiments of Elton Mayo (1924), an Australian-born psychologist, researcher and theorist. At Roffey Park Institute, we talked about him as a major influence in the evolution of organisational thinking and theory, key to the human relations movement who challenged the orthodoxy of Frederick Winslow Taylor's approach to Scientific Management. At that time, this dominated and set the tone for approaches to people and organisations that were typified by the notion of organisation-as-machine (Morgan, 2006; Taylor, 1911). Time and motion studies? Thank Taylor for those as well. An engineer, his observations of people engaged in manual work enabled him to redesign tasks to be more efficient. As I mentioned in an earlier chapter, key to Taylor's principles was that the manager was responsible for organising work, not the worker. He (for at that time it would be a he) designed roles, trained people and monitored performance. Mayo was different:

> "Twenty years later, Elton Mayo … found that working groups performed at their best when their members were motivated (Mayo 1933; Morgan 2006). The task of the manager thus became binary. The manager was now responsible not only for designing efficient tasks but also for ensuring that the people performing those tasks are motivated. This binary scoping of the leader's role is still popular today, such as definitions of leadership based on the individual's ability to 'get the job done' and 'bring people on the journey'." (Lawrence in Bachkirova *et al.*, 2021: 4)

Mayo's fame, and resultant impact, is largely based on the Hawthorne work and his seminal work in 1924 at a Philadelphia textile mill which had been experiencing a high rate of staff turnover. His hypothesis was that repetitive work consisting of routine tasks was impacting the mental state of workers and introducing rest periods might reduce turnover. What became known as the Hawthorne Experiments in the 1920s and 1930s are regarded as seminal in helping us understand the importance of groups in organisational behaviour. The Hawthorne studies "are significant as a precursor to our understanding of organisation change", suggested Warner Burke (2002: 33), for reasons that demonstrating the influence of psychological or human factors on worker productivity and morale; worker autonomy; the importance of feedback and that "they ushered in more humanistic treatment of workers on the job" (ibid.).

While at face value these were laudable findings, Mayo is an example of how theories and theorists tend, over time, to have their failings and inconsistencies edited out and minimised, to reduce anxiety and cognitive dissonance. The net result is the further fuelling of the idea that a particular theory or methodology, or the person behind them, offers a neat solution or Silver Bullet.

Stewart argues that the evidence is that Mayo's research was not rigorous, rather it was a working hypothesis and results "were quietly altered wherever they failed to make the right point" (2010: 119). Stewart notes that it was not until independent researchers took a fresh look at the evidence did the lack of rigour in Mayo's research become apparent. "His posthumous critics eventually described the Hawthorne work as 'worthless scientifically' and 'scientifically illiterate'. But by then it was too late to prevent the myth of Hawthorne from wreaking its profound effects on management thought and the social answers" (Stewart, 2010: 120).

Stewart's critique is useful, because he makes a direct link between how a researcher and his theories can take on a life of their own, and we become fixated on the idea that the theory is complete and that it answers our questions.

This could be argued is the problem with mainstream positivist academia: that the object of research (the thing being studied) is observed to analyse 'it' and, thereby, test, prove, verify and validate the hypothesis of new knowledge as theory. It's an 'outside-in' process and allows us to keep what may be dissonant or disconcerting at bay. Thingification is endemic in organisations and theories about them, and 'management speak' is dripping with abstractions and nominalisations (verbs solidified into abstract nouns), e.g.:

- Organisation – take away the people and it ceases to exist;
- Culture – the whole construct of 'culture change' is arguably a fallacy as it assumes culture is both homogeneous and a thing;
- Change – 'land the change', 'drive change', etc. The notion of 'driving change' is problematic, as it requires a selected group to enforce the change on those who might harbour reservations, reluctance or resistance in the face of a plan crafted elsewhere and visited unthinkingly upon them;
- Management – bye-bye to managing, hello to management consultants, education and training;
- Leadership – what was once the practice of leading has been similarly commodified.

A constructivist approach is different, for it is 'inside-out'. Here the learner learns through experience rather than swallowing whole. They notice, recognise or discover; realise and acknowledge, and then make sense of their own experience. The data of evidence is interpreted subjectively in relation to the experience and the significance of the research-practitioner's findings in order to choose what to do next.

This is how action researchers make their own theory from their practice: *how I am* with *how it is* determines *what I'm doing, how I'm doing it*, and *why it matters to me*. Now the theory is 'inside-out'; not just subjective, it's downright personal in being simultaneously unique and universal. What matters to me matters to us. What matters to us matters to us all.

Silver Bullets here become objects that we create to manage anxiety, projecting our hopes and fears into and onto the thing that will alleviate pain. They allow consultants to see people in organisations as objects ('doing things to people') rather than subjects (whereby people in organisation are the originators of action not the practitioner) – after all, if people are the originators of action what is the point of a consultant? Consultants must be seen as 'doing the doing' and Silver Bullets legitimise that, and theories and methodologies are integral to this process.

To come back to Mayo, he is an example of how theories become containers of anxiety, in that *if* he is right, then he answers the criticisms of Taylor and gives us permission to think of people and organisations in a more human(e) way. The narrative and evolution of how we think about the world of work is neatened and makes sense. So, "the Hawthorne effect, in short, has become a

189

'principle' that explains whatever it is about people that defies explanation" (Stewart, 2010: 127).

Stewart helps us make sense of the themes in the last chapter, where he notes that:

> "The most vocal, if not always the most informed, advocates of Mayo's vision in recent times have been the popular management gurus. The buzz words and catchphrases that most excite today's gurus – empowerment, responsible freedom, the wisdom of teams, the new organisation – hailed from the time of Mayo and his Hawthorne experiment, even if their promoters are not always aware of the fact" (Stewart, 2010: 127).

In the introduction to *In Search of Excellence* (2004), the back cover of which boldly states it is "a must-have for the boardroom, business school and bedside table", Tom Peters (one of the most famous management gurus) and Robert Waterman make a direct link to Mayo: "For us, the very important message of the research that these actions spawned is that it is *attention to employees*, not work conditions per se, that has the dominant impact on productivity" (Peters & Waterman, 1982, in Stewart, 2009: 130)

Stewart, a former management consultant himself, comments on this introduction: "Having a PhD from Stanford is no guarantee that one will not harbour a thoroughly distorted view of the foundations of one's own discipline. Mayo was never a 'rationalist' ... [he] wasn't anywhere near Hawthorne when the elimination experiments took place; and these experiments did not in any case produce meaningful results ... Central to the functioning of the legend is the notion of Professor Mayo as a disinterested scientist (a 'rationalist' even), that Hawthorne was his road to Damascus and that the result of his labours is just a scientific finding of great significance" (2009: 130–131).

A further shift towards liberal democracy, against the backdrop of two horrendous world wars, meant that Mayo's thinking emerged as a perfect ideological conceit to reassure employees across the developed sections of the global economy that they mattered. The modality of power changed – Scientific Management to Human Relations – but only so that power could remain untouched at the heart of our human society. So did he have a 'positive' impact? Yes, if you assume that the way we organise and the economic system that underpins that is fit and fair. Depressingly, in January 2024 Elton Mayo was featured in *Forbes* magazine in a fawning homage that linked his work to Diversity, Equity and Inclusion (DEI). The article asserted that "over seven years, the team's experiments led to a profound re-evaluation of prevailing assumptions about efficiency and productivity in the workplace" ('A Century-Old Study Shows That Whatever We Call It, DEI Will Always Be With Us', Forbes.com, 29-01-2024). While there is some truth in suggesting that the Hawthorne Experiments began a process of revealing the importance of social processes, the problems with Mayo's research methodology and findings are conveniently edited out. Also lost in the mists of time is this eviscerating review of the Hawthorne Experiments from 1967, that highlighted how the conclusions were unsupported by the evidence.

> "Questions are raised about how it was possible for studies so nearly devoid of scientific merit, and conclusions so little supported by evidence, to gain so influential and respected a place within scientific disciplines and *hold this place for so long* [my italics]." (Carey, 1967: 403)

Carey was prescient, and over forty years later one might well ask again how it is Mayo is still held in such esteem. The challenge is that Mayo's legacy is contested rather than settled. For every author who suggests the Hawthorne experiments are flawed and Mayo's legacy problematic (e.g. Baritz, 1960), another can be found that says, maybe, after all, his reputation is being unfairly tarnished (Smith, 1987). Perhaps the problem is that "psychologists show an undeserved respect for the conclusions associated with this classic research. The errors of the interpretation seem to reflect an uncritical acceptance" (Bramel & Friend, 1981: 867). In a world that increasingly favours the reduction of complexity to zeros and ones, good and bad, right and wrong, it is the lack of criticality and willingness to inquire that is the real danger.

Ultimately, the attraction of rationality is key, as it links to the need to explain away that which is confusing, inconsistent, distressing or uncontrollable. The more we neaten, the greater the likelihood that a model or theory will become disconnected from reality. As Dan Ariely has demonstrated, human beings are "predictably irrational", and "our irrationality happens the same way, again and again" (2008: xx). When it comes to organisations and complex challenges, there is no better example of predictable irrationality than believing that a model or theory offers a Silver Bullet. It is the validation of needy realists, who expect evidence-based practice to work again and again, essentially embodying a wonderful contradiction in terms.

When in doubt, buy a methodology

A few years ago, I was working with a global fast-moving consumer goods (FMCG) corporation, both designing and delivering an OD practice programme, and consulting directly to my client. This was a long-term engagement, and in the background the organisation had made the decision to use Prosci, a well-known change management methodology, as its primary vehicle for 'delivering' change. My client paid for me to do the Prosci accreditation, so that I could better support the work of her team and understand their context, and, before I headed off to spend three days on the certification programme, she quipped, with no little amusement, "I bet you'll hate it …"

Prosci describe their change management certification as "a proven, people-focused approach to developing an agile, change-ready organisation."[148] The homepage is littered with the rhetoric of change – "Change is accelerating. Are you ready?" (a nice way of evoking anxiety as a motivator), "pace", "agility", "flexibility", "get really good at change" (which makes learning how to 'do' change a bit like going on a pasta-making course) – along with language that will make a C-Suite twitchy at how on earth they might change their organisation to actually sit up and beg – "grow", "succeed" and the logically flawed "cultivate a flexible, change-ready culture" (just … ick, plus culture is not a thing). It is marketed as evidenced-based, and indeed it is supported by a lot of research, although arguably skewed to the Global North.

It is clearly positioning itself as a Silver Bullet, best epitomised by the line:

> "Prosci's Change Management Certification Program gives participants the knowledge, skills and tools to drive successful change initiatives—no matter how complex or urgent."

If I was a CEO and not sure how to catalyse/lead/facilitate/'do' change, that would soothe me. Which begs the question: what are 'change capabilities' and how do you build them?

---

148. www.prosci.com

It's a little bit more complex than a three-day certification

The word 'change' in corporate contexts hides a multitude of sins. Fundamentally, human existence – indeed all existence – runs along the axis of time and is founded on how we 'manage' change as things happen. Instead, it is the organisation which is a static and unhelpful aberration, not the people doing the organising. So how do we help them? Often we send them on a course to learn about an approach that promises to make change manageable, ideally with guarantees that it will work. Prosci epitomises how a client's Silver Bullet thinking is fed by a solution provider who knows how to hit all the right notes. It is an exquisite example of the functional collusion that goes on between the two, and it reveals several issues. To be clear, I believe there is utility in the Prosci approach and have met (and worked with) some excellent Prosci consultants. What distinguishes them, however, is that they have a wider *change practice*, rather than merely what they have learned on a three-day course.

To break it down a bit more, let's start with my lived experience on the certification programme. The cohort consisted of a mix of people, all either external consultants wanting to gain a certification to support their practice or internal people who, typically, were working in organisations that had adopted Prosci as the favoured approach to change.

The facilitator was an experienced Prosci consultant and trainer, and I rapidly concluded that this was someone who really understood how change works in human systems. He did his best with nearly 300 slides of content, and by the end of my time in the basement of a West London hotel, he had done a good job of getting us to understand the *methodology*, if not how to deal with the subtleties and real mess of change.

I commented at one point that change in organisations is fundamentally a function of conversation and interaction, and unless you have the relational skills to work with that, all of what we were learning was moot. The trainer said:

"You are right. Seventy per cent of this depends on dialogue."

Wow.

There I am soaking up the tools, yet the difference that makes a difference is the art of conversation, the magic 70%. It left me wondering why we were only paying for the 30%.

The irony in that statement was that dialogue or indeed anything that might help the participants in the room to facilitate it more effectively was utterly absent from the slides and materials. Yes, there were plenty of models, frameworks and tools, but scaffolding conversations to support inquiry and dialogue is an art in itself, and requires practice, which was neither explained nor offered.

> "Prosci Certification is like getting your Learning Permit to drive a car. There is absolutely no way you can acquire the skill and knowledge involved in leading an effective change initiative in a three-day course."[149]

Almost as if to bring this tension to life, in the room we had two people who had been sent by an organisation that had adopted Prosci as their approach to change management. One of them commented that when they mentioned to colleagues at work they were going on the course, several said they too had done it. My fellow participant had no idea, she said, that so many people had been certified, and confirmed that there was no real interaction, communication, or collaboration, let alone a coherent approach to change, in her organisation. In other words, certifying people in a methodology is useful but not sufficient, particularly if a leadership team thinks that all change requires is getting a few people skilled up so they can be made responsible for what happens. Funnily enough, I have never seen that work. The contrary, in fact. One internal OD practitioner observed that until recently the NHS promoted a Culture and Leadership Programme for Trusts that were deemed to be needing improvement.

"A self-selecting cohort of people from up, down and across the organisation was recruited to engage with the wider workforce as part of a discovery exercise, with the aim of identifying themes of concern that needed to be addressed. This cohort would cohere around this task and invariably were given rich data from the warp and weft of the organisation, because they were seen to be part of it. Once a report was drafted by the cohort, the process fell apart, because they were then expected to pass their findings to the Executive for the directors to produce a strategy for change … and the cohort was disbanded and sent away."[150]

This is not an outlier. I have seen a similar pattern in an organisation that asked me to design and implement a series of interventions framed as

---

149. https://www.ocmsolution.com/is-Prosci-certificate-worth-it/#Negative-Prosci-Customer-Reviews
150. Email 10th October 2023

'Culture Conversations', as part of a place-based leadership initiative. It proved impossible to get the primary client to engage with the importance of ensuring that there were feedback loops between these conversations and senior leadership. For all the talk I often hear about the importance of ensuring change is 'done with' and not 'to' people, it is remarkable how rare it is to hear about initiatives that are successful in creating the conditions for dialogue. Change methodologies that do not bridge that gap are part of the problem rather than the solution. Other criticisms that might be levelled at Prosci are:

- It fails to acknowledge the centrality of leadership and leadership culture. It assumes that leaders set the direction, know what they are doing and understand change in human terms.

- ADKAR, the model for personal change that forms the spine of the approach, is linear, and that is out of step with much current thinking about change. It colludes with a set of assumptions that change is linear, plannable, A to B, manageable, etc. Nonetheless, I have worked with clients that have found it incredibly useful.

- It is predicated on a scientific approach to change, and offers little in terms of the 'art' of leading and facilitating change.

- If your organisation does not subscribe to a structured approach to change, it will jar.

- It is linear. If you are going through lots of digital transformation, or lots of cultural change at multiple levels, it may well struggle.

- Part of that is due to the focus on individual level change. In part that is down to the specific cultural context it grew out of, i.e. the US.

In many ways it is absurd that organisations rely on, say, a three-day certification as the key vehicle for organisational learning and change. Developing a change practice that is more than glorified project management requires *personal* as well as professional development, not least because you need to learn how to navigate power, politics and culture, as well as understand how to influence patterns of behaviour and interaction at multiple levels.

My experience of working with my FMCG client supports the above. In spite of the large numbers of people who were certified, during my time there the challenges that internal change agents typically brought up were all to do with how to navigate interpersonal relationships; power and politics; working with senior stakeholders; how to contract rigorously and what it takes to hold senior stakeholders to account; dealing with the weight of expectation; plus the often unrealistic demands placed on them as responsibility for change(s) got pushed further down from those who actually needed to do the work. Reflecting on the Prosci qualification, there was little in it that talked to these types of challenges.

In writing this chapter, I reconnected with an internal change manager I both coached and supervised over a couple of years in this organisation.

> "We still struggle to align sponsors to their role. Roles and responsibilities alignment across the board tends to be the root causes of many issues when you really get down to it on most transformation programmes [here]. Taking time to contract and gain full alignment isn't where we want to go. We are a culture of doers/implementers."[151]

There is little in Prosci that will help people develop their practice to have those 'necessarily unnecessary' conversations, so it is no Silver Bullet, and does not "give participants the knowledge, skills and tools to drive successful change initiatives — no matter how complex or urgent". It highlights how the user of 'the tool' – in this case Prosci – is somehow forgotten or demoted to servant, with the tool becoming master, rather than the two combining (and improvising and adapting) for whatever purpose.

The Grandaddy of Change Theories

It is worth noting that Prosci sits within the context of a wider field of change theory. Arguably the most influential theory of change is the three-stage change process that people have lifted from the far wider and more nuanced body of work by Kurt Lewin, namely that of Unfreezing, Change and Refreezing (1947). It has heavily influenced several fields, including Change Management, Organisation Development and Organisation Design. Many change models created by others are effectively re-badged or reframed versions of the same thing. The most obvious and well-known example of that is probably John Kotter's eight-step model of change, which I will return to later. There is a problem with all this emulation and adulation, however.

Firstly, it misses the fact that Lewin was particularly interested, in the aftermath of WW2, in social conflict and how to resolve tensions between people. He was deeply interested in Field Theory, Group Dynamics and Action Research, all of

---

151. Email 1st February 2023

which, the more you learn, are anything but simple and linear. In a sense, what we have done with Lewin is what has happened to Elton Mayo: if the latter's reputation was burnished over time and inconsistencies glossed over, Lewin's work has been oversimplified and, arguably, misrepresented.

The wonderful irony is that more recently Cummings *et al.* have questioned whether Lewin ever developed a three-stage model, suggesting it came into being *after* his death (2016: 1). They mused further on how these three steps took on a life of their own in the nascent field of change management and have come to have such influence. Tellingly, they suggest:

> "This foundation of change management has less to do with what Lewin actually wrote and more to do with others' repackaging and marketing." (Ibid.: 3)

There again is that neatening. It is a lot easier to simplify Lewin's work, to squeeze out the mess of group dynamics and implications of the work that doing action research as part of a change initiative involves, than wrestling with complexity and mess. This has a big impact on how organisations set themselves up to deal with change, and what that means for change practice and practitioners, which is where the people who deal with the mess resulting from the failure of Silver Bullet solutions end up picking up the pieces (more on this in Chapters 9 and 10).

Lapping up the new, shiny and sexy

Another facet of Silver Bullet-type theories are those that get leapt on as being shiny and new, or even sexy. There are many examples to be found, starting with Scientific Management. As Niels Pflaeging notes, "this concept became wildly successful and transformed not only organisations, but also the way we looked at work. The search for efficiency and the 'one best way' to do anything that Taylor pioneered became defining for the 20th century"[152] and its principles can be seen in how Elon Musk has reorganised Twitter (now 'X') since he acquired it in 2022.

Frederick W. Taylor is in no small part responsible for both the growth of business schools in the US, and the management consulting industry, having set himself up as an independent "consulting engineer for management" (Stewart,

---

152. https://www.linkedin.com/pulse/management-belongs-onto-garbage-heap-history-niels-pflaeging

2010: 29). All this even though the project on which his fame is based, at Bethlehem iron works, ended when Taylor was ordered to stop all his work. From that point onwards, no organisation followed Taylor's suggestions from this project, Taylor did walk away "with a total of $100,000 in consulting fees (about $2.5 million in today's money)" (Stewart, 2010: 50).

Taylor was skilled at self-promotion and creating enough noise around his theory that it took hold and became incredibly valuable as a vehicle for advancing his career. To be clear, there is nothing wrong with marketing your ideas to earn a living. The issue is when the marketing leads to a glossing over of inconvenient truths or misrepresents, failing to inquire/research more deeply. More current examples of that include:

- Growth Mindset – from the initial 2006 book and TED Talk by Carol Dweck, a whole industry was born. As psychologist David Yeager of the University of Texas commented "any popular idea in education gets spread way ahead of how ready the science is".[153] Yeager and Dweck started working together in 2019, "becoming aware of all the ways that it [Growth Mindset] might be misunderstood or not implemented in a compelling way. *One thing we've learned in the past five to ten years is how the nuances matter* [my italics]."

- Engagement – as a term, this has largely supplanted 'motivation' in HR circles. The problem is, says Amy Armstrong, senior faculty at Ashridge at Hult International Business School, "there's more than sixty different definitions and no universally accepted definition of what it means … It's something that has been looked at in organisations since the late '90s and there's been more than 2,000 studies in it but each study has looked at something slightly different."[154]

- Agile – regularly I hear clients struggling to define what they mean by the word. It has become a catch-all for concepts such as flexibility, adaptive capacity and responsiveness. The connection to the real value in Agile Scrum, namely how it created the conditions for collaboration, iteration and self-management is often missed. As Eva Appelbaum commented: "Agile in its original design was there to solve a set of problems but only in the context of software development. And when you bring that into, say, leadership problem solving, it just doesn't work because it doesn't fit

---

153. https://bit.ly/3STMmz3
154. https://www.hrmagazine.co.uk/content/features/is-engagement-fact-or-fiction

the culture".[155] Dr Richard Claydon sums up the problem with Agile: "In the two decades since its conceptualisation, Agile has itself morphed into a utopian promise that generates undiscussable absurdities. It is now being sold as THE way to speed up productivity while reducing cost in organisational-wide frameworks for all projects in all environments no matter the context. Yet, since its widespread implementation, productivity has flatlined" (2023: 15).

- Myers-Briggs Type Indicator (MBTI ®) – one of several personality tests based on Carl Jung's work on psychological types, alongside Insights and Disc, two other well-known psychometric instruments. To criticise MBTI ® is to enter a minefield. However, research more than a decade apart by Prof. of Psychology David Pittenger, suggests that "there is insufficient evidence to support the tenets of and claims about the utility of the test" (1993: 467) and "while offering much intuitive appeal, [MBTI ®] may not yet be able to support the claims its promoters make" (2006: 210).[156]

- Leadership styles – a 2023 paper in the *Journal of the Academy of Management* calls into question seventy years of thinking. The "limitation rests on specifying behaviours as inherently positive or negative and leads to mixing the description of the content of leadership behaviours with the evaluation of their underlying intentions, quality of execution, or behavioural effects … this conflation leads to amalgamation, construct redundancy, and … causal indeterminacy, *which calls into question the entire evidence base of leadership style research* [my italics]" (Fischer & Sitkin: 2023).

- Self-management – the buzzword of the past fifteen years, promoted as a radical way of transforming teams and organisations. As Joost Minnaar of Corporate Rebels pointed out in a blog post, "the academic roots, and empirical evidence of, self-managing teams can be traced to the 1950s when British scientist, Eric Trist, reported on self-regulating coal miners" ('The Self-Management Hype: Aren't We Just Reinventing The Wheel?' 18-03-2023). Trist's work was built on and include "Scandinavian

---

155. Interview 8th June 2020
156. There is a plethora of research out there that talks to the fragile and contradictory evidence base for the instrument. A useful starting point is this comment by Joseph Devlin, on a post he wrote re what he terms the 'neurobollocks' of MBTI, where he lists a number of useful research papers on the topic. https://bit.ly/3Mqsa5r

experience with semi-autonomous teams in the 1970s, self-managing teams at the American Gaines Dog Food plant in the 1980s, and self-managing organisations like Morning Star, Zappos, Valve, FAVI, Haier, Handelsbanken, and Buurtzorg" (ibid.). Various myths have arisen over time, including that self-managing organisations have no structure. As Lisa Gill observed in an aptly titled Medium post, 'Three Myths about Self-managing Organisations, Debunked' (16-10-2019), "in reality it's quite the opposite. Successful self-managing organisations have very explicit structures, perhaps even more so than old-guard, top-down organisations." Two other myths Gill highlights are that there are no leadership or hierarchies involved, and that everyone has to agree on everything. A more fundamental problem may simply be us humans: "research seems to indicate that flattening workplace hierarchy is not only much more complicated than it seems, but that people prefer a pecking order. One Stanford study found that egalitarian work structures were disorienting … [Another] looked at why hierarchical structures in the workplace have such staying power, [and] concluded … Hierarchies work. They are practical and psychologically comforting" ('Why Are So Many Zappos Employees Leaving?' Bourree Lam, The Atlantic, 15-01-2016).

Case studies: the fast food of thought leadership

"The 'Spotify Model' is victim of a bandwagon effect. The same happened with Agile and Scrum. Before you know it, uninformed people create a Frankenstein monster out of it. And this is where it starts to derail." Willem-Jan Ageling ('You want to adopt the "Spotify Model"? I don't think it means what you think it means!', 23-01-2019)

There is a problem when individual examples of the application of a model or theory are mythologised. For example, Spotify as an organisation has been held up as an example of how to 'do things differently'. It is "a people-driven, autonomous framework for scaling 'agile' while emphasising the importance of culture and network. This methodology uses Squads, Tribes, Chapters, and Guilds – the foundation of which is the Squad, which acts like a Scrum team."[157] Corporate Rebels have documented the Spotify approach in both

---

157. Atalassian are a software company that sell software that supports Kanban and Scrum, two of the most prominent Agile framework." https://bit.ly/3INPPKK

their blogs and book, and certainly the culture of the organisation seems markedly more progressive than many conventional organisations. Agility and adaptiveness are embodied in how they think and behave:

> "We would rather spend our time and energy on adjusting, and quickly recovering, than on futile attempts to predict the future." (Katarina Berg, HR Director Spotify, quoted in Corporate Rebels *Make Work More Fun*, 2019: 106)

The 'Spotify Model' arguably does not exist as an example that can be followed or model to be copied however, as Tom Nixon, author of *Work with Source*, commented in an exchange with me on Twitter:

Tom Nixon
24th June 2020

Lots of folks tried to adopt Spotify's Squads, Tribes, Guilds model but it was basically a matrix with funky names.

Tom Nixon
24th June 2020

Spotify's magic was not actually about the org structure but other things and they moved on from this model anyway.

The problem with looking to case studies is that they fail to consider two things. Firstly, as noted earlier, what works in one context is likely to fail in another, however similar. Secondly, it denies human nature, and if we do not see that clearly, others and our own, we are stuffed. So, case studies may make for interesting reading, but when they descend into an obsession for case studies, when we read about these wonderful companies and their innovative ways of working and then proclaim 'but that would never work with our people because they are not prepared/equipped/skilled, etc. enough', then they are pointless.

The kicker

Progressive theories about how to change organisations, whether that be Teal (based on the work of Frederic Laloux, 2014), agile, self-management, 'feedback cultures', 'psychologically safe cultures' and more, all require people to develop greater levels of emotional intelligence, the capacity to operate in more adult ways, rather than replicating endless cycles of parent/child relational dynamics and get (more) comfortable with working with paradox and contradiction.

That is not straightforward work, and it is no surprise therefore that those offering a shortcut to that will get welcomed into most organisations. The alternative is to wrestle with reality: namely what am I faced with, what are the implications and options, and what can I do. This mirrors what is sometimes referred to as Reflection in Action, based on Donald Schön's work (1983), and boils down to a series of questions that get to the heart of what it means to wrestle with complex challenges:

- *How is it now?*
- *How am I with how it is now?*
- *How do I feel?*
- *What do I think?*
- *What am I doing – or not doing – about how it is now?*
- *And what do I want to do about that?*[158]

What tends to happen is that we eschew engaging with such questions and paying attention to our lived experience and crave the certainty of theories.

If we look at Mayo briefly once more, the social psychologist Richard Nisbett, in a 1998 *New York Times* article entitled 'Scientific Myths That Are Too Good to Die', described the Hawthorne effect as "a glorified anecdote", and "once you have got the anecdote, you can throw away the data". The study claimed that that *any* changes in break time (longer, shorter, more, fewer) increased productivity. The problem is that the sample size was five, and two of those workers had to be replaced, ironically for low output. If that is not skewing the data, I am not sure what is.

This raises a specific question of how robust the evidence base underpinning change theories is, or within individual fields of practice such as Organisation Development or Human Resources. Add to that another tension: to what extent are consultants and practitioners willing to engage with that question? How often do we suggest an intervention and alongside that evidence to support why it might be useful? I notice in my own practice two things work against that. One is the fact that this represents more work for me, and the other is

---

158. This list was devised by another consultant, Alastair Wylie, as part of his own research for his PhD that included Reflection in Action and Schön's work.

that clients like things to be succinct and preferably simple. The need for speed, to move to action, maybe flavoured sometimes by a wee bit of anxiety as to whether, if we dig too deeply, we might find that many of these change interventions *really are* experiments at heart, and that outcomes are not guaranteed.

Fields of practice can also shy away from thinking too deeply about such things. I once did a workshop on family constellations, an approach to mapping family members and histories devised by German psychologist Bert Hellinger that has been adapted for organisational contexts also. During that workshop, I asked the facilitator whether there had been any research into how exactly constellations work and whether there was any evidence for their impact. (As an aside, it is an approach that for some is esoteric and woo woo to say the least, although I admit I find it useful.) She said that there were two contrasting views in the constellations community when it came to research. One group believes it behoves them to research the practice, both to understand it better and to evidence impact. The other resists that, as it 'might spoil the magic'. Organisation Development has a problem here sometimes, as it is not unusual to hear the phrase 'the magic of OD', which colludes with the idea that this is a mysterious art that only the initiated will understand, and feeds the idea that mythical solutions are available … such as Silver Bullets.

Referring to change interventions more widely, Thomas Rhys Evans suggests that "there is not a universal blueprint for optimal outcomes", and instead what is required is an approach of ongoing negotiation regarding "the relevance of various factors to the specific organisational and change context" (2020: 4). In other words, contextual and organisational variables are in such flux that a Silver Bullet designed for one moment in time and one context will rapidly lose contextual relevance and thus potency.

Evans (2020: 5) goes on to suggest there are three main factors which cause problems for organisations dealing with change:

1. The use of ineffective or inappropriate models and tools.
2. The use of inappropriate or ineffective implementation methods.
3. Misunderstood environmental factors and issues

All of which screams out: what is the evidence base for these various models, theories, tools, methodologies, etc.?

The lack of evidence for many change models

Rhys Evans highlights a 2014 systematic literature review of 563 academic studies on change interventions that found only ten pre-test/post-test randomised control studies of organisational change, and that 77% "were evaluated using poor quality methods" (Rhys Evans, 2020: 5). To translate: two thirds of studies use unreliable and frequently invalid measures.

It gets worse. If we come back to the most popular and (still) commonly used Kotter Eight-Stage Change Process, this was found not to adequately represent the reality and complexity of the change process in organisations and "is most frequently applied as a post-hoc structure to explain change case studies, rather than being the primary theoretical driver of organisational change interventions" (Rhys Evans, 2020: 6).

Most damning is Evans' observation (2020: 6) based on Dawson (2003: 37):

> "From a theoretical perspective, change is often presented using a rational approach, as 'neat linear prescriptions on how to best manage change', however the reality more clearly represents a 'complex muddied political process consisting of competing histories and ongoing multiple change narratives which may vie for dominance'."

It is in this mulch of client-side anxiety and helper-side (occasionally overly simplistic) positivity and puppy-ish energy that the base metal of many a Silver Bullet can be found.

Evans' 2020 paper also confirms my earlier assessment that many change models, tools and techniques are derivative. Many 'newer' models "overlap in their shared assumptions" with each other to such an extent that there is little to distinguish them from each other. For example, a 2013 study found that thirteen of the most widely used planned change models replicate and echo Lewin's three-step model, which itself has little empirical basis (Evans, 2020: 6).

Zombie stats

Lack of evidence can also apply to individual statistics, which is a problem when they become mythologised, spread like fungus and became the basis for a slew of further ideas that are built on sand. A prime example of this is the oft quoted statistic that 70% of change programmes fail. Often attributed to John Kotter's 1965 article in the Harvard Business Review on *Leading Change*, the first problem we encounter is that he never actually used that figure. Further fuel was poured on the fire by another HBR article entitled '*Cracking the Code of Change*' in 2000.

Kotter's 2008 book *A Sense of Urgency* is sometimes regarded as a more reliable origin story, but the popularisation of this 70% failure rate was fuelled by a self-published paper from Bain & Co in 2008 and McKinsey's publication in 2009 entitled *The irrational side of change management*.[159]

The evidence base for this is weak to say the least, and The Oxford Review have produced a short and detailed rebuttal of the dominant narrative, and it is worth a watch.[160] The bottom line is that while there is undoubtedly a popular narrative of 70% organisational-change failure, "there is no valid and reliable empirical evidence to support such a narrative" (Hughes, 2011: 452).

It is worth considering why there is so much emphasis on this statistic, and how it is that, for example, McKinsey are happy to host that 2009 post on their website to this day. What is the commercial benefit? I would suggest it is simple: if that failure rate *is* true, it further legitimises the business case for buying in external support and help due to the (apparent) lack of change capability inside organisations. It also serves to fuel the anxiety of clients already worried that they may not know what to do themselves, preparing the ground for the reassuring balm of a consultant's slide deck and the impending arrival of hordes of associates.

If it sounds rational, it must be right. Right?

Given the anxiety at play, and the psychological factors that drive the need for certainty identified in Chapter 2, it is hardly surprising that organisational change models often strain to represent a rational approach, offering client and practitioner ways to organise or manage change that, at face value, are (reasonably) neat and linear.

The reality is that when change requires wrestling with power, politics, multiple and conflicting narratives, anxiety, fear, conflict and more, coupled with goals, agendas, hopes, dreams, aims and objectives that may be misaligned or in competition, change is anything but linear.

---

159. https://www.mckinsey.com/capabilities/people-and-organizational-performance/our-insights/the-irrational-side-of-change-management
160. https://bit.ly/3uPPdB2

It leaves me wondering whether what has been missed in our worshipping the 'greats' of organisational theory and practice, either in the fields of leadership, management or change, we may be missing something. What if, at some level, Taylor, Mayo, Kotter and others were all trying to manage their own existential anxiety, and their theories are to varying degrees a mass of projection, deflection and denial? However, that is a difficult hypothesis to test out without a clairvoyant or time machine.

Theories as memes: from fad to fashion and back again

Management and organisational practices are the 'tools of the trade', "yet they have been known to wax and wane in popularity, often quite unpredictably, with one technique following the other in wave-like fashion" (Piazza & Abrahamson, 2020: 264). They are all underpinned by theories, and often associated with particular names, as we have seen. Why, though, are Taylor and Mayo, for example, still talked about, and many others are not? Why are Quality Circles and Business Process Reengineering, once models du jour, now largely forgotten? Eric Abrahamson, who is interested in the mess of organisations,[161] asks a useful question: "what explains waves in the popularity of management practices, which emerge suddenly, flow extremely rapidly, broadly, and transiently, and then crest, ebb, and vanish equally rapidly, sometimes without a trace?" (ibid.).

Abrahamson has been researching this area for thirty years, and his 2020 paper with Piazza is a fascinating read, given how it sits at the intersection of many of the questions this book is concerned with. They say: "we use the term 'management practices' because, although scholars of fads and fashions differ on what they call such concepts, they tend to agree what goes in and out of fashion are labels denoting *linguistic behavioural prescriptions* – that is, theorisations – describing new and more efficient means to new and more effective ends for managing organisations and their stakeholders." Lurking beneath that are Silver Bullets, and it is telling that Piazza and Abrahamson also pick up on the role of rationality, referencing Meyer and Rowan (ibid.: 266):

> "Management practices generally take hold because they are believed by organisational stakeholders to be rational ways of managing organisations; that is, they 'identify various social purposes as technical

---

161. https://business.columbia.edu/faculty/people/eric-abrahamson

ones and specify … the appropriate means to pursue these technical purposes rationally'."

This connection between managerialism and rationalism is important. To take a radical political position, does management shroud itself in the cloak of reason to mystify itself to justify its existence, in terms of a hierarchy that is occupied by people whose primary role is seen to be to 'supervise' others? Thinking back to Martin Parker's argument, that management education is predicated on the assumption that there is one way of organising – market managerialism – it takes a particular rationale to legitimise that, not least around power. So, what does it take for a new practice or idea to get a look in? Tellingly, Piazza and Abrahamson go on to say (2020: 266):

"… the appearance of rationality is not enough for a new management practice to appeal to organisations and their stakeholders: rather, it must also be underpinned by norms of progress, thereby representing 'a significant departure from the state-of-the-art at the time it first appears' (Kimberly, 1981: 86). In other words, novel management practices must be framed as improvements on the state-of-the-art."

'Progress' has an element of subjectivity to it, however. Who gets to decide on what it is, based on what assumptions? From the perspective of the differing sides of the political debates of today, who is 'on the right side of history' – and therefore represents 'progress' – is going to be up for debate, and a thwack on the side of the head with a placard if you answer the wrong way. I wonder also how we construe progress when working with clients to help them learn. As we will see in Chapter 9, the fields of practice all have their own assumptions around what may constitute success or be construed as progress. In Organisation Development, progress is woven tightly into the fabric and measured ultimately against a set of specific values (Cheung-Judge & Holbeche, 2015: 19):

- Democracy and participation
- Openness to lifelong learning and experimentation
- Equity and fairness – the worth of every individual
- Valid information and informed choice
- Enduring respect for the human side of enterprise

I applaud the humanistic and socially responsible nature of these and wonder if sometimes we are overly certain that our interventions will make things better, when – for some clients, sitting sucking glacier mints and supping fizzy water in artificially lit subterranean hotel conference rooms – the reality may feel very different.

Think back to the NHS's quest for the 'right' leadership theory as outlined in Chapter 3, or the growth of Agile, or the growth of interest in self-managing teams and organisations. All of them have their champions and standard bearers, hailing them as the way we need to go, sometimes with some useful data to support that. The sting in the tail is that not all these fads and fashions stick, as "when a given practice has achieved widespread diffusion, it will undergo either *selective retention* or *abandonment*" (Piazza & Abrahamson, 2020: 268).

The mechanism by which ideas either stick or fade has changed over time, and central to Piazza and Abrahamson's argument is the role of technology in enabling the promotion, discussion and dissemination of ideas.

They contend that it is not enough to create new practices and theories to guarantee success, they "must be broadcast by supply-side organisations – consulting firms, multinational corporations (Kern et al., 2019), magazines, business schools (Engwall & Wedlin, 2019),industry associations, social media and software companies – if they are to have a chance of becoming fashionable" (Abrahamson, 1991: 271).

To give you an idea of the scale of the dissemination of ideas, between 1980 and 1996 McKinsey consultants alone published over fifty books (Mazzucato & Collington, 2023: 129). That is on top of all the various thought leadership articles and blogs, the recipe for which one of my interviewees, a former PwC consultant, distilled down into:

"Have the headlines of a proposal. So here's the thought leadership issue, we researched everyone, here's some amazing analysis, we summarise the main issue as follows. What people want is this, the following needs to happen. The following all play a part of the solution, and some things need to be brought to the fore. The following should also be accelerated.

Finally, we should pay attention to this, contact us to find out how we can help."[162]

In their seminal text on management gurus, *The Witch Doctors,* Micklethwait and Wooldridge (1997) document in detail the incestuous relationship between

---

162. Interview 9th March 2021

academics, business schools, consultants, consultancies and how that dovetails in a quest to "link … new ideas and profit" (1997: 54). They also point out that we have many former business leaders who leap on the bandwagon, amplifying the pattern as well as the organisations they lead. The functional collusion is neatly described by Micklethwait and Wooldridge:

"A taste for management theory allows companies to present themselves as 'go ahead; and even gives them a chance to earn money. One way for a company to get noticed is to present themselves as a 'centre for excellence' … and charge people for watching it perform … Another … is to promote oneself as a small business school in one's own right." (ibid.: 56–57)

If thirty years ago this broadcasting took place through books, journal articles, newspapers, magazines and public events, the growth in social media – and the speed at which ideas can both be disseminated and shared – means that LinkedIn, X, Instagram, blogs, etc. are how ideas get amplified at scale. It also means that the need to generate new content, fast and in digestible form, increases the pressure to make the ideas being presented as simple and easy to consume as possible. That in turn squeezes out the complexity, and makes it easier to justify the omission of data and facts that might make an otherwise less clear picture less attractive. After all, a Silver Bullet is nothing if it is not easy to understand, incontrovertible and offered without any lack of self-confidence and certainty. By nature, they tend to be of their time – populist, consumerist, just-in-time, over-the-counter, a quick fix that is intended to allay our fears, manage our short-term anxiety, and prevent us from having to confront uncertainty and confusion.

A perfect of example of this is a Gallup blog, by their Chairman no less, in May 2021,[163] entitled 'Gallup Finds a Silver Bullet: Coach Me Once Per Week'. I leave you to enjoy the certainty and oversimplification in peace via the link below.

> There really is a silver bullet to running a culture of high performance and high development.
>
> It's always the manager.
>
> ⎯
>
> Gallup has discovered -- through studying what the best managers do differently -- that great managing is an act of coaching, not one of directing and administrating.

---

163. https://bit.ly/3xaHZII

What's hidden behind the curtain of neatness

Donald Schön (1983) argued that "complex professional action cannot be arrived at through the model of 'technical rationality', and that such an approach to professional development leads to over specialisation and an unhelpfully narrow view" (Jackson in Bachkirova *et al.*, 2021: 33).

As I finish this chapter, reflecting on Schön's ideas, my mind goes back to the 30,000 people who liked the Simon Sinek post I referenced earlier. It suggests to me that to question and challenge binary thinking and oversimplification, to shine a light on apparently narrow thinking, to ask what is behind this, is often to put you in a minority. It is a short hop, skip and jump to the defensive behaviours that lead to whistle-blowers being scapegoated.

The bottom line, when it comes to our reliance on theories and models as Silver Bullets is that: "… the problem with conceptual frameworks is that they readily become temples into which the light of experience does not enter. They extend the umbrella of non-falsifiable certainty over claims that can and should be subject to empirical scrutiny, and thus they provide a refuge for dogma and hidden agendas. They often have to be unlearned – at great cost" (Stewart, 2020: 179).

Models and theories, even ones that purport to help us make sense of complexity run the risk of "training our brains actually to do the opposite of what is required. And that's *dealing with* constant uncertainty, and pretending not to have the answers is a good state of mind (to foster real learning)", according to Alex Boulting, who has extensively researched change theories.[164] Boulting is essentially pointing out that the greater the reliance on theories and models, or case studies that demonstrate best practice, the less the grunt work. Joost Minnaar talked to this:

> "Many leaders have no clue about what options they have, and they have no clue about how Buurtzorg[165] for example really works. And you don't figure that out by reading Laloux's book or reading our book. You really need to go there, talk with people, then your frontline people.

---

164. Interview 18th September 2020
165. https://reinventingorganizationswiki.com/it/cases/buurtzorg/ is a good place to learn more about Buurtzorg. This Substack post by Matthew Kalman Mezey is required reading if you want to get a sense of the reality of implementing these approaches, in this instance in health and social care: https://bit.ly/3thUfFt

Talk with people from Buurtzorg and talk about the good stuff and the bad stuff. I think the only thing we scholars or writers or whatever can give is inspiration, and we can only give this first view or the first steps … But if you really want to understand then you have to go there, just like we did."[166]

Minnaar's comments are echoed by Paul Jensen, who used to work for Buurtzorg UK & Ireland, who cautions that there "is a risk that being inspired by one such example and wanting to replicate its model because of its great outcomes, will divert your transformation process away from your own journey and into the path of 'implementing' your source of inspiration into an environment which isn't quite suited or quite ready for it" ('Lessons from going Dutch in the UK' by Paul Jensen, 04-12-2020).[167] This is the antithesis to the certainty that often accompanies Silver Bullet solutions, whether models, tools, methods or the pronouncements of experts and thought leaders. The reality is that experimenting with new approaches to organising, and even more importantly what it takes to make them work, is not as simple as leaders saying, 'oh goody that looks like a new and sexy approach, I'll have some of that for my organisation'. As Brendan Martin from Buurtzorg UK says:

> "Examples of … long-term radical organisational changes are few but significant because they depend on robust long-term leadership commitment to making the organisational changes required to grow and sustain a new approach." (Quoted in 'The possibility of autonomous Buurtzorg care teams across the UK: tantalising hope vs organisational rigidity (Part 1)' by Kálmán Mezey, 24-11-2023)[168]

This means leaders who are prepared to be and do the radical, to show up in ways that are different to the norms of existing schools of thought epitomised in Chapter 3 and the learning institutions featured in Chapter 4.

In the next chapter, we look at the role consultancies – and by extension the consultants that work within them – play as part of the 'broadcast industry' and feedback loop for Silver Bullets.

---

166. Interview 18th May 2020
167. This post is well worth a read. It offers first-hand experience and lessons of implementing self-management. https://trust-works.co.uk/blog/f/lessons-from-going-dutch-in-the-uk
168. https://matthewkalmanmezey.substack.com/p/the-possibility-of-autonomous-buurtzorg

Reflective Questions

- What are your 'go to' theories and theorists?
- Amidst the many mainstream theories, to what extent do you step out of your intellectual comfort zone to explore critical theories in respect to the history and nature of the socio-economic system in which we find ourselves?
- To what extent are you managing your own anxiety with an over-reliance on theories?
- How evidence based is your practice?
- What assumptions underpin your choice of theories in your work?

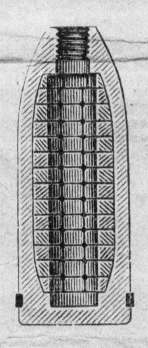

SILVER BULLET NO. 6

EXPENSIVE CONSULTANT

a.   I cost a lot, yes, and the reason is I have a lot of models and slide decks
that you really need. I also have many associates who need work, so let
me help you to understand why your business needs them.

THE ROLE OF CONSULTING FIRMS IN PERPETUATING THE SILVER BULLET MYTH

OR: THERE BE A LOT OF MONEY IN THEM THAR HILLS

Chapter 7:
The Role of Consulting Firms in Perpetuating the Silver Bullet Myth

One of the interesting questions is how Silver Bullets are constructed, and who does the constructing. In one sense, the construction is often a projection: anxiety drives the client to edit out complexity and project their hopes of a panacea onto the person or thing that best fits the projection. Nonetheless, we might look for an example of how they are constructed in the world of large consulting companies, such as McKinsey & Co, Boston Consulting Group (BCG) and Bain & Company (the 'Big Three'), and the global accountancies, namely EY, KPMG, PwC, Deloitte (the 'Big Four'), and the raft of supporting players such as Accenture, Tata and PA Consulting.

The revenues they generate are staggering: "In 2021, estimated at almost $700 billion to over $900 billion" (Mazzucato & Collington, 2023: 2).

This is set against a background of regular stories about the apparent ills of the consulting industry, the extent to which consultants bleed public sector coffers dry and milk their corporate clients. The literature is deep and broad, and I do not intend to do a full review of it, other than to suggest Mazzucato & Collington's *The Big Con* (2023) and *When McKinsey Comes To Town* (2022) by Walt Bogdanich and Michael Forsythe as useful starting points. The latter includes a chapter on their relationship with the NHS, and should be read in conjunction with research over the past few years from the University of Bristol that repeatedly highlights the largely negative impact of consultancy services. More recently a 2021 report ('A consultancy habit? The use of external management advice in the NHS') concluded that the "use of paid management consultants in the NHS has become habitual despite having a negative impact on efficiency". Their overall findings, based on research with 120 hospital trust (so not a small sample) are striking. I have highlighted a few sections as they relate directly to what follows in this chapter:

- High levels of use of consulting services in the past are linked to greater use in the future **despite no efficiency gains**.
- Continually hiring consultants is not a result of a shortage of management because the biggest users are those trusts with relatively more managers. It is also not associated with the poorest performers.

- While it seems unlikely that clients knowingly bring inefficiencies in through consultancy use, the precise reasons for doing so remain unclear. It could be linked to the **high status of many consulting firms,** fuelled by their **promotional activities** and **close relationships with potential clients**. More concretely, there is the **appeal of having new and instant resources available who will promise efficiency** and **rarely challenge the 'hand that feeds them'**.

The relationship between the consulting sector and the NHS is now so intimate that KPMG and PwC, along with the Management Consultancies Association (MCA), were tasked in 2023 with redesigning one of the most longstanding leadership programmes, NHS Leadership Academy's Nye Bevan programme.

> "The programme supports senior healthcare leaders who aspire to become Executive Directors. It sits at the heart of NHS talent management in England, building leadership skills through expert-facilitated inputs, practical exercises, and peer-assessment." (Management Consultancies Association, 'KPMG And PwC With NHS Leadership Academy Bevan Programme', 11-05-2023)

The NHS has outsourced the cultivation of critical thinking and reflective practice skills to three organisations who have a vested interest in (not building too much) capability. When you consider that the MCA "is dedicated to supporting member interests and promoting the value of consultancy",[169] you have to wonder how this one passed the conflict-of-interest sniff test.

Reading the Bristol report, I wondered for a moment if someone had read an early draft of this book, as it uncannily mirrors the themes within it. Given all this, why do organisations keep coming back for more?

To be clear, there are many excellent, principled and effective people who work in these organisations. They are not evil. What I want to do here is shine a light on the *systemic* patterns, and how they relate to Silver Bullets. This chapter has been influenced by Geoff Marlow, who has had a long career in consulting, including a stint at Arthur D. Little, which was one of the first consulting firms founded in 1886. A story Geoff told me locates us at the heart of the client/consultant dance, so we start there.

---

169. https://www.mca.org.uk/about-us

Once upon a time …

Imagine you are the Head of Group Planning in a global petrochemical business. You have responsibility for all scenario planning, and you come to understand – rightly I would suggest – that the world is so unpredictable and uncertain that you can't come up with a single strategy to control the world and plan for all eventualities. The challenge is to think about which of the political, economic, social, technological, legal and environmental drivers you need to pay attention to, and why, given the way they are varying, unpredictably so. You could use an approach like the PESTLE[170] analysis, which, ooo! look at that, is a tool that allows the busy consultant or executive to study the key external factors that influence an organisation.

The next step is to come up with several scenarios that seem to map out the likely territory, which is a pragmatic way of preparing your organisation to be truly agile, in the sense that it is aware of unpredictability and uncertainty and has the adaptive capacity to respond rather than react.

A former Group Head of Planning at Shell described this scene to Geoff Marlow when they both served on the Board of the Society for Organisational Learning, further detailing how those scenarios were developed and presented to a committee of managing directors, essentially the top management of the organisation across all countries they operated in. The meetings would go well, with no obvious problems, and then:

> "…he could guarantee that what would happen is, after they've done all the formal stuff, they'll be in the bar in the evening together and more than one managing director would come up to him and say something like:
>
> 'Hey, great presentation, really like it, but between you and me, which scenario do you think is the most likely to come about?'
>
> Because what they wanted was the one thing that they could plan for."[171]

---

170. PESTLE is based on an idea from Francis Joseph Aguilar, an American scholar of strategic planning and general management, in the 1960s. Originally PEST, it has spawned many variants. Like many easy-to-remember frameworks, it offers a shortcut for the busy executive or consultant but inhibits wider thinking that would be unbounded by the categories that can be arranged into a convenient acronym. This Silver Bullet-like magnifying glass leads to an intense focus on certain things, and a blindness to peripheral matters that might potentially be influential. That's not to say that focusing is not useful; when it becomes less a filter and more a sieve to remove uncomfortable grit even if relevant, that is a problem.
171. Interview 24th May 2023

This mirrors the pattern that I observed at the Corporate Rebels event I described earlier in the book, the need to believe that, despite the agreement that there is complexity, uncertainty and mess, there must, after all, please, go on reassure me, let there be a Silver Bullet.

For Geoff, who has a particular focus on the notion of 'future fit culture', this chimes with his observation that "most people have a framing already set up in their head into which a single strategy fits. They're convinced such a strategy must exist, they just need to find it." And here is the kicker:

> "They're not looking to change the frame that they carry around about what the solution might look like. They want the single point solution that I just need to find and then it'll all be easy. They'll be able to breathe a sigh of relief, and it will be wonderful."[172]

It is this belief system that consultants and consultancies feed off, and mostly amplify.

'Nobody ever got fired for hiring PwC'

We need to tick off a (largely) simple truth to begin with, namely that the aphorism that 'nobody has ever been fired for hiring PwC' (or McKinsey/ Bain/BCG/KPMG, etc.) is largely true. The most likely outcome, one that I have heard on several occasions, is that the expensively produced report and accompanying recommendations are quietly filed in a drawer, until the next consultancy is hired, then rinse and repeat. That report might simply be a slide deck, consisting sometimes of one slide and costing a six-figure sum (yes, even for a slide or two) and, in one case I was told about, a seven-figure sum that left an organisation decidedly underwhelmed.[173]

Marlow offers a useful twist on this and suggests:

"Most senior executives aren't looking for an answer, they're looking for a defensive shield to protect their position and future career aspirations. When they hire McKinsey or whoever, what they gain is plausible excusability for the failure to change. 'Don't blame me, I hired McKinsey'."

In Chapter 10, we will see just how this manifests in reality.

---

172. Interview 24th February 2023
173. Interview 20th September 2021

Hello anxiety, my old friend

Even when a top team executive does genuinely want to bring about change, they may have top team peers who like things just the way they are. Marlow's experience was that, even if they agree with the need to change, many senior executives will continue to act in ways that perpetuate the status quo. "Some do this knowingly. Others unknowingly. Old habits die hard."

It's not just habits, it's attachment to status. The irony is that senior leaders are tasked with leading organisational change – but can, at a personal level, be the most change-resistant people in an organisation. This is understandable, for two main reasons. Firstly, they have little incentive given the high-status and salary they enjoy: it would be irrational to give that up willy-nilly. Secondly, sometimes habits are hard to change because to do so would mean letting go of long-held assumptions, e.g. that the strategy that led our organisation to where it is today, that I helped design and deliver, is wrong; that I might not have the answers, etc. So the status quo is actually quite attractive.

The decision-making process that informs why consultancies are hired is key. I worked with a major retail business for several years, building Organisation Development and change capability, and most of that time working closely with someone who had a long history there and had retained the capacity to think critically. In my interview with her, I asked about the relationship between senior leaders and consultancies in her organisation. Her answer was beautifully nuanced and talks to the co-dependent relationship that can arise between client and consultant.

From the organisation's perspective, "they sometimes make the connection to the consultancy via one of their existing relationships … they seek them out to help them make the decision that they know they're going to make anyway. But they like somebody from outside to tell them that it's the right thing to do. And they like to use the big-name consultancies to do that."[174]

Her reflection on the behaviour of senior leaders is telling, and reveals just how much fear of making a 'wrong decision' drives things:

> "… there's something about not trusting ourselves, and sometimes thinking the outside world knows better. So, we ask the outside world. But what the outside world usually tells us is what we currently know anyway." (Ibid.)

---

174. Interview 1ˢᵗ May 2020

That old cliché about hiring consultants to take your watch and use it to tell you the time? More than a grain of truth, although it is also worth pointing out some clients do forget how to tell the time or need to be reminded to wear a watch, but that is another story. And sometimes they walk away with your watch as well!

The dysfunctionality in the relationship is further evidenced by her follow-up observation:

> "The other thing is, they can blame the other people when it goes wrong. Or they can choose to ignore it if it's somebody from outside the organisation that is suggesting it to them, and it doesn't feel right. Or they don't think it's the right thing to do. They can just say, 'Oh, well, we can ignore it because that's somebody who's not us telling us that'."

If that sounds both childlike and game playing, it is probably a bit of both. There is a need to please and/or not be found out, which talks to the strong parent/child dynamic in many organisations, and this one in particular. This links to some of the patterns discussed in Chapter 2, the way in which behaviour in the present is coloured by our relationship with authority figures from our childhood. It shows up most obviously in the (many) organisations where I observe an over-egged deference to authority, typified by the (often unconscious) acquiescing to the views of the most senior person in the room. It is why rigid hierarchies, and command and control cultures, proliferate. It also reveals the game that is being played: 'we all know what needs to change, but we can't say, or be seen to actually do anything about it'. Emperor/boy/no clothes anyone?

This may be in part because most senior executives may, at heart, not be all that interested in change because they got where they are based on the current model. If you change that, they might not be good enough to be at that level and earn well. So, there are powerful forces at work that almost incentivises them to maintain the status quo, even if deep down they might know it's got no longevity to it. At a macro and rather depressing level, this probably reflects decision making at government and corporate level when it comes to climate change.

The ethics of consulting

> "There are no generally recognised professional standards for management consultancy." Shaw (2019: 54)

The narrative in much of the marketing is that clients get customised and tailored solutions, and that they will have their internal capabilities enhanced. The reality is more nuanced, containing ethical tensions that I will consider before looking at what it is that systemically creates the conditions for these tensions to arise.

I spoke with several current and former consultants from well-known firms, and what is revealed is the other side of this co-dependent relationship that consultancies sometimes rely on to generate revenue.

To begin with, there is nothing inherently wrong with cultivating a close relationship with a client. The question is, when does that slip into something that has less to do with what the client organisation *needs,* and more with ensuring the consultancy remains in poll position to upsell and extend. This talks to the closeness of the relationship between senior leaders, particularly at C-Suite level but also lower down, and consultancies.

I have two clients who have crossed over from large consulting firms to the other side. The first worked for several years at Accenture and said the belief that big consulting firms are good in part stems from how much they cost, i.e. the more they charge, the better they must be. "They must be good at this stuff, right? They've created white papers and research papers, and they seem to have some pretty certain answers for things, and they seem to have an approach. You know, what my internal guy is telling me it's more complicated than that. You follow this linear step-by-step guide. They've got the playbook. Bring them in, they've got all the answers."[175]

It was revealing to hear him say what it was like to be the person selling that narrative:

> "I've done it myself. You sell, literally, a predictable methodology, where you say 'follow this, and we will give you predictable outcomes'. So, I have absolutely been there myself, you're a salesperson at the end of the day, to some degree, and part of what you're selling is certainty, predictability, guarantees." (Ibid.)

---

175. Interview 18th May 2020

A former PwC consultant, now working at a corporate FMCG business, commented to me, "some of these consultants are so embedded, they're in the ears of some of the most senior leaders and have access that other people in our organisation just don't have. They're Machiavellian. And they create an unhealthy dependency.[176]

This dependency also shows up via one of the voices that Mark Cole and John Higgins spoke to in *The Great Unheard at Work* (2023: 151): "Consultants rarely tell us anything we don't know but somehow their 'expertise' is listened to more than those who have worked in the organisation for many years." The consultant comes in because senior leaders are concerned presumably about discussion around improvement being distorted by vested interest, but do not recognise the way in which their own vested interests shape and distort the decisions and actions they take around change. Senior leaders therefore come to depend more on external voices to tell them what to do than the people they pay to create value within their organisations.

The former PwC consultant mentioned above went on to further reveal the relational dynamic between her consulting firm and their clients.

> "The people who thrive at senior levels [here] are people who are adept at giving reassurance, of showing enough of what's inside the 'Black Box', but not giving the tools [to clients] … It's about: here's the methodology, showing you enough, but not giving you the tools of the trade to actually do it for yourself. It's ensuring that there's dependency and never equipping the client to take care of themselves." (Ibid.)

For 'Black Box', read Silver Bullet, the creation of mystic and magic and an air of infallible expertise. She went on to shine a light on a particularly fascinating part of the psychological process at play. In PwC, her managers would encourage consultants to make 'the problem' even more complex:

> "… [T]o almost debilitate the client. And then you come in with the Ta-dar! I know all the answers, and here's what we're going to do. But you don't actually show them what's behind the methodology. You talk about results, outcomes, blah, blah, blah, but you don't show them the ingredients of how you get there …" (Ibid.)

---

176. Interview 18th June 2020

Was this a one-off? No. "I've seen it time and time again, where you're the boots on the ground, doing the doing at the project level, and then you've got this Partner who swans in for their client meeting every couple of weeks, and you're escalating risks and issues, and then they're schmoozing instead of having 'crucial conversations' because they don't want to jeopardise the contract" (ibid.).

Another internal change practitioner, with substantial experience of working with and alongside external consultants, echoed this:

> "I'm trying to persuade my current employer not to bring large consultancies in to help with our transformation. Smaller firms and individuals are often able to add greater value because they are more creative and flexible. There's so much bias though, partly because of the networking of the people at the top."[177]

However, it is the need to create dependency that is central to the Finders, Minders, Grinders consulting business model (Maister, 2004, 'The Anatomy of a Consulting Firm[178]') which I will be exploring in more detail shortly. You never want the client to mobilise their own people, or you might never be needed again. This sense of questioning the value that large consulting firms offer was a key refrain from ex-employees of large and medium firms.

This is a beautifully functional collusion, the meshing of dysfunction, fear and anxiety in the client system with those that would like to help by creating evermore dependency. If it sounds like a quasi-abusive relationship, it's probably because it is, in that it matches exactly the definition of gaslighting, which can be defined as "a manipulative tactic in which a person, to gain power and control of another individual, plants seeds of uncertainty in another person's mind. The self-doubt and constant questioning slowly cause the individual to question their reality."[179] In essence, it is because of the business model of many consultancies, which is predicated on providing answers. What happens if someone in one of these large firms attempts to build capability, then?

> "I'll never forget in my very early days ... facilitating a conversation with the client in a 'coaching style'. And then the senior manager, who was in the meeting at the time, took me aside afterwards and said, 'I can see you've got great coaching skills. You're at [this firm] now, you're

177. Interview 22nd February 2023
178. https://davidmaister.com/articles/the-anatomy-of-a-consulting-firm/
179. https://bit.ly/42Z4vQz

a consultant now, and people are not paying you to help them find the answer within themselves. They're paying you to come with a point of view and expertise. So, stop the coaching and come in with a point of view and an answer.'"[180]

What compounds my own unease is the apparent unwillingness of this vast and growing industry to enter into a genuine dialogue about some of the ethical tensions and contradictions. How was it deemed acceptable, for example, for consulting firms in the US to simultaneously advise the government on how to lower the cost of prescription drugs whilst helping drug companies to maximise profits. (*Magic Consultants* Episode 4, BBC Radio, 17-08-2023). In the last episode of this excellent radio documentary series, it was revealed that the big six consultancies in the UK either didn't respond to requests to comment or refused to take part in the series. The only contributor from *within* the consulting profession was the CEO of the Management Consulting Association, who seemed incapable of accepting the possibility that there are problems within the sector and with how they serve their clients.

The partner view

As I said earlier, there are people in large firms who see the tension here. A partner at one of the Big Four consulting firms told me:

> "So much of what I see out there is people that are desperate, as you have said, for a Silver Bullet, for the answer to be categorical. And that doesn't work ... What does that do for you as a consultant if you don't have the answer? Well, actually, it's an uncomfortable place. But for me the journey is more important than the destination ... the biggest challenge really is being able to get over yourself, enough to realise that maybe you don't have to have the answers anymore."[181]

They also shone a light on the conversation that can go on in a large firm, describing how a new hire from another consulting firm proposed a 'new strategy' that transpired to be one of "no longer sell(ing) stuff to clients that we didn't know added value". Their response was one of shock and reveals that this is a both/and dynamic, not an either/or: consultancies have people who have strong ethical stances and others who don't.

---

180. Interview 18th May 2020
181. Interview 26th May 2020

"We never ever dreamt to position anything with a client that we didn't believe would really add value and would move them to a better place. ... it was not anywhere near the culture of the organisation. There is not a chance in hell we would sell something just to sell it, just to make money, just to get something moving.

Now, that's not to say that three, four weeks, three months, four months into the project, we didn't realise it was a bag of shit and it was never going to deliver value and the extent to which people called that out and stopped or continued, you know, that was a challenge. But you would never sell something and proceed with the start something that you knew would not work." (Ibid.)

My conversation with this partner was powerful, because he had the humility and honesty to shine a light on a profoundly human aspect to life as a consultant.

"... this is where people's humanity and humility disconnect and engages with their apparent professionalism ... there's a split around emotional awareness and emotional intelligence. I think people give up emotional intelligence for what looks like professionalism, which is basically to close off every emotional trigger ... in order to sell something, anything ... you become a corporate machine." (Ibid.)

The challenge for clients is to pay attention less to the brand and the label a consultant comes with, and more to the human being that they might be working with. That, however, requires you to dig a little deeper and go beyond superficial questions or the glitz of a slide presentation to find out what lurks behind that, and wrestle with reality. Specifically: in the dominant consulting model you typically only spend enough time with a senior consultant to secure current and future sales. The people you'll 'be working with' are fungible junior consultants.

Co-created dependency

It is all too easy to blame consultants and consultancies for the vast sums of money that pass between them. This is a co-created dependency, and clients are the other party. Whether they are ill-equipped or afraid, or both, clients are sadly culpable also. There is the failure to ask more probing questions, to challenge those selling solutions more deeply, and generally to get into a conversation that moves beyond the neatness of the Silver Bullet on offer. As we will see in Chapter 10, this can lead to incredibly poor and costly outcomes, and sabotage change at the outset.

This is how we end up with, for example, the UK public sector awarding £2.8bn worth of consulting contracts in 2022 (Elgot: 2022), up 75% on 2019.[182] Some of that money was well spent, some less so no doubt. The question is, how does the functional collusion show up here? In the course of my work, I was told a story that illustrates this beautifully.

A large UK government department wanted to initiate a significant behavioural change programme. A senior leader within this organisation engaged with a large consultancy, who – correctly in my view – insisted on a diagnostic phase, including shadowing people on the front line. The client said that was not possible, and a stand-off ensued, with the senior person in the consulting firm not bidding for the work, insisting that without listening to the people doing the front-line work, i.e. the people whose behaviour they wanted to change, they were not going to learn what was really going on.

The consultant told the government department it would be awfully convenient for them to come in and tell them they had 'the answer', and to ask £4m for that. However they told the client the answer was in their organisation. The consultant offered an approach that might get that answer out, which entailed working with the front line to listen to them, to use that to inform a behaviour change programme based on the lived experience of employees. The client agreed, and the irony is the change programme didn't work.

The moral of the story here is twofold:

1. Not all interventions, however well designed and thought through, will work.

2. There is no Silver Bullet for behaviour change, so why are you surprised if it does not work?

How did we get here?

The first organisational consultancy was founded in 1886 by Arthur D. Little (ADL), who was a chemical engineer. He saw the advantage of helping organisations understand the 'chemistry' of their own organisations, i.e. their

---

182. https://bit.ly/3T8w9pG

products, processes, etc. It was the genesis of the idea of business advisory services, to help people to run their businesses better.

Fast forward to 1926 and the foundation of McKinsey, who were a product of Scientific Management, and called themselves 'management engineers' in the early days, capturing the zeitgeist. Consulting grew in parallel to the growth in management education and the 'professionalisation' of leadership and management. Then in the 1960s, the seeds of what we have now were sown. Up until then, it is probably fair to say that the primary role of the big consultancies was to do analysis of markets, opportunities and competition, a cerebral activity more than anything else.

Geoff Marlow described his own experience:

> "When I did some of the training at ADL, they taught you things like the pyramid principle, which is how to structure an argument so that you can persuade people with the logic of the argument. You make sure that you've got the data to build up the argument and then present it to senior people, so you're not overloading them with too much data but they can make well-informed decisions. That was what the finders/minders/grinders consulting business model was set up to do, and it did it very well."[183]

Bruce Henderson, who left ADL to found one of the other behemoths of the field, the Boston Consulting Group (BCG) in 1963, felt that you could do more to proactively grow consulting to have a bigger impact. The key was this: if you're able to showcase your thinking to senior executives, rather than just be a firm that they hired when they've got problems, then it is a professional service like law or accounting. Thus began a period when consulting was about having a long-term relationship before it moved to more of a marketing-led 'smoke and mirrors' business model. Marlow observed that "claiming the intellectual high ground was the sort of jargon that we used to hear inside ADL – is your model, concept, etc. salient? Does it capture the attention of senior executives? *There's a difference between salience and truthfulness* [emphasis added]" (ibid.). Thinking back to the chapter on gurus and thought leaders, the notion of salience is hugely relevant there too: in an age of celebrity culture, being noticed trumps saying something true or useful, a pattern that shows up increasingly in political discourse, sadly. Salience matters, but so does truthfulness, because without that, what we are left with is bullshitting, in the technical sense. Harry G. Frankfurt,

---

183. Interview 24th February 2023

whose work on defining 'bullshit' (2005) deserves more attention, is worth mentioning here. He suggests 'bullshitting' is speech intended to persuade with little regard for the truth and makes a distinction between the liar and the bullshitter. The former cares about the truth and attempts to hide it, whereas the latter is not bothered either way.

> "For the essence of bullshit is not that it is false but that it is phony. In order to appreciate this distinction, one must recognise that a fake or a phony need not be in any respect (apart from authenticity itself) inferior to the real thing. What is not genuine need not also be defective in some other way. It may be, after all, an exact copy. What is wrong with a counterfeit is not what it is like, but how it was made. This points to a similar and fundamental aspect of the essential nature of bullshit: although it is produced without concern with the truth, it need not be false.
>
> The bullshitter is faking things. But this does not mean that he necessarily gets them wrong." (Frankfurt, 1986: 14)

That last sentence is key here: there is much bravado and machismo, strutting and preening, posturing and pontificating, when it comes to leadership, organisations, management education and, yes, consulting. The knack is to notice our own part in that, and to call it out when it is getting in the way of the 'work proper', a term coined by the late Brendan Reddy and Chuck Phillips of NTL in their Group Process Consultation (GPC) model. In Brendan Reddy's book *Intervention Skills* (1994), he talks about two distinct phases in GPC work: the entry phase and the work proper phase, with a contracting gate in between the two. What I notice when I work with clients who are developing their consulting skills is that the latter phase sometimes is skipped over. There is a desire to move from the ease of entry – essentially building rapport – to 'doing something', without taking the time to have the conversation about the *real* nature of the work at hand. Again, anxiety has a part to play, as consultants who are, say, less comfortable with conflict or afraid of upsetting someone in a more powerful role may play it safe.

The thing about the 'work proper' is that it is often, well, hard. It challenges. It may frustrate and induce anxiety. All of which makes the lure of a 'solution' the more attractive.

The intoxication of a good consulting model

Salience in consulting, therefore, is all about capturing attention, and is crucial for consulting firms' own survival. Hence the need I noted in the last chapter, that management practices "must be broadcast by supply-side organisations … if they are to have a chance of becoming fashionable" (Abrahamson, 2020: 271). It is vital to catch a client's eye, ideally with something that not just interests them but also catalyses a sales conversation. Provoking thinking – and learning – is arguably less useful than creating a sales opportunity, as the former risks educating clients and reducing dependency. Hello ethical tension, my old friend.

Much of the language and many of the models of modern organisations stem from consulting: 'deep dive', 'change management', 'purpose driven', 'low-hanging fruit', 'impact/effort matrix', 'onboarding', 'running up the flagpole', 'OKRs', 'KPIs', 'SWOT analysis', 'omnichannel', 'b2b', 'b2c' and all things digital, digitalised and digitally transformed.

One of the best examples of this is BCG's Growth Share Matrix, the prototype for all 2x2 models. It invites the client to ask useful questions, e.g. which products do you invest in? Which ones do you use as cash cows to provide the money to explore the products of the future? Which parts of the business do you sell off or close? etc. One of the key innovations here, Matthew Stewart suggests, is that it validates a key concept of Henderson's view of consulting, namely that consultants do not need to have any specialist knowledge of the businesses they advise, rather they can apply general principles (2009: 161). A more cynical view of 2x2s is that they oversimplify a complex world and reduce it to two axes and four quadrants. That generates the illusion of knowability and offers what looks to be a prompt to action (i.e. find a way to move yourself from the shit square in the grid to the shiny one).

The attractiveness of this idea was not lost on others, and imitators quickly followed, starting with McKinsey reinventing itself as a strategy consulting firm and coming up with its own three-by-three model (when in doubt, adding some boxes or alliterate is another common technique in the imitation game). That this pattern persists to this day was highlighted while I wrote this chapter, when I saw the table in a post from Dave Ulrich which neatly demonstrates how, in the HR field, consultancies attempt to differentiate themselves,[184] all the while talking about, well, largely the same thing.

---

184. https://www.linkedin.com/pulse/what-makes-effective-hr-function-value-logic-dave-ulrich/

Overview of Views of the HR Function Themes and Focus

Firm	Theme	Focus
Accenture	Business operating model	• Resilience / make the change • Six key capabilities: agile, technology, configure, ecosystem, decision making, reskill
	"High-Res"	• Six CHRO skills: systems thinking, financial acumen, leadership, technology/data, strategic talent, business acumen
Academy to Innovate HR (AIHR)	HR operating models	• Five HR operating models from HR centralization to decentralization • Best practices: link to business strategy, collaborate, map competencies, redesign operating model and structure
Deloitte	High impact HR operating model	Core elements/philosophies or base assumptions: 1. HR customers: workforce experience 2. Digital workplace empowers the workforce 3. Workforce insights inform business strategy 4. Fluid interactions: breaking silos 5. HR operational services: deliver data and services 6. Business HR: deploy workforce solutions 7. Communities of expertise: relevant, data-based, experience-designed workforce solutions 8. External networks to add workforce solutions 9. HR leadership sets vision and priorities 10. HR enablers
Gartner	Agile HR: Flexible	Agile principles: 1. Create space for strategic thinkers 2. Implement customer-centric model 3. Manage portfolio, not set agenda HR operating role: 1. HR business partner 2. HR problem solvers 3. Agile COEs 4. HR shared services center for service delivery HR technology: 1. Connect with employees 2. Manage employee performance and productivity 3. Conduct workforce planning and deployment
Josh Bersin	HR Capabilities (competencies)	• 94 individual competencies in 20 domains • Priorities: · Develop leaders and managers · Change management and communication · Apply principles of organization design · Coach individuals for performance · Operate as business partner · Understand global cultural issues · Terminate senior executives
KPMG	Pathfinders	HR functional model: • Remove boundaries • Meet employee expectations • Digital drives processes Lessons: • Live values, connect with employees • Evolve/adapt employee experience • Lead with humanity • Adapt to change Areas of impact: • "S" in ESG: talent pool • "Total workforce": talent management, personalized employee experience, skill gaps • Reimagine the world of work: employees adapt, workforce, employee experience Priorities: • HR strategy/operating model • Workforce strategy • Experience • Talent marketplace
McKinsey	HR operating model	Five HR operating model options: 1. Ulrich + 2. Agile 3. Employee experience 4. Leader-led 5. Machine powered
Mercer	Target interaction model	• People-centric HR operation model: · Employee lifecycle · Place people needs at front of HR agenda · HR transforms around people · Measure employee satisfaction • HR customer: candidate, external workforce, employee, people leader, top management • Operations: people operations platform, personal support, functional expertise
PwC	Shaping next-generation HR	Next-generation HR: • Adapt to pace of change • Put advisors close to business to adapt to business needs • Be flexible and resilient Roles: • HR experts • HR advisors • HR leadership • HR partners

This is a good example of the productisation of processes that turns unique and bespoke 'hows' into the ready-for-rollout, replicable 'whats' of Silver Bullet products, and sometimes these products are elaborate practices and methodologies. A former consultant summarised the process neatly:

> "They all work on value propositions. And a value proposition is something we can commercialise, and can be scaled. And then always indicate that yes, we believe that this is industry standard, this is best practice, this will work for everyone.
>
> I don't think that we will get them to admit it, but I think for them, it becomes the Silver Bullet. Because [if] I can scale, I can commercialise, and that's how we're going to make millions ..."[185]

A lot of the Silver Bullets proposed by consultancies are just the next salient thing that apparently claims the intellectual high ground. If BCG comes up with something that resonates with clients, a lot of clients who are currently paying Deloitte or McKinsey move to BCG, and then Deloitte and McKinsey have to come up with their new sexy thing that is going to be the thing that lures clients back. This is the game, or to be more precise the 'marketing game'. The wider game also includes the need to keep lots of Grinders (junior and delivery consultants) billable with very few handholding Minders (client managers), so the Finders (partners) can fully focus on filling the future business pipeline. These roles are key in the consulting business model.

Finders, Minders and Grinders

Fundamental to the way in which a market for Silver Bullets continues to be cultivated by consultancies is the way in which they are set up. David Maister is often regarded as the person who has best defined the leverage model that professional services firms use, defining three roles that typically show up in law firms, accountancies, banks and, of course, consultancies. These roles – Finders, Minders and Grinders – not only show up in these organisations, they also strongly influence how they are scaffolded and run, to maximise the value and return on investment to the professional services firm itself.

---

185. Interview 8th November 2021

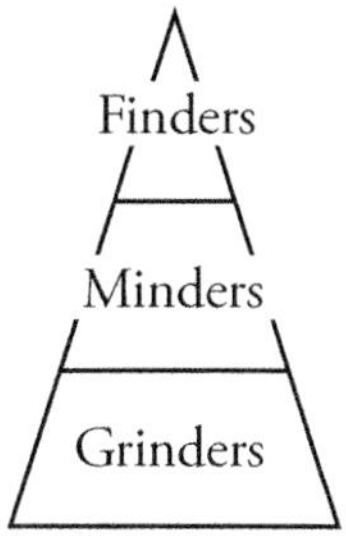

Consulting	Audit	Law
Partner	Partner	Senior Partner
Manager	Manager	Junior Partner
Consultant	Staff	Associate

The Finders[186]

In simple terms, Finders are in sales, while managing the business and ensuring a future pipeline is in place. These are the relatively small number of senior people at the top of the pyramid whose primary role is to go out and find clients. Typically equity partners, they are owners of the business and therefore success for the business equates directly to personal financial gain. This can create an 'in-it-to-win-it' culture, and they hunt for a living, roaming the plains to home in on the biggest beast they can and bring it down to feed the firm. Most of their time is spent on business development and account management, cultivating the long-term relationships that mean that when a client moves organisation, they are well placed to move with them.

To be clear, that is part of the inherently relational nature of work, and I have clients who I have worked with in different contexts. I hope that they work with me because I am the best person for the job and not because I am good at schmoozing. I can shark with the best of them at conferences and networking events, but over the years that has left me feeling … dirty – and not in a good way. The tension is an ethical and moral one, and I know several clients who stopped going to conferences because they were tired of having to slough off consultants who had homed in on them like dementors from Harry Potter. I understand the need to generate business, I can feel the tear in me occasionally (want … to … talk … to … them … about … business … must … resist …) but at heart I believe most of us know when we are being sold to under the pretence of human curiosity.

It should be no surprise that there is evidence that the most Finders and Minders are skilled at the three phases of what is termed 'Rapid Relationality' (DiBenigno, 2018: 29):

186. Professor John Kim's website is a useful resource here https://www.consultantsmind.com/

- Phase 1: rapid connection building.

- Phase 2: rapid proving of capability (e.g. demonstrating commitment with free time/resources/knowledge etc.).

- Phase 3: continual relationship building.

The bottom line, however, is that the primary role of Finders is to hunt. Matthew Stewart (2009: 61–72) uses the allegory of hunting whales, illustrating in detail the process by which clients are hooked, harpooned and reeled in, all the while being convinced the solution on offer is the right one.

It's a somewhat cynical view, and the stages echo key elements of the dance that I have had described to me and seen first-hand. As Dr Richard Claydon says:

> "… very few consultants are quite so devilishly manipulative. Most genuinely believe that their models are the best thing on the market. But make no mistake, it's 'best practice' models they are selling."[187]

The ritualistic dance of the pitch process reaches its climax, where the steps are well choreographed and known to all, to the extent that they seem to be unconscious and unquestioning. A former PwC Director echoes this view: "There's not one single project that I did when I was at PwC that left a client with [new] capability to do the same project again").[188] Revealingly, he went on to suggest that clients are "in on that":

> "… that's exactly what the client wants … the question you get asked at proposal time, when you're pitching, most often is: where has this been done before? What lessons can we learn from other examples? What's the best practice? That's what the client wants to know." (Ibid.)

The relational dynamics can be coloured by a particular machismo as well:

> "You're in a process of competition and presentation … you put enormous bollocks on the table and say 'I have bigger bollocks than anybody else'. Basically, that's what you're doing: 'we've done this more times than anybody else. We know more about this subject than anybody else. We have the very best people'." (Ibid.)

---

187. https://www.linkedin.com/pulse/do-you-want-dirty-clean-consulting-dr-richard-claydon/
188. Interview 9th March 2021

Is it any wonder some clients find it hard to say no, or that too often consultancies end up selling context-free methodologies and frameworks that create more problems than they solve?

The Minders

A smaller group, these are the senior managers, engagement managers and line managers who oversee those doing the client work. Their motivation is often to become a partner themselves, so pleasing those above and currying favour is not uncommon, which can create cultures of patronage.

Think *Game of Thrones* or *The Crown*, but with less nudity and fewer crowns. Also, no dragons, but clients may still get burned.

The Grinders

Often bright young things, fresh out of university. Smart, eager to please, energetic, impressionable and perfectly placed to work long hours and/or burn out, depending on their managers and their own anxiety levels. They are the people interviewing clients' employees, gathering requirements, drafting presentations, crunching data and generally doing the grunt work. One client observed to me that you know a Grinder by the fact that they need a bottomless cup of coffee throughout the day to fend off the fatigue of unhealthy working hours. Their company grafts a laptop on to them, so that they can swim around your company like a whale gathering plankton, capturing the data that they'll collate and then pass up the line to the person above them who will produce your expensive slide deck.

The value exchange for them, at least superficially, is based on hard work in return for learning lots and increasing their employability substantially. It also can come at a cost, given the number of ex-consultants from professional services firms I have met who are exhausted.

There is more of a shadow here, however, and a key part to how the model sustains itself. Fundamentally it's an illusory promise of learning because Grinders have to do handle-turning projects (e.g. the equivalent of producing sausages) that have been de-risked. The other promise is big money, travel, expense accounts, the potential to become a partner, and even if they fail to make it to partner (most don't due to the 'up or out' policy that stops there being too many Minders) they get outplaced to client organisations … where they hire back their old firm, thereby ensuring a future supply of ready clients.

Maybe the most revealing feature of how Grinders are recruited is that some large consultancies explicitly look for 'insecure overachievers'. One of my interviewees talked himself out of a job at McKinsey because he said he was quite secure in himself. If consultancies are recruiting for this quality, it suggests that shame is being baked in early on for some who choose consulting as a career, and the next generation of fragile helpers are being groomed. The lived experience of one former consultant who joined PWC early in their career was that large consultancies are "a breeding ground for insecure overachievers and chew them up and spit them out. They play on your insecurities and that is why you get hooked."[189] This, maybe, is how the succession planning works. As one ex-director of a professional services firm suggested, it was telling that a colleague of his once said, "all senior partners are paranoid".[190]

Got … to … get … me … some … leverage …

Now we come to the nub of Maister's work, and how professional services firms operate. In a nutshell, *leverage* is how consultancies make money. In simple terms, there is Low Leverage, based on what he called a Tall Pyramid. This might consist of one partner, one manager and one consultant, and typically would be focused on a more strategic or specialised assignment.

High Leverage revolves around Flat Pyramids, with maybe one partner, a few managers and herds of consultants.

It is the ratio between the three groups that determines the shape of the pyramid, where a Tall Pyramid suggests a lower leverage ratio, therefore it will take more time for the fewer number of bodies to deliver.

A Flat Pyramid, by contrast, has a higher leverage and more bodies. You may bill a gaggle of bright young things out at a lower rate, but the more of them you deploy, the greater the profits. It turns out that the way you ensure that your business is profitable as a consulting firm operating that model is you need to mobilise large numbers of Grinders with a small number of Minders. And that machinery needs to be fed by the Finders whose primary job is to (up)sell large assignments that mobilise large numbers of junior people. Natch.

---

189. Conversation 19th February 2024
190. Conversation 5th September 2023

This is where professional services firms make their money, making a margin on every consultant they can deploy through a process of 'land and expand'. At its best, this means you can buy in resource when you need it. At its worst, it is an incentive for more self-serving consultancies to create dependency and need.

Fine lines

In a column in *The Times*, journalist Pravina Rudra observed that while consultants' charge high day rates, only a third of that constitutes their actual pay. The balance covers costs to the consultancy. "What clients really pay for is the intellectual property that comes in the consultant's briefcase — spreadsheets, templates and case studies" ('Consultants play the role of therapists to government', *The Times* 30-10-2020).

This tension is illustrated by my client who had previously worked for Accenture. He beautifully described the Flat Pyramid:

> "You literally sell a predictable methodology, where you say 'follow this, and we will give you predictable outcomes'. So, I have absolutely been there myself, you're a salesperson as a consultant, to some degree, and part of what you're selling is certainty, predictability, guarantees. And, to be fair, you are also selling a huge amount of experience and expertise you're bringing to it."[191]

That, in a nutshell, is the sales pitch for many professional services firms. The shadow is not far away, however.

> "I got to the point where I needed a change; I realised that I would get more rewarded as a consultant for selling on three months of work for a project team than I would get for actually helping the client to effectively manage change, and to create some kind of more sustainable kind of approaches or answers for itself.
>
> That's where it started to stick in my craw: I realised I could get more rewarded for selling on bodies and project work than I could do for actually being more genuinely client-based." (Ibid.)

The business model here is prone to fluctuations that can easily send the consultancy from profitability to loss-making if hourly billing shifts even a few

---

191. Interview 18th May 2020

percentage points. For Grinders you go from making shedloads of money and getting massive bonuses to looking like you might not be around soon: the first to go will be unutilised grunts.

It is a business model that is very sensitive to 'billability' and driving junior consultants is key to that. Now, they're bright and inexperienced so if most of the work is intellectual analysis, you can standardise and create 'one size fits all' methodologies that edits out the risk and requires little management because it's repetitive. You turn the handle, *á la* the organ grinder and their monkey, and make money. Consultancies approach their work in the way that they do partly because they're part of the structures that support the Silver Bullet myth. This is reinforced by the fact that their establishments and simplified models interact to generate greater turnover and possibly profit for them. Their approach in the world is distorted by the fact that a reductionist model isn't just more sellable to senior leaders: it can be managed by the simplified but billable activity of a significant chunk of your workforce.

This approach works for the client until they are faced with more complex and messy questions, such as should we diversify, which market should we go into, culture change, behaviour change or any number of challenges that human systems throw up.

Consultancies don't help clients build capability

"It is difficult to get a man to understand something, when his salary depends on his not understanding it." Upton Sinclair (1934: 109)

The huge systemic flaw in the relationship between many consultancies and their clients boils down to the dependency it creates: if the primary service you are providing is one that does not enable the organisation to learn, you are creating the conditions for learned helplessness. Waisberg and Nelson suggest consultancies that use step-by-step and template-driven approaches give "the *illusion* of customised, bottom-up, and client-driven solutions when, in fact, the junior consultants were encouraged to simply reuse prior solutions" (2018: 426).

In one sense it is totally understandable. You've got senior people in a consulting firm, the Finders, who are co-dependent with client-side senior executives, because the senior executives need the consultants to answer the complex problems, normally because the senior executives don't talk to their own people who could tell them the answers. A good example of this is every episode ever of the TV programme *Undercover Boss*, where the moral of the story is typically 'leader-learns-something-really-important-they-would-never-have-known-had-they-not-spoken-to-the-people-who-actually-create-value-in-their-organisation'. It is a wonderful example of how things are simply not joined up in many organisations, and no wonder senior executives need the plausible deniability of a consultant, sometimes one after the other overriding what came before with newer, shinier presentations and models.

The problem comes when you want real change, and even more of an issue if it is change that you want to learn how to facilitate/influence/create/lead yourself. That requires capability building, and, as we have seen above, that cuts right against the business model.

Bringing this back to the Wizard of Oz, he is not really a magician, although everyone thinks he is, and yes, he helps the other characters get what they want (a heart, brain, courage and to go home). The moral of the story is that all of them did not know where to look or have confidence in their own answers. Like the wizard, a consultant's "value often just lies in validating their client's own decisions pointing the way or just giving clients confidence to act on their own knowledge" (*Magic Consultants* Episode 5, BBC Radio, 18-08-2023). To be fair to the wizard, he probably didn't charge upwards of £10,000 per day, which is a conservative estimate for a partner at a large firm. The collusive aspect is that some clients will only work with consultants if they charge that much. One consultant I know of had to charge a global bank £10,000 a day because if he charged them his normal £2,000, they would not think he was good enough …

'Future fit'

Geoff Marlow believes it is vital:

> "… to differentiate between the traditional perspective on culture as a case of 'cultural fit' versus the need for 'future fitness'. In the former the question is 'will you fit in to what we already have?' In the latter it's 'will you contribute to developing the muscles we'll need in the future, even though no one knows what they'll be?'
>
> You've got to build up new muscles, you have to exercise them, your muscles for being innovative, for being agile, for interacting in ways that

are adaptiive … All of that muscle building has to be done by the people in the organisation."[192]

That last line is key, because it loops right back to the tension that the professional services business model has baked into it: profit and scaling is dependent on selling in more products, services and bodies, *not* helping clients to do things for themselves. That is not to say that the pitch from a consultant will not promise capability building, but that is not necessarily the offer or intent. The client-side perspective from a Chief Human Resources Officer was that:

> "… what they do very little of is talk about the issues around culture and the difficult things that might impede a programme working successfully, because it's a bit messy and a bit grey … it's harder to sell a solution for that, so they focus on the stuff you can handle, which is mostly some kind of financial metric."[193]

Consulting firms are possibly at their most disingenuous here, in that if they did genuinely build capability, they would be cutting their own throats. In the same way that planned obsolescence became a business strategy for manufacturers from the 1950s onwards, so creating the need, from a capitalist perspective, to maintain the learned helplessness of organisations and perpetuate dependency.

It helps to know the role your consultant is playing, and whether you agreed to it

It is worth lingering for a moment on one of the classic texts in consulting, Peter Block's *Flawless Consulting* (1999). Block's work as a consultant and author is seminal and has influenced both the theory and practice of consulting in multiple fields.

Ed Schein, Block says, identified "three ways consultants work with line managers: in an expert role, a pair-of-hands role, or a collaborative role. The choice depends on individual differences in management style, the nature of the task, and the consultant's own personal preference"[194] (Block, 2000: 21).

---

192. Interview 24th February 2023
193. Interview 26th June 2020
194. The thinking around consulting modes has moved on very little since Schein's initial thinking in the 1960s, although in the next chapter, as I consider consulting practice and ethics at an individual level, I will touch on where there has been some evolution of thought.

Pair-of-hands mode

Solve a technical problem, using the client's model of change

This is the role Grinders typically play. In this mode, the consultant operates as an extra pair of hands for the client and manages a technical change on their behalf. The client (or manager) has control, having already diagnosed what needs to be achieved and the change methods. The consultant's role is to apply their specialist knowledge to 'manage the change'.

The consultant may provide recommendations to the client for them to review, as in the expert mode below. If the client doesn't accept those recommendations, or they fail, this is where problems of ownership and accountability could arise. The consultant is at risk of being scapegoated, when in truth the solutions put forward are dependent on the client's diagnosis and model of change.

Often, it's a task that is felt to be unpalatable, of course, such as downsizing. The leader has to maintain the currency of trust to ensure that they can count on the workforce to be followers. Hence, they literally get someone in to do the dirty work, so that they can appear untarnished by the process they patently kickstarted.

Expert mode

Use specialist knowledge to design bespoke solutions

In this mode the consultant is responsible for data gathering, diagnosing the problem and typically developing bespoke solutions. This mode is relevant for process or system changes where cause and effect are predictable or change parameters are known.

Whether the solution is fit for purpose depends on the accuracy of the diagnosis; how much the consultant understands the business; if the client has shared data openly and honestly; or if the consultant has the right expertise for this problem.

The challenge with this approach is that implementing new changes usually requires a change to working practices. There is often the assumption the consultant will 'sell in' their solution, yet the client might not be ready to adopt it. Crucially, the consultant isn't expected to develop the client's ability or readiness to adopt the change and take ownership of it beyond delivery.

Collaborative mode

Empower the client to own the change.

In this mode, the consultant facilitates the client's readiness for, and ownership of the change. The consultant knows that change agency lies with the client. The client is responsible for identifying issues and building a common perspective around these throughout their organisation.

The consultant starts where the client is in their readiness/maturity and facilitates the client step by step to implement a process that solves the problem, considering all influencing factors, e.g. strategic direction, success factors, cultural climate and the external environment. The intention is to make the change sustainable by developing the organisation's readiness and capacity to own the change during and beyond implementation.

This mode demands a high level of trust-building with the client. Challenges arise if the client becomes dependent on the consultant as expert if they feel challenged in their capability. It is also going to test just how much the consultant really is up for genuinely being in partnership, or is really trying to disguise the dependency that may be emerging.

Block's thinking in relation to the Collaborative mode are worth quoting in full here:

> "When consultants work through a collaborative role, *they don't solve problems for the manager. They apply their special skills to help managers solve problems. The distinction is significant.* The key assumption underlying the collaborative role is that the manager must be actively involved in data gathering and analysis, in setting goals and developing action plans, and, finally, in sharing responsibility for success or failure." Block (2000: 25) (My emphasis.)

Contrast that with the cases I highlighted earlier from ex-consultants, describing the reluctance to engage in genuine capability building. It also raises a question in terms of how consultancies market themselves. If you read the sales collateral of most consultancies – large and small – they tend towards promising certainty and answers. Typically, they sit comfortably in the Expert position, and the broadcasting they do through multiple channels amplifies this narrative.

They are also skilled at selling a Pair of Hands, particularly the large professional services firms, where deploying people in numbers is key to their sustainability.

What you see less of is the third mode, Collaborative, understandably so, because that is not where the money is. As Geoff Marlow succinctly puts it:

> "In the Finders/Minders/Grinders firms the grey hairs are the Finders whose sole focus is to sell large teams of Grinders, not to help managers solve problems. Doing the latter would be doubly counterproductive – firstly it would reduce the need for consulting firm help, and secondly it would divert the Finder's attention from filling the sales pipeline. Finders would be (doubly) insane to even contemplate operating in Collaborative mode."[195]

The psychological dependency that underpins this

The consultant modes can also be used to reveal something of the psychological processes inherent in the client-consultant relationship. Alastair Wylie, an experienced consultant who has worked across multiple industries and with many consultancies, mapped the consultant modes to the ego states in Transactional Analysis. His idea is simple.

The Expert mode is largely a function of the Adult and Parent ego states in a consultancy engaging with the Child ego state of the client. It appeals to the helplessness they feel, and there is a parental quality to the 'consultant knows best' stance that some clients slip into to assuage their anxiety.

The Pair of Hands mode is the reverse. The client knows what the problem is, they know how they want it handled, they just want to buy in the skills and/or bodies to do the job. 'Client knows best', so they become Parent.

The Collaborative mode is the only one that invites both sides into an adult/adult relationship, where the invitation to both parties is to share responsibility for identifying the problem and working out how to address it.

---

195. Interview 24th February 2023

The challenge with the Collaborative mode is that it requires both sides to work harder to both work out what is wrong and how to tackle it which may require some crunchy conversations. It might require assumptions being challenged and could entail some risk taking and experimentation.

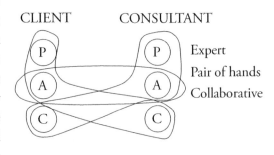

Is it any wonder many clients prefer the ease of the first two and many consultancies are happy to collude with that, even if it is not what is going to make a difference?

My own experience is that there can be a blurring of the modes, sometimes for good or ill. I was once asked to conduct a review of a finance function's operations (Expert) but the actual agenda was that the client wanted me to provide evidence to support the replacement of the Finance Director. There was a fine line here: I drew this out and told the client if I found no such supporting evidence I would not collude with that agenda, to which they agreed. The point was moot, as they were right unfortunately.

I have also worked on projects where I have agreed to work in all three modes, moving between them depending on task and context. This blurring of the boundaries and more nuanced approach is less easy to sell, however, and requires consultants to be fleet of foot and humble enough to move one moment from a position of expert to that of service.

That's the 'big boys' but what about the rest

The focus in this chapter has been on large firms, rather than small to medium consultancies because it is with the former that functional collusion and dependence is most clearly seen. None the less, many of the same observations could be made of smaller firms who draw on the discourse of certainty. Maybe that should not be a surprise, as the revolving doors between firms large and small often see the same people and therefore thinking moving between them.

There are outliers, the boutique consultancies and mavericks who collude only so far or flat out refuse to play that game. I work with a number of these, and do have relationships with some larger entities where there is a tension between how I see the world and the ways in which they collude with their clients' anxieties. In the next chapter, I will explore the implications for individual practitioners.

The systemic nature of the problem

In this chapter, I have laid out some of the ways that consulting firms are not only part of the functional collusion around Silver Bullets for complex problems, but may also be invested in perpetuating it.

If large consultancies and professional services firms were to reconsider their approach, to fundamentally question the Finders/Grinders/Minders model, then they would likely be very different organisations; the way they talk about change would not be the same and they would probably be smaller. They would probably consist more of Finders, fewer permanent Minders and Grinders and a more dispersed network of resources that they would call on as needs arise, and, therefore, would be able to respond to emerging and new challenges more effectively because they would not be wedded to selling the skills and capabilities they have in-house, nor to a set of models, tools, frameworks and methodologies they have expended considerable time and money on in the name of demonstrating their 'thought leadership'.

Again, this is not to say that there are not instances where a large gaggle of bright young things would be just what is needed, rather there is a need for a rebalancing in the way organisations engage with consultancies, how they contract and what they contract for.

Turkeys do not vote for Christmas

Behavioural economist Dan Ariely and colleagues conducted some fascinating research into the impact of different-sized bonuses on performance. The results were clear, demonstrating a motivational double-edged sword:

> "For tasks that require cognitive ability, low to moderate performance-based incentives can help. But when the incentive level is very high, it can command too much attention and thereby distract the person's mind

with thoughts about the reward. This can create stress and ultimately reduce the level of performance." (Ariely, 2011: 36)

The research subjects were in India, to make it possible to replicate the different levels of bonus in an affordable but meaningful way for the subjects and researchers. Ariely acknowledges that one view might be that in the 'real world', employers and compensation boards would account for lower levels of performance and not offer incentives that would degrade performance. The problem is, further research demonstrated that "the negative effect of high bonuses is not something that people naturally intuit" (Ariely, 2011: 37), and we need to rely less on inkling and more on empirical research.

More damning are Ariely's experiences of engaging with executives and boards to test out whether they would be prepared to abandon their assumptions around bonuses. The answer is they are not; they tend to regard themselves as 'super special' people who work well under stress. Invited to come to Ariely's lab to engage in experiments to test that out, one group of execs refused: "it was impossible to tempt them to take part in our experiments or to offer them a bonus that would have been large enough to be meaningful for them" (ibid.: 38).

Consider the implications of this at an ethical level for a moment. Senior executives in consulting firms, who earn large bonuses while selling 'data-driven/informed services', telling their clients how important it is to do an organisational diagnosis and crunch the numbers, who make lots of money advising on how to transform culture – and therefore by definition values and beliefs – seem remarkably immune from anything that disrupts their business model.

That unwillingness to challenge one's own assumptions is mirrored on the client side, with a reluctance or inability to move beyond anything other than perpetuating a functional collusion. In turn, that sustains both status, power and privilege while maintaining the pretence that there is no alternative, feeding the market for Silver Bullets.

The bottom line

There is a peculiar irony in all this. On the one hand, the need to build capability is greater than ever, and the systemic flaws (e.g. the leverage structure, the tendency to create evermore dependency, an over reliance on insecure overachievers, etc.) in the consulting business model work against that. Yet as the pressure to grow increases, so too does the rhetoric, and in turn the desire to look for – and sell – Silver Bullets. Critiquing consulting and consultancies can lead to accusations of axe grinding or that you have a political point to make. What if both were true? What if that was a response to the vast amount of PR in favour of the industry, and the cosiness of relationships, e.g. between public sector bodies and consultancies? What if critiquing systemic flaws does require questioning the fundamentals of how we organise and do business? After all, what happens in organisations does not do so in a vacuum, it reflects the norms, values and priorities of us all.

Part of the structural issue lies in the unregulated and opaque nature of the industry. It has its tentacles – for good or ill – in many places, yet is unregulated, other than when their activities stray into accounting or legal adjacencies. Sometimes there are efforts to manage these tensions. For example, partly to address the concerns about the relationship between government and the consulting industry, a UK government consultant hub was established by the UK government in 2021. Its purpose was to help reduce the amount that the government spent on consultancy. After less than two years later, it was quietly scrapped.

Should consulting be a profession? Maybe. You can sue an accountant, lawyer, doctor or teacher, as professions like these have standards they are expected to adhere to. Consultancies would argue they have values. Yes they do, although that does not seem to have prevented issues arising.

The various scandals that get reported are less down to a lack of technical competence, rather it is a specific shortfall in capability: the capacity for robust and open conversations that do not shy from discomfort, and which may evoke shame in either client and/or consultant. Those conversations may be about why there is no easy answer, or a need to hold a mirror up to dysfunctional behaviour at senior level, or to fundamentally question a business model rather than take the money to sustain it. These are conversations that necessarily rub up against power, undiscussables, what is taboo, hidden, denied and shameful. The cost of not talking about these is too often hidden out of sight, as the cases in Chapter 10 will illustrate, and talk to the painful truth that it is the collusion between leaders and organisations that pay for solutions and the consultancies that offer them: both buyers and sellers are part of this dance.

The irony is we have many people *outside* of organisations with the very skills that are required *inside*. There are hordes of consultants and practitioners doing very well *not* being on the inside. Many of them have a vested interest in maintaining that dependency, even while they may talk about capability building. That can create an ethical tear when you are asked to do something that is more about revenue generation and less about building genuine capability. This plays out at the level of the individual consultant or practitioner of change, raising several questions about those of us who operate in that space.

A larger question, which is worthy of further inquiry, is whether consultancies, particularly larger ones, actually 'consult'. The word originally comes from the Latin for 'take counsel', which itself means 'discuss a problem'. It does not mean take at face value the Silver Bullet on offer, or shy away from talking about messiness.

We need to start to describe what they do in a different language to many of their smaller competitors who are not bound by the same need to sustain a monolithic business model at all costs, and equally acknowledge that ethical and unethical practice can show up in any one of us.

Reflective Questions

- What makes you think you do not already have the capability you need in your own organisation? How do you know?
- Do you find yourself privileging external voices and, if so, why do you think that might be?
- How aware are you of collective and individual anxiety as you make decisions on whether to buy in external support? Is that even discussable?
- What would it take to trust your own decision making and people before bringing in outside support? What capability building and learning might you need to undertake to enable that?
- How much of a day rate is too much before you ask yourself whether anyone, really, is worth that much?

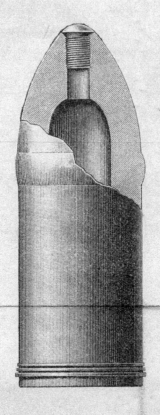

SILVER BULLET NO. 13

FANCY SLIDE DECK

This slide deck has taken a team of five consultants a couple of hours to put together.
It really is very whizzy with lots of transitions and some impressive models.
That is why we are charging you a six figure sum for it.

HOW THIS UNFOLDS AT THE LEVEL OF INDIVIDUAL CONSULTANTS AND PRACTITIONERS OF CHANGE

OR: WHY WE ARE ALL CULPABLE

Chapter 8:
How this Unfolds at the Level of Individual Consultants and Practitioners of Change

Given the scale of the consulting industry, and not just the large players, the reality is that *individual* consultants and experts are often the people involved in initial conversations with clients regarding a solution, and/or are brought in to help find or implement one. The simple reason for that is that Silver Bullets are most sought for when anxiety in the client system is at its highest, and the belief is strongest that the solution must lie outside.

The *practice* of consulting (or management consulting as it is often framed in an organisational context), the expertise and ethics that accompany that, and the intentionality of individual consultants, are crucial to understanding how the functional collusion sustains itself. It would be all too easy to blame gurus, theories, theorists, business schools, the purveyors of solutions and various consultancy firms for what happens. That lets those of us who sit on the helping side of the relationship with our clients off the hook, for ultimately these are ethical questions that unfold at an individual level.

Why organisations engage consultants

An ethnographic and literature review-based study by Waisberg and Nelson (2018: 433–434) found that organisations turn to consultants to obtain and use external knowledge when employees, for example:

1. Do not have the skills or the time to search for relevant information, or have the skills to make external knowledge applicable to their organisational situation.
2. Do not have the capability to transfer knowledge across organisations and organisational silos and units.
3. Are bound by the politics of the organisation.
4. Have sufficient experience across different organisational boundaries to contextualise knowledge.

Notice how much of the list above is in effect driven by the *lack of capability* client-side, and, once an organisation focuses on building capability, the need for external support declines. Let's assume however that a client has good need to hire an external consultant. What, exactly, is it they look for?

What organisations *think* they are buying is not the same as what they *get*

David Shaw, a former management consultant who is now a writer and researches around organisational change and consulting, conducted a meta-analysis of research in 2019. It found that what organisations look for, and expect, are broadly:

1. expertise; and
2. a bespoke and customised service and solution(s) to their issues.

In short, organisations think they are buying expertise, namely people who 'know their stuff' and know how to customise it to their situation/problem. Thus the 'bespoke solution' becomes the key motivating factor when it comes to engaging an external expert.

What is interesting about Shaw's paper is it starts to peel the onion on the ethical dilemmas and tensions at play, predicaments that unfold at both consultancy and an individual level.

To take expertise for a moment, I know from my own work that clients often want me to establish what I am an 'expert in'; given how my practice has evolved in recent years, that is often framed as inquiring into the extent to which I have expertise and knowledge in Organisation Development and culture change. I notice a need, often, for clients to be able to label me, to locate me within a frame of reference that allows them to a) know what I am expert in, in relation to what they are looking for, b) assess my credibility, and c) the extent to which that means I can help them.

That is all well and good, and sometimes I sense an abdication of responsibility, or a hope that I will come with The Answer. I was once asked, at the start of a two-day consulting skills programme, why the group should listen to me. I found myself laughing as I answered: "You shouldn't. I have some questions, a few suggestions, I know some stuff, but if you think you 'should' listen to me because I have the 'answer', I do not."

This is one overt example of an invitation from a client to step into a functional collusion and a dependent relationship, and was a seminal moment for me, as it clarified for me what kind of consultant I wanted to be.

It also hints at practice maturity. Early-career consultants and organisational practitioners understandably have a greater need to acquire knowledge and 'tool themselves up'. I find myself colluding on consulting skills programmes with that need, until such a point when I can begin deconstructing the mythology that tools in and of themselves are what make the difference.

Tensions that consultants wrestle with

Shaw (2019) further looked at the impact management consultants and consultancies have on change projects, suggesting four primary conflicts or tensions are at play:

1. Implementing recognised industry 'best practice' versus innovating and being 'cutting edge'.
2. Creating change versus meeting expectations and instructions.
3. Engaging in and dealing with the politics in the organisation versus giving impartial and professional advice.
4. Reusing industry-standard change methods versus creating bespoke solutions.

These tensions, and how consultants choose to work with them, create a form of 'routinised knowledge', that constitute something of what lurks in the shadows of the client/consultant relationship, and is often undiscussable. It also talks to the pattern identified in the last chapter, namely that it is in the interests of consultants and consultancies to create dependency. So, how this knowledge is used, or rather not, is directly related:

- It is rarely made explicit and open to clients.
- Good knowledge management practices are rarely applied.
- They are rarely open to challenge.
- They are rarely systematically informed by peer-reviewed research.

Lastly, and representing a thread that connects this and the previous three chapters, Shaw found that consultants tend to dress up 'routinised knowledge' as cutting edge, innovative and based on research when it isn't.

Hello Silver Bullet, my old friend…

Consultant as magician

In a sense we are arriving back where we started, namely in the magical and mythical realm. If Silver Bullets are the stuff of folklore and beast-slaying Buffy-esque[196] popular culture, then consultants have an air of mystique also.

Clark and Salaman's seminal 1996 paper compared the dance of management consultants and gurus to that of witch doctors. Both have a high need to create 'magic' and 'mystery' to protect their knowledge, simultaneously using it to create a performance – the dance – designed to impress the client. Think less of a bird of paradise spreading its wings to woo a mate, but more a cross between John Travolta as Tony Manero in *Saturday Night Fever* with a touch of Joey Tribbiani from *Friends* chatting someone up with a 'How YOU doin'?'

Farrington and Clark's (2000) wonderfully titled article '*Snake oil, science, and performance products*', found that consultants often purposefully avoid or obviate a focus on whether their solutions work and make things better, instead choosing to major on client satisfaction. This connects with what you may have picked up in the last chapter, namely the tendency of consultancies to avoid rocking the boat and to stay out of trouble rather than risk damaging the client relationship, and hence jeopardise their income. This is about impression management, and many consultants have been found to focus on that and more subjective measures, according to Wright & Kitay (2002: 277), whose interviews of both consultants and clients highlighted:

> "… the continued centrality of the informal and subjective aspects of organisational change. Indeed, many of the consultants we interviewed were well aware of the need to carefully manage client impressions."

Wright and Kitay's findings from their interviews with clients and consultants (from individual, small-, medium- and large-sized organisations) go on to suggest that the larger consultancies have been offering 'bottom-line' measures of results in response to criticisms of consultants, which, when actually analysed, are usually fairly simplistic and infer causal relationships where none exist. Again, the consultancies are caught between wanting to show cause and effect, for impression purposes, while managing client expectations. They argue such measures have been found to raise client expectations, thus requiring even greater impression management efforts.

---

196. *Buffy The Vampire Slayer*, a popular teen drama series.

This is a fundamental ethical and moral malaise. While much has been written about the ills of the consulting industry, and a smaller but nonetheless significant body of literature exists that talks to what 'having' a consulting practice requires, there is less written about the psychological factors that might be at play that result in consultants being less principled than they like to believe they are.

The Unholy Trinity

I want to touch on what might be termed an Unholy Trinity of Shame, Ego and Narcissism. These are all at play in a leadership context, but let's consider how they show up for consultants and practitioners of change more widely, regardless of the label they may adopt. Let's start with the key terms:

- *Ego*
  Who we take ourselves to be. Made up of self-images and ego ideal (Superego).

- *Shame*
  The feeling of failing to live up to ego ideals and fearing rejection and inclusion.

- *Narcissism*
  1. The process of identifying with self-images and ego ideals.
  2. The process of manipulating the environment to maintain self-images and ego ideals through narcissistic supplies.

The structures, processes and experiences of all three are in our shadow to the extent that we are not aware of them and they 'have us'. As we become aware of them, we can 'have them' and we have more choice about whether we are run by them – if we name them, we can tame them.

What happens when we are not comfortable with the idea of getting uncomfortable, is that this Unholy Trinity starts to bend us out of shape. It can manifest in several ways, not least:

- a pervasive anxiety about being good enough;
- self-doubt;
- tendency to judge self and other;
- grandiosity as a defence against the above;
- preoccupation with appearing 'good' in others' eyes; and
- perfectionism.

Take a moment to consider, if you are reading this from the perspective of a client, how some of these might show up in you, or if you have experienced them in others, particularly consultants. A clue will be how you felt at the time. If you read this as a practitioner, what resonates with you? Ever had feelings and thoughts of 'not good enough-ness', or had those amplified by interactions with clients? Do you ever judge yourself? Clearly you never tend to grandiosity, eh?

How this shows up

If that is the internal wrestling that the Unholy Trinity can spark, the key question is how that manifests in practice. The following is a list that emerged from reflections with my colleague Simon Cavicchia, as we reflected on how the Unholy Trinity might show up in our work.

- *Preoccupation with status* – living up to self-images and ego ideals – think for a moment about 'thought leadership', both the ego that sometimes is on display, and the narratives at play around what it takes to 'become one'. In professional services, it shows up in the Finders/Minders/Grinders model, and is baked in.

- *Difficulty with not knowing* – given knowledge capital is an ego ideal in client systems e.g. that moment a client asks what you would recommend, and you don't know.

- *Denial of human vulnerability and the lonely hero/strong man narrative* – this links back to Chapter 3, and how we still – socially, culturally, politically and in organisations – seem addicted to heroic leadership. Consultants are not immune, and that aspect of our own shadow can be evoked particularly with a client that is unconsciously seeking to be rescued or parented.

- *Terror of dependency* – the corollary of the above, this is when we fear becoming dependent on others. Our patterns of behaviour become characterised by a need to remain independent, and inhibits our capacity for intimacy and relationships. Not ideal when what is needed is a genuine trust.

- *'Facipulation'* – a word Simon Cavicchia coined by combining 'facilitation' and 'manipulation' during our work to describe how our own unconscious need for control or self-protection, or worse still unhealthy desire for domination, leads us to manipulate our clients through the use of our skills and practice.

- *Intoxication of client projections, with 'expertise' the most common* – there is a difference between a client seeking evidence of knowledge and credibility, or of appropriate appreciation for services rendered and impact, and colluding with the idea that you are able to do things they would never be able to/know things they will never know/are better at something than they will ever be. I love an ego stroke as much as anyone, and there is a healthy aspect to this. When our egos get fluffed to the point of narcissistic self-love and grandiosity, then there is a problem.

- *Over reliance on control and less support for the unknown and emergent* – another aspect of our own anxieties derailing us, consultants can be prone to lean on models, theories, tools and methodologies not just because they are sales collateral. They are a good way of pretending that we are more in control than we really are. If both client and consultant are anxious, is it any wonder Black Box solutions and Silver Bullets are so appealing?

- *Overemphasis on forces for compliance rather than risking differentiation* – low innovation/thinking outside the box – innovation requires experimentation and risk taking. That might mean challenging norms *within* consultancies. For example, one consultant I know, with thirty years' experience across multiple firms and sectors, was advising a client to move to the cloud using Amazon Web Services. His firm were developing its own host cloud solution and "didn't even have a thing that worked at that point. And they didn't have any customers." As a result, the consultant sold the client several million £s of Amazon services. "I got called into the office by one of the senior people – they just said 'what the hell are you doing?', when I thought I would get a 'well done'. They wanted me to sell in our solution, and I pointed out it wasn't even ready. The response I got was 'when I have that kind of issue, what I tend to do is I look at the top of my payslip and see whose logo is on it'."

- *Avoidance of anything that might risk a rupture in relationship, e.g. straight talking, feedback, challenge* – this links back to the psychological defences we use as defences against anxiety, as well as the fear of risking losing business.

- *Defence of superiority if people don't 'get' what we are offering* – sometimes I can sense my own ego feeling a little bruised if a client doesn't understand what I think is obvious. That is normally data about me first, and the client second. Not the other way round.

- *We talk about reflective practice but avoid it* – while there is much talk in practitioner communities about reflective practice, I am often surprised at either how little is *actually* done and the lack of depth. I totally understand this, because to genuinely inquire into your practice and impact requires a willingness to go furtling in your own shadows and, yes, maybe even things like your relationship with your mum and/or dad, etc. It is not for everyone, or necessary all the time. If, however, we are to be of service to our clients we need to be willing to work on our own shit if we are going to be working with others at what may often be the moments of stress and anxiety when their own unconscious and unresolved issues come into play.

- *Deeper shadows, e.g. gender, race, sexuality etc.* – often these may be undiscussable, and the fact they are undiscussable may in and of itself be undiscussable (Argyris, 1980: 206). As a white, straight, middle-aged, middle-class man, I am aware that my client relationships will evolve differently to a peer who is possibly female, in their thirties and a person of colour. Even at gatherings of supposedly equally enlightened brethren, I have noticed how conversations around difference are remarkably uncomfortable once we move beyond the superficial to exploring what we are really thinking and feeling.

An ethical blind spot

In the past few years, I have developed a working hypothesis about the consulting profession, that spans all disciplines and specialisms within it: we have a blind spot when it comes to doing our own work on our 'stuff', which in turn means, at best, we are not as effective as we could be.

At worst, we advocate medicine that we are not prepared to take ourselves, e.g. 'you need to improve the self-awareness and capacity for constructive conflict in your leadership team', while simultaneously not working on our own fear of conflict. I know that tension well: as the son of an alcoholic, it took me a long time to understand how my relationship with conflict – and avoidance of it –

permeated my relationships, personal and professional. Was it easy work? No. Did it take a session or two of coaching to resolve? No: it was years of ongoing inquiry and therapy, yet incredibly fruitful, and hard, and revelatory, and uncomfortable, and liberating, and more.

I start with the assumption of positive intent on the part of any practitioner working with a client, regardless of whether they are a McKinsey or PwC consultant, boutique or small firm, or an independent and unaffiliated. In the literature on organisational change, there is a view (which I subscribe to also), that the consultant is in effect an intervention in and of themselves, e.g. Cheung-Judge and Holbeche (2021), Cheung-Judge (2001), Block (1981). Merely by walking in the room, they are introducing a difference, even if they say nothing.

In the field of Organisation Development, this idea is central to the philosophy of change. There is the notion of 'self as instrument' (Cheung-Judge, 2001), and the idea that the OD practitioner needs to model something of the difference that the system needs.

> "Often, OD people in organisations add value by standing for or modelling something important that is a little different to the mainstream of the organisation. Whether it's a 'big picture', whole-systems orientation, a focus on people and values or some desirable aspect of the organisation's culture the OD person often becomes a standard-bearer for it. *This is not always a comfortable place to be. It can feel lonely and carries political risks. Wise practitioners develop strategies for resilience and support* [my italics]." (Martin Saville, 2014: 43)

That is the theory at any rate. Unfortunately, my experience is that few of us – whether internal or external – find the courage to challenge up as well as down. Organisations and those that help them with change typically load the responsibility for change onto those at the bottom of the pyramid, under direction of those above us and/or who hold the purse strings. That is a dynamic not without its complications.

How then do we take care of ourselves? Where do we go to do the work on ourselves when the anxiety and mess in our relationship with clients impacts us? If the discomfort we experience resonates with our unresolved or archaic distress, how do we learn to acknowledge and work with that while remaining of service to our client? Erik de Haan, Director of the Hult Ashridge Centre for

Coaching, suggests that "supervision is where we wipe the sweat from our brows and the dirt from our faces, wash our hands, look at ourselves in the mirror and get ready to become an 'ordinary' person again, without a 'role' or 'function'" (2012: 1). If we look in adjacent fields, we see that there is a strong culture for supervision, by which I mean "disciplined reflection-in-relation wherein case history and principles are transformed into new potential for action and skills" (de Haan, 2012: 2). In other words, a space where we get to make sense of our client work, ourselves and any crap that evokes in us, before we go back out into the world. Therapists and counsellors, clinicians, mental health professionals, etc. – all typically are offered supervisory space.

In the coaching world, it has long been advocated that coaches need a supervisor, although many do not. There are several places you can go to get a qualification in coaching supervision. There are many places to get certified, the most well-known being the International Coaching Federation (ICF), the European Mentoring and Coaching Council (EMCC) and less well-known bodies such as the Association for Professional Executive Coaches & Supervisors (APECS).

However, when it comes to *consulting* supervision, the picture is very different. Places to learn how to become a consulting supervisor are few, and notable exceptions are the Tavistock Institute for Human Relations (where I qualified) and Ashridge Hult. An accreditation scheme for this I have yet to find (if you know of one, please let me know).

As my own supervision practice has developed, I have explored with peers and clients why this is this case. What has emerged is that it is not that common for consultants to be in regular supervision. Given that our work directly impacts people, it is extraordinary that we do not attend more to talking with another in a formal relationship about what we see, hear and feel, what we are asked to do, what we end up doing, and how that is experienced by others.

I know through inquiring with supervisors in my network that there are large and small consulting firms that both encourage and facilitate supervision for their consultants, but it is nowhere near as common as coaching supervision.

Does this matter? In one sense no, if you assume that how consultants operate is largely fine as it is, that how we work with clients is with a genuine intention to be of service and build capability (which I suggest the consulting industry is not really that interested in, given much of the evidence), and that we are self-aware enough to know when we are not being present or are hooked by our own 'stuff'.

On the other hand, it matters because it goes to the heart of whether we are willing and able to challenge our clients, and not collude with them when all they really want is us to fix things for them, even if that fix leaves them ever more dependent on others and/or is a delusion, i.e. that the solution is no such thing, and is merely a panacea to allay anxiety for a short period of time.

These conversations, uncomfortable as they may be, go to the heart of our psychological well-being and capacity to engage in deep conversation to work through tensions and difference.

Do you tell a client what they *want* to hear or what they *need* to hear?

Mee-Yan Cheung-Judge told a story at a workshop I attended that described her work for a Singapore government organisation, and how she created a detailed project plan for the senior leadership team, to help them understand the work she was tasked with delivering. The kicker was this project plan was a fiction: she created it solely to allay their anxiety; she had no need for it herself. The question here is whether this merely serves to reproduce and amplify these expectations, leaving the status quo unchallenged while offering no challenge upward, or is a skilful way of managing the client's anxiety.

Cheung-Judge herself was aware of the importance of speaking truth, even if that might be uncomfortable. One of her regular challenges to OD consultants and practitioners was the extent to which we are willing to 'spit in the soup'. The metaphor was developed by the therapist Alfred Adler, who recognised that stirring up change can be difficult.

> "To motivate reorientation, I employ a mirror technique, confronting the patient with his goals and intentions … When the patient begins to recognise his goals, his own conscience becomes a motivating factor. Adler called this process 'spitting in the patient's soup'." (Dreikurs, 1973: 12)

Another way of thinking about this is to ask what it actually requires to change behaviour, particularly when that is underpinned and driven by anxiety, which is often the case when organisations are most desperate for a Silver Bullet.

That kind of learning is sometimes deemed transformational, although true transformation in organisations is a rare thing, because it is a little like having your suit dry-cleaned while you are still wearing it.[197] There is also a hitch with this kind of organisation-wide behaviour change. The very idea of 'changing hearts and minds' in a corporate context is overshadowed – particularly in respect to culture – by a strong sense of totalitarianism. You are either with us, or against us, is the subtext.

I see 'spitting in the soup' as a form of compressive intervention, which has a specific meaning. Consultants and facilitators Keith Jones and Tessa Sharp, in their book on transformative facilitation, *Provoke*, describe compression as:

> "… the point at which a learner encounters their past behaviour as a possible obstacle to achieving their desired objective, before moving into a more here and now experience of how changing that behaviour could change the outcome." (Jones, 2019: 158)

To work in this way is challenging. It requires role clarity, and even if you have been invited in to reveal what is really going on, it can still seem that the consultant is being set up to fail. Consultants are often heard telling stories of being shut down once they have lifted the carpets to reveal some of the dirt that lies beneath.

Lurking here again is the ethical tension, one that talks to the fragility of the consultant born of the ultimate existential fear, namely that of being fired, something that is rarely acknowledged or discussed, not least because it talks to our shame. Keith Jones told me, "I can think of times when I've adapted, agreed with what are palpably bullshit requests, knowing full well that whatever it is that they're asking for, would never be achieved within the structure that they're asking for. And I've agreed to do it, knowing full well it's bullshit, for fear of being rejected".[198] It is hard for a consultant to reveal their fragility to a client they know well, and vice versa, but, with sufficient trust and respect, it may be possible. With a new client, I suggest that would be nigh on impossible, and would require a high degree of emergent trust and a self/other awareness. I think we are a long way from that being anything other than a rare occurrence.

---

197. Hat tip to Robin Charney for that wonderful metaphor. "The irony is that digital transformation has so far proved pretty much impossible. I can't think of any established business that has ripped up its business model and replaced it with a new one, and still kept its doors open. The challenge is just too great; it's like dry-cleaning your suit while you're still wearing it." https://bit.ly/3o8MyP0

198. Interview 28th October 2021

Back to the beginning

Let's loop back to where we started, i.e. what drives that need for certainty? If you are a client faced with a complex organisational challenge and you have a choice as to whether to wrestle both with your own anxiety that might be getting in the way of your making an accurate assessment of both the problem and how to address it, or paying someone to do it for you, ideally with a guaranteed quick fix, is it any wonder that the market for Silver Bullets flourishes?

In that moment, what is our responsibility as the consultant or indeed any kind of helper they have approached? To challenge? To gently point out the emperor is wearing no clothes? To point out candidly absurdity or contradictions? Or is it to collude, go along with or stroke them, whether that be because we value the business more than anything else or are simply too scared to say anything challenging due to our own unresolved issues?

This brings to life the tensions inherent in the mantra of 'speaking truth to power'. It's a lovely idea, and certainly important. There are also plenty of people who have found their heads on spikes – literally and metaphorically – over the years having had the temerity to suggest that those in power may not be infallible.

One of my observations, having both been an internal and external change agent and consultant, worked alongside many and been a client, is that to be at the centre of change is to put yourself in the spotlight. The better you are at your job, the stronger the light that shines on you; often you can become a node through which the crazy flows, as being an effective change agent puts you front and centre as people make sense of what is happening. The projections and expectations are likely to be at their most acute at this moment, and it is then when we learn to what extent, truly, we are prepared to stand out from the crowd and take a contra position.

Unless you have something of the contrarian about you, you are little use to your clients

In early 2023, I had a series of exchanges with a peer about how they experienced me as being contrarian, to such a degree sometimes that they were nervous if they saw I had commented on one of their posts on LinkedIn. This sparked a fruitful inquiry.

Firstly, what is contrarianism? Adrian Furnham, a professor of psychology at University College London, pithily outlines the inherent tension here:

> "There are various synonyms for contrarianism, some positive, some neutral, some distinctly negative. Contrarians may be seen as courageous, unconventional, counterintuitive thinkers, able to withstand herding pressures and even abuse from crowd-following conformists.
>
> Others may see them as maverick, out-of-touch, denialists 'living on another planet' and unable to see the obvious. Some rejoice in the title while others shun it. It can be a label of both praise and condemnation.
>
> What makes an individual a contrarian? Why are they able to resist pressures to conform? And is this position always desirable? Psychologists and sociologists have been studying these questions for years, but have a radically different take on it.
>
> Sociologists are likely to see contrarian(s) … as deviants, while psychologists may see them as healthy, 'independent' thinkers."[199]

The Hans Christian Anderson story of *The Emperor's New Clothes* offers a vivid example of contrarianism, as well as a prescient satirical take on the relationship between some consultants and their clients. In the fairy tale, an emperor hires two tailors who promise to make him a set of remarkable new clothes that will be invisible to anyone who is either incompetent or stupid. When the emperor goes to see his new clothes, he sees nothing at all — because the tailors are liars, cheats and swindlers, merely pretending there are clothes. Afraid of being judged incompetent or stupid, the emperor pretends to be delighted with the new clothes and 'wears' them in a grand parade through the town. All the townsfolk pretend to see them, until one – contrarian – child yells out, "He hasn't got any clothes on!"

Throughout history through to today, there are multiple examples of people who have been described as contrarian for speaking out of turn:

- Galileo – for having the temerity to suggest the Earth orbits the sun.
- Václav Havel – the former dissident who became President of Czechoslovakia.
- Christopher Hitchens – author and journalist who became known for, among other things, his contrarianism in the face of religious orthodoxies.

---

199. https://www.ipe.com/ahead-of-the-curve-the-psychology-of-contrarianism/10033018.article

- Germaine Greer – feminist and academic who has found herself being labelled as contrarian at different points for different reasons in her career.
- The inaugural winner of the Contrarian Prize was Michael Woodford, the former CEO of Olympus who exposed a $1.7 billion fraud at the heart of the company and was sacked for doing so.

Whistle-blowers are inherently contrarian, as they go against a dominant narrative and challenge conventions and established ways of doing things. Often at huge cost to themselves. They can also be arrogant, self-serving, narcissistic and/or cruel, as can often been seen in the form of self-appointed populist moral arbiters of what is right and wrong, whether they be purveyors of retrograde forms of masculinity, former reality TV show contestants or louche and loud stand-up comedians. Some big names in organisational thinking and leadership are experienced or labelled as contrarian, or self-label as such. Dave Snowden, for example, sits in the mainstream, and is one of the most significant voices in modern complexity and systems thinking. He doesn't step back from challenging ideas to which he takes exception and is a self-described curmudgeon.[200] That makes him uncomfortable to some, but discomfort the contrarian wrong doth not make.

Making it personal

What is missing from this is an explicit recognition of the projections that are at play, for one person's contrarian is another's kindred spirit. The brutal unnuanced version of that shows up in the culture wars that play out on social media, but they are also present in more mundane settings. Bringing this back to myself, and my reflections on practice, more questions come up:

- Am I too challenging sometimes?
- To what extent have I leaned too far into my desire to highlight contradictions and what is being overlooked?
- Am I becoming predictable?
- When am I 'too much'?
- What, exactly, does it mean to be a contrarian, and is it a good or bad thing? If so, why?

Where this took me was to a place of considering the extent to which consultants need to be contrarian, or as a minimum have access to that

---

200. https://thecynefin.co/the-art-science-of-being-a-curmudgeon/

capability, if they are to be of any use. If they cannot take a contrarian position, then they will tend towards agreeing and ultimately colluding with their clients, even if at some level they know that may not be the most useful thing to do. Or they hold that part of themselves in check for fear of being rejected, expelled, attacked or any number of other imagined fantasies.

I chewed on this for a while, taking my inquiry to a peer group, out of which deeper questions arose. Is contrarianism:

- A label that we put on ourselves – which can be liberating (or not)?
- A label we put on others – which might lead us to dismiss them, if we're uncomfortable with what we experience as a challenge to our world view/current perspective/ideas etc?
- A role that we might adopt when we want to open things up – and therefore a skill?
- A stance of intellectual curiosity?
- A stance we might take just for the hell of it?

Robert Holley suggests that contrarians are valuable as "they can help avoid potential mistakes by presenting alternative viewpoints" (2019: 334). He goes on to point out that "management literature and general opinion are overly weighted to stress harmony and consensus as organisational values" and suggests that contrarians represent an important antidote to those who "take action without sufficient critical analysis, overlook threats to the organisation, predict overly optimistic results, and hamper diversity" (ibid.).

Mark Cole's work on power, voice and silence has led him to conclude that those who challenge the norm are othered in one of three ways.[201]

1. They may be seen as a Maverick, a person whose reflections and expressed views might be felt to run counter to the organisational fabric at this time but they are tolerable, amusing and (ultimately) ignorable, dismissible as a joker/clown.
2. They might be categorised as a Rebel, a slightly edgier and abrasive version of the Maverick, although still seen to be someone in the fold rather than outside of it.
3. They might be defined as a Trouble-Maker, which will see their manager on the phone to HR, asking how they can manage the person out of the organisation (even though the trouble they are making may simply be

---

201. Email 13th October 2023

to question the status quo in a way that reflects their annoyance at how things are around them in corporate life).

Lurking within that is also the suspicion that whether you are labelled as a Maverick or Trouble-Maker may come down to something as simple as whether you are white or black in some organisations …

My belief is that unless we understand contrarianism, in ourselves and others, we are further contributing to cultures where what matters is buried beneath layers of assumptions and story. Positions become entrenched, fears multiply, anxiety grows and the need to assuage that creates the conditions where it is easier to look for something that will make the pain go away rather than engage in inquiry, dialogue and debate, even if that is heated.

Silver Bullets show up in two respects here. Firstly, they may be pacifiers and instruments for anxiety management – 'take one of these and the pain will go away'. Secondly, they are the hallmark of the arrogant contrarian who knows (or thinks they know best): 'here take this, I have the answer, and I believe I am right.'

A model for contrarianism

This is one of the aspects of the functional collusion I describe in this book that requires us to take a whole system approach, to consider how, in this instance, contrarianism shows up for good or ill both in client and in consultant/help/ guru, etc. My own contrarianism I trace back to my father's status as a perennial outsider, a man in touch with his own essential and existential absurdity, caught in his own shadow and who struggled with his demons to the end.

While I am far from the troubled outsider he was, I was influenced by his relationship to the world around him. I have a microchip in my head that is not labelled 'Intel', rather it has the word 'Really?' etched in. It activates when I experience something contradictory and/or absurd, and the more absurd it is, the more there is a sense that people are unaware that, metaphorically, the emperor may be wearing no clothes, the louder it is, with increasing numbers of question and exclamation marks. It is this which has resulted in the creation of what I term the 'Really?' Continuum.

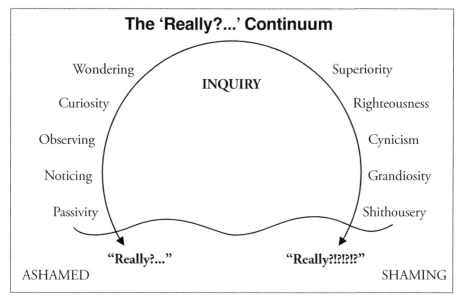

Essentially what we have here are two extremes: a contrarianism that tends increasingly towards passivity and another that moves to aggression, once they drop below the line. In between is a place of inquiry, but once you get too close to the poles, there is little room for dialogue, inquiry or understanding. Both extremes are a way of avoiding dealing with uncomfortable thoughts and feelings, or of being lost to them.

Total passivity and unwillingness to speak truth even when, say, you know that what is being offered to a client will not help them or is simply creating greater dependency, may evoke feelings of shame (*self-contempt*).

At the other extreme, increasing levels of grandiosity result in the flipside of shame (*contempt for others*). Remember the consultant in the last chapter faced with selling a client a solution they did not believe was appropriate – that had the potential for one or other extreme.

Contrarianism as dissent and speaking truth

There is something here about our capacity to speak truth to power,[202] and willingness to name the proverbial elephant in the room. This means working with the shadow side in organisations, which Gerard Egan describes as:

202. It is important to note that I am writing this from the perspective of someone in the Global North. The whole 'speaking truth to power' thing we are fond of here has a very different dynamic in, say, Asia Pacific, where the notion of face means that challenging a leader in public is deeply frowned on. Social norms require different approaches depending on context. A truism, but important to say here.

"All those things that substantially and consistently affect the productivity and quality of the working life of a business, for better or worse, but which are not found on organisation charts, in company manuals, or in the discussions that take place in formal meetings." (1994: 7)

This takes us again to the question of what is undiscussable, what is not being discussed that should/could be, what is taboo, what we are too afraid to name and more. This tension is at the heart of the contrarian role consultants play, for to name the undiscussable is to embody contrarianism. This can be unbearable for others, IF they are not ready to work with what is being named. Hence the many whistle-blowers who find themselves out of a job, as they are torn by conflicting loyalties, namely one to the organisation and the other to their own sense of moral duty (Jubb: 1999).

This tension is, I suggest, at play within consultants as well: to whom and to what are we most loyal? And based on what assumptions?

Chris Argyris neatly summed up how all this unfolds at the organisational level forty years ago, and it seems as true now as then:

"… the undiscussable games that people have learned to play for years will have to be dealt with. Moreover, we must deal with the organisational consequences of these games such as the win-lose group dynamics, the rivalries among coalition groups, and the double binds that many people report … Of course, only people who are concerned about honesty and loyalty get hurt. The others learned long ago to de-emphasise these factors in order not to get upset." (Argyris, 1980: 207)

That is a subtlety in the relational context in which client and consultant meet. The question is how both contract, and the extent to which unspoken assumptions are (genuinely) aired and worked with. Do they collude with one another or get dirty?

Clean vs Dirty Consulting

Dr Richard Claydon (2017) offers what is, for me, one of the most helpful ways of distinguishing between consulting that purports to offer neat solutions, and that which embraces the messy reality of organisational life. He posits that there are essentially two modes: Clean and Dirty.

Clean Consulting

Claydon suggests that this has its roots in Taylor-ism and specifically the notion of 'one best way' and 'first-class men'. The assumptions underpinning Clean Consulting:

> "… allow the consultant to avoid dirty work or negative feedback. The model is 'proven' best practice. Thus, if the model fails, it is not the consultants' fault – rather it's that the organisation doesn't have the 'first-class employees' who can deliver the expected outcome. You just have to find those that can. Then everything will be hunky-dory."[203]

Responsibility and accountability are abdicated down, to HR and managers, and I would go further and say they are also passed on to whoever the organisation decides to task with 'doing' change work, often *internal* Organisation Development, change, transformation practitioners/consultants or Human Resource Business Partners (HRBPs).

The cleanness also comes from rituals, symbols and artefacts of consulting, namely "lots of colourful slide decks promising a beautiful outcome – rational, logical, predictable, ordered, manageable" (ibid.). That 'cleanness' goes so far as how people walk and talk, and to what have now become well-established ritualistic dance moves.

A PwC partner in conversation with one of my interviewees described how they were "taught to walk into a room and own it". Part of developing that ability was drilled into the partner at a young age in the firm by being taught, quite literally, how to walk, talk and sit. He was coached to slow his speech to a cadence that drew in clients, through a measured tone and calmness that signalled surety and credibility. In some firms, beards were for a long time unacceptable, and in some cases still are. After all, clean consulting is nothing if not clean shaven. How susceptible are clients to this behaviour? One of my NHS clients remembered watching a group of senior leaders chatting, as McKinsey were pitching for work from their organisation.

> "… the change in the behaviour of the senior leaders was pathetic … The Finance Director turned into something akin to Gordon Gekko. He's sitting there and saying 'Good to see you. Thanks for coming in. And, you know, if you look at our headcount, we've still got some slack in there, we can take out 10% …'

---

203. https://www.linkedin.com/pulse/do-you-want-dirty-clean-consulting-dr-richard-claydon/

I thought, I've never heard him talk about this before. I've never heard him talk in internal settings like this before. And I don't think he's checked this with any of these other execs. But he's here because it's McKinsey. It was an alpha person in the room and the Finance Director was behaving in a really peculiar way."

Clients are wooed. Complexities and contradictions are glossed over if too challenging to the neat narrative, differences between the client and other organisations downplayed, as are those around comparative size, market, industry, purpose, etc. all while the value of the one best way approach is maximised. In the context of a pitch like that, best practice is an intoxicating and compelling offer. It may also be so impressive that whether a client *actually understands* what is being sold to them is moot. Organisational change specialist Susanne Evans shared with me her experience of clients "hanging off every word of some consultants".

> "I was working with a big government department and they wheeled in some [consultants] who did a presentation. And it was very impressive. When they left, my client turned to me and said, 'Susanne, what was all that about? I didn't understand what they had to say.' I had to translate, but no one seemed to mind that they didn't understand. It had just been a very impressive experience for the client."[204]

Keith Jones, who has consulted for years, including extensively with professional service firms as clients, suggested to me:

> "It's possible to hypnotically induce the client into agreeing to stuff that the consultant knows full well we'll never achieve. The thing that I find most interesting about it is that the moment you say to a consultant, you know, this is what I think about some of the things that are peddled out in our profession. They go, Yeah, I know that. Yes, that's true."[205]

Much as we may like to delude ourselves, the ethical questions are never that far away.

Dirty Consulting
Claydon offers[206] an alternative with less polish and collusion: the Dirty Consultant, who has a 'problem' in the sense that their label accurately reflects reality rather than the myth of fixability:

---

204. Interview 11th November 2020
205. Interview 28th October 2021
206. https://www.linkedin.com/pulse/do-you-want-dirty-clean-consulting-dr-richard-claydon/

> "[S/he] doesn't have an immediate answer for the complex problem vexing the client [and] has no flashy best practice model s/he strongly believes in. No shiny slide deck that outlines a defined future state."

Claydon argues that what the Dirty Consultant *does* have is a research process. Essentially, they are offering the client the opportunity to inquire together into the problem, jointly finding out all the dirty and messy reasons for why things are going wrong:

> "This involves two processes – **(1)** working out where the inefficiencies and absurdities are, and **(2)** finding out who knows how to solve them.
>
> This is a dirty process because it can uncover all manner of things that can cause emotional and psychological strain." (Ibid.)

This is consulting that does not deny anxiety; rather it assumes it is part and parcel of organisational life, and the human state more generally. Clean Consulting sells itself in part because it seeks to sanitise or deny this mess rather than embrace and work with it.

I link this to the notion of the 'Craft of Change' that Jesse Segers, Dean of SIOO Business School in Holland, described to me in a conversation:

> "The Dutch school [of Organisation Development change practice] is called the 'Craft of Change', because you cannot manage change. And so, it's not change management. It's craft, which is more about the practice."[207]

Parking for a moment the question of whether you can 'manage change' (personally I think it is an oxymoron, in large part because of the assumptions that often accompany it, but that is for another book), this notion of the 'craft of change' I like. What distinguishes the craft movement from professionalisation is that it is never about perfection or mastery – it fully embraces the evolutionary nature of the craft. You are in a constant relationship with drawing things out of the material. It never ceases to be a process of experimentation, innovation, failure, learning and experimentation. And as soon as you 'have it' you encounter a piece of gnarly wood and you have to start again. Crafting is a process of lifelong learning, and working with change and the human dynamics of organisations is similar.

---

207. Interview 20th April 2023

Note the process that the Dirty Consultant must follow, according to Claydon. It is dirty because:

1. It involves speaking truth to power – "a delicate process that can result in the immediate removal of the consultant if done without panache."

2. The "processes of experimentation look messy, confusing and unstructured from the outside" – and as they are experimental, guess what? They won't always work, again creating jeopardy for the consultant if the client is not in on and with the messiness of experimentation.

3. Unlike the Clean Consultant promising novelty and uniqueness, the Dirty Consultant "will be borrowing from many different experiential and theoretical domains, twisting and melding models so they can fit the issues". That is going to blow the minds of some clients, and can be emotionally exhausting.

4. The Dirty Consultant "has to work hard to shut down failures and ramp up successes" as they experiment, inducing more anxiety potentially as it may kill off ideas some people are attached to, creating more defensiveness and evoke shame or embarrassment – a challenging process as it involves killing off people's idea-babies.

5. Lastly "it initiates a period of change with no clearly defined target to aim at". Change catalyses plenty of emotional and cognitive responses at the best of time, and the uncertainty of no guaranteed outcome. That just amplifies things. (Ibid.)

When we talk about consulting, therefore, the Clean Consultant deludes both themselves and their client about the neatness of working with complex challenges. The Dirty Consultant understands this is about relaxing our attachment to expertise. They focus on relatedness and relationality in a fundamental coming together, and working collaboratively on things in their real-world context.

That, however, is counter cultural, going against the interests of those who have a vested interest in buying and selling solutions (however unfit for purpose they may be when they meet reality) and is a more challenging and uncomfortable proposition for clients who would rather not face the potential psychological and emotional strain that Claydon rightly says may ensue. Far easier to find a Clean Consultant with a slide deck of neat solutions and quick fixes.

Where does this leave us?

For all the window dressing and baubles (e.g. certifications, associations, suits, slide decks, communities of practice, expense accounts, etc.) that consultants and practitioners favour, when we boil this down the challenge is a profoundly human one. It reveals us – both the client being wooed and the consultant doing the wooing – as needy, deluded, fearful, wanting to be liked/loved, hopeful and excited as any human being can be. We are also as worried about being found out that we are not as clever as we or others think we are, or discovering that we may, in fact, be wrong. As Kathryn Schulz, author of *Being Wrong: Adventures in the Margin of Error* notes:

> "a whole lot of us go through life assuming that we are basically right, basically all the time, about basically everything … As absurd as it sounds when we stop to think about it, our steady state seems to be one of unconsciously assuming that we are very close to omniscient." (2011: 4)

Ask yourself: how often have you heard senior leaders or consultants admit straight out that they are wrong? Without qualification or excuse. It is understandable in some ways given the potential jeopardy and our societal fear of failure and intolerance of mistakes. I would argue a healthier position to cultivate is one of 'doubtful certainty', that enables us to have the courage of our convictions – whether as client or consultant – while embracing the potential for our as yet undiscovered wrong-ness. This echoes Edgar Schein's notion of 'humble inquiry' (2013), with its emphasis on asking questions rather than leading with what we know and think the client needs to know.

For this need to be right, the inability – even terror – of admitting we may be wrong, permeates organisations and creates the conditions for shame and embarrassment to be evoked. It links straight back to Chapter 2, and how the human condition drives the need for certainty, and that applies to those of us who say we are there to help clients. Peter Block cuts through all the noise at the end of *Flawless Consulting* when he says:

> "In the end it is our authenticity, the way we manage ourselves, and our connection to our clients, that is our methodology, our marketing strategy, and the fruit of our labour. The fact that we show up with a briefcase, a resume, and a conceptual framework is more a function of habit than necessity. It will be enough if we simply show up. And that is the heart of the matter." (2011: 342)

The more we deny the wonderfully dirty nature of that, the greater the likelihood we are part of the functional collusion, that we, too, orientate towards oversimplifying the complex to minimise the anxiety.

Reflective Questions

- To what extent, really, do you want to build capability, if it means you may earn less?
- How willing are you to be fired?
- How does the Unholy Trinity play out in your practice, as a consultant or leader?
- How important do you think it is to cultivate your 'Inner Contrarian'?
- To what extent does the desire to belong overwhelm the urge to speak truth to power?

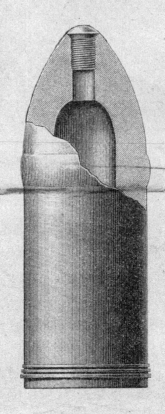

SILVER BULLET NO. 11

CUTTING EDGE TECH

Implement our software and optimise your processes, reduce head count
and increase customer satisfaction. Well, that is the theory anyway
until you realise some of those people are still required.

FIELDS OF PRACTICE OR WARRING TRIBES?

OR: HOW WE GET HUNG UP ON LABELS

Chapter 9:
Fields of Practice or Warring Tribes?

Ask most professionals and experts which field they are associated with, and they will probably tell you. The related term 'field of practice', which does not actually have a dictionary definition, is commonly used in various professional contexts, particularly law, medicine, engineering and social sciences. Within psychology alone, there are many: social, cognitive, research, clinical, educational, sports, workplace and more.

In an organisational context, we also have a variety of fields, the most well-known and prominent being HR, Organisation Development, Organisation Design and Change Management. Various professional bodies play a role in amplifying the importance of some fields, particularly those such as the Chartered Institute of Personnel and Development (CIPD) and Organisation Development Network (ODN), the US-based progenitor of many regional OD bodies.

For some, Learning and Development, Talent Management, Digital Transformation and more are also fields. The challenge about 'fields of practice' is that the term does not have a specific origin in the sense of being attributed to a single person or moment in time.

A fairer assessment is that this idea of dividing 'professional' domains into distinct areas of expertise of practice has evolved over time as human beings specialised. A good example is Organisation Development and Organisation Design, which are arguably in adjacent spaces (although be bloody careful if you attend conferences that are aimed at one or the other and ask which is a subset of the other ...). The former preceded the latter, which really started to emerge as distinct from the 1980s onwards, differentiating itself increasingly as those that orientated to working at the level of structure sought to define what they did as a distinct practice.

This is a good example of managing the tension of ever-expanding bodies of knowledge and how to boundary/contain them within distinct areas/categories, to both make them easier to describe and offer an appropriate focus for conversations about quality. So, we end up with 'fields of practice' as a way of describing specialised areas within what we decide societally are discrete professions. It sets the context for where people with particular skills and disciplines both can validate their practices and build community.

The nature of these fields intrigues me. Differentiating needs and forces in professional practice are at play, and the recruitment into them, plus the explicit and opaque nature of the criteria applied in being brought in/kept out of them, is rarely discussed. They are social constructions, many relatively young – certainly in relation to those pertaining to organisations and organising – and they all take us toward something good/needed/longed for e.g. notions of professionalism, competence, excellence, collegiality, community, safety, etc. The human desire for membership leads us to accept the rules that exist within them: we do what it is accepted to do, and challenge what sits outside of that boundary. This feels like a primal response in contrast to a reasoned judgement.

Ultimately these fields of practice are thought collectives and play a subtle role in the perpetuation of Silver Bullets.

Like attracts like

The idea of 'thought collectives' comes from the work of Ludwik Fleck in the 1930s (1979 – reprint of 1935 text) and is key to understanding how the idea of a Silver Bullet for complex problems is so pervasive. I came across the term through conversation with Dr Graham Curtis, Director of Operations at Roffey Park Institute.

Curtis (2018: 80) describes how Fleck "presents an argument for how people come to take up ideas from their specific context and regard them as taken for granted truths". This happens through the social processes *within* thought collectives, that in turn have their own thought style. For example, a "thought collective of scientists will make claims for their truth being universal and social processes of enforcement are then used to criticise any argument that undermines their paradigm" (ibid.). This is a form of confirmation bias, of finding ways to 'make' ideas psychologically fit our frame of reference.

Thus, the influence of a thought style "means one cannot think in any other way" (Fleck, quoted in ibid.). What Fleck is pointing to is something of how power works in social systems, what it means to belong, what it requires of members to stay part of a group, and simultaneously it sets the conditions for what it means to be a heretic when you challenge perceived core truths.

This points to the risk of totalitarianism in any thought collective if it assumes a greater authority, monopoly on truth, etc. than any other. We need to recognise that thought collectives all offer something as well as missing/overlooking things that others might pick up on, who in turn miss other things, and so on ad infinitum. In human society, monopolies on wisdom and truth are in short supply, so too in thought collectives, however much there may be a tendency to echo the Mandalorian creed from the TV series of the same name: "This is the Way ..."

Organisations as thought collectives

There is a difference between belonging to an organisation, as opposed to a field or community of practice. The former offers greater containment; the latter tend to be more loosely coupled, so the question arises as to whether, in these spaces, we huddle together to compensate, and minimise our differences to fit in.

The Catholic church is an example of this, but heresy does not just show up in faith organisations. We see this in politics when Republicans in the US get labelled as RINOs (Republican in Name Only) or UK when 'Remoaners' engage with 'Brexiteers'. *The Guardian* newspaper has seen a very public version of this play out around trans rights and indeed the trans debate is one that is constellated by particularly strong thought collectives who exercise power against those they deem to have departed from a truth they hold dear. Academia is rife with thought collectives and you only have to do a cursory search online and you will find many others, for example, within the Systems Thinking world, variously engaging in debates around what is and is not true.

Many thought collectives appeared in earlier chapters: business schools, universities, academia more widely; individual consulting and professional service firms; adherents of theories and models; followers of gurus and thought leaders and more. A good example of this was in Chapter 5, in how someone at an Organisation Development conference was challenged for merely deigning to critique the work of a key figure in the field: this was heresy in action.

They also show up in organisations (e.g. working at *The Guardian* and Roffey Park Institute was to experience being part of incredibly distinct thought collectives bound by brand, history, values, location, language, ritual and more); individual teams or functions (ever met, say, an IT or marketing or finance department that appears to operate to its own set of principles, for good or ill?);

leadership teams (particularly influential in terms of the conditions they set). In short, they are everywhere, and part of the warp and weft of how humans organise. It starts early as well: we learn which thought collectives we are born or invited into as we arrive in our families and schools, which sets conditions for later life.

To illustrate how thought collectives show up, Martin Parker, who is both a member of academic thought collectives *and* critiques them, described elegantly how business schools fit the pattern:

> "… they sediment particular expectations and certain sorts of identities. When we're talking to academics about why they need to change … their instinct is to hunker down into a particular version of themselves, who they think they are and what they think their roles and responsibilities might be. [This is] despite the fact that we talk about innovation and producing new knowledge."[208]

This reinforces particular thought styles that continue to dominate:

> "… despite the fact that they very often talk about ideas to do with change and newness, they base this on some very archaic mediaeval notions of the university as a fortress of knowledge." (Ibid.)

In all the above, to think in ways which deviate from received wisdoms is to be seen to be a heretic, subversive, to be an outsider, to be at risk of expulsion. The contrarianism I discussed in the preceding chapter is in part a process of navigating the boundaries of thought collectives, because it tests out the extent to which we are willing to risk losing our place within a group or groups, or indeed what happens when we are invited in.

Joining the Freemasonry of Organisation Development

Within a couple of months of working at Roffey Park Institute I had begun to be drawn into the part of the institute that focused on Organisation Development practitioner programmes, a core part of the offering and, to some extent, what defined the organisation. Shortly after this, one of my new colleagues commented, "You are one of them now." Their experience was that they had never been 'invited in', so it begged the question: why? Had I inadvertently offered the right handshake, worn my trousers with one leg rolled

---

208. Interview 24th May 2021

up appropriately or waggled a flip chart marker pen in a way to signal I was of the right stock?

Hold in mind that up until that point in my career I had no idea what Organisation Development was; I did not mention it in my job application, and I did not describe myself as an 'OD Practitioner'. Nonetheless, I apparently qualified according to a set of criteria which I was ignorant of and was welcomed into a lovely OD thought collective within the wider Roffey Park Institute one. I am eternally grateful for that, as in no small part it marked the start of a transition in my own career that led to where I am now.

The wider OD thought collective

> "The OD community as a whole has got many fascinating strands to it. Many different philosophies within it. Many, many tribes and many sectorial groups, and there is a risk that each of those believes they've got their own Silver Bullet." Linda Holbeche[209]

A couple of years later, I stood for the board of the OD Network Europe, an association for OD practitioners, and then for three years I was Co-chair of the organisation and therefore deeply embedded within that thought collective. I still move in and out of the community, and value being part of it, not least because of the values that underpin the field. There is a paradox here, in that the more we stand for something, the clearer it becomes to see what it might be heretical to say or do. That is true in social groups more generally; in this context, I found myself increasingly aware of what connected me, and of what might lead me to be seen as a heretic. I am certainly seen by some as that, as in 2023 a colleague mentioned to me that one of my peers in the OD community does not like me because I "speak out of turn …"

As I reflect on OD as a field, and how it manifests as a thought collective, I notice how often conversations arise within it as to:

- What is OD? Art? Science? Profession? All three? (A need to perpetually reassert an identity, while simultaneously a testament to the fact it is an evolving, fluid, dynamic field of inquiry and no one-size-fits-all. Quite the recipe for anxiety as well.)

- How is it different to, e.g. HR? (A need to self-differentiate.)

---

209. Interview 15th June 2020

- Where should OD sit within an organisation? (A need to know our place in the world, maybe born of an existential anxiety around continuing relevance.)

- How do the different flavours of OD relate to each other, e.g. Diagnostic OD, Dialogic OD, Agile OD, etc.? (As differences emerge, how does the whole stay together? When does a 'new' take mean the thought collective will struggle to accept the difference?)

- How do we convey the 'magic of OD'? (When what is valuable in a field or discipline morphs into faith and fervour.)

- • How do we develop a global competency framework, to standardise practice? (Because turning practice into another abstraction is going to help.)

None of this is wrong; it is all profoundly human stuff, maybe in part reflecting a lack of confidence, and is as much about managing tensions and polarities as anything else. However, one of the unintended outcomes of this is an (often unspoken but not always) assumption about why a particular field or practice is 'better', 'more ethical', 'more useful' or paramount to another, such as how Organisation Development and Organisation Design practitioners can sometimes be overheard discussing which is subordinate to the other. Which in turn mirrors the same debate between HR and Organisation Development folk in other contexts.

This reflects a propensity in thought collectives to be somewhat inward looking. Thought styles give primacy to certain ideas that can turn into truths that become articles of faith, rather than shared assumptions open to challenge and change. An example of this is the belief I noticed many OD practitioners held pre-COVID that it is not possible to work at depth in a virtual environment. It has been remarkable to see that widely held shared assumption soften and change.

Leadership teams are equally prone to this and can have serious consequences if that goes unchallenged for extended periods. Wilful blindness, the phenomenon I mentioned whereby people bystand behaviour that they know to be wrong or unethical, which Margaret Heffernan discussed in depth in her 2011 book, is a powerful example of what happens when thought styles become particularly fixed on one version of truth.

Monty Python understood this

This can feel a bit like the scene from Monty Python's *Life of Brian*, with the warring factions of the Judean People's Front and People's Front of Judea.[210] More widely, the many fields of professional practice are more akin to the guilds in Terry Pratchett's *Discworld* novels. He conjured the idea of professional guilds, such as those for the Accountants and Usurers, Historians, Lawyers and Teachers jostling for space with more esoteric ones like the Guild of Assassins, Guild of Fools and Joculators (and College of Clowns), Haberdashers Guild, Priests, Sacerdotes and Occult Intermediaries Guild, and Guild of Victims. We have the Guilds of Change Mangers, Organisation Development Consultants, Organisation Design Consultants, Digital Transformation Consultants, Agile Coaches, Executive Coaches, Facilitators and more, all to varying degrees seeking to differentiate themselves from each other while simultaneously needing to acknowledge and work with the similarities. Although none are yet to merge, which is telling.

Pratchett's books demonstrate an acute awareness of social and political issues in contemporary society. They are a satirical take on the tribal nature of human societies and how we organise into thought collectives at multiple levels. They also talk to how power plays a role, in terms of the relative status and internecine conflicts within and between guilds, and echo how power relations and our need to belong manifest in real-world social and professional affiliations and relationships.

The theologian Matthew Fox (interestingly a maverick expelled from his religious order) has a lovely metaphor for this (2001). He says spirit is like an underground river and all the world religion are wells which offer a way towards that which we long for. It becomes problematic when individuals compete as to which well is best and become more preoccupied with the well than the river.

The quest for a 'seat at the table'

One of the most visible manifestations of how the fields of practice both influence what happens in organisations and mirror things outside are the debates, in OD and HR particularly, around where they 'sit' in an organisation. The HR community perennially wrestles with this (e.g. *Four Reasons HR Deserves a Seat At The Table*, Forbes 10/09/2021; *What HR Needs to Do to Get a*

---

210. https://youtu.be/a0BpfwazhUA

Seat at the Table, HBR 27/11/2014; *What does it take for HR to be ready for a seat at the table?* Ernst &Young 16/08/2022) and I have been to many conferences where this and similar questions arise. A recent example was at the 2023 CIPD Festival of Work, where one session revolved around whether HR needed its own PR to elevate its status. This was strikingly divorced from a conversation about what HR's client organisations actually need and, in many instances, do not receive – another example of the importance of context, i.e. we do not practise in a vacuum.

Organisation Development has a slightly different anxiety, most often showing up as one of place: while HR shows up as a function and typically will often have an exec level representation, OD is often an adjunct to HR, or coupled with Talent, maybe even with L&D, or with Organisation Design, or Strategy, or maybe consist of merely one or two lone people with 'OD' in their job title, floating in the ether …

Why this may matter

Simon Cavicchia suggests that "the preoccupation with professional boundaries and professionalism is individualistic and protectionist.[211] He suggests that being concerned with what clients might need and thinking together with them "to co-create approaches that are context relevant is more relational. That is not to say relational is best, rather that relational ideas offer a meta perspective in which tensions and differences can be held and thought about" (ibid.).

Maybe this is just a load of professionals and practitioners debating concerns that relate to their own anxieties around their place and influence and has less to do with what their clients might need. As the fields of practice gather at their conferences or networking events, conversations orientate towards how to maintain, sustain, expand and/or defend their 'field'. The question of what is of most service to clients is no longer foregrounded, rather a need to elevate a given field to a place where its value is self-evident and the existential threat of being disbanded or deemed to no longer be relevant can be assuaged.

This requires a simple question to be dodged, and one I asked a panel of HR leaders at a conference which garnered an uncomfortable collective response: if HR did not exist, and we needed to create a field of practice or function to meet client needs, would we create what we have today? If so, how would it be the

---

211. Conversation 11th March 2022

same or different, and what would we call it? (You could ask the same question of Organisation Development as well.) The response from the panel was one of collective confusion and deflection, and an unwillingness to countenance the possibility that their guild may not have as much relevance as they thought, or that it might need to evolve.

Labels: do clients care?

If you read this as someone who relies on one or more of the fields, whether contracting internal practitioners or teams, or bringing in externals, then it is important to recognise that what is happening at a relational level is not simply one of where you are buying a service or solution.

What gets missed – I would suggest more often than is ideal – by the professionals clients buy from is that first and foremost they are there to *serve* you. I question whether clients really care which flavour of Organisation Development is being offered, or how different HR and OD are, or whether you are a Transformation Consultant or a Digital Transformation consultant.

In 2018 I co-hosted an event for the OD Network Europe and the European Organisation Design Forum (EODF) on the theme of 'Labels: Do clients care?'. We had several client representatives in the room. During one exchange, a senior leader from a bank made the comment that all that was important to her was whether a consultant "understood change and knew how to work with it". I delved a bit deeper, and clarified whether what made the real difference was:

1. a consultant who understands the nature of change in human systems; and
2. knows how to intervene in human systems; and
3. that the label was irrelevant: they would be judged on the above and nothing else in effect.[212]

She confirmed that was the case. In other words, which thought collective the consultant identified with was of little relevance. It was also clear, as my co-host for the session, Nick Richmond, at the time Chair of the EODF, commented on our blog post after the event, that clients appreciated three things:

---

212. https://www.linkedin.com/pulse/whats-label-lot-whether-orgdev-hr-orgdes-any-other-steve-hearsum

- Diversity of thought to help provide provocation.
- Helping the client to see what's really going on to better qualify the problem.
- Curiosity and learning over 'solutionising'.

The parallel process at play

This need for self-differentiation is mirrored on the inside of organisations, as HR teams are reconfigured, Organisation Development comes and goes, as different teams and their labels get moved around and uncoupled or coupled. One internal Organisation Development and Design practitioner shared with me a list of all the roles she had considered that contained, ostensibly, a responsibility for Organisation Development:[213]

- HR projects
- HR change specialist
- Transformational change consultant
- Business change
- Learning and collaboration specialist
- Learning and OD consultant
- Organisation effectiveness
- Performance and development
- People and organisational capability
- Op model design specialist
- Culture and experience people change manager
- Organisational change consultant
- Leadership development and OD
- Human capital consultant
- Organisational capability
- Organisation design specialist

This confusion is further evidence of a human need to establish identity and differentiate, while at the same time trying to codify how a role may best be described in relation to both various fields and organisational context. There is a tension here. Organisations rely on symbolic exchange, and things only become things when they have a label attached to them, which bounds and defines – and that crucially allows corporate functions to quantify them. Equally, there is what Neil Morrison describes as a "kind of fragmentation", expanding on this to say:

---

213. Email 28th June 2023

"I constantly tell my teams [that] my CEO and my business doesn't recognise OD, talent, resourcing: they recognise my one team. Nobody cares. Only you care, nobody else cares. It really doesn't matter … I think that fragmentation gives us a level of inertia that doesn't help."[214]

I recognise that inertia *inside* organisations that become overly focused on labels rather than what people can *actually* do and the impact they might have. It partly explains why I have worked on several large capability-building programmes that have been quickly followed by the client organisation moving the furniture around and making redundant or disempowering the very people they have 'equipped' to help with change, something I will touch on again.

This inertia also shows up *outside,* however. The more fields of practice orientate towards negotiating around their differences, rather than asking what would most serve clients, then the fragmentation increases. The absence of dialogue around how they are similar, or, God forbid, what the value in merging together might be, is telling.

Separating the signal (what is useful) from the noise (ego- and anxiety-driven self-protection), becomes tricky. Try this for a thought experiment: in terms of the fields of practice and hordes of consultants out there, what in recent years has emerged as genuinely novel? More importantly, is the question really about a need for novelty (often a synonym for 'new and sexy'), or rather a profound need to recognise, paraphrasing Matthew Stewart again, that our practices are built on ideas barely a century old. Our need to label ourselves derives from a delusion that what we are wrestling with is something other than that which human beings have been working on for centuries. Namely, social processes, relationships, working with difference, existential angst and more.

Lurking in the shadows here is that our professional identity becomes entwined with our personal identity mainly because of values. Therefore, it is hard to separate the two, or separate these in turn from our own (unresolved) issues and self-narrative.

A call for more permeability

I believe the boundaries of fields need to be permeable, to allow expertise to flow between them more, with less defensiveness and snobbery around which is better than another. Put simply, I would rather never hear another story

---

214. Interview 26th May 2020

like that from a client who is a highly experienced – and effective – NHS HR practitioner, who was deepening her knowledge and skills in Organisation Development only to be snobbily told by one of the most well-known OD teams in the NHS that, to all intents and purposes, she was not 'one of them'. People's Front of Judea stuff all over, and an example of fields becoming cults of expertise, the need to defend territory (repel those HR borders!), of right and wrong.

Organisation Development is a field that paradoxically applauds taking a 'pick and mix' approach – it is often described as a 'Magpie practice' by practitioners and at the same time seems to want to hold onto its distinctness. When that distinctness depends on permeability, there is a tension, and yet there is a power and no little learning in letting your professional identity and frames of reference broaden.

There is a need to transcend the silos that the fields become. Yes, they are necessary places of safety to hang out and experiment and learn, but they need to have open and flexible boundaries and remember why they exist and who they serve so as not to become obsessed with petty differences when the client just wants help.

As Toby Lindsay, an experienced change and OD practitioner, once quipped to me, "fields are important for growth, yet the boundaries and hedgerows are where I want to look and much flourishes!" The challenge is that hedgerows are messier and may have hidden qualities. There is a distinction to be made between defining and refining. OD, like coaching, is relatively new and so has necessarily been preoccupied with defining and differentiating. As practice evolves, we need to shift the focus to looking at what *actually happens* in practice, what supports meaning making and meaningful change to happen and how we need to go on cultivating our approaches in light of this knowledge. It is not just about what the discipline or the practitioner can 'do' for you, which is still an endemic preoccupation, but what use can the client make of the practitioner and their approach. It is hedgerow work.

The risk

To recap. We have fields of practice that, to varying degrees, have a need to self-differentiate, part of which can entail holding a stance of why what they offer is more appropriate than another's. 'More appropriate' may on occasion be driven by a need to ensure credibility and relationship is maintained, and by extension relevance and reward, which is not necessarily the same thing as what serves a client.

Within the fields there is a tendency towards orthodoxy, as part of the need to protect identities, which then limits challenge, inquiry and the possibilities for emergent change *within* the thought collectives, and certainly would be unlikely to include dissolution even if that was a natural step. The audience for what emerges from a thought collective is often the collective itself, feeding defensiveness as it reinforces thought styles and the narratives that perpetuate its very existence, even if that presence is no longer needed.

Add into this a competitive element, something that seems to be paid little attention. It is self-evident people within given fields may compete with each other; that competition may be present between, say, Organisation Development and Organisation Design, or HR and Talent, or in many other dyad and triad relationships, is not as obvious. Inside organisations, that is likely to be characterised as politics, and the jostling that goes on will be all too familiar to some readers.

Naomi Stanford's critique of the fields of practice is interesting, given how she is perceived as being closely aligned with Organisation Design: "... the different splinter groups try and defend something which is not defensible, because there's no academic rigour underpinning any of it. It's all hot air and different takes on a similar sort of thing".[215] She built on that, observing how many of the fields that tend to business and organisations – whether that be leadership development, Organisation Development, HR or any other – are essentially anthropological, which is a field in and of itself (ironically).

The jostling outside fields is more subtle. In simple terms, this may show up in conversations where a consultant is making a case for a particular approach, which is in turn associated with a particular school of thought or field. A very visible example is when a client is looking for someone to support culture work. There are many different approaches to working with culture, and these vary not only because of which field you engage with, because the assumptions about the nature of change in organisations colours the solutions offered. To offer one clear juxtaposition, the choice to go with someone offering an approach from the world of Change Management such as Prosci will take you to a very

---

215. Interview 24th July 2020

different place than if you engage with someone whose practice is informed by Organisation Development principles, or those who label themselves as 'culture specialists', or who eschew any label at all other than 'change'.

Place these variances into a competitive tender environment, and the need to self-differentiate, to convey how and why, exactly, your approach is right, dials up the propensity to assert that what is offered will work, that it is a solution to a client's problem, that it is, in fact, a Silver Bullet.

This connects directly to the need for certainty on the client's part touched on elsewhere, and it is matched by the need for certainty in the solution provider. That confidence can in turn be amplified by the field of practice that the provider may locate themselves within. To be clear, not all do, although often it is possible to reverse engineer identifying where they sit the more the underlying assumptions they hold are surfaced.

The comfort of the familiar is not the same as what is needed

In summer 2023, I was part of a pitch for a leadership development programme for a UK government client. The brief articulated a need for an intervention that was, to a large extent, conventional and traditional, e.g. it articulated very clear outcomes, talked about 'best practice' in other organisations, and much of the language reflected the assumptions of a world view that 'outside in' development was needed, i.e. offer the learner template for what 'good' looks like and help them become more like that.

The consultancy I was working with take a practice-based learning approach. In simple terms, this entails working with clients to help them come up, at each individual level, with a question that talks to something that they want to address or develop in their leadership practice: something like 'how can I become better at X, in the context of Y?' Done well, this is deep development and helps clients get to the heart of behaviour change, which is ultimately what most leadership development is about.

Our approach was to not collude with requests for costs for a programme we had not helped design or wholeheartedly agreed with philosophically. Asked to provide a positioning paper, we made some of the arguments that appear in Chapter 3.

What was interesting was that one of the other providers we were up against, who were rejected in the first round, made a case based on the idea that they had run many similar leadership development programmes so it would be easy to roll a version of that out here. Their expertise in that field amplified the case for a particular type of Silver Bullet, in this instance a Leadership Development flavoured one: 'you need one of these, because our experience and expertise in this field mean it is the right one'. It was a 'cookie cutter' approach, another of those favoured by the purveyors of Silver Bullets.

In the end the choice came down to us and another provider with a programme that they had run before. The client said, "We had a choice between someone offering us off the shelf, and you who would challenge us. We have decided to go with you." I suspect this client is somewhat of an outlier.

So what?

We need to understand the psychological and social processes involved, and how that then impacts how we interact with clients because the more we orientate to navel-gazing in our guilds, the greater the possibility that what the client needs may be lost in the need to protect individual and collective identities.

It is less obvious why clients should be concerned about the identity crises and politicking among people they hire on a temporary basis, or on some limited cases appoint into internal roles, HR being possibly the most obvious.

Trying to articulate *why* this matters in any way to the reader who is coming at this chapter from the client side feels a little like juggling jelly. Bluntly, who cares? Fields of practice are, to greater or lesser degrees depending on context, engaged in iterative cycles of sense making, trying to work out who they are, what they are for, who they are for, what skills they need, how that differs to their peers and how to sell that. The risk is that becomes a "public masturbation of words", as Keith Jones archly put it to me.[216]

In parallel, clients are faced with problems and challenges, attempting to categorise what kind of problem they have and who they can go to that might help, and, oh look, there are all these fields of practice that appear to be making it easier to categorise my problem … Phew … That simplifies things because if my problem is one of X, then I can go to the thought collective that is doing such a good job of articulating that they are the professionals best placed to help.

---

216. Interview 28th October 2021

In summary: fields of practice assert they have the answer to a client's problem, and to manage their own existential angst and need for significance, they end up in a dance with clients, and on occasion other fields. 'We are the experts. We know stuff.' To admit that a field may NOT have a monopoly on answers, or a Silver Bullet, is to accept you may not be as important or as valuable as you thought. Fields are therefore part of a wider psychological process aimed at managing the existential anxiety of not knowing. The greater the uncertainty, the more attractive the field of practice becomes that signals it knows what to do in the face of that. We can breathe easy at that point.

Ultimately there is a blind spot in the way humans organise in response to solving complex problems. The journalist and author Mathew Syed points out the extent to which homophily (i.e. the tendency for people to seek out or be attracted to those who are similar to themselves) is pervasive:

> "Our social networks are full of people with similar experiences, views and beliefs. Even when groups start out with diversity, this can be squeezed out by a process of social osmosis as people converge upon the dominant assumptions." (2019: 55)

In other words, the dominant thought styles lead the collective, however positive its intentions and intellectual strength of its membership, to be less than the sum of its parts precisely because it seeks to reinforce its distinctive identity. Syed rightly invites us to be compassionate towards the individuals involved, suggesting that this is not a criticism rather it is important "to note that when smart individuals have overlapping frames of reference, they become collectively myopic" (ibid.: 56). My own experience is similar: the more I have found myself in groups that tend to a particular map of the world, the greater my sense that I am missing something.

If the aim of many of the fields of practice is to be centres of wisdom, they are missing the point, for wise groups:

> "… are not clone like. They do not parrot the same views. Instead, they are more like groups of rebels. They do not agree for the sake of it, but bring insights from different regions of the problem space. Such groups contain people with perspectives that challenge, augment, diverge and crosspollinate." (Ibid.: 56)

That sounds like a place where contrarians, questioners, dissenters, wonderers, critique-ers, rebels or punks of all kinds congregate. Where there is enough similarity to bring them together, and sufficient permission for difference to create the possibility that wise thoughts might arise.

Now what do we do with that?

The rub is that the need here is not to 'do' anything, rather it is to notice, and for all of us to think more critically. It behoves members of fields of practice to be less preoccupied with differentiation and asserting their professional credentials/identities and consider whether a client may need something from elsewhere, or even has a problem that does not neatly 'fit' within one specialism. Simultaneously while communities are great, they can stifle creativity and innovation by squeezing out different perspectives, so fields and communities of practice need to be more skilled at ensuring that they either welcome in genuine diversity of thought, or find ways to rub up against others who can bring that.

For clients it is harder. Under pressure to get things done, often with boards, shareholders, customers, employees, regulators and/or peers demanding things happen fast, and to a certain standard, who wouldn't lean into the reassuring arms of a clearly labelled helper? All of that feeds the need for certainty outlined in Chapter 2. The conditions are ripe then for clients to look for a Silver Bullet and for fields of practice to collude with that. What we do in light of this we'll come to in Chapter 10.

What this means for practice

Linking back to the ethical questions raised in the last chapter, Neil Morrison suggests that as a good practitioner, the ask is to get up each day "prepared to be sacked".

> "… and I don't think enough of us have that, [or] the courage to go in and say 'if today is my last day then so be it, I'm going to bring the level of honesty, openness and integrity to this that is required to be successful. I'm not going to just go along with whatever the plan that my leadership team is heading down, and my CEO thinks is right'."[217]

To adopt the label of a particular field of practice does not mean that the individual ethical concerns apply any less. Fields of practice invite us to ask important questions of ourselves when it comes to standards and ethics.

---

217. Interview 26th May 2020

They offer clients a topography to help them navigate what is being offered and by whom.

What these thought collectives do without awareness, however, is co-create the conditions for (yet more) Silver Bullet thinking, where we conspire with the idea that a given body of knowledge or people have The Answer. A good example of this is how the thinking about change capability manifests in organisations, in particular how to build it. In the next chapter, we see what happens when organisations, theories, fields, consultants, practitioners and the various players collude unconsciously, and the impact that has on clients.

Reflective Questions

- Which tribe or guild do you most associate with?
- What would it be heretical for you to say within it, and what stops you?
- How attached to your labels are you, and how do you know if your clients care?
- If you are a consultant or practitioner of any sort, where do you go for supervision? If you do not, where exactly do you take your ethical wrestles and client challenges to make sense of them?
- How easy it is in your thought collective or tribe to talk about your shadows?

SILVER BULLET NO. 14

Our solution not only looks big, it is. That's why it costs so much.
Plus it costs a lot to make it shine.
It is very big and shiny. Because you are worth it.

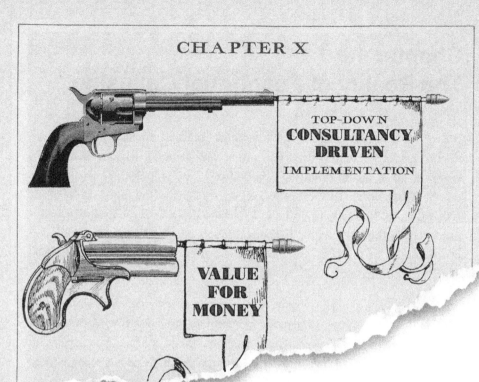

THE REALITY OF FUNCTIONAL COLLUSION

OR: SHINING A LIGHT ON WHAT LURKS IN THE SHADOWS

Chapter 10:
The Reality of Functional Collusion

It is worth reminding ourselves of 'functional collusion' at this point. These are the unconscious patterns of relating, and accompanying behaviour, that people engage in to avoid uncomfortable emotions. Prime among these is shame, as people collude in an attempt to be seen as competent. The functional element is that the collusion serves a purpose, namely to defend against anxiety. It is also functional in the sense that it happens through people acting in specific roles, in the context of this book these being the buyers and sellers of Silver Bullets, which often means senior leaders and the experts who cater to them.

The challenge all along in writing this book has been that underpinning the patterns I am attempting to describe are the dynamics of shame. Brené Brown (2013: 68) defines shame as "the fear that something we have done or failed to do, an ideal that we've not lived up to, or a goal that we've not accomplished makes us unworthy of connection". Cavicchia and Gilbert suggest that "shame, and its milder form, embarrassment, are the feelings which can alert us to when we might have transgressed an acceptable range of behaviour in a particular context and then imagine or experience the context as being less welcoming or even rejecting towards us as a result" (2018: 148). What we will see in this chapter is precisely what happens when individuals teeter on the edge of what they experience as a transgression.

By its very nature, shame is not something that human beings are comfortable discussing. Given that functional collusion is essentially an attempt to describe patterns of relating that set out to hide and/or deny uncomfortable feelings and are not often in the open, you must dig for it or see if you can spot where it might be lurking beneath the surface, and, if you are lucky, meet someone who is prepared to talk freely about their experience. For Cavicchia and Gilbert (2018: 147), things to look out for in individuals include:

- "a preoccupation with self-image and sensitivity (at times acute) to the perception of others (and particularly feedback) based on the need to have self-images constantly shored up and reinforced by mirroring from others;

- exhaustion as a result of a constant workaholic striving to be perfect; a lack of meaning and purpose in their personal and professional lives as a result of having disconnected from what they desire;

- the inability to set appropriate boundaries for fear of what others may think of them if they say no."

The ex-politician and government minister Rory Stewart eloquently described how the above manifests at a human level for political leaders:

"I think it is because the gap between the way that MPs are encouraged to present themselves to the public and who they really are is almost unsustainable.

It's mad, because you're pretending to be all-knowing, perfect, dynamic, confident. You are pretending that you've got the answers to everything, and that I know where we're going. The truth is, this is a country of 70 million people, and politicians don't really know what's going on. And yet we pretend to the public that we do." (*The Guardian*, 11-09-2023)

This would seem to me to be a fairly accurate description of what it must feel like to be a leader trapped in a pattern of functional collusion, where the fear of failure is set against the fear of not being able to meet expectations, and the shame that results. In the context of politics and the political system more widely, in the UK at least, Stewart is bringing all of us into this dance. For it is the *collective* expectations – both realistic and unrealistic – that set the boundaries.

The NHS offers us a clear example of what happens when the impossibility of a task meets the humans responsible for delivering it. In 2019, the median tenure for NHS chief executives was reported to be three years and the mean average was four years (Chambers & Exworthy, 2020: 7). Fast forward to 2023 and the *Health Service Journal* reported that "nearly two-thirds of trusts have a 'first-time' chief executive, while one-third of the sector's CEOs have been in their current post for 18 months or less" (HSJ, 23-08-2023). The jeopardy within NHS boardrooms is clear, as Sue Sjuve, a former chair of an NHS trust, told me:

"There is a frightening fast turnover of CEOs in the health service [and] there is this tendency to look for an individual to blame … if there is some sort of patient safety scandal, the chief executive will go, the chair will go. Sometimes the whole board is cleared out."[218] [219]

The trust she became Chair of in 2017 was found to be in breach of its license in 2016, and that is what happened: most of the board was culled, and with them went all the organisational knowledge.

> "… there is a definite feeling that you're looking constantly for that Silver Bullet in terms of a leader who is going to bring the answer rather than accepting that a leader or leadership group is always going to have some failures." (Ibid.)

The attachment to heroic leadership is deep within the NHS, as it is elsewhere. Hold in mind that this is an interconnected set of many different organisations that in turn make up the whole. Leadership development and learning within the NHS has for years emphasised the importance of systemic leadership, systems working, collaboration, working at multiple levels and anything and everything that is in many ways the antithesis of heroic leadership.

If heroic leadership does not work, of course, there is always one other tried and tested route, suggested Sjuve:

> "… when something goes wrong, the first thing the NHS hierarchy do is reach for one of the Big Four consulting firms to come in and sort it out. I am told by people who've worked in the Big Four consulting firms that they see the NHS as a real cash cow, that the NHS will pay huge amounts of money for PwC or Deloitte or somebody to come in and write a report …
>
> And then we'll use the recommendations of that report … often to clear out senior leadership and bring in new people rather than invest in supporting the people who are already there to help them to be successful." (Ibid.)

I am having an awful sense of déjà vu at this point, and as Sjuve mused:

> "But is that really belief that there's a Silver Bullet or is it just covering your rear?" (Ibid.)

---

218. Interview 15th September 2023
219. This reminds me of an event I co-hosted on the NHS as a hostile environment. A former NHS CEO in the group recalled how regulators used terms that seemed closely related to medieval torture.

When I am told stories by people in the NHS of senior executives jumping ship into the arms of professional service firms and now relentlessly marketing their health practices, then this reaching for the Big Four Sjuve highlights is not surprising. It is working incredibly well, functioning in fact, and there is a real sense of collusion. What follows reveals something about the games that are played in corporate life, all the while hidden beneath the tarpaulin of rational and informed decision making.

Finding the words for something hard to talk about

Since my research methodology is implicitly qualitative, I can only reflect the landscape as I see it; I cannot prove or disprove a hypothesis. After all, the idea that things can be objectively true, measured and manipulated is what underpins the pursuit of the mythical Silver Bullet.

Towards the end of my research, one of the final interviews I conducted was with Thomas Wilde, an English consultant now based in Canada. Our conversation crystalised a key element of my inquiry, as in case after case he shared experiences that demonstrate just how powerful the patterns of relating underpinning functional collusion are, and the way in which decision makers are bent out of shape by shame has serious consequences in both human and financial terms.

In revisiting the role of large consultancies covered earlier, it is merely because it serves to neatly illustrate the point, not to pick on them in particular. Through a series of case studies, I want to bring the reality of functional collusion to life and reveal a little of the real-world impact it has. Doing so through the eyes of one consultant may seem a narrow data set, except the stories that follow are all subtly different, yet reveal functional collusion at play with the same witness each time.

Towards the end of my research, one of the final interviews I conducted was with Thomas Wilde (a pseudonym), an English consultant now based in Canada what Curtis means by functional collusion, and his response was that it made sense of everything he had experienced in the events he was describing to me. While he had known something was going on, that it signified something, he was unsure what, other than it being yet more examples of organisational and leadership dysfunction.

Case 1: Once upon a time in Europe …

Wilde is an anomaly, a rare kind of person who early on in their career was skilled at spotting inconsistencies and absurdities and pointing them out to others. Hold in mind he was in his early twenties, a young Asian man in a predominantly white, male industry, which made him even more of an oddity when added to his willingness to speak up.

Wilde's career started in the early 1980s in the UK arm of a global motor manufacturing business. Having made a name for himself by asking awkward questions around the amount of money the organisation was making in its negotiations with unions, he was spotted by the VP of HR who liked his approach. He asked Wilde to look after the finance operation for a large and high-profile IT training programme being run by a global consultancy that has since been subsumed into another, which in turn was part of a far larger IT systems implementation.

Value for money

Wilde noticed that the consultancy was sending in large invoices, with poor evidence of material benefit. This piqued his curiosity, as he observed little activity other than partners "wining and dining" with senior executives of the client organisation. He started looking at the programme and discovered that the part he was responsible for – IT Training – represented £5m per year of a several £100m IT project. His initial impression of the consultancy slowly changed:

> "… at one level it was this amazing company because they were very well presented, I'd never met anybody like them. I'd seen suited and booted people, [but] never seen people so professional, so very articulate, and I learned much later in life the whole thing was a performance. Anyway, at the time I was: 'Wow, these guys really are like from the movies', but then I start digging deeper …"[220]

What he found were offices full of young Grinders, bright young people his own age, and on closer inspection noticed that the skills and experience promised in proposals did not match that of the young consultants. On questioning this, Wilde was in effect told 'you do not understand' and the young consultants

---

220. Interview 10th July 2023 – all other quotes in this chapter from this unless otherwise stated

were barred from fraternising with him by their Minders. This galvanised Wilde. For example, he would turn up at consultant meetings on site to ask what they were discussing, and if client-related. If they were discussing client matters, he would insist on staying. If it was consultancy business, he would then ask for a justification for why the business was being billed for that time.

He dug into the work further and found £200k a month for translation services, although the organisation already had in-house capability for this (hold in mind that all consultancies do a diagnostic phase, so likely would have known this). The head of translation services who Wilde approached said, "This is what we were set up for" and the work was pulled from the consultancy.

The twist

The next thing Wilde did was start to network with multilingual consultants in the areas that the organisation needed IT training and challenged them to form a consortium to bid for the work. This they did and came back with a proposal for £500k per year. Instead of the £5m the client was being charged …

> "… for the same level of service delivery, and better quality of service. We got rid of a ton of stuff they shouldn't have been doing. They were doing prototypes and all kinds of stuff that weren't even useful. And they were running focus groups which weren't being listened to.

> Then of course they were doing Translation Services, we saved some money there. So, we've stripped out stuff they didn't need to do. The new consortium came in and suddenly boom! All across Europe, people were just so happy, because they were being heard [and] getting training on time."

If this were simply a case of 'smart guy spots his employers being rinsed', then it would not be that unusual. You would imagine that Wilde would've been in line for a pay rise, but no. The VP of IT hauled him in and said he would be "fired for insubordination" for "jeopardising the project". This is such a powerful reminder of how speaking up in corporate contexts comes with an extraordinary level of risk to the person giving voice to both concerns or indeed new ideas. The very term 'insubordination' derives directly from the hierarchy on which workplaces tend to rely.

Despite offering evidence of the value of what he had negotiated, and pointing out how far the project was behind and so was being jeopardised by the consultancy themselves, the threats persisted. The VP of HR, who had brought him in initially, backed him as he had done exactly what he had hoped, and the fight moved to the boardroom. Overall, however, the consultancy retained the overarching contract, and for all Wilde's efforts the symbiotic relationship remained largely undisturbed.

This is a lovely example of what I described in Chapter 2, where the unconscious task is to collude with the organisation ideal, the system version of individual ego-ideal. Here we see the need to maintain the image of both the commissioning and consulting organisations as competent, honest and knowing what they are doing.

By holding up a mirror to data which challenges this narrative and burst the collusive bubble, Wilde gets scapegoated. All of these dynamics explain why whistle-blowing is so hard, dangerous and threatening. Shame and the fear of rejection for speaking out police what people feel they can and cannot talk about. This is an anti-democratic, totalitarian process and it is rife in organisations.

Case 2: A Game of Thrones

Wilde's early experience of the relationships between consulting partners and senior client leaders was not an outlier, as the pattern has not changed much over time. The idea that consulting firms are simply brought into complete specific tasks or projects is not entirely true. Sometimes the machinations at board level are strikingly close to *A Game of Thrones*, albeit minus all the nudity and dragons.

In one well-known US telecoms business Wilde worked with in the 1990s, a leading global consultancy was brought in by the then CEO. The CEO brought them in because the board were "idiots", in his view. Proposals the CEO made to the board would be questioned and rejected. By bringing in consultants, giving them his strategy and asking them to rebadge it as theirs with all the bells and whistles of their trade – and without changing a word – it would be gleefully accepted by the board, and the global consultancy hired to carry out the work. While the CEO had successfully got approval for the strategy he wanted to adopt, it was at the cost of having to pay a consultancy to be, in effect, an expensive Trojan Horse.

In effect, dysfunction and incompetence masked by engaging a consulting firm to provide a fig leaf, a further form of collusion in the true sense of the word.

This echoes the comment one of my clients made to me regarding the intimacy she observed in "each member of the senior leadership team [having] their own consultant whispering in their ears".[221] This creates another problem, identified by a different client, "as we might have more than one consultancy in but each consultancy is working with a different group of leaders. So we're not getting the overlap."[222]

As David Shaw notes:

> "The continuing tendency for consultancy services to be procured through relationships between particular senior managers and consultants, rather than through rational, criterion-based procurement processes whereby an organisation's purchasing function mediates between its senior managers and their consultants, enlarges the scope for opportunistic behaviour by consultants in responding to the commercial pressures that they face." (Shaw, 2019: 56)

Wilde's experience mirrors this, in that he will sometimes find his work in an organisation ends the moment the senior leader responsible for a project leaves, and the new incumbent wants to bring their own consultant(s) in.

That is not unsurprising, and at the same time it is worth noting that, sometimes, these decisions are not made based on a robust assessment of value and impact, rather they are a function of relationship and the need for senior leaders to manage their anxiety by having (another) person who they trust/are comfortable with, who will tell them what they want to hear, and/or will enable them to make their own mark.

As Jeffrey Sonennfeld noted when looking at the patterns within boards that had failed, it is the ability to tolerate, cultivate and value useful dissent that makes the difference (2002). Removing challenge from the room just means that you are less likely to have someone point out when you are wearing no clothes, as per Hans Christian Anderson's fairy tale. Sonnenfeld argues that what is required is a culture of open difference, stressing that "perhaps the most important link in the virtuous cycle [of Respect, Trust, and Candour] is the capacity to challenge one another's (and one's own) assumptions and beliefs" (2002: 6).

---

221. Interview 18th June 2020
222. Interview 1st May 2020

My own experience of senior leadership teams is that calls for candour are common but translating that into a reality where group members work through their differences, and any heat that may ensue, is challenging. David Wilkinson, an organisational consultant and founder of *The Oxford Review*, suggests that "no holds barred" team cultures are at the route of high performance, because they are orientated on learning.[223] While rare, his work with the Red Arrows and in a major bank demonstrated what can be achieved when relationships and relatedness is taken to mean working through differences and perception gaps. The difference that makes a difference, Wilkinson observed, was having a positive intent around collective learning: mistakes are OK, so shame is less likely to be evoked. This links back to Mintzberg's observation earlier in the book (2004: 41) regarding the failure of business schools to teach 'soft skills', which are in fact nothing of the sort. The ability to talk about shame, whether that be at an individual or collective level, is sorely lacking in many of us.

It is symptomatic of a wider systemic failure in education and learning, as the curriculum for children, with its overemphasis on STEM subjects, does nothing to equip people with the skills to navigate the relational dynamics of organisational life. Much management and leadership development, while at face value sometimes professing to address that gap, is still an exercise in futility if the dynamics of the boardroom are not addressed. There are also significant cultural differences, for example in societies where the notion of 'saving face' is deeply embedded. I say boardroom specifically because many of the decisions that result in the purchasing of Silver Bullet solutions are made by the most senior people in organisations.

Case 3: Mutually assured destruction

Lurking beneath the stories in this chapter is a relational dynamic that might at first sight appear to be founded on mutual benefit, a 'you scratch my back' dynamic that benefits all parties involved, if not necessarily wider stakeholders in the client organisation, customers or society more widely.

Sometimes, however, it is more the threat of mutually assured destruction that maintains the functional collusion. The following case also illustrates in stark terms why it is much easier to get £100m or £300m to pay for an extremely big technology solution and a lot harder to get £5 million to pay for behaviour change. Digital transformation? Have a big cheque. Culture? What now? Can't

---

223. Interview 19th July 2023

HR do that, or can we have a tick-box online course to address diversity and inclusion issues please?

Shortly before COVID hit, Wilde was invited by the CEO of a major US retail organisation to become their VP of Global Trends for two years, to see through the organisation's response to the growing threat posed by Amazon. Despite the attractive offer, Wilde respectfully declined. What then emerged was the real story. In the previous two years, prior to the CEO's arrival, they had spent $200m on digital transformation with a global consulting firm which had failed. So another of the global professional services firms was engaged, and a further $400m spent.

The CEO told Wilde that in the first year the consultants came in and made lots of these promises, and the next year the new consultancy similarly struggled to deliver.

At this point, Wilde inquired why the client did not sue the consultants, or at the very least try to recoup some of the money spent. The answer?

> "'… there will be backlash. I can't sue the people I bought in because I'm tethered to them'. I said, 'Well, that sounds ridiculous. But that means there's zero accountability.' He said that it's 'like hush money because if they fail, you can't sue them for not delivering because you were the one who signed the cheques and brought them in'."

That plus the CEO believed it would mean he would never work at a senior level again if he took on one of the major consulting firms for a failure to deliver. It served both parties to keep the failure secret and hidden, if possible, to protect both their reputations. When Wilde asked whether the CEO had carried out a post-mortem, his response was: "No, I'm not going to do that. Why would I document my failures?"

This is a psychological protection racket based on the need to maintain ego and organisation ideals. Wilde's final comment here was particularly disheartening and damning:

> "There isn't really even a blackmail, there's no kind of threats, there's not even veiled threats. It's just the way this is structured at that level of an organisation."

In other words, this level of dysfunction, waste, incompetence, fear of failure and incredible human fragility in the face of having made mistakes, is just a given. Deal with it. It is a shame-driven version of '*omertà*', the Mafia code of silence. A former PA Consulting consultant offered a view from the other side, that chimes uncannily:

> "I was pitching some work for Goldman Sachs a few years ago. I knew one of the clients quite well, and he said, 'I don't mind working with you. But I can't take the risk of bringing in PA … I'm ex-Accenture. My boss is ex-Accenture. If I go with Accenture and they fail, nobody will look at me and say you did a bad job. If I go with a new company, and they don't deliver the value, they will look at me and say "why did you choose them?"'."

This reflects the fragility of the consultant, the fear of being fired plus the sense that you are only as good as your last client engagement and deliverable. If the latter can be framed as having been a guaranteed success, a Silver Bullet no less, all the better. As de Vries and Miller archly put it: "An exalted self-image is usually difficult to sustain in the light of external circumstances such as disappointment and failure" (1985: 592).

Ex-consultants moving client-side (more common than the reverse) can deepen the patterns of functional collusion. As John Whittington, a consultant and facilitator who specialises in using systemic constellations as a way to map human systems, said on a workshop I attended that he led, a dysfunction in one part of the system is a perfectly functional expression of a dysfunction elsewhere. This is a shining example of that idea, for even failure is rewarded as it fulfils a function of minimising distress and shame. The psychological processes are what I am most interested in here, linking to shame, ego and narcissism (see Chapter 2).

The thing about narcissism is that it is profoundly ordinary. Yes there are pathological versions of it (hello loud and orange US president) and the day-to-day version when we are in thrall to an idealised version of our own ego, rather than how things really are. In *Narcissistic Process and Corporate Decay* (1990), Howard Schwartz highlights how individual ego ideals become fused with the ideals of the organisation in which people work. This means that individuals, often out of conscious awareness, become preoccupied with living up to the expectations the organisation places on them, and its cultural norms. They also focus on maintaining the particular image the organisation wishes to promote to the world. That is how we end up with the gap that many in organisations experienced as the gap between espoused and lived values. When values are laminated rather than lived, some form of narcissism is at play.

Case 4: When shame meshes with power

Wilde was moved to share the following final story directly after I read him the definition of 'functional collusion', and it proved to be an exquisite example of the phenomenon. Many of the threads from preceding chapters show up.

We have the psychological and human elements; the desperate desire to find the thing that works; questions are raised by implication in terms of what on earth CEOs are being taught if this is what happens; how theories, ideas and methodologies are wielded as weapons of influence and persuasion; once more, the role consultancies and consultants play and how powerful thought collectives become when an idea takes hold.

It is also a profoundly human story where the shame was no longer hidden.

A bank in trouble

The CEO of a Canadian bank asked Wilde to help with a restructure. They were eighteen months in, and "in trouble", according to the client, despite the efforts of the large consulting firm they had hired. They were seeing no progress, and the CEO was under pressure from the board.

Wilde suggested an approach based on Whole Scale Change, a methodology that looks to change organisations by involving those who are likely to be affected – it is change 'done with' rather than 'done to'.

Central to this is finding the key protagonists in all parts of a business, and Wilde spent several months working across the organisation, meeting people and bringing them together. He began by teaching them how to do design work, helping them develop both the mindset and skills to become effective internal change agents, and by the end of this phase, there were twenty-five people ready. He tasked them with coming up with three or four innovative and potentially viable design approaches for the bank. The intention was that these would be 70% ready, to allow for them to start work literally the next day and iterate, rather than questing for the Silver Bullet of an org design that is 100% right on paper but never gets implemented because it is always being refined.[224]

The team of change agents presented to the board, and by the end of that Wilde told the CEO they could start implementation immediately.

Ghosted

From this point on, Wilde waited to get started. He called each day, to establish whether they had a green light. None of his messages were answered or calls returned. After a while, he simply gave up and put it down to experience: clients change their minds, consultants are disposable. You move on.

Three years on, and Wilde received an invitation to the CEO's leaving do. Out of curiosity, he went, and his former client met him. She began crying as she told him what actually happened. As Wilde spoke to me, he choked up, his own shame mirroring that of his client in the story he was telling:

> "'I've got to apologise to you,' she said. 'I've wasted three years of my life. And what happened was when you left, [the consulting firm] came in. They took your work, and said it was their work, that it was part of what they were planning to implement, and that you'd sat down with them and interviewed them. [They said] you'd taken these confidential documents, you'd given them to the change agents the week of the presentation and done a 'big smoke and mirrors' job'.
>
> And they said to her, 'How do you think people with no education and background in design could come up with that stuff by themselves?' She was apologising, because she had no faith. Forget the process, forget me, that wasn't an issue. She had no faith in *her* people. And she trusted them [the consulting firm]. She said, 'You're right. How can people who've never done work on design come up with such amazing solutions?'
>
> So I said, 'Why didn't you call me?'

---

224. As an aside, a colleague of mine spent two years on an organisation design project for a US business developing a Target Operating Model (TOM) that, by the time the consulting team felt it was ready for release, was so out of date as to be useless. TOMs are another example of useful ideas that get turned into Silver Bullets. They are very seductive, and clients often like them because the neatness, on paper, of a TOM squeezes out all the mess, e.g. emotion, angst, politics, etc.

She said, 'I felt ashamed … I just didn't know how to call you. So we went through another year, year and a half, two years go by … They carried on trying to implement the solutions that your teams came up with. And they failed. Because they couldn't implement it effectively because they were trying to do a traditional top-down implementation. Not engaging people, not getting the whole system working together … they were just top down. So it failed.'

I said you could have called me. She said, 'I couldn't – I'm now saying to you face to face: I apologise.'

I wasn't going to comfort her, and I said, 'It is not me you have to apologise to, I didn't lose anything out of it, but your people did. The people that you should have worked with, to engage in this process to make change happen.'"

I asked Wilde why he thought the client believed the consulting firm, and his sense is that they did what persuasive consultants do well: they showed up and successfully persuaded her that Wilde had fraudulently taken their methods and repurposed them as his own. They offered her certainty, reinforcing the narrative that their methodology, scale and approach was the one the bank needed. It was also an approach that maintained the control they were at risk of losing.

The consultants here were also projecting onto Wilde what they themselves had done, simultaneously disavowing their own unethical behaviour. It is a form of what some psychologists characterise as DARVO when describing abusive behaviour – deny, attack, reverse victim and offender.

The client made no attempt to verify if this was true, and three years on, when there was no possible consequence for the business or the consulting firm, her shame was sufficiently close to the surface, and she had enough self-awareness, to at least acknowledge her part of the dance. Shame here became conscience and the need to acknowledge the truth.

Picking the learning out of this

What shows up across these stories and others I did not have space to include are several patterns:

- Fear of failure and 'getting it wrong'.

- High need for protection of an ego ideal and organisation.

- Self-protection and displacement of uncomfortable and unbearable thoughts and feelings.

- Covering up of incompetence, whether that be one's own or that of others.

- Fear of conflict and working through differences.

- Fear of – and an unwillingness to – challenge core assumptions about change and leadership.

- A yearning for someone – anyone! – to please have a solution that can be bought off the shelf that simply works.

- And if someone has the Silver Bullet, phew, I get to dodge the bullet of being fired.

- The obsession senior leaders have for new and shiny, coupled with a tendency to apply conventional thinking to post-conventional problems.

- An issue of trust – employees are not trusted to come up with answers. As one client commented: "We don't trust the views of our own people. [Also] our own people don't always trust our leaders to keep us safe when we're putting forward the ideas because often it is the person who came up with the idea and suggested it to their most senior leaders that the senior leaders will get rid of when it goes wrong. That's quite a big risk to take if you wanted to stay with the organisation."[225]

When faced with these tensions and the need to alleviate the anxiety they induce, reaching for the first (apparently) viable Silver Bullet makes sense. What is also clear is that, not only do they not exist, the continuing reluctance and failure by buyers and sellers of quick fixes to acknowledge these tensions is causing more problems, often making things worse rather than helping.

At the relational boundary between consultant and client, the real dysfunction and functional collusion emerges. Shelly Hossain, an experienced Organisation Development practitioner, reflected in conversation with me on whether "we have got to a point of not being good enough", the 'we' here being all involved in the process of change.

---

225. Interview 1st May 2020

"It is about you doing the work that is required. You grow in order to do the societal work better (and to make change happen in organisations), it is not about hanging about in our own glory … I worked with a very influential organisation who brought us in, and then said, 'You are not doing what we wanted'. I said, 'We are but we are working with what emerged.'"[226]

The client could not bear the discomfort of something unexpected or unwanted emerging, so cancelled the project, and Hossain then saw the same tender going out multiple times in the following months. As she wryly observed:

"This is the absurdity. People are not prepared to do the internal work."

Everybody knows the game (probably)

I found myself wondering the extent to which a form of wilful blindness permeates client/consultant relationships that we are largely in denial of. Repeatedly, I heard stories that implied a sense of acceptance or resignation that this is just how things are. For example, one client commented:

"We spent a huge amount of money on something with McKinsey that we then never did anything with at all. And I think McKinsey supported us well … They did all the things I would expect them to do, but they didn't care whether we used it or not."[227]

I asked her why she thought that. She replied, "Because of how quickly they let it drop when we let it drop. They were still working with us. They still had opportunities to continually ask us what we were doing with it. But they didn't, they pushed us a bit and then dropped it."

This same organisation has also worked with the following in the past fifteen years or so:

- Deloitte
- PwC
- EY
- BCG
- Accenture
- Bain

226. Conversation 26th July 2023
227. Interview 1st May 2020

That and a melange of mid-size and specialist consultancies. At one point, I asked a different client in the same organisation to count the number of consultancies working in the business at that moment in time. We stopped counting when we hit double figures.

I asked my first client whether any consultancy had ever named the merry-go-round and the apparent lack of any progress, and she said, maybe unsurprisingly, no. It seems turkeys are still reluctant to vote for Christmas.

Yet you cannot blame consultancies, according to the former PwC Director, for "developing salve for the brow of the chief executive who wants that level of confidence and assurance that the people that they are working with can wrap their arms around them and say 'it's okay, we've done this before. We know how this works. We know how to do this.'"[228]

I agree, it is more evidence however of a very well-developed and entrenched pattern of functional collusion.

Reflective Questions

- What does it take for you to admit when things go wrong and learn from that?
- How accepting are you personally of error and mistakes – or do you cleave to a standard that sits very close mentally to the idea of perfection?
- How aware are you of what most evokes shame in you? How do you defend against that?
- What strategies have you consciously or unconsciously used to minimise anxiety? What might the cost have been of that?
- What work might you need to do on yourself to both better understand your unconscious behaviour and take better care of yourself?

228. Interview 9th March 2021

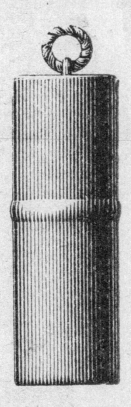

SILVER BULLET NO. 7

2X2 BOX

Our 2x2 model is different to all the others.
It is new and sexy although it does use many of the same words,
just in a different order.

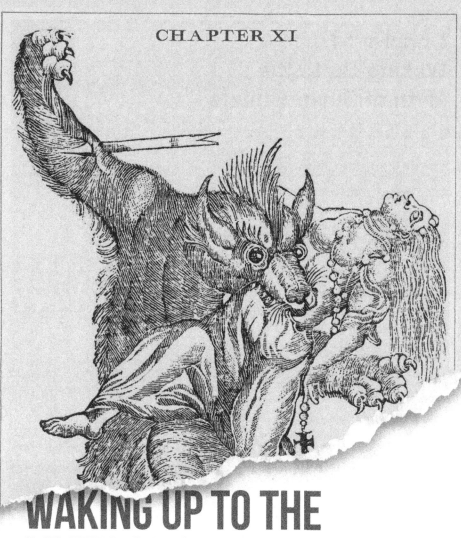

WAKING UP TO THE MYTH OF SILVER BULLETS

OR: WHAT TO DO WHEN REALITY BITES US ON THE ARSE

Chapter 11:
Waking Up to the
Myth of Silver Bullets

"It is easy to say 'avoid Silver Bullets' and be a curmudgeon or naysayer about what is wrong with much of our faddish field; it is more difficult to parse out the relevant and useful from the noise." Dave Ulrich[229]

What to do if there are no Silver Bullets

Now we come to the crunch question. I said at the outset that I am not going to offer a Silver Bullet. I also wanted to resist the invitations to fill a large part of it with suggestions of what we all might do in the absence of easy answers, and I remain steadfast in my refusal to rescue you from any anxiety and discomfort you may be experiencing.

I also do not think there is a great need to offer oodles of suggestions, not least because the internet, bookshops, universities, business schools, gurus, thinkers and others already offer many 'solutions' and 'answers'.

More useful, in my view, is to offer, *tentatively and with no promise of easy answers,* some ideas to provoke your thinking, a few starting points in relation to some of the issues raised in the book, and some gentle signposting to people and resources that might be useful.

It is also true that, in *some* contexts, with *some* problems, *some* solutions have a high chance of success. If they did not, nothing would work.

The options

I am not offering you something to replace the Silver Bullet as a thing, rather I want to encourage you to think more deeply about what our options might be when we realise pursuing the myth of the Silver Bullet takes us on a fool's errand. I'll start by offering a selection of suggestions from my research subjects, who I asked whether they believed there was a Silver Bullet to complex problems, and if not what the next best thing might be. No one said there was

---

229. Email 20th December 2020

one, rather there was a definite pattern of people saying that with emergent and complex change, the idea there could be a Silver Bullet was inherently absurd.

The starting point for some was a recognition that often the nature of the problem is not that clear, even when a client may think it is. Gervase Bushe's view is that you first have to "figure out what kind of problem is the technical problem, which is an adaptive challenge [i.e. a problem that is often unknown or hard to identify, and tied to deeper patterns or dynamics. The solution is unknown, which requires learning] … you always need to do that".[230] Bushe is also an advocate of inquiry:

> "If we authentically engage the people who work here around a question they care about, they'll figure out a way to make it work. And you just need to get out of the way. And then when they're starting to try to make it work you need to be very present and doing everything you can to support what might help them make it happen." (Ibid.)

He points to the gnarly challenge that for major problems that leaders face, "they need to look inside and create the opportunity for the collective intelligence that exists to get surfaced, and to figure out what's going to work for them here and now" (ibid.). Bushe articulated his approach, which he calls a generative change strategy, more fully in *The Dynamics of Generative Change* (2020). It is based on the premise that when dealing with complex, adaptive challenges, no one knows what the right answer is, so the best strategy is to engage stakeholders in trying many changes at the same time and learn as you go. He points out that this strategy has been employed under different labels for decades with generally positive results, and importantly highlights what leaders must do *before* and *after* encouraging the people who must change, including how they need to act.

Lucian Hudson, with a long career as a senior leader and operating in multiple executive teams, suggested what is needed is "a better collective appreciation of [where] the leader or leadership team can exercise enough agency for themselves to play their full part, yet also create the space where others can also contribute. This ultimately can result in a more collaborative endeavour, recognising that we are social selves rather than individual selves.[231] Again, notice the thread of inquiry that runs through that.

---

230. Interview 6th May 2020
231. Interview 31st July 2023

Diana Wu David suggested what is required is an iterative approach and the capacity to adapt: "It's being able to say: here's one small step you can do, and you can just focus on that one and tune a lot of the rest out. And here's the second step that builds on the first step. And you can do that and all of a sudden you find yourself ten weeks later thinking, 'wow, I made so much progress'." This is reminiscent of the idea of Trojan Mice, which were described by Peter Fryer on his (now sadly no longer available) website[232] as:

> "Much change is of the 'Trojan Horse' variety. The planned changes are presented at a grand event (the Trojan Horse) amid much loud music, bright lights and dry ice. More often than not, however, a few weeks later the organisation will have settled back into its usual ways and rejected much of the change.
>
> This is usually because the change was too great to be properly understood and owned by the workforce. Trojan Mice, on the other hand, are small, well-focused changes, which are introduced on an ongoing basis in an inconspicuous way.
>
> They are small enough to be understood and owned by all concerned but their effects can be far-reaching. Collectively a few Trojan Mice will change more than one Trojan Horse ever could."[233]

Trojan Mice are the antithesis of Silver Bullets and echo several of the approaches suggested to me during my research. Dr Richard Claydon's ideas are in this territory, in that "the closest thing I have to a Silver Bullet is if you run interventions and trainings that are highly enjoyable for people, the chances are, the answer will emerge … your people will know how to solve your organisation's problems if you just let them. And it's a matter of giving them the courage to speak up".[234]

The Chief Human Resources Officer I interviewed concurs: "I can't think of many cases where there's like one solution that suddenly fixes everything. It's normally lots and lots of different often small steps or changes of behaviour, or trying and failing that actually leads to the ultimate breakthrough".[235]

---

232. An internet archive of the relevant page can be found here: https://bit.ly/3P2Zq3M
233. A helpful graphic explaining the concept can be found here: https://jarche.com/2012/10/on-trojan-mice/
234. Interview 4th May 2020
235. Interview 26th June 2020

Naomi Stanford agreed, with a warning: "If you accept that there's no Silver Bullet, that is one thing that will give you 'an answer'. But there may be multiple things that could get you somewhere, so inquiry might work. But you'd have to be rather careful about how you frame the inquiry and who is participating."[236]

Three suggestions from Glenda Eoyang: "Firstly iterative inquiry-based, very short cycles of data collection and analysis and action. That's one thing. The second thing is that they stay in inquiry. They don't get stuck in their own answers constantly looking for the better question. And the third thing is pattern logic [a particular approach to sense making in Human Systems Dynamics] that they get really good and conscious about individually and collectively, seeing and understanding patterns."[237]

I liked the pithy simplicity of Alex Boulting's response: "If there is a Silver Bullet, the Silver Bullet is starting that conversation",[238] which paradoxically cannot be a Silver Bullet because no conversation has a predictable outcome. It is also a conversation that does not happen at one moment in time. Susanne Evans, whose PhD research was about what it takes to successfully change organisations, suggests:

> "The conversations that we as consultants need to be having with clients is to help them move away from thinking something is going to help in that moment … [when] in six months' time that might not be the thing anymore. There might be something else that they need … leaders and organisations need to be okay with that, and not be trying to look to solve everything all the time."[239]

To do that, however, takes us back to the need to get comfortable with not knowing, to the possibility of being wrong and the limits of human agency in a complex world. Eek!

Maybe we need to embrace the paradox of organisational life, for as Dr Richard Claydon says, "the ironist just sees the absurdities and says, 'well, we should deal with this because it doesn't make any sense. I don't necessarily know what the answer is. But wouldn't it be good fun trying to define and then engage a whole bunch of people in that and in that experimentation'."[240]

---

236. Interview 24th July 2020
237. Interview 5th May 2020
238. Interview 9th September 2020
239. Interview 11th November 2020
240. Interview 4th May 2020

Naomi Stanford echoes Claydon in observing that her utility often lies in being able to act as the "ironic employee", asking lots of questions that get under the skin of things to reveal contradictions and absurdities, and ultimately surface what may actually be going on.[241]

Rob Briner is a proponent of evidence-based practice. 'There is too much concern about WHAT we should do (e.g. search for the magic solution) rather than the WAY WE GO ABOUT making decisions about what to do (evidence-based practice). It's not a Silver Bullet but it's the nearest thing we have to one."[242]

Ultimately, we may be in the realms of philosophy, something Perry Timms, an influential UK HR practitioner and thinker suggested. While his view is that there are no Silver Bullets in a practical or mechanistic sense, there *may* be a philosophy or way of thinking that serves that purpose, but we haven't discovered it yet).[243] I would argue that the risk here is of further reifying ideas, and it might be more helpful to think about work and the workplace philosophically without coming up with a whole new belief system.

Shifting the focus from a heavy emphasis on action ('that's enough chat, let's do something') to one that balances thinking, discussion and experimentation is a key challenge for everyone in and around organisations. So, pace needs to be dialled down (something that consultants often look to accelerate), room needs to be created for people to connect beyond the lines on the organogram, and people's voices need to be respected rather than just invited so that the environment doesn't just look involving and engaging, rather it actually is.

The client perspective

Client-side perspectives do not differ hugely, merely adding extra texture and nuance. Bernd Zimmermann, formerly a Director of OD for Siemens, observed that "the 'guaranteed solution' is to understand that there always needs to be an 'as well as' solution … the problem is you will never have all the data, and time to digest that data").[244] The implication being that things are in such flux that what works in one moment may no longer be fit for purpose in another, therefore there is no certain solution.

---

241. Interview 24th July 2020
242. Email 17th February 2024
243. Interview 15th September 2020
244. Interview 5th May 2020

One client offered a nuanced take that echoed this, suggesting that there might be localised Silver Bullets, but he qualified that: "Temporarily you can have a Silver Bullet. Over the long term, I think you would have to seriously question as to whether you've still got the right one, in fact that would be a risk. When you think you've got your bullet, at risk of expanding the analogy, you'll start firing it off in every situation. And you might find that what you start hitting isn't the target you intended for."[245] Therefore, by definition, it is not a Silver Bullet, if it runs the risk of collateral damage.

Neil Morrison, from the perspective of having worked in multiple industries, offered a take that talks to the risks of hubris, the pitfalls of thinking we know more than we do: "The answer is not the one you think it is, the answer is one you discover. And you can only discover by feeling, asking, sensing, discussing, testing, trying. And none of that comes from walking in and saying 'here's the answer'."[246] There is also the difficulty inherent in having a conversation with someone who 'knows what they are talking about'. Whenever we think we have an answer, we lose the generativity of exploration and emergent discovery. 'Answers' need to come, at a minimum, with an accompanying recognition that there may simultaneously not be one, even if we cannot see it yet.

What started to emerge from these conversations is that if *inquiry* is key, then the capacity – and willingness – to *experiment* is not far behind. Experimentation, however, is the antithesis of a Silver Bullet, given that experimenting comes with a readiness to not know and to fail, which some organisations profoundly struggle with; it is anathema to them. The Head of Innovation in one global motor manufacturing company once told me that in her organisation, all innovation business plans had to demonstrate how they would ensure success. If you cannot bear failure, shame is probably close by.

The Chief Human Resources Officer I quoted earlier said, "I can't think of any cases where there's one solution that suddenly fixes everything. It's normally lots and lots of different, often small, steps or changes of behaviour, or trying and failing, that actually leads to the ultimate breakthrough."[247] Again, iteration and experimentation are to the fore.

A senior HR leader from the private health industry suggested that in the absence of a Silver Bullet, "it doesn't matter how much data you've got, how

---

245. Interview 18th May 2020
246. Interview 26th May 2020
247. Interview 26th June 2020

much you've done it before, unless you are able to make decisions through a filter of emotional intelligence."[248] Which again talks to the importance of relational approaches to change and problem solving.

The bottom line

Returning to Matthew Syed's work on the significance of diversity in thinking, he neatly draws a few threads together:

> "If … experts bring similar backgrounds and training (and, by implication, similar frames of reference), they are likely to share the same blind spots. Sometimes you need to look at a problem in a new way, perhaps with the eyes of an outsider.
>
> The critical point is that solutions to complex problems typically rely on multiple layers of insight and therefore require multiple points of view." (Syed, 2019: 20)

By implication, having lots of consultants may at face value bring a wealth of experience. However, they will typically come with similar social backgrounds and life experience, plus share assumptions about the nature of change coloured by the field and/or organisation they identify with. The diversity is superficial, and even where there *is* useful difference that spawns creative responses to the problems clients face, the pressure to conform, assimilate, join and be accepted into a group will always be present. Holding a position on the periphery – spatially, contractually, emotionally, philosophically – becomes key, and that, again, requires one to learn how to dance.

There is a risk also that clients are drawn to consultants and helpers who are similar to them, too similar sometimes, and vice versa.

For clients, the ask here is harder. Faced with the need to find their place within their organisation's culture, to be similar enough so as not to be expelled by the organisational immune system, nor to feel their difference so strongly as to walk away, similarity often trumps difference. The need to 'join', to be accepted, becomes the primary task, and the primary risk becomes the fear of rejection, of being seen when we are feeling vulnerable. In some organisations, a regime exists which in effect refutes the rights of those within them to use their voice, compounding the problem.

---

248. Interview 7th July 2020

Considering this dynamic, is it any wonder that organisations struggle to bring together diverse and different voices when they most need them in the same room?

If you cannot accept the 'emperor is wearing no clothes', you have a problem

The choice is actually quite simple. It is entirely possible to carry on believing – or colluding with the idea – that the emperor is not wandering about with his crown jewels on show for all to see. There is a comfort in that, but then ostriches feel safe with their heads in the sand apparently. The need is to be willing to be open to a reality that recognises Silver Bullets do not exist, and that the emperor is indeed wearing no clothes. We might even need to 'get naked' ourselves by revealing our fragility and uncertainty.

This requires us to develop the intellectual and emotional capacity to accept the world is more complex and ambiguous than simple models and tools, methodologies and theories, experts and thought leaders would have us believe. It requires letting go of illusions of mastery, control, domination and power over others. It means eschewing manipulation and exploitation and learning to dance with the complex, the unknown, the emergent and the possible. That may mean a tango, a waltz, rhumba, cha cha, funky chicken or body popping. Who knows, but you will need to learn how to dance differently.

It calls for learning to learn, learning how to reflect and think, how to make meaning together, in dialogue. Alongside learning (or perhaps development might be a better term) sits the ethical judgement and choice to embrace these ways of being different in terms of presence and practice in the workplace – and, of course, beyond. I can learn to reflect and to think, but then eschew that in my day-to-day life.

Yes, this will require courage, boldness or failing that a willingness to jump off the edge of a metaphorical cliff. It means thinking more deeply about oneself and one's behaviours, how we show up and impact others, what we embody and the nature of our relationships. It is only by connecting with others that we might hope to amplify creativity, imagination and the experimentation and innovation needed to respond to today's organisational and global challenges.

For both clients and consultants of any flavour, this requires reflexivity, and of a form that bridges the gap from the learning space to practice and application, rather than residing solely in the safety of a comfortable off-site residential, bite-size learning model or modular programme that spoon feeds theory to manage anxiety through the promise of knowledge acquisition.

The ask

As change practitioners, coaches, consultants and leaders, the ask is to create conditions where these moves might become possible. Note *might*, as there are no guarantees, only the knowledge that maintaining the status quo will not bring out the radical step changes in perspective and behaviour that giving up Silver Bullets requires.

Nested in that is also the 'work proper' of addressing patterns of functional collusion, namely working with our own shame, furtling in the undergrowth of our own individual and collective narratives. Is that easy? Not often, and the alternative is more of the same.

If we turn this into specific practices, they might look like this:

- Practitioners and consultants developing the capacity to co-create conditions with clients for containing anxiety. This also requires working on themselves to learn to contain, think about, relate to and express their own anxiety. In my own work, this has led me increasingly to name what I experience in the moment in terms of transference, counter transference and projection.

- Supporting clients to develop the knowledge, confidence and skills for reflecting on their presenting issues and making meaning from them together. That means challenging the rhetoric of, say, confidence to talk about the specifics of what would increase a client's surety in some facet of their experience of self.

- Helping clients and their systems to relax egoic attachments to narcissistic ego and organisational ideals of 'being right', greatness, mastery, perfection, winning, etc. That's difficult to do without a combination of courage and a radar for absurdity.

- Helping clients develop the capacity for pluralism, recognising and even valuing the different perspectives individuals hold on reality. For me, this means I need to develop my own capacity for hearing and considering other perspectives, adding another layer of complexity to the process of deciding when to challenge and when not.

- Supporting clients to tolerate increasing levels of ambiguity and uncertainty and develop the capacity to go on thinking and responding. Without self-compassion, hard nay impossible to do for clients.

- Cultivating a degree of trust in the capacity to navigate uncharted territory rather than having to find a quick fix. That means embodying one's own relationship with not knowing. I do that by explicitly saying I come with more questions than answers.

- Working to reveal the pitfalls and blind spots of Silver Bullets – why we are attracted to them, the psychological functions they serve and what they defend against. Hard to do if part of you is hooked by a need to appear like you have the answer/know a lot/do not want to get fired.

- Creating contexts of containment – where anxieties can be named and thought about so that they do not need to be so quickly evacuated into the pursuit of certainty. This means understanding the subtle distinction between 'psychological safety' and 'enough psychological safety'. Total safety is an illusion.

- Creating contexts for human connection – fostering empathy and developing knowledge, confidence and skill in relationship building and maintaining relationships, adopting a stance of radical hospitality to that which we experience as 'other', different, novel, strange. Not easy. I notice my defensiveness is normally a clue I have work to do here.

- Holding meanings lightly and allowing room for knowledge and perspective to evolve – creating the conditions for an ongoing dialogue between experience and the sense we make of it. That means slowing down and resisting the pathological need for speed.

- Teaching others how to learn while continuing to learn ourselves – from a leadership perspective, and from the helping perspective, that means not expecting others to do work we are not willing to do ourselves. If our consulting is a partnership, we do not necessarily have access to teachable material; instead, we commit to being co-learners, sitting alongside those with whom we work as part of a collective inquiry for which we offer the space and safety.

- Developing reflection skills and capabilities – and the crucial skill of reflexivity, which can be defined as "the ability to notice, understand and use constructively one's own process of thinking and feeling as well as the psychological, social and systemic influences that condition them" (Jackson in Bachkirova, 2021: 28). This book, for example, is one long reflexive process for me.

- Waking up to our bodies and to the rich data they hold rather than maintaining the fallacy of the body-mind split – everything is data, yet 'rationality' and 'intellect' remain often the sole lens for inquiry, even when reality is screaming for a different conversation.

- Be suspicious of the term 'data', having just said pay attention to it. During my research, I was introduced by an interviewee to '*verstehen*', an approach to making sense of the world that does not seek to interpret what people are telling us (let alone aggregate it into digestible research results). Instead, we listen attentively so as to understand their specific experiences. To then label this as data is a commodification and sets us up as the seers who can read the entrails. Much as I'd look great in a long robe and Gandalf beard, I am more hobbit than wizard.

- Seeing all theories, models and tools as navigation aids while remaining committed to understanding the unique contours of any given situation – all of these constructs are ultimately scaffolding for an inquiry and conversation, they are not blueprints for rigid adherence to predetermined action.

- Challenging the commoditisation of knowledge and the impact of colonial and extractive capitalist principles that underpin this – if that sounds a bit political, no apologies are on offer. Market managerialism still dominates our ways of thinking about organising and is not doing a good job of helping us adapt to changing contexts.

- Committing to the democratisation of adult learning as opposed to the creeping totalitarianism of thought collectives – from early years education through to higher education and adult learning in the workplace, there is a need to hear and think about multiple perspectives.

- Encouraging an emancipatory and empowering ethic – where all change practices (including the thought collective of Organisation Development that sometimes appears to hold a monopoly on notions of working with difference while struggling with that in actuality) are focused on equipping individuals to learn and develop in knowledge, confidence and skills.

- Refusing to foster commercially motivated dependencies — if we haven't learned that that is a zero-sum game and leads to ever worse outcomes, we have learned nothing as people interested in the functioning of organisations.

- Putting *being* before *doing* — if that sounds cliched, it is because it bears repeating. No reflection and deep learning comes without getting into *being*. Which precedes knowing, because we often lose sight of that. This is particularly the case with leadership development, which obsesses about people knowing things and knowing how to do things.

The risk of not engaging with these things is that you stumble headfirst into messy reality. It is all well and good finding a model or theory you like, but what looks simple on paper is usually a little more complex. Joost Minnaar has seen organisations …

"… on a path of trying to become more progressive or they just read Laloux's book on *Reinventing Organisations* (2014). They start to introduce this kind of stuff and to believe in things like 'organically emerging behaviour' and often you see that it ends up in chaos. If you have no clear view of where you want to go and there's no clear structure and there's no clear accountability, or conflict handling, etc., that actually doesn't work."[249]

In other words, the ask requires working with and in mess and discomfort. As Minnaar is keen to emphasise, self-management, one of the most popular new Silver Bullet-y ideas of the past ten years, is actually harder work than 'traditional' ways of managing organisations.

How this translates in the real world

Eschewing again the invitation to list, case by case, what to do when we realise there is no Silver Bullet, here are some basic questions that underpin how you might approach complex challenges when you feel the urge to tap up your dealer for a quick-fix panacea.

---

249. Interview 18th May 2020

None of these are particularly mysterious or clever, and many have been used in real client conversations. You may know some/all of them, because, as noted earlier, the truly new, novel and sexy is rare …

What's the question you are trying to answer?

That may seem an obvious question, but it surprising how often, when I have posed that question, the response has been a blank stare. I have spoken to colleagues who have used that question with leadership teams, asking them to write down their individual responses, only to find that they all appeared to be thinking about something different.

If you cannot define the 'exam question', how do you know what to buff up on, or who to go to for some help? I asked this question of a client early in my consulting career, as I was about to sign (another) three-month contract. It was a large IT change project, and I said to my client, "Can you tell me what question this programme is seeking to answer, and when will you tell everyone in the organisation?" To which they said, "Good questions." That week I signed my extension, the next day the project was shelved and my paternity leave was, in effect, paid for as they honoured the contract. They never answered my questions.

What do you want to be the same and different?

This is not about a binary opposition of same and different, rather it is a way of inquiring into context, to sift for meaning and to reveal assumptions. With that, there is greater possibility of identifying patterns of behaviour, activity and value creation that need to be dampened or amplified.

If you can, sharpen this to find the 'difference that makes the difference'. That one thing, that when push comes to shove, will have the biggest impact if only it were realised.

A few years ago, I asked a client for a brief on something they wanted me to do. I received a two-page document. It said all the right things, hit all the appropriate notes in terms of business speak, and was rich in rhetoric. The problem was it was impossible to tell what was critical, although I had my hunch. I facilitated a 'Same and Different'[250] inquiry with the key clients. This was a simple process that invited the client to list all the things they wanted to remain the same post the intervention, and what they wished to be different. Drilling into the differences, I invited them to consider what, when push came

---

250. You can find details of how to access this in the Resources chapter later on.

to shove, would be the 'difference that made the difference'. It turned out to be something nestled in a paragraph at the end of page one of the brief, and not the preceding corporate riff.

What do you want to see/hear/feel six/nine/twelve months after the programme has finished?

A variation on the last question, it is another way into the same territory. To paraphrase Shakespeare's Macbeth, the language of leadership, management, change, consulting and organisations in general is a bit like "… a tale told by an idiot, full of sound and fury, signifying nothing." Too often the emphasis is on slide decks, models, methodologies and case studies, the glittering paraphernalia of anxiety management.

The simplest questions are often the best, and a personal favourite of mine is this see/hear/feel one. I once moved a potential client from thinking of my organisation as a bit-part player to having a lead role in a large change leadership development programme when I asked her what she wanted to be different once the participants had finished the year-long programme. She said that they "should emerge as the next generation of potential senior vice presidents and general managers". I then asked her what she would see/hear/feel that would tell her that they had achieved that.

Silence.

"That is a really good question, Steve, and I don't know how to answer that. I will have to think about it and come back to you."

That one question was the difference that made the difference, and I was lucky to have a client that understood the value of critical reflection, and comfortable with admitting she did not know. The risk with this question, of course, is that it sets up what looks like a 'knowable' before and after. It implies a linear cause and effect dynamic if you are not careful. The value here lies in asking the question to surface underpinning assumptions and meaning making. I have had the odd client stumped by the language, who prefers the safety of KPIs and abstractions. That is normally a clue that they either have not thought deeply enough about the problem, and/or anxiety is leading them to shy away from naming what they really need/fear.

Who owns the budget, *how* they choose to spend it, based on what *assumptions*?

This is a gnarly ball of string, and the interplay between budget ownership and how decisions are made is imperative. It takes you into power and politics, and I am familiar with the contortions some of my clients go through to work with me, e.g. spending money before year end to make sure the budget is not lost; contracting me through a third party to bypass business rules; paying for my services out of their own budgets rather than a central L&D budget because they refuse to be dictated to in terms of who they can/cannot work with[251] and, occasionally, follow the rules.

The key here is to be clear how the power and politics influence what happens and can in fact be one of the most significant factors in perpetuating the pattern of buying Silver Bullets, as budget holders use their influence to favour particular solutions and providers. Power in particular overshadows things, as the quest for a Silver Bullet is often a way of finding an intervention that reinforces existing power relationships, in part through its approach to knowledge. It is also reflective of hierarchical structures, in light of who gets to commission things, and reinforces the position and status of the leader. It allows them to assume an aura of competence by eschewing direct involvement in running the company for fear of ending up with dirty hands (in, for example, a re-organisation that requires redundancies). Instead, they get to exercise – and reinforce – their power by being seen to 'bring in the right person for the job'.

As we saw in Chapter 2, anxiety drives many decisions that result in reaching for quick fixes, and that manifests in the moment you decide to spend money. Lurking beneath the language of 'value for money' and 'cost benefit analysis', however, are the psychological processes that result in clients and solution providers finding ways to mitigate risk not just financially, but also in terms of shame, ego ideal and reputation. Hence the examples earlier in the book of just how far clients and consultancies will go to move on from failures, without admitting and/or learning from them.

Leadership development is construed differently by the various players. HR, the board, individual senior stakeholders and participants, all may have slightly or significantly different assumptions. Surfacing expectations around the following is key:

---

251. I am fully aware that this may in and of itself be a problem. What is of most service to a client? Is it to 'follow the rules' and not work with me, or bend them? I can make a choice that I believe I add value, equally it is also indicative of a dysfunction, possibly within the client system.

- The nature of change in human systems.

- Defining what is meant by 'capability building' and …

- … the absence of virtually any conversation around what this might mean for senior executives and leaders.

- How to work with the anxiety that may emerge, or even to admit it may exist.

- Resistance, which is too often used as a label to crudely pathologise those who are 'not on board', rather than as an opportunity to find out why they might be energised against a plan.[252] I suspect that 'resistance to change' has now become a theory meme, where inconvenient complexities and differences are ignored to fit a simplistic narrative and make it easier to sell change interventions.

- To acknowledge that any 'solution' is likely to have unintended consequences that in turn create problems.

The unwillingness to explore some of these is probably because they are messy and may not result in closure. They are, in part, about sharing philosophical positions and values. Done well, they are a crucial part of forming genuine partnerships rather than unequal and dysfunctional co-dependent relationships.

Ask better questions
Speaking as a consultant, and reflecting on what colleagues tell me, I am sometimes surprised at the lack of rigour that goes into deciding to work with people like me. Contracting conversations tend to be biased in favour of transactional factors, e.g. financial, legal, establishing credibility, ascertaining whether I have a solution, etc. Taking leadership development as one example, a more robust and useful way forward might be to ask your potential provider things like:

- *Do you do development or training, and understand the difference?* – If there is no clear answer, or a sense they do not see the difference, walk away.

---

252. As an aside, most conversations I have with clients about 'resistance' reveal they have not actually considered that those labelled this way are highly energised and care, albeit they have a different view of the world. That perception gap is what needs to be inquired into. The real problem in change is those that are apathetic.

- *How will we both know whether this intervention has made a difference?* – Both parties will have assumptions about what success looks like. In the gap between the two lies data as to whether you are sufficiently aligned.

- *What experience have you got of designing experiential programmes?* – You need to understand whether your provider gets that the learning participants' needs are not going to come if everything is 'safe'. Developmental learning tends to happen when there is sufficient edge and stretch, and useful discomfort. No stretch, and all you get is better sameness.

- *How is your design going to work in our context?* – I don't mean everything has to be bespoke, but where it is not, there needs to be clear reasons why that is so. The most useful thing might be to say that the design will be *determined by context* and not, say, the curriculum of an off-the-shelf programme someone wants to wheel in because they 'know it has worked well elsewhere'.

- *To what extent does your design allow space for action learning and inquiry-based approaches?* – A programme that does not create space for participants to bring real challenges into the learning space and to be supported and challenged to develop their capacity for sense making, inquiry and critical thinking is pointless.

- *How will this activity build leadership capabilities, and when will we know it has worked?* – The word 'capabilities' runs the risk of being too vague. Moving from abstract notions of 'we want people to show up as leaders' or 'be better at offering feedback' does not get sufficiently under the skin of what is required behaviourally or developmentally.

- *How will we get a sense of the people involved feeling more confident in respect to stepping into leadership in a range of organisational contexts?* – This means they develop their sense-making capabilities and learn how to translate that into action.

- *To what extent will you help us do work at the level of individual and collective identity?* – If you are looking for genuine change, that often requires working at a deeper level, including that of identity, which in turn might require inquiring into and raising awareness around ethics, morals, power and difference.

- *What is the rationale for starting 'at the top'?* – I believe that unless senior leaders model any change, what follows is likely to fail. Equally, what is the rationale for saying that people at the top need developing first, or if they do is it enough to just develop them? If budgets are limited, is the most value *really* going to be created by blowing it on a few of the elite, or can you both have a bigger impact by spreading the money further and changing the narrative about who is valued the most? Or maybe even better, bringing the *entire* leadership community together at once.

- *How can you help us have conversations that go beyond discreet layers and groups?* – The separation of target groups by organisational level (e.g. Board, heads of, middle management, junior management, everyone else, etc.) maintains hierarchy and colludes with a narrow set of assumptions about how power both works AND how to help people learn. It is absurd that we often separate people out into cohorts to develop their capacity to 'work systemically' or 'collaborate more' or 'improve the culture' but do so by replicating siloes. In a nutshell, instead of, say, talking about collaboration and the need for people to challenge more upwards, create a laboratory where there is permission and protection to experiment.

Some further resources

As I said earlier, there are already many people out there offering services, ideas, approaches, models, questions and more that can help. I want to resist the temptation of saying 'these are the people you really need to look at because they are the best'.

What I have signposted on the website that accompanies this book are a number of things that, in my humble opinion, are probably worth checking out. Some are people I know personally and may have worked with; others are people I encountered while writing this book. Others still I have not spoken with or met and will not know they have been mentioned here until someone tells them how they came to find them.

All have something to offer, in the absence of a Silver Bullet, and you can find them here https://www.hearsum.com/no-silver-bullet/resources.

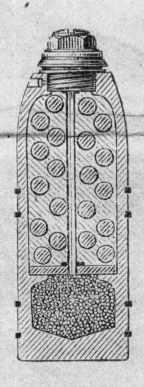

SILVER BULLET NO. 4

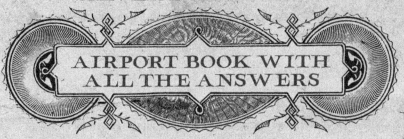

AIRPORT BOOK WITH ALL THE ANSWERS

With years of experience behind me, I know the answers
to leadership challenges in modern organisations.
Don't think for yourself: I have done that for you.

CONCLUSION

Conclusion

"From the management industry's viewpoint, the beauty of the system is that none of the formulas works – or, at least, none works as completely as the anguished or greedy buyers had hoped." Micklethwait & Wooldridge (1997: 63)

The definition of success in a complex world is not just whether you succeed, it is also how quickly you do so. Everything is stacked against an approach that suggests that, maybe, rushing to action and grasping for what seems to be a Silver Bullet might not be the right answer. Heroic leadership still holds us largely in its (mostly hairy and ever so masculine) vice-like grip, and the attempts to encourage more reflective and reflexive practices run up against the need to assuage conscious and unconscious anxieties.

More challenging is that the psychological processes that most impede the capacity for genuine learning are rooted in shame. Eliat Aram suggests that as adults "we do not like the feeling of shame and also attempt to resist or avoid it in many ways" (Aram, 2001: 9). Given how hard it is to process shame at an individual level, let alone in teams or organisations, is it any wonder that functional collusion permeates how we as human beings organise and think about work? Add to the pressure and jeopardy that senior leaders often encounter, and you have a recipe for a market in Silver Bullets. Bertrand Russell once said that "not to be absolutely certain is, I think, one of the essential things in rationality" (1949: 3). We are expecting people to be rational often at moments when, for some, that is the last thing they are capable of being, but to admit that is the case runs the risk of intensifying the shame even further, burying dysfunction even deeper.

It is at moments like this that pedlars of Silver Bullets tend to wander into view, proffering 'solutions' confidently and authoritatively. After all, who would believe in magic beans or Silver Bullets if the person selling them did not sound sure of themselves? The humble, insecure, diffident and shy snake oil salesman is as rare as the unicorn, the surety of the pitch stemming in no small part due to the fact they often use 'selling' rather than 'solving' language.

Selling a 'simple' solution inherently means using a limited vocabulary to make it easier to swallow. Or at the other extreme garnishing it with glitter, glitz,

340

impressive words and a four-box grid or two in a necessarily fancy slide deck. In both cases, shout louder, rinse and repeat.

Someone offering an approach that seeks to explain the subtlety with which one might need to approach complex challenges will need to be nuanced, careful and ethical. That may not come across as classically 'confident', but it is often what is needed. When you lean into the mess, you are using an entirely different language grounded in inquiry, investigation and curiosity, and requires a comfort knowing that things might not be resolved in an entirely satisfying way.

Not all helpers really help

For totally understandable reasons, we seek help when we do not have an answer and believe that none of our peers or employees do, which in itself can evoke shame: 'I *should* know what to do …' That means there is a market for helpers, which is what all the various players I write about in this book are essentially: whatever the intrinsic or extrinsic motivation, they are positioning themselves as helpers, and in some cases that is in the form of something that purports to be a guaranteed solution.

The crucible of thought leadership that is the *HBR* carried an article by Archie N. Turner in 1982 entitled 'Consulting Is More Than Giving Advice'. It suggested there is a hierarchy of purposes. Notice what sits at #2 and what is way down at #7.

1. Providing information to a client
2. Solving a client's problems
3. Making a diagnosis, which may necessitate redefinition of the problem
4. Making recommendations based on the diagnosis
5. Assisting with implementation of recommended solutions
6. Building a consensus and commitment around corrective action
7. Facilitating client learning—that is, teaching clients how to resolve similar problems in the future
8. Permanently improving organisational effectiveness

Forty years on, I do not think much has changed: we are stuck in a paradigm of organisational learning that starts with the assumption that 'helping' is primarily about meeting leaders where they are at, defining problems through a lens of their world view, and, even when 'diagnosis' extends to all levels in a client organisation, decision making rests with the same thought collective, i.e. leadership teams.

The various guilds of solution providers, practitioners and consultants are largely orientated to colluding with the idea that their primary role is to come with 'the answer', 'the solution', 'the model', 'the methodology', 'the theory', 'the intervention', etc. that will fix things, rather than starting with an inquiry about how things really are, however confusing and untidy that is. It is the commodification of branded products to solve clients' problems, with stalls laden with shiny gewgaws and gadgets – a market based on appearance and the pitch-ability of the products.

As we have seen, when the 'solution' does not work, there can be another whole cycle of denial rooted in the need to defend the fragile egos and reputations of all involved. And there is a lot of vulnerability at play that drives behaviours, and it boils down to some profoundly human stuff that is as real in a school playground as it is in a boardroom. When Allan Katcher, an American psychologist, asked senior executives what they would "least want their subordinates to know about them, in nineteen out of twenty cases" they "feared that their subordinates would learn how inadequate they felt in their jobs" (Micklethwaite & Wooldridge, 1997: 60).

I am not immune to that. I have had three clients in my career (that I know of, there could be others who have just not told me) who have said they do not want to work with me again. My own learning has been richest when I have chewed on not just what I might have done differently (the level of task) but have also rummaged around in what these experiences have meant to me in terms of my identity, self-image, shame and self-narrative.

While it is reasonable to hold helpers to account and interrogate them as to whether what they offer will make a difference, that is very different to having a conversation about how things *really* are and what *might* be possible.

There is a chronic need to move beyond seeing the problems between clients and helpers as being primarily about poor practices in consultancies or shoddy procurement and decision-making processes in organisations. As Mazzucato and Collington (2023: 30) suggest, these patterns are "indicative of deeper contradictions" in consulting and contemporary capitalism.

Yet the challenges here are in some ways remarkably and painfully human. Michael Jenkins, the former CEO at Roffey Park Institute, told me a moving story that illustrates this.

"I was teaching recently, and somebody from a large bank said that people basically evolved strategies to manage bosses who are inconsistent. One of them shared a story about 'The Big Boss'. His PA has a toy panda and she keeps it on her desk. When, in the morning, people stride in thinking, 'right, I'm going to go and see the boss and share my great idea with him', the first thing to look for is the panda. If the panda is facing the wall, that is the sign that the boss is not in a good mood. And therefore, if you've got a great idea, maybe you should save it for another day. So because she does this, it saves a whole lot of pain in terms of people thinking 'Oh, panda's not facing out today. So I'll be on a hiding to nothing if I try and engage the boss in a discussion about the idea that I had.'."[253]

Consider for a moment the implications of such behaviour: for all the leadership development, thousands of books, gobbets of thought leadership and myriad advice from consultants, at a human level people find simple panda-based ways of navigating the undiscussable. They collude, ever so functionally, to manage their individual and collective anxieties.

In the absence of the availability of wise PAs and toy pandas in all organisations, I want to offer a few challenges, provocations and the odd tentative suggestion for how we might begin to approach things differently, while simultaneously developing a greater capacity for generative thinking.

1. Develop reflexivity

The Heath Brothers (2011) use the metaphor of the elephant and rider to describe how leaders might more usefully work with change in organisations. The elephant is emotion, and the rider the leader. We can appeal to the rider's rationality to suggest how they might 'steer', they can clear the path to encourage the elephant to go the direction the rider wants them to, or the third way is to simply hang on for dear life when its mount is spooked.

Given the rhetoric about the ever-increasing pace of change, an elephant seems to me to be a tad on the slow side. Maybe when faced with complex challenges, leaders are more like a monkey on a greyhound. The greyhound pointlessly chases an electric hare in circles and never quite catches up. Meanwhile the monkey clings on for dear life, but is content to think that, because they're on top, they must be in charge. In practice, this means slowing down long enough, even it

---

253. Interview 29th January 2024

343

means ungracefully throwing ourselves off a speeding hound, to consider what might actually be going on.

Heifetz and Laurie (1997) popularised the idea of 'Going to the Balcony', which is the art of getting high enough 'above' a situation to see the patterns to work out where most usefully to intervene. While it can be framed as the strategic skill of seeing the 'bigger picture', it can be more profound. I worked with two groups of senior leaders in a global motor manufacturing business for fourteen months, and the takeaway for most of them was this idea of stepping back by moving up onto the balcony. For them, though, it was a process of being able to slow down to notice what they were feeling and sensing, identifying entrenched patterns in the organisation, and reflecting on how they might respond. It was genuine *reflexivity.*

The difficult part of reflexivity is the recognition of one's immersion in the context. For leaders, this is crucial: one has to be willing to step into the space where you recognise your place in the system – and the impacts that your presence has in terms of the constellation and events in that place.

While there is much talk in leadership development about critical reflection, and some of the organisational fields of practice are preoccupied with it, we need to shift the conversation from the abstract. What we might be noticing about ourselves and each other, often in conversations *outside* of the workplace, e.g. a coaching conversation, development programme, etc. is insufficient unless we move towards deeper and more meaningful dialogue, even if it is harder and at times painful. Without that, we will simply achieve better sameness.

These conversations need to take place at the level of the group and not the individual. The individualism of the Global North and much Western thinking in general colludes with the idea that the primary unit of change in organisations is the individual. The problem with that is that change happens in organisations primarily at the level of the group, and our capacity to deal with our self-narrative, feelings and shame needs to increase if we are to work these through such that conversations *between* people evolve.

2. Rethink internal capability building

How we think about capability building is fundamentally flawed and rarely works. This boils down to a combination of how it is construed, and who it is convention believes needs to have their 'capabilities built'.

'We need specialists!'

> "That's where it all falls over: change is shoved into a programme office or a change unit. But it isn't really, it's just a programme office with people who are good at doing charts. And they drive the changes and it's all in the wrong place." Susanne Evans[254]

When organisations embark on large-scale change, particularly when there is recognition it may involve cultural and behaviour change (which essentially means every change project, unless your organisation employs nothing but robots), there is often a view that they need to upskill a core number of people. This may be framed as skills in consulting, change, transformation, communication, facilitation, people and more. It may be associated with something like Organisation Development or Organisation Design as well.

I wonder if what is actually going on here is a psychological split: leadership teams appoint teams of specialists 'qualified' to deal with the issue(s) so they do not have to think deeply about it.

I have worked on many such initiatives, and a common pattern, particularly in corporates, is that as soon as the development has taken place, the very people who have had their 'capabilities built' to help with change are included in restructures and consultations, and large numbers end up leaving. Often, their previously change-orientated roles become more conventional ones, e.g. HRBPs, Learning Partner, etc. Earlier in my career, I thought this was the exception; now I know it is the norm. I also experienced it first hand, when my internal consulting role at *The Guardian* was made redundant, as the team of three I was part of that had developed substantial change capability over three years was disbanded among a raft of redundancies across the organisation.

As I have explored this further, it has become clear that organisations typically do not have a clear idea whether they want (and need) either context-specific specialists who can move between spaces in response to need, or 'centres of excellence' so everyone knows what 'good' looks like. Add to that the fact that in many instances consultancies are either pulling the strings or working in parallel, and you have a recipe for further mess.

What *is* clear to me from many conversations with leaders is that they know how important these skills are. As one senior leader said to me about the

---

people I was about to start developing, "We want them to be far more skilled at support and challenge and acting at a level above their paygrade."[255]

Which begs the question: are the skills of those at several grades above fit for purpose?

There is no culture of capability building for senior leaders
It is virtually impossible to get clients into a meaningful conversation about what capabilities senior leaders might need to develop *in parallel* or *with* their change practitioners. As Mazzucato and Collington sharply observe:

> "The use of consultants to develop or deliver a core function … assumes that capabilities can be conjured up at will, and knowledge can simply be purchased, as though off the shelf. It assumes learning in the contracting organisation is not an incremental and collective *process*, but a *transaction*." (2023: 157)

The risks might be mitigated if what happened in such situations was that the people being 'equipped' to 'deliver' change on behalf of senior leaders were viewed as being genuine partners in making change happen. That requires consistent and ongoing dialogue and contracting at task and relationship level. The pattern, however, is consistently one of keeping the most qualified change practitioners as far away as possible from the people, arguably, they need to have the most permission and protection from, and yet are the very people they are likely to need to support and challenge. This takes us back to the notion that senior leaders decree that those around – and especially beneath – them need to embrace the change that they prescribe, but they are deemed to be immune from the necessity of change. Commanding the change makers to institute change while not remaining alongside them is an abdication of responsibility. 'The plan was exquisite, but the execution was disastrous', means leaders have agency without accountability. Bringing in consultants adds a further layer of plausible deniability.

This is not a nice-to-have. One 6,000-strong global organisation I encountered in 2015 restructured from a divisional to matrix structure. I asked how it had gone. The response?

> "Nothing has changed – the top thirty people are all behaving in the same way."

---

255. Interview 5th August 2020

We need a fundamental rethink of what is meant by 'change capability' and capability building more widely. It must encompass senior leadership and be accompanied by a radical change to the contract between those initiating and those tasked with delivering change. As Dr Wendy Shepherd from Cranfield University said to me, "If you are developing people in the middle range and expecting them to change, without actually thinking about the behaviours and the performance of people at a more senior level, then that can be an uphill battle."[256]

Ultimately this requires a more honest conversation about the fragility of the egos in some senior leadership teams, and a compassionate and appropriate approach to working with shame. It also requires more honesty about how long it takes to develop the necessary skills, and a greater recognition of the nature of change in organisations.

3. Evolve our thinking and institutions

Institutional theory offers us the idea of sedimentation, which is "a process that fundamentally rests on the historical continuity of structure, and especially on its survival across generations of organisational members" (Tolbert & Zucker, 1996: 184). Institutions become sedimented in how they produce certain sorts of identities and strategies and ways of seeing. This establishes thought styles that allow them to understand the world and themselves in particular kinds of ways.

There is a stagnation in some of our institutions that sustains the market for Silver Bullets. Leadership and organisational theories perpetually reinvent themselves. Management thinking as practised in universities and business schools is stuck in a feedback loop augmented by thought leaders and gurus both inside and out, particularly in consulting firms. We look to the wandering buffalos of big business to write books and tell us their secrets, and hope new gurus have the answer. The various guilds where practitioners gather tend to mirror this sedimentation into layers of thinking that means they ossify rather than reinvent.

While Martin Parker's suggestion that we bulldoze business schools may not come to pass, I am with him in the hope that we become less precious in our romanticisation of the sacred cows of organisational thinking, theory and practice.

---

256. Interview 29th September 2020

What might that look like? Maybe some fields and institutions will merge; some might disappear. Perhaps we will move to seriously embrace the idea of 'craft', whether that be the craft of change, the craft of consulting or the craft of leadership. That would require us to lessen our egos and be more comfortable with not knowing.

4. Get (more) comfortable with not knowing

One of my former colleagues once quipped that working at the level of groups in organisations, in particular working with anxiety, requires one to metaphorically ski off-piste downhill on a black run, while both blindfolded and with our hands tied behind our back. While not all complex challenges require that, read between the lines of some of the stories in this book and you may appreciate there is a requirement to let go of certainty and get used to not being in control (think monkey on greyhound again).

The opposite is to find solutions that you believe are the answer, without doing the work to understand 'how it is' really. For solutions imposed on others inevitably evoke resistance: individuals do not feel involved, included and can experience being impinged upon by the authority structure, being told how to think, feel and act. In a sense this is akin to what the Romantic poet John Keats (Keats, 1899: 277) referred to as "negative capability":

> "… that is, when a man is capable of being in uncertainties, mysteries, doubts, without any irritable reaching after fact and reason."

All human beings need to belong, which inevitably involves a degree of compromise in relation to individual preferences and needs. At the same time, individuals need to have their uniqueness acknowledged, welcomed and included. Imposition of a solution from the authorities can feel like an abuse of power, leaving people compromised in their sense of self. This approach leans dangerously in the direction of corporate totalitarianism.

To put this in simple terms, whenever I ask clients in the context of change what they do when they are under pressure and do not know what to do, most go to a place of wanting to exert more control, over people and things. It is the same regardless of whether they are in change or leadership roles, although as an aside it should be noted that *all* leadership roles ultimately require role holders to understand change to some degree. That's why we have so many 'how to lead change' programmes and no 'how to lead stability' ones.

5. Own our fragility

Executive fragility is an under-researched area. There is much on the challenges of leadership, and many surveys suggesting what CEOs believe is needed or not in modern organisations and business. I am less certain that we have seen an open conversation that talks to how fragility at senior leadership levels leads to shame-driven defensive behaviours or bullying and tyrannical rule. The way we think about how we organise, how power and hierarchy works, is remarkably old-fashioned.

Alongside this there is possibly an equally under-researched area in relation to the fragility of the helpers. Yes, there is a sizeable literature on consulting and change practice, but I see little evidence of linking how the two patterns might relate to each other. So we end up with cycles of restructure and behaviour change that repeat forever. These manifest in a dance at executive level, sometimes fed by consultants, and with a myriad of internal and external change practitioners of various types brought in to mop the blood up a bit, without addressing why so little seems to really change. The functional collusion is embedded, and I wonder if part of the reason for that is, fundamentally, that "shame is an intrinsic part of any authentic learning process" (Aram, 2001: 1), which is precisely what learning to live without Silver Bullets entail.

6. Inquire, and then inquire some more

Co-operative inquiry – the capacity and capability to work with others to explore and change your world – is key. Everything else is largely window dressing, upselling and/or the organisational equivalent of an opioid to numb the pain. As Jon Heron and Peter Reason, both key figures in the world of experiential learning and participatory research, put it:

> "Co-operative inquiry is a way of working with other people who have similar concerns and interests to yourself, in order to: (1) understand your world, make sense of your life and develop new and creative ways of looking at things; and (2) learn how to act to change things you may want to change and find out how to do things better." (2001: 179)

In one sense, simple, eh? It's also the antithesis of a slide deck festooned with models and promises of solutions and change that can be easily 'delivered', 'implemented', 'landed', 'driven' and more. My contention is there is a need to respect those who live and work in a territory as opposed to those who merely visit it. The power of dialogue, as a means of making sense of what is going on, in the specific context and circumstances of supporting our collective intelligence, and creating space for people to explore their ideas, is crucial. That means creating the conditions for people to come together and talk, even if it is not easy.

There is a certain irony in me of all people saying this, as someone who is sometimes contracted to be a consultant, but consulting in its Silver Bullet format is an alien presence in organisational life. The 'work proper' resides with those *in* the organisation and can be heard via the voices of those who do it. Let them speak and make sense of things, together. If we can't do that, then prepare for better sameness.

The challenge is to 'stand in inquiry', as it is all too easy to get entangled in our own stories. I find the Human System Dynamics simple rules for inquiry[257] a useful scaffold for this work:

- Turn judgement into curiosity
- Turn conflict into shared exploration
- Turn defensiveness into self-reflection
- Turn assumptions into questions

The discipline and practice these require is well worth the effort.

7. All of which requires a lot of the 'C Word'

Curiosity as a word has become something of a cliché, and I wonder if we sometimes fully embrace the implications of it when it might be most needed. The word essentially talks to the idea that one has a strong desire to *know* or *learn* something. The wrinkle when it comes to some of the more intractable problems in life is that alongside desire may be a smidge of trepidation, dash of fear or dollop of anxiety at what we may come to know or learn. We might learn, for example, there is not a straightforward answer, or we do not have as much control, power or influence as we thought, or even that others can see how inadequate or helpless we feel.

Complexity and its various bedfellows – uncertainty, volatility, ambiguity, brittleness, anxiety, nonlinearity, incomprehensibleness, etc. – can be hard. A likely emotional response to it might be 'aaaaaargh!', but to avoid a fight, flight or freeze response, other responses might be useful. One such is curiosity, a

---

257. https://www.hsdinstitute.org/about-hsd-institute/simple-rules.html

genuine wonderment at that which faces us, a desire to understand what *might* be happening and how we *might* respond. Even if part of us is freaking out.

In doing so we cushion the anxiety and discomfort of not knowing by (partly) replacing it with curiosity and a sense of venturing. I hesitate to say adventure because that tends to have positive connotations of unusualness and excitement. Venturing embraces a sense of risk taking and daring. It is a form of questing, and like all good quests, there be monsters sometimes, and we need to get more comfortable meeting them, both those out in the world and in ourselves.

8. Get more comfortable with nuance and ambivalence

As political and social discourse becomes ever more characterised by binary, either/or, black/white thinking, where one is expected to both have and take a position on something, and know what one is for or against, nuance is becoming increasingly different to express.

It is also becoming a riskier position to adopt, not least as it is increasingly acceptable to colour debate with strong emotion. 'Othering' is legitimised as a function of intolerance for difference, whether that be the expression of views or worse embodied difference. Culture Wars are the most obvious examples of this, and the labelling of others as 'woke', 'radical left', 'radical right', etc. simply lazy ways of discounting other's opinions and/or identities.

The irony is that working with and in the mess of organisations, wrestling with the complex problems that arise, this requires an artful level of skill at both appreciating and working with nuance. Even more radically, it on occasion requires us to be ambivalent about possible choices or strategies, because there may be no obvious 'best option' or 'right way'.

Linked to this is a need to be more comfortable with being wrong, because, in the absence of Silver Bullets, and I hate to tell you this, you may find yourself making mistakes or being wrong *before* it becomes clearer how you might best tackle what you are wrestling with.

9. Develop an evidence-based approach

Rob Briner, unsurprisingly given his research specialism, suggested to me that the mistake many organisations likely make is a failure to take an evidence-based approach, meaning:

a) They fail to clearly define the question they are answering (whether a problem or opportunity).

b) They do not use the best available evidence from multiple sources and of multiple types to first understand the problem and then do the same to identify a potential solution.

c) Do not take a structured approach.

"If you don't do these three things it massively increases the chances of bias driving the process and hence things like fads and fashions, quick fixes, etc."[258] Think back to the beginning of this book and the idea of functional stupidity: evidence-based practice is the antithesis. And as we have seen, we may *know* logically what to do but we are not always rational, even in organisations, regardless of our seniority, age or length of service. Even if you do have an evidence-based approach, you still need to decide what construes valid data. For example, do you have a bias towards quantitative or qualitative data? Are numbers more important to you than stories? How will you decide? Based on what assumptions?

10. Experiment and then experiment some more

Essentially all the above prepares the ground for some form of experimentation. Remember that the only form of failed experiment, ultimately. is one from which no learning can be derived. This reinforces the need for inquiry and asking questions, and doing this at a moment when anxiety may be high. Not least we may be wrestling with acting while uncertain of the outcome, when there is the potential for failure, and what that will say about us personally, the team or the group that we are most identified with, and/or the organisation that we represent or are in service of. At moments like this, talk is cheap and the allure is great for something that will, at least superficially, reduce the risks. The acid test comes when, in the face of the uncertainty, ambiguity and the unknown, we still choose to act.

In experimenting, whether you are a leader or consultant, you are potentially at the edge of your comfort zone, and developmental stretch is what is required if you are both to meet the challenges you face and become more skilled in your practice.

---

258. Email 17th February 2024

And no, this is not a Top 10 because I could keep on adding to the list. Top 10s are just another mechanism to manage anxiety, signalling to the reader that all possible eventualities have been considered and this is all you need hold in mind. My encouragement? Use this list to feed your own inquiry. And here is #11.

11. This is about developing your *practice*

All of the above is within the wrapper of how you show up and the impact you have, in different contexts, in service of something. TThe error many learning interventions make, whether that be a leadership programme, change management intervention, guru talk, consultancy deployment and more, is not connecting learning to practice. Methods that might support this include coaching, supervision, mentoring and action research. All of these have something in common: they are about human relationships.

As Richard Hale notes, "peers wrestling with their own leadership challenges beat a business school professor [or 'expert', or 'guru', or 'thought leader', etc.] hands down in being able to provide practical help for development ... Skilled facilitators of practice-based development can add real value in supporting leaders to do meaningful work on themselves, or the self, and by recognising the wider human context of teams and organisations." 255 Absent that, we are in the performative not genuinely developmental space of change, capability building and learning.[259]

And so on …

I have, ahem, no Silver Bullet. Sorry to burst your bubble. The ask is for us to pay attention to what might *actually* make a difference to our collective experience of work and organising. I wonder whether ultimately this all boils down to:

- *Community* – how to come together in ways that embrace similarities *and* differences, rather than as a means of justifying exclusion. Community here is not some idealised love fest: communities cohere, and tensions will always arise. Can we develop the capability to work through those?

---

259. Places to do practice-based learning are few and far between at present. Richard Hale's work is worth exploring, and also the master's in People & Organisation Development run by Mayvin through and accredited by the University of Chichester are worth exploring. Disclosure: I am on faculty for said master's, so clearly I think it is brilliant. https://mayvin.co.uk/masters/

- *Connection* – building bridges where none exist or are at present are rickety. The antithesis of the fight-y, playground and 'Ya! Boo! Sucks!' nature of much public discourse, this means moving towards rather than away from others when things feel sticky.

- *Relatedness* – appreciating that everything in organisations happens through relationships and relating, whether we like it or not. Organisations are relational systems, deny that and you are attempting to deny reality. Yet that is what many do, often most visibly in narratives that focus on a task without acknowledging that this on its own is useful but rarely sufficient, and certainly isn't when community and connection fray. This means working at a deeper level in groups, and developing an understanding of social defences against anxiety, our own and other people's.

- *Knowing* – not knowing in the sense of knowledge, more an experiential, tentative and always provisional way of knowing and a willingness to inquire into why we experience the world the way we do. Key to this is becoming more at ease with working in liminal spaces, and yes that can be anxiety inducing.

- *Co-creation* – none of this happens in isolation. Realising the co-created nature of many of the challenges in organisations can be terrifying, as it means facing into a reality: that we may be part responsible for that which we do not like, and to attend to that means wrestling with stuff we would much rather leave in its box, thank you very much. Far easier to make someone or something else responsible and edit out our part in the dance.

- *Trust* – all of this stands or falls on whether we can create more trust between those leading and being led. What gets missed in much of the discourse on trust is that it arises as a function of talking about what we don't want to talk about: we need to create the conditions to discuss the undiscussable. That means taking risks, being bold, and being open to the possibility that things may get bumpier before they get easier. One thing I am certain of: there is no Silver Bullet for this work.

The above requires reflexivity. Without that, Silver Bullets will remain incredibly popular, delusional panaceas and illusions, and emperors and empresses will continue to happily flaunt their crown jewels, oblivious to how absurd they

354

look. So too the Wizard of Oz will stay hidden behind the curtain, amplifying his voice to make ever bolder pronouncements about his power and cleverness, using brighter lights and more smoke to impress. He may well help, but he will probably charge you a very high day rate for the privilege.

As long as we fail to pull back the curtain or compassionately point out the delusion of invisible regal attire, we too are colluding, ever so functionally, possibly even stupidly. I am up for removing the curtain, for pointing out nakedness, and I will get it wrong sometimes: that is always a possibility when you name what is undiscussable or hidden. Sometimes too, monsters will be lurking, and at other moments they will be harmless furry mammals. I'd like what is in the shadows to be talked about more; I'm up for that. Are you? I am a bit fearful, but let's do it anyway.

The alternative is evermore better sameness. At best.

Appendix 1

Great Man Theory (1840 onwards)
Often attributed to the Scottish philosopher Thomas Carlyle, this is a 19th-century idea that history can largely be seen through the lens of the impact great men have had on the world. The sexism here is upfront: there is no Great Woman Theory of leadership, even though there are plenty who would feature. The fact that it is framed as masculine creates an inbuilt filter that invites us to think only of men, discounting and ignoring their female counterparts.

The nub of the idea is that leaders are born and not made (and clearly cannot be female, which while an outmoded thought seems to pass some people by). The Great Man Theory is strong in individualistic cultures, particularly in Western industrialised countries. In the past hundred years, figures such as Winston Churchill, Nelson Mandela, Steve Jobs and Jack Welch follow in the footsteps of their forebears such as George Washington, Julius Caesar and Alexander the Great. Their achievements always overshadow their failings, so Churchill's overt racism is conveniently forgotten, and Alexander's massacring of natives become worthy of a footnote at best. Popular culture also has a role to play. John Wayne, as the archetype of a tall, decisive, quick-thinking, strong man is just one figure who reinforced the idea of what a leader should look like, sound like, how they needed to be and what they needed to do. Albeit he is a strong man who does not say very much. Jim Collins' book *Good To Great* (2001) has a lot to answer for as well, in terms of perpetuating Great Man Theory.

Behavioural Theory (1950–1970)
Are you born a leader, or can you be made into one? The nature vs nurture question comes into play and the idea that, with the right conditions, a leader may emerge as a result of their environment as well as nature. Engagement and the motivation became a consideration as well, but what was still missing was an understanding of why behaviours varied across tasks and situations. This move from charismatic ideas of leadership above to behaviour was nudged by business school research in the last century, the beneficiaries of that being … business schools and their Executive Education arms.

Contingency Theory (1967–1990)
The good news is the next wave of theorists took on the question of the contextual variables, e.g. the people involved, tasks, situations, organisation

and other factors. Shock horror, there is the beginnings of an awareness that no single style of leadership or type of leader is perfect for every situation. Fielder (1967; 1971) identified the importance of leader-member relations, task structure, position power and key managerial components. Hersey and Blanchard (1969) were among the first to posit that (surprise surprise) the development levels of leaders influenced their effectiveness (if only someone could have sent Alexander the Great on a leadership programme, maybe he wouldn't have felt the need to kill so many people).

Leader-Follower Theory (1970 onwards)

Robert Greenleaf's work on Servant Leadership (1970) was one of the early catalysts of a school of thought that said that leaders are there to 'serve' their followers, thereby creating the conditions for the latter to live and work to their full potential. There was a social agenda to this as well, as the least privileged in society were ultimately seen as beneficiaries of the 'servant leader'.

Other work in this area saw research that looked increasingly at the quality of the relationships and interactions between leaders and followers, and the extent to which they created or undermined trust.[260] Servant Leadership is the antithesis of much of the muscular heroic leadership that is increasingly prevalent in wider society today. There is also a darker version: the leader who purports to serve, using the rhetoric of service to justify a more subtle totalitarian or selfish agenda. As Paul Babiak and Robert Hare – the latter renowned for his work on psychopathy – observe: "The general state of confusion that change brings to any situation can make psychopathic personality traits – the appearance of confidence, strength and calm – often look like the answer to the organisation problems" (2007: xii). That may show up as heroic leadership, and at the manipulative end, it can hide in plain sight as service.

Transformational Leadership Theory (1985–2010)

This was the idea that leadership is not simply about transactional change – *outputs* – it can also be transformational – *outcomes*. Both are needed, and the latter adds a moral and ethical dimension, as there is a difference between, say,

---

260. Books like *The Art of Followership: How Great Followers Create Great Leaders and Organisations* (Riggio *et al.*, 2008) and articles such as Robert E. Kelly's 1988 HBR article 'In Praise of Followers' form part of this cannon, and you can still see the popularity of the idea of followership today. Derek Sivers 2010 TED video a man happily dancing in a field and attracting lots of 'followers' became a mainstay of development programmes and a popular meme in the 2010s. Equally, Simon Sinek's LinkedIn feed reveals a strong interest and advocacy of Servant Leadership.

the output of oil from the ground and the outcome of climate change. Bernard Bass (1985; 1998) is largely regarded as having popularised the theory through his model of the '4 Is':

- **Idealised Influence (II)** – in 'walking the talk', the leader embodies the qualities that he/she wants in his/her team, which builds trust.

- **Inspirational Motivation (IM)** – the ability to inspire and motivate followers through having a vision and presenting that vision.

- ***Individualized Consideration (IC)*** – *the leader demonstrates genuine concern for the needs and feelings of followers, and helps them self-actualise.* So, transformation is extended to followers, and trust is deepened further.

- **Intellectual Stimulation (IS)** – the leader challenges followers to be innovative and creative. There is permission to challenge the status quo, and the leader is not on a pedestal. Power is here exercised with humility in service of higher performance.

System Leadership Theory (2005 onwards)

While a Senge, Hamilton and Kania article in 2015 is often credited, the idea of Systems/System Leadership predates that. Core to it is the idea that leaders of an organisation (which might also be considered a human system, or an agglomeration of systems, which in turn create the space wherein connections are made and work is done) need to be able to solve complex problems and, crucially, have a strong collaborative practice. That in turn requires the ability to work with and in conflict, as collaboration ultimately means working with difference(s). A multitude of theories and theorists in adjacent spaces all feed into Systems Leadership, Ronald Heifetz's approach to Adaptive Leadership (2009) and Glenda Eoyang's work in the field of Human Systems Dynamics (2013) being examples.

Bibliography

Abrahamson, E. 1991. 'Managerial Fads and Fashions: The diffusion and rejection of innovations'. *The Academy of Management Review.* 16(3). pp. 586–612.

Ageling, W-J. 'You want to adopt the "Spotify Model"? I don't think it means what you think it means!' *Medium.* Jan 23rd 2019. Available at: https://medium.com/serious-scrum/you-want-to-adopt-the-spotify-model-i-dont-think-it-means-what-you-think-it-means-7df4316081f. <Last Accessed Feb 18th 2024>.

Alvesson, M. & Spicer, A. 2016. *The Stupidity Paradox*: The power and pitfalls of functional stupidity at work. London: Profile Books Ltd.

Anderson, C. 2014. 'What HR Needs to Do to Get a Seat at the Table'. *Forbes.* Nov 27th 2014. Available at: https://hbr.org/2014/11/what-hr-needs-to-do-to-get-a-seat-at-the-table. <Last Accessed Feb 18th 2024>.

Anon. 2024. 'Did Peter Drucker Say That'. *The Druker Institute: Claremont Graduate University.* Available at: https://drucker.institute/did-peter-drucker-say-that/. <Last Accessed Feb 17th 2024>.

Anon. 2023. 'KPMG and PWC With NHS Leadership Academy Bevan Programme'. *MCA.* May 11th 2023. Available at: https://www.mca.org.uk/consulting-case-studies/kpmg-with-pwc-bevan-learning-nye-bevan-executive-leadership-programme. <Last Accessed Feb 18th 2024>.

Aram, E. 2001. *Shame as an integral part of a potentially transformative learning process.* (Unpublished paper).

Aram, E. 2006 *The complexity of experiencing learning: panic, shame, and the potential transformation of identity* (unpublished book based on 2001 PhD thesis).

Argyris, C. 1980. 'Making the Undiscussable and Its Undiscussability Discussable'. *Public Administration Review.* 40(3). pp. 205–213.

Ariely, D. 2009. *Predictably Irrational: The hidden forces that shape our decisions.* London: HarperCollins.

Ariely, D. 2011. *Upside of Irrationality: The unexpected benefits of defying logic at work and at home*. London: HarperCollins.

Babiak, P. & Hare, S. 2007. *Snakes in Suits: when psychopaths go to work*. London & New York: Harper.

Barber, P. 2006. *Becoming a Practitioner-Researcher: A Gestalt approach to holistic inquiry*. London. Middlesex University Press.

Baritz, L. 1960. *The Servants of power: A History of the Use of Social Science in American Industry*. Middletown, Conn. : Westleyan University Press.

Bass, B. M. 1995. 'Comment: Transformational Leadership: Looking at Other Possible Antecedents and Consequences'. *Journal of Management Inquiry*, 4(3), 293-297. Available at: https://doi.org/10.1177/105649269543010

Bass. B. M. 1998. *Transformational Leadership: Industrial, Military, and Educational Impact*. Mahwah, NJ: Lawrence Erlbaum Associates.

Bazalgette, J. & Harrison, S. 2020. 'FE and Skills and Shame in Organisational Life'. *Further Education Trust for Leadership*. May 2020. Available at: https://fetl.org.uk/wp-content/uploads/2020/05/2992_FETL_Shame-within-organisational-life-web-1.pdf. <Last Accessed Feb 18th 2024>.

Beer, M., Finnström, M., & Schrader, D. 2016. 'Why Leadership Training Fails - and What to Do about It'. *Harvard Business Review*, 94(10), 50–57. Available at: https://dialnet.unirioja.es/servlet/articulo?codigo=5696059 <Last Accessed March 24th 2024>.

Benner, P. 1982. 'From Novice to Expert'. *The American Journal of Nursing*. 82(3). pp. 402–407.

Bennis, W. G. 1959. 'Leadership Theory and Administrative Behaviour: The problems of authority.' *Administrative Science Quarterly*. 4(3). pp. 259–301.

Binz, M. & Schulz, E. 2023. 'Reconstructing the Einstellung Effect'. *Computational Brain & Behavior*. 6(3). pp. 526–542.

Block, P. 1999. *Flawless Consulting: A guide to getting your expertise used*. San Francisco: Jossey-Bass/Pfeiffer.

Bogdanich, W. & Forsythe, M. 2022. *When McKinsey Comes to Town: The hidden influence of the world's most powerful consulting firm*. New York, NY: Doubleday.

Bolton, C. 2017. 'Silver Bullet Syndrome and Richard Pascae's Management Fads'. WhatsthePONT. May 14th 2017. Available at: https://whatsthepont. blog/2017/05/14/silver-bullet-syndrome-and-richard-pascales-management-fads/. <Last Accessed Feb 18th 2024>.

Bolton, C. 2017. 'The Life Cycle of a Silver Bullet'. WhatsthePONT. May 29th 2017. Available at: https://whatsthepont.blog/2017/05/29/the-life-cycle-of-a-silver-bullet/.

<Last Accessed Feb 18th 2024>.

Bosch, I. 2022. 'The Messenger Review of NHS leadership: what you need to know'. *NHS Confederation*. June 8th 2022. Available at: https://www.nhsconfed. org/publications/messenger-review-nhs-leadership. <Last Accessed Feb 18th 2024>.

Bramel, D., & Friend, R. 1981. 'Hawthorne, the myth of the docile worker, and class bias in psychology'. *American Psychologist, 36*(8), 867–878. Available at: https://doi.org/10.1037/0003-066X.36.8.867

Braun, W & Agerbech Petersen, D. 2022. 'What Does it Take for HR to be Ready For a Seat at the Table?' *EY*. Aug 16th 2022. Available at: https://www. ey.com/en_dk/workforce/what-does-it-take-for-hr-to-be-ready-for-a-seat-at-the-table. <Last Accessed Feb 18th 2024>.

Brown, B. 2013. *Daring Greatly*. London: Penguin.

Buber, M. 1970. *I And Thou*. Translated by Walter Kaufmann. New York, NY: Free Press/Simon & Schuster.

Buckingham, H., Reed, S., Kumpunen, S. & Lewis, R. 2023. 'People, Partnerships and Place: How can ICSs turn the rhetoric into reality? *Nuffield Trust*. Briefing January 2023. Available at: https://www.nuffieldtrust.org.uk/ sites/default/files/2023-01/1674472419_nut-integration-briefing-web.pdf. <Last Accessed Feb 18th 2024>.

Bushe, G. 2010. *Clear Leadership: Sustaining real collaboration and partnership at work*. Boston, MA & London: Nicholas Brealey Publishing.

Bushe, G. 2019. Generative Leadership. *Canadian Journal of Physician Leadership*. Vol. 5, No. 3. pp. 141–147.

Bushe, G. 2020. *The Dynamics of Generative Change*. North Vancouver: B.M.I. Publishing.

Çakmak, E., Öztekin, Ö., Karadağ, E. 2015. 'The Effect of Leadership on Job Satisfaction' in: Karadağ, E. (Ed). 2015. *Leadership and Organizational Outcomes: Meta-analysis of empirical studies*. Heidelberg, New York, Dordrecht & London: Springer, Cham. pp. 29–56.

Campbell, W.K., Hoffman, B.J., Campbell, S.M. & Marchisio, G. 'Narcissism in organizational contexts.' *Human Resource Management Review* 21. 2011. 268–284

Carey, A. 1967. 'The Hawthorne Studies: A radical criticism. American Sociological Review. 32(3). pp. 403–416.

Cavicchia, S. & Gilbert, M. 2018. *The Theory and Practice of Relational Coaching: Complexity, Paradox and Integration*. Abingdon, Oxon & New York, NY: Routledge.

Cavicchia, S. & Vogel, M. 2020. Leadership Supervision: Reframing coaching for turbulent times. *Association for Coaching Journal*. Issue 27(2). pp. 52–58.

Chambers, N. & Exworthy, M. 2020. 'Long serving NHS CEOs: What makes them tick and what keeps them going?' University of Manchester. Feb 2020. Available at:

https://pure.manchester.ac.uk/ws/portalfiles/portal/177914392/Long_serving_NHS_chief_executives_report_final_Feb_2020.pdf. <Last Accessed Feb 18th 2024>.

Cheung-Judge, M-Y. & Holbeche, L. 2021. *Organization Development: A practitioner's guide for OD and HR*. 3rd Edn. London: Kogan Page.

Cheung-Judge, M-Y. 2001. 'The Self as an Instrument'. *OD Practitioner*. 33(3).

Clark, T., & Salaman, G. 1996. 'The Management Guru as Organizational Witchdoctor. *Organization*. 3(1). pp. 85–107.

Claxton, G. 1998. *Hare Brain, Tortoise Mind: Why intelligence increases when you think less*. London: Fourth Estate.

Claydon, R. 2023. 'Irony & Absurdity, Together in Imperfect Harmony' in *OD Publication*. November 2023. pp. 7–15.

Claydon, R. 2017. 'Do You Want Dirty or Clean Consulting?' LinkedIn. June 12th 2017. Available at: https://www.linkedin.com/pulse/do-you-want-dirty-clean-consulting-dr-richard-claydon/. <Last Accessed Feb 18th 2024>.

Clifton, J. 2023. 'Gallup Finds a Silver Bullet: Coach me once per week'. *Gallup.* Oct 4th 2023. Available at: https://www.gallup.com/workplace/350057/gallup-finds-silver-bullet-coach-once-per-week.aspx. <Last Accessed Feb 18th 2024>.

Cole, M. & Higgins, J. 2023. *The Great Unheard at Work: Understanding voice and silence in organisations.* Abingdon, Oxon & New York, NY: Routledge.

Collington, R. & Mazzucato, M. 2023. *The Big Con: How the consulting industry weakens our businesses, infantilizes our governments and hijacks our economies.* London: Penguin.

Collins, J. 2001. *Good To Great: Why some companies make the leap… and others don't.* New York: HarperCollins.

Cooperrider, D. 1985. *Appreciative Inquiry: A Methodology for Advancing Social Innovation.* PhD Dissertation. Available at: https://aicommons.champlain.edu/educational-material/appreciative-inquiry-toward-methodology-understanding-enhancing-organizational-innovation/. <Last Accessed Feb 18th 2024>.

Cooperrider, D. & Srivastva, S. (Eds). 1990. *Appreciative Management and Leadership: the power of positive thought in organizations.* San Francisco: Jossey-Bass.

Cummings, S., Bridgman, T. & Brown, K. 2016. 'Unfreezing change as three steps: Rethinking Kurt Lewin's legacy for change management'. *Human Relations.* 69(1). pp. 33–60.

Curtis, G. 2018. 'Functional Collusion in a UK Non Governmental Organisation: Processes of shame and exclusion from the perspective of an organisational development practitioner'. *University of Hertfordshire Research Archive.* Available at: https://uhra.herts.ac.uk/handle/2299/21079. <Last Accessed Feb 18th 2024>.

Dawson, P. 2003. 'Organisational Change Stories and Management Research: Facts or fiction'. *Journal of Management & Organization.* 9(3). pp. 37–49.

De Berker, A. O., Rutledge, R. B., Mathys, C., Marshall, L., Cross, G. F., Dolan, R. J. & Bestmann, S. 2016. 'Computations of Uncertainty Mediate Acute Stress Responses in Humans'. *Nature Communications.* 7(1), pp. 10996–10996.

De Haan, E. 2012. *Supervision in Action*: A relational approach to coaching and consulting supervision. Berkshire & New York, NY: McGraw-Hill.

Denworth, L. 2019. Debate Arises Over Teaching "Growth Mindsets" to Motivated Students'. Scientific American. Aug 12th 2019. Available at: https://www.scientificamerican.com/article/debate-arises-over-teaching-growth-mindsets-to-motivate-students/. <Last Accessed Feb 18th 2024>.

de Vries, M. F. R. K. & Miller, D. 1985. 'Narcissism and Leadership: An Object Relations Perspective'. *Human Relations.* 38(6). pp. 583–601.

DiBenigno, J. 2018. 'Rapid Relationality: How peripheral experts build a foundation for influence with line managers'. *Administrative Science Quarterly.* 65(1). pp. 20–60.

Di Carlo, G. S. 2015. 'Pathos as a Communicative Strategy For Online Knowledge Dissemination: The case of TED talks'. Journal of Language Teaching, Linguistics, and Literature. 21(1). pp. 23–34.

Dignan, A. (2019). 'Brave New Work: Are You Ready to Reinvent Your Organization?'. United States: Penguin Publishing Group.

Duffell, N. 2014. 'Why boarding schools produce bad leaders'. The Guardian June 9th 2014. Available at: https://www.theguardian.com/education/2014/jun/09/boarding-schools-bad-leaders-politicians-bullies-bumblers.   <Last Accessed Feb 18th 2024>.

Egan, G. 1994. *Working the Shadow Side*. San Francisco: Jossey-Bass.

Engel, N. 'There's No Silver Bullet to Carbon-Free Energy But Hydrogen Could Be Part Of The Solution'. *Politics Home.* March 26th 2023. Available at: https://www.politicshome.com/thehouse/article/theres-no-silver-bullet-carbonfree-energy-hydrogen-part-solution. <Last Accessed Feb 18th 2024>.

Eoyang, G. 2001. 'CDE Model: What is it and where did it come from?' Available at: https://www.hsdinstitute.org/resources/cde-model-dissertation.html. <Last Accessed Feb 18th 2024>.

Eoyang, G. & Holladay, R. 2013. *Adaptive Action: Leveraging uncertainty in your organization*. Stanford, CA: Stanford University Press.

Evans, T. R. 2020. Improving Evidence Quality For Organisational Change Management Through Open Science. *Journal of Organizational Change Management*. 33(2). pp. 367–378.

Farrington, J., & Clark, R. E. 2000. Snake oil, science, and performance products. *Performance Improvement*. 39(10). pp. 5–10.

Fischer, T. & Sitkin, S.B. 2023. 'Leadership Styles: A comprehensive assessment and way forward'. *The Academy of Management Annals*. 17(1). pp. 331–372.

Fleck, L. 1979. [1935]. *The Genesis and Development of a Scientific Fact*. Chicago & London: University of Chicago Press.

Fonagy, P., Gergely, G., Jurist, E. & Target, M. 2002. *Affect Regulation, Mentalization and the Development of the Self*. NY: Other Press.

Fox, M. 2001. *One River, Many Wells: Wisdom Springing from Global Faiths*. Los Angeles: Jeremy P. Tarcher.Hersey, P., & Blanchard, K.H. 1969. 'Life cycle theory of leadership'. *Training & Development Journal*, 23(5), 26–34.

Frankfurt, H. 2005. *On Bullshit*. Princeton, NJ: Princeton University Press.

Furnham, A. 2019. 'Ahead of the Curve: The psychology of contrarianism'. *IPE*. Sep 2019. Available at: https://www.ipe.com/ahead-of-the-curve-the-psychology-of contrarianism/10033018.article. <Last Accessed Feb 18th 2024>.

Georgieva, K. 2024. 'AI Will Transform the Global Economy. Let's make sure it benefits humanity'. *International Monetary Fund*. Jan 14th 2024. Available at: https://www.imf.org/en/Blogs/Articles/2024/01/14/ai-will-transform-the-global-economy-lets-make-sure-it-benefits-humanity. <Last Accessed Feb 18th 2024>.

Ghoshal, S. 2005. 'Bad Management Theories are Destroying Good Management Practices'. *Academy of Management Learning & Education*. 4(1), 75–91.

Gill, L. 2019. 'Three Myths about Self-managing Organisations, Debunked'. Available at: https://medium.com/culturati/three-myths-and-misconceptions-about-self-managing-organisations-2f23c298c79b. <Last Accessed Feb 18th 2024>.

Gino, F., Sharek, Z. & Moore, D. A. 2011. 'Keeping the Illusion of Control Under Control: Ceilings, floors, and imperfect calibration'. *Organizational Behavior and Human Decision Processes*. 114(2). pp. 104–114.

'Government failed to act on its security plans for a pandemic'. *UK Parliament Committees*. Dec 18th 2020.

https://committees.parliament.uk/committee/111/national-security-strategy-joint-committee/news/137998/government-failed-to-act-on-its-security-plans-for-a-pandemic/. <Last Accessed Feb 18th 2024>.

Greenleaf, R. K. 1970. *The servant as leader*. Robert K. Greenleaf Publishing Center.

Grimm, J. & Grimm, W. [1812]. 2011. *Grimm's Complete Fairy Tales*. United States: Knopf Doubleday Publishing Group.

Grint, K. 2010. 'Wicked problems and clumsy solutions: The role of leadership' in: Brooks, S. & Grin, K. (Eds). 2010. *The New Public Leadership Challenge*. Hampshire & New York, NY. Palgrave Macmillan. pp. 169–186.

Hall, M. n.d. 'The history of NLP, part 3: The Gestalt base of NLP'. *The Coaching Room*. Available at: https://thecoachingroom.com.au/blog/the-history-of-nlp-part-3-the-gestalt-base-of-nlp/. <Last Accessed Feb 18th 2024>.

Harmeling, S. 2024. 'A Century-Old Study Shows That Whatever We Call It, DEI Will Always Be With Us'. *Forbes*. Jan 29th 2024. Available at:

https://www.forbes.com/sites/susanharmeling/2024/01/29/how-the-100-years-old-hawthorne-studies-foreshadowed-dei/. <Last Accessed Feb 18th 2024>.

Harvey, W. S., Mitchell, V. Jones, A. A. & Knight, E. 2021. 'The Tensions Of Defining And Developing Thought Leadership Within Knowledge-Intensive Firms'. *Journal of Knowledge Management*. 25(11). pp. 1–33.

Haslam, S. A., Alvesson, M. & Reicher, S. D. 2024. Zombie Leadership: Dead ideas that still walk among us'. *The Leadership Quarterly. In press*.

'Healthcare Leadership Model: The nine dimensions of leadership behaviour'.

NHS Leadership Academy. Leeds: West Yorkshire. Available at: https://www.leadershipacademy.nhs.uk/wp-content/uploads/2014/10/NHSLeadership-LeadershipModel-colour.pdf. <Last Accessed Feb 18th 2024>.

Hearsum, S. 2015. 'What's in a label? A lot - and not a lot - whether #OrgDev, #HR, #OrgDes or any other'. *LinkedIn*. Sep 24th 2018. Available at: https://www.linkedin.com/pulse/whats-label-lot-whether-orgdev-hr-orgdes-any-other-steve-hearsum. <Last Accessed Feb 18th 2024>.

Hearsum, S. 2015. *Whistleblowing: removing the wilful blindfold*. HR Magazine. Feb 5th 2015. Available at: https://www.hrmagazine.co.uk/content/features/whistleblowing-removing-the-wilful-blindfold/. <Last Accessed Feb 18th 2024>.

Heath, D. & Heath, C. 2011. *Switch: How to change things when change is hard*. London: Random House Business Books.

Heffernan, M. 2011. *Wilful Blindness: Why we ignore the obvious*. London: Simon & Schuster.

Heifetz, R., Linsky, M. & Grashow, A. 2009. The Practice of Adaptive Leadership: Tools and tactics for changing your organization and the world. Boston: Harvard Business Press.

Heifetz, R.A. & Laurie, D.L. 1997. 'The Work of Leadership'. *Harvard Business Review*. 75(1). pp. 124–134.

Heim, J. A. & Compton, W. D. 1992. *Manufacturing Systems: Foundations of World-Class Practice*. Washington, DC: The National Academies Press. Available at: https://www.nap.edu/catalog/1867/manufacturing-systems-foundations-of-world-class-practice. <Last Accessed Feb 18th 2024>.

Heron, J. & Reason, P. 2001. 'The Practice of Co-Operative Inquiry: Research with rather than on people' in: Reason, P. & Bradbury, H. (Eds.). 2001. *Handbook of Action Research: Participative Inquiry and Practice*. London: Sage. pp. 179–188.

Herzberg, F., Mausner, B. & Snyderman, B. 1959. *The Motivation to Work*. 2nd edn. New Brunswick, N.J: Transaction Publishers.

Highsmith, J. 2013. *Adaptive Software Development: A collaborative approach to managing complex systems*. New York, NY: Dorset House Publishing.

Holley, R. P. 2019. 'The Contrarian Manager: The importance of alternative viewpoints'. *Journal of Library Administration*. 59(3). pp. 334–341.

Hughes, M. (2011). 'Do 70 per cent of all organizational change initiatives really fail?' *Journal of Change Management, 11*(4), pp. 451–464.

Jackson, P. 2012. 'Supervision for Enhancing Reflexivity' in: Bachkirova, T, Jackson, P. & Clutterbuck, D. (Eds). 2011, Coaching and Mentoring Supervision Theory and Practice. Maidenhead: McGraw-Hill/Open University Press. pp. 28–39.

Jacques, E. 1951. *The Changing Culture of a Factory: A Study of Authority and Participation in an Industrial Setting*. London: Tavistock.

Jansen, P. 2020. 'Lessons from going Dutch in the UK'. *Trust Works*. Dec 4th 2020. Available at: https://trust-works.co.uk/blog/f/lessons-from-going-dutch-in-the-uk. <Last Accessed Feb 18th 2024>.

Jaques, T. 2023. Why There is No Silver Bullet for Qantas' Reputational Crisis. *Smart Company*. Sep 27th 2023. Available at: https://www.smartcompany.com.au/opinion/qantas-reputational-crisis-solution/. <Last Accessed Feb 18th 2024>.

Johnson, K. 2018. 'What Amazon's Board Was Getting Wrong About Diversity and Hiring'. *Harvard Business Review*. May 14th 2018. Available at: https://hbr.org/2018/05/what-amazons-board-is-getting-wrong-about-diversity-and-hiring. <Last Accessed Feb 18th 2024>.

Jones, K. & Sharp, T. 2019. *Provoke: The art of transformative facilitation*. London|: Alchemy Worldwide.

Jubb, P. B. 1999. 'Whistleblowing: A Restrictive Definition and Interpretation'. *Journal of Business Ethics*. 21(1). pp.77–94.

Kafilat. n.d. 'How to Make Leadership Training Cross-Culturally Relevant'. *Oxford Review Briefings*. Available at: https://oxford-review.com/how-to-make-leadership-training-more-cross-culturally-relevant/ <Last Accessed Feb 18th 2024>.

Kahneman, D. 2012. *Thinking, Fast and Slow*. London: Allen Lane/Penguin.

Kastenbaum, R. 2015. *Death, Society and Human Experience*. United Kingdom: Taylor & Francis.

Keats, J. 1899. *The Complete Poetical Works and Letters of John Keats, Cambridge Edition*. Boston: Houghton, Mifflin & Company.

Kegan, R. & Lahey, L. 2009. *Immunity To Change: How to overcome it and unlock the potential in yourself and your organization*. Boston, MA: Harvard Business School Publishing Corporation.

Kelly, R. 1988. 'In Praise of Followers'. *Harvard Business Review*. 66(6). pp. 142–148.

Kemmis, S. 2010. 'Research for Praxis: Knowing doing'. *Pedagogy, Culture & Society*. 18(1). pp. 9–27.

Keswin, E. 2022. '3 Ways to Boost Retention Through Professional Development'. Harvard Business Review. April 5th 2022. Available at: *https:// hbr.org/2022/04/3-ways-to-boost-retention-through-professional-development*. <Last Accessed Feb 18th 2024>.

King, A. 1990. 'Evolution of Leadership Theory'. *Vikalpa: The Journal for Decision Makers*. 15(2). pp. 43–56.

Kituno, N. & West, D. 2023. 'Revealed: 60pc of trusts have a 'first-time' CEO'. *Health Service Journal*. Aug 29th 2023. Available at:https://www.hsj.co.uk/ workforce/revealed-60pc-of-trusts-have-a-first-time-ceo/7035420.article. <Last Accessed Feb 19th 2024>.

Kolata, G. 1998. *Scientific Myths That Are Too Good to Die*. New York Times. Dec 6th 1998.

https://www.nytimes.com/1998/12/06/weekinreview/scientific-myths-that-are-too-good-to-die.html. <Last Accessed Feb 18th 2024>.

Kotter, J. *A Sense of Urgency*. Boston, Mass: Harvard Business Review Press.

Kotter, J. 1996. *Leading Change*. Boston, Mass: Harvard Business School Press.

Kubler-Ross, E. 1969. *On Death and Dying*. London: Routledge.

Kulhari, R. 2021. 'Four Reasons HR Deserves a Seat at the Table'. *Forbes*. Sep 10th 2021. Available at: https://www.forbes.com/sites/ forbeshumanresourcescouncil/2021/09/10/four-reasons-hr-deserves-a-seat-at-the-table/?sh=4ef6adaa6690. <Last Accessed Feb 18th 2024>.

Laloux, F. 2014. *Reinventing Organizations: a guide to creating organizations inspired by the next stage of human consciousness*. Brussels: Nelson Parker.

Lam, B. 2016. 'Why Are So Many Zappos Employees Leaving?' *The Atlantic*. Available at: https://www.theatlantic.com/business/archive/2016/01/zappos-holacracy-hierarchy/424173/. <Last Accessed Feb 18th 2024>.

Lave, J. & Wenger, E. 1991. *Situated Learning: Legitimate peripheral participation.* Cambridge: Cambridge University Press.

Lawrence, P. 'Supervision for working systemically' in: Bachkirova, T., Jackson, P. & Clutterbuck, D. (Eds). 2011, *Coaching and Mentoring Supervision Theory and Practice.* Maidenhead: McGraw-Hill/Open University Press.

'4 Reasons to Invest in Leadership Development'. *Centre for Creative Leadership.* Nov 21st 2021. *Available at: https://www.ccl.org/articles/leading-effectively-articles/ why-leadership-development-is-important-4-reasons-to-invest/.* <Last Accessed Feb 18th 2024>.

Leroy, H., Anisman-Razin, M. & Detert, J. 2023. 'Leadership Development Is Failing Us. Here's How to Fix It'. *MIT Sloan Management Review.* Dec 6th 2023. Available at: https://sloanreview.mit.edu/article/leadership-development-is-failing-us-heres-how-to-fix-it/. <Last Accessed Feb 18th 2024>.

Lewin, K. 1939. 'When Facing Danger' in: K. Lewin, L. *Resolving Social Conflicts: Field theory in social science.* pp. 116–121.

Lewin, K. 1939. 'Field Theory and Experiment in Social Psychology'. *American Journal of Sociology.* 44(6). pp. 868–896.

Lewin, K. 1947. 'Frontiers in Group Dynamics: Concept, method and reality in social science; social equilibria and social change'. *Human Relations.* 1(1). pp. 5–41.

Ludewig, J. 2017. 'TED Talks as an Emergent Genre'. *Comparative Literature and Culture* Web. 19(1). pp. 1–9.

Mabey, C. 2013. 'Leadership Development in Organizations: Multiple discourses and diverse practice'. *International Journal of Management Reviews.* 154). pp. 359–380.

MacLean, P. 1990. *The Triune Brain in Evolution: Role in paleocerebial functions.* New York & London: Plenum Press.

Maister, D. 2004. 'The Anatomy of a Consulting Firm'. *davidmaister.com.* Available at: https://davidmaister.com/articles/the-anatomy-of-a-consulting-firm/. <Last Accessed Feb 18th 2024>.

March, J. G. 1991. 'Exploration and Exploitation in Organizational Learning'. *Organization Science.* 2(1). pp. 71–87.

March, J. G. 1994. 'The Evolution of Evolution' in: Baum, J & Singh, J (Eds). 1994. *Evolutionary Dynamics of Organizations*. New York, NY: Oxford University Press. pp. 39–52.

Maslow, A. H. 1943. 'A theory of human motivation'. *Psychological Review*. 50(4). pp. 370–396.

Mayo, E. 1933. *The Human Problems of an Industrial Civilization*. Cambridge, MA: Harvard University Press.

Menzies-Lyth, I. 1960. 'A Case Study in The Functioning Of Social Systems as a Defence Against Anxiety: A Report on the study of the nursing service of a general hospital'. *Human Relations*. 13(2). pp. 95–121.

Messenger, G. 2022. *Leadership for a collaborative and inclusive future*. https://www.gov.uk/government/publications/health-and-social-care-review-leadership-for-a-collaborative-and-inclusive-future/leadership-for-a-collaborative-and-inclusive-future <Last Accessed March 24th 2024>.

Mezey, M. 2023. 'The Possibility of Automonomous Buurtzorg Care Teams Across the UK: Tantalising hope vs organisational rigidity (Part 1)'. *Glimpses of the Horizon*. Nov 24th 2023. Available at: https://matthewkalmanmezey.substack.com/p/the-possibility-of-autonomous-buurtzorg. <Last Accessed Feb 18th 2024>.

Mickelthwait, J. & Wooldridge, A. 1997. *The Witch Doctors: Making Sense of the Management Gurus*. New York: Times Books.

Miller, D. & Hartwick, J. 2002. 'Spotting Management Fads'. *Harvard Business Review*. 80(10). pp. 26–27.

Minnaar, J. 2018. The Self-Management Hype: Aren't we just reinventing the Wheel?' Corporate Rebels. Mar 3rd 2018. Available at: https://www.corporate-rebels.com/blog/reinventing-the-wheel. <Last Accessed Feb 18th 2024>.

Morgan, G. (2006). *Images of Organization*. United States: SAGE Publications.

Nohria, N. & Beer, M. 2000 'Cracking the Code of Change.' *Harvard Business Review*. May-June 2000. Available at: https://hbr.org/2000/05/cracking-the-code-of-change. <Last Accessed Feb 28th 2024>.

O'Hara, M. & Leicester, G. 2012. *Dancing at the Edge: Competence, Culture and Organization in the 21st Century* Axminster: Triarchy Press.

Onkvisit, S., & Shaw, J. J. 1991. 'Marketing Theories, Models and General Issues: Is Services Marketing "Really" Different?' *Journal of Professional Services Marketing.* 7(2). pp. 3–17.

Paine, A. B. 1912. *Mark Twain: A biography.* https://openlibrary.org/books/OL26222320M/Mark_Twain_a_Biography

Parker, M. 2018. *Shut Down the Business School.* London: Pluto Press.

Parlett, M. 1991. 'Reflections on Field Theory'. *British Gestalt Journal.* 1(2). pp. 69–81.

Pascale, R. T. 1990. *Managing on the Edge: How the smartest companies use conflict to stay ahead.* New York: Simon & Schuster.

Pentland, A. 2012. 'The New Science of Building Great Teams: The chemistry of high-performing groups is no longer a mystery'. Harvard Business Review. 90(4). pp. 60–70.

Pfeffer, J. 2015. 'Why We Don't Get the Leaders We Say We Want'. *Porchlight.* Sep 16th 2015. Available at: https://www.porchlightbooks.com/blog/changethis/2015/why-we-don-t-get-the-leaders-we-say-we-want- <Last Accessed Feb 18th 2024>.

Pflaeging, N. 2014. *Management Belongs onto the Garbage Heap of History. LinkedIn.* Dec 27th 2014. Available at: https://www.linkedin.com/pulse/management-belongs-onto-garbage-heap-history-niels-pflaeging/. <Last Accessed Feb 18th 2024>.

Pflaeging, N. 2015. 'Why we cannot learn a damn thing from Toyota or Semco'. *LinkedIn.* Sep 14th 2015. Available at: https://www.linkedin.com/pulse/why-we-cannot-learn-damn-thing-from-semco-toyota-niels-pflaeging/. <Last Accessed Feb 18th 2024>.

Piazza, A., & Abrahamson, E. 2020. 'Fads and Fashions in Management Practices: taking stock and looking forward'. *International Journal of Management Reviews.* 22(3). pp. 264–286.

Pink, D. 2011. *Drive: the surprising truth about what motivates us.* Edinburgh: Canongate Books.

Pittenger D. J. 2005. 'Cautionary comments regarding the Myers-Briggs Type Indicator'. *Consulting Psychology Journal Practice and Research.* 57(3). pp. 210–221.

Pittenger D. J. 1993. 'The Utility of the Myers-Briggs Type Indicator'. *Review of Educational Research.* 63(4). pp. 467–488.

Poly, V. 'There Is No Silver Bullet For Hiring, But These 5 Principles Can Help Improve Your Odds'. *Forbes.* Mar 16th 2023. Available at: https://www.forbes.com/sites/forbesbusinesscouncil/2023/03/16/there-is-no-silver-bullet-for-hiring-but-these-5-principles-can-help-improve-your-odds/. <Last Accessed Feb 18th 2024>.

Quiggin, J. 2012. *Zombie Economics: How dead ideas still walk among us.* Princeton, NJ: Princeton University Press.

Raelin, J. A. (Ed). 2016. *Leadership-as-Practice: Theory and application.* New York, NY & Abingdon, Oxon: Routledge.

Reddy, W. B. 1994. *Intervention Skills Small Groups Teams: Process Consultation for small groups and teams.* San Diego, CA: Pfeiffer & Company.

Rhys Evans, T. 2020. 'Improving Evidence Quality for Organisational Change Management Through Open Science'. *Journal of Organizational Change Management.* 33(2). pp. 367–378.

Riggio, R, Chaleff, I. & Lipman-Blumen, J. (Eds). 2008. *The Art of Followership: How great followers create great leaders and organizations.* San Francisco: Jossey-Bass.

Rogers, C. 2021. *Wiggly World of Organization: Muddling through with purpose, courage and skill.* London & New York: Routledge.

Rooke, D. & Torbert, W. R. 2005. 'Seven Transformations of Leadership: leaders are made, not born, and how they develop is critical for organizational change'. *Harvard Business Review.* 83(4). pp. 66–76.

Rudra, P. 'Consultants Play the Role of Therapists to Government'. *The Times.* Oct 30th 2020. Available at: https://www.thetimes.co.uk/article/consultants-play-the-role-of-therapists-to-government-rxwql9fzb. <Last Accessed Feb 18th 2024>.

Russell, B. 1950. [1949]. *Am I an Atheist or an Agnostic?* Girard, Kansas: E. Haldeman-Julius Company.

Times of India. April 22nd 2023. Available at: https://timesofindia.indiatimes.com/world/us/theres-no-silver-bullet-for-ukraine-against-russia-top-us-general/articleshow/99684201.cms. <Last Accessed Feb 18th 2024>.

Saville, M. 2014. 'The Practitioner at the Heart of OD' in Griffin, E, Alsop, M, Saville, M & Smith G. (Eds.) *A Field Guide for Organisation Development.* London: Gower.

Sayed, M. 2020. *Rebel Ideas: The power of thinking differently.* London: John Murray Press.

Schein, E. H. 2013. *Humble Inquiry: The gentle art of asking instead of telling.* San Francisco: Berrett-Koehler Publishers Inc.

Schön, D. 1983. *The Reflective Practitioner.* New York: Basic Books.

Schultz, K. 2011. *Being Wrong: Adventures in the margin of error.* London: Portobello Books.

Schwartz, H. S. 1990. *Narcissistic Process and Corporate Decay: The theory of the organization ideal.* New York: New York University Press.

Seidman, D. 2023. 'What It Means to Be a Moral Leader'. Harvard Business Review. Sep 22nd 2023. Available at: https://hbr.org/2023/09/what-it-means-to-be-a-moral-leader. <Last Accessed Feb 17th 2024>.

Sharp, R. 2019. 'Is Engagement Fact or Fiction'. *HR Magazine.* Available at: https://www.hrmagazine.co.uk/content/features/is-engagement-fact-or-fiction. <Last Accessed Feb 18th 2024>.

Shaw, D. 2019. 'Partners And Plagiarisers: Dualities in consultants' influence on organisational change projects.' *Journal of Organizational Change Management.* 32(1). pp. 51–66.

Shaw, P. 2003. *Changing Conversations in Organizations: A complexity approach to change.* London & New York: Routledge.

Sheard, S. 2003. 'Life Cycle of a Silver Bullet'. *CROSSTALK The Journal of Defense Software Engineering.* July 2003. pp. 28–30. Available at: http://freyr.websages.com/Life_Cycle_of_a_Silver_Bullet.pdf. <Last Accessed Feb 18th 2024>.

Siegel, D. 1999. *The Developing Mind: How relationships and the brain interact to shape who we are.* NY: The Guilford Press.

Sinclair, U. 1934. *I, Candidate for Governor: And how I got licked.* New York: Farrar & Rinehart.

Sinek, S. 2011. *Start With Why: How great leaders inspire everyone to take action.* London: Penguin Books.

Singhal, D, Davis, M. C & Voss, H. 2023. 'Rethinking Business School Education: A Call for Epistemic Humility Through Reflexivity'. *Business & Society.* 0(0). pp. 1–6.

Sivers, T. 2010. 'How to start a movement'. *TED.* Feb 2010. Available at: https://www.ted.com/talks/derek_sivers_how_to_start_a_movement.   <Last Accessed Feb 18th 2024>.

Skovholt, T. M., Hanson, M., Jennings, L. & Grier, T. 2016. 'A Brief History of Expertise' in: Skovholt, T, M & Hanson, M (eds). 2016. *Master Therapists: Exploring expertise in therapy and counselling.* New York: Oxford Academic. pp. 1–16.

Smith, J. H. 1987. 'Elton Mayo And The Hidden Hawthorne'. *Work, Employment & Society, 1*(1), 107–120. Available at: http://www.jstor.org/stable/23745146

Snowden, D. & Boone, E. 2007. 'A Leader's Framework for Decision Making'. *Harvard Business Review.* 85(11). pp. 68-76. Available at: https://hbr.org/2007/11/a-leaders-framework-for-decision-making. <Last Accessed Feb 18th 2024>.

Sonnerfeld, J. A. 2002. 'What Makes Great Boards Great'. *Harvard Business Review.* 80(9) pp. 106-113. Available at: https://hbr.org/2002/09/what-makes-great-boards-great. <Last Accessed Feb 18th 2004>.

Stacey, R. 2012. 'Tools and Techniques of Leadership and Management: Meeting the challenge of complexity'. Abingdon, Oxon & New York, NY: Routledge.

Stein, M. 2021. 'Defences against anxiety' in: Lawlor, D. & Sher, M. 2021. *An Introduction to Systems Psychodynamics: Consultancy Research and Training.* London: Routledge. pp. 226–244.

Sternberg, R. J. 1996. 'Costs of Expertise' in: Ericsson, K.A. (Ed). 1996. *The Road to Excellence: The acquisition of expert performance in the arts and sciences, sports, and games*. Hillsdale, NJ: Lawrence Erlbaum Associates, Inc. pp. 347–354.

Stewart, I. & Joines, V. 1987 (2005). *TA Today: A new introduction to Transactional Analysis*. Nottingham: Lifespace.

Stewart, M. 2010. *The Management Myth: Why the experts keep getting it wrong*. New York, NY: W. W. Norton & Company.

Sturdy, A. & Veronesi, G. 2021. 'A consultancy habit? The use of external management advice in the NHS'. *University of Bristol*. Policy Briefing 98: Feb 2021. Available at: https://www.bristol.ac.uk/policybristol/policy-briefings/external-management-nhs/. <Last Accessed Feb 18th 2024>.

Syed, M. 2019. *Rebel Ideas: The Power of Diverse Thinking*. London: John Murray Publishing/Hachette UK.

Taylor, F. W. 2011. *The Principles of Scientific Management*. New York, NY & London: Harper & Brothers.

Teece, D., Peteraf, M. & Leih, S. 2016. 'Dynamic Capabilities and Organizational Agility: Risk, uncertainty, and strategy in the innovation economy'. *California Management Review*. 58(4). pp. 13–35.

'The Future of Leadership and Management in the NHS: No more heroes'.

The King's Fund. Report from The King's Fund Commission on Leadership and Management in the NHS. pp. 1-38. Available at: https://www.kingsfund.org.uk/insight-and-analysis/reports/future-leadership-management-nhs. <Last Accessed Feb 17th 2004>.

Tolbert, P. S. & Zucker, L. G. 1999. 'The Institutionalization of Institutional Theory'. *Studying Organization. Theory & Method*. 29(1). pp.169–184.

Turner, A. N. 1982. 'Consulting Is More Than Giving Advice: By building on a hierarchy of goals, consultants and managers can work toward mutual interests'. *Harvard Business Review*. 60(5). pp. 120–129.

Vaynerchuk, G. 2009. *Crush It!: Why NOW is the time to cash in on your passion*. New York, NY: HarperCollins.

Vaynerchuk, G. 2013. *Jab, Jab, Jab, Right Hook: how to tell your story in a noisy social world.* New York, NY: HarperCollins.

Vaynerchuk, G. 2018. *Crushing It!: How Great Entrepreneurs Build Their Business and Influence-and How You Can.* New York, NY: HarperCollins.

Veli Korkmaz, A., van Engen, M. L., Knappert, L. & Schalk, R. 2022. 'About and Beyond Leading Uniqueness and Belongingness: A systematic review of inclusive leadership research.' *Human Resource Management Review.* 32(4). pp. 1–20.

Waisberg, I. & Nelson, A. 2018. 'When the General Meets the Particular: The practices and challenges of interorganizational knowledge reuse'. *Organization Science.* 29(3). pp. 432–448.

Walker, P. 2023. 'Some MPs came close to suicide, says ex-Tory minister Rory Stewart. Guardian. Sep 11th 2023. Available at: https://www.theguardian.com/society/2023/sep/10/some-mps-came-close-to-suicide-says-ex-tory-minister-rory-stewart. <Last Accessed Feb 19th 2024>.

Weick, K. 1993. 'The Collapse of Sensemaking in Organizations: The Mann Gulch Disaster'. *Administrative Science Quarterly.* 38(4). pp. 628–652.

Western, S. 2019. *Leadership: A critical text.* 3rd edn. London, Thousand Oaks, CA, New Delhi & Singapore: SAGE.

Westfall, C. 2019. 'Leadership Development Is A $366 Billion Industry: Here's why most programs don't work'. *Forbes.* June 20th 2019. Available at: https://www.forbes.com/sites/chriswestfall/2019/06/20/leadership-development-why-most-programs-dont-work. <Last Accessed Feb 18th 2004>.

Wheatley, M. 2006. *Leadership and the New Science: Discovering order in a chaotic world.* 3rd Edn. San Francisco, Calif & London: Berrett-Koehler.

Wilcox, D. & Tapsfield, J. 2022. 'Suella Braverman Warns There Is No 'Silver Bullet' To Solve Channel Migrant Crisis And Small Boats Won't Be Stopped 'Overnight' As She Defends New £63million Deal With France To Stop People Smugglers'. *Daily Mail.* Nov 14th 2022. Available at: https://www.dailymail.co.uk/news/article-11426821/Suella-Braverman-warns-no-silver-bullet-solve-Channel-migrant-crisis.html. <Last Accessed Feb 18th 2024>.

Winnicott, D. 1958. *Collected Papers: Through paediatrics to psychoanalysis.* London: Karnac.

Winnicott, D. W. 1958 'The capacity to be alone'. *The International Journal of Psychoanalysis*, 39, 416–420.

Wizard Of Oz 1939 [Film]. Directed by: Victor Fleming. Metro-Goldwyn-Mayer.

Wooldridge, A. 2023. McKinsey's Missteps Point to an Industry-Wide Mess. Bloomberg. Jan 24th 2023. Available at: https://www.bloomberg.com/opinion/articles/2023-01-24/mckinsey-s-missteps-point-to-a-bigger-management-consulting-mess. <Last Accessed Feb 18th 2024>.

Wright, C. & Kitay, J. 2002. '"But does it work?" Perceptions of the impact of management

Consulting'. *Strategic Change.* 11(5), 271–278.

Printed in Great Britain
by Amazon

40157647R00215